Evolutions in Sustainable Investing

Founded in 1807, John Wiley & Sons is the oldest independent publishing company in the United States. With offices in North America, Europe, Australia, and Asia, Wiley is globally committed to developing and marketing print and electronic products and services for our customers' professional and personal knowledge and understanding.

The Wiley Finance series contains books written specifically for finance and investment professionals as well as sophisticated individual investors and their financial advisors. Book topics range from portfolio management to e-commerce, risk management, financial engineering, valuation, and financial instrument analysis, as well as much more.

For a list of available titles, please visit our Web site at www.wiley finance.com.

Evolutions in Sustainable Investing

Strategies, Funds &
Thought Leadership

Editors

CARY KROSINSKY

with

NICK ROBINS
STEPHEN VIEDERMAN

WILEY

John Wiley & Sons, Inc.

Published by John Wiley & Sons, Inc., Hoboken, New Jersey.
Published simultaneously in Canada.

For general information on our other products and services or for technical support, please
contact our Customer Care Department within the United States at (800) 762-2974, outside
the United States at (317) 572-3993 or fax (317) 572-4002.

Wiley also publishes its books in a variety of electronic formats. Some content that appears in
print may not be available in electronic books. For more information about Wiley products,
visit our web site at www.wiley.com.

Library of Congress Cataloging-in-Publication Data:

Evolutions in sustainable investment : strategies, funds and thought leadership / Cary
Krosinsky, editor ; with Nick Robins & Stephen Viederman.
        p. cm. – (Wiley finance series)
    Includes index.
    ISBN 978-0-470-88849-0 (hardback); ISBN 978-1-118-15790-9 (ebk); ISBN
978-1-118-15791-6 (ebk); ISBN 978-1-118-15792-3 (ebk)
    1. Investments–Social aspects.   2. Investments–Environmental aspects.   3. Social
responsibility of business.   4. Investment analysis.   I. Krosinsky, Cary.
    HG4515.13.S87 2012
    332.6–dc23

                                                                    2011029130

Printed in the United States of America.

10 9 8 7 6 5 4 3 2 1

To not only the next generation, but perhaps especially two generations forward—and those beyond:

May we find a way to build a successful bridge to your future.

Contents

CHAPTER 7
Domini and BP 81
Colm Fay

CHAPTER 8
The Story of Calvert 91
Sam Brownell and Sara Herald

CHAPTER 9
Winslow 107
Amrita Vijay Kumar

CHAPTER 10
Portfolio 21 115
Ashley Hamilton

Acknowledgments

Many thanks are required here, but likely I will touch successfully only on some. Thanks to the thought leaders who took time out of their busy schedules to contribute to this book, including Paul Hawken, Dan Esty, Roger Urwin, et al. Your dedication to the ideals we share is valued greatly. Also great thanks to the academic institutions whose MBA students contributed to the book, including the University of Michigan, Duquesne, Presidio, Marlboro, the London School of Economics, the University of Maryland, and Columbia University. It was great to have the final chapter contribution come from Lloyd Kurtz of the Haas School at Berkeley. Lloyd was in many ways the first-ever researcher in this field. Thanks also to the peer reviewers, especially Dana Krechowicz of Sustainable Prosperity and my friend and colleague at Trucost, Dr. James Salo. Great thanks as well to Amr Addas of Concordia University for his extensive and thoughtful peer review. Amr is a member of the Core Faculty at the John Molson School of Business responsible for developing the Sustainable Investment Professional Certification (SIPC), the first certification of its kind for professionals in the finance, investment, and corporate world. I wish them every success with this groundbreaking new program. Thanks as well to my wife, Valerie Brown, who added her own thoughts and edits and put up with my efforts off hours to get this book accomplished. Thanks to the great folks at John Wiley & Sons, including Debra Englander, Susan McDermott, Jennifer MacDonald and Natasha Andrews-Noel. And thanks most of all to Nick Robins and Stephen Viederman. These two visionaries helped shape this book. Their thinking and investment philosophies are reflected throughout and are always in mind, and their ongoing insights and counsel are greatly appreciated.

About the Editor

Cary Steven Krosinsky is coeditor and author of *Sustainable Investing: The Art of Long Term Performance* (Earthscan, 2008).

He was a member in 2005 of the 70-person expert group that helped oversee and create the United Nations Principles for Responsible Investment.

Since 2008, he has been senior vice president in North America for U.K-based Trucost and has served as a senior advisor to the well-received *Newsweek* Green Rankings. Trucost maintains the only comprehensive global database that objectively quantifies the environmental impacts of public and private companies.

Cary also teaches sustainability and investing at both Columbia University's Earth Institute as well as an MBA class at the University of Maryland's Smith School of Business.

He originally worked in collaboration with Trucost in 2005 on its Sustainable City award–winning Carbon Footprint study of U.K. portfolios and on the International Finance Corporation–sponsored Carbon Counts Asia report in 2007.

Cary has a background in data management and analysis, and has served on the management committees of three data and analytics companies: Trucost, CapitalBridge, and Technimetrics.

He is a frequent speaker at universities, including the Massachusetts Institute of Technology, Columbia Business School, Darden School of Business (University of Virginia), the Northstar Initiative (University of Minnesota), and many more.

Cary's other honors and memberships include:

- Member, Circle of Advisors, Marlboro College Graduate School MBA in Managing for Sustainability Program
- Advisor, Bard College MBA Sustainability (scheduled for 2012)
- Technical Advisor, Investment Work Group, STARS (Sustainability Tracking, Assessment and Rating System) for Universities
- Member, Advisory Board, Association of Climate Change Officers
- Founder/Director, Investor Watch
- Advisor, Dwight Hall SRI Fund, Yale University

- Editorial Board Member—*GHG Measurement and Management Journal*, Earthscan
- Editorial Board Member—*Journal of Sustainable Finance and Investment*, Earthscan

About the Contributors

Adam Blumenthal is cofounder and managing partner of Blue Wolf Capital Partners LLC, a private equity firm specializing in investments in middle-market companies in which managing relationships with government or labor, or resolving financial or operational distress, is critical to building value. He is a director of four portfolio companies, including American Builders Supply Co., Finch Paper LLC, Northern Resources Nova Scotia Corporation, and Gloucester Engineering Co., Inc. Prior to Blue Wolf, Adam served, from 2002 to 2005, as first deputy comptroller and chief financial officer for New York City Comptroller William C. Thompson Jr., and held positions including president and vice chairman of American Capital, a publicly traded business development company, from 1989 to 2002. Adam has an MBA from the Yale School of Management.

Howard Brown is founder of dMASS.net and chairman of o.s.Earth Inc. For more than 20 years as chief executive of RPM (Resource Planning & Management) Systems, Inc., in New Haven, CT, he worked with companies such as Duracell, Avery Dennison Corp., Exxon Mobil Corp., General Electric Co., Pfizer Inc., Warner-Lambert Co., and Whirlpool Corp. to establish or enhance their environmental practices and performance measurement.

Sam Brownell received his MBA from the University of Maryland's Robert H. Smith School of Business in May 2011. Born and raised in Washington, DC, he attended Loyola University in Baltimore, where he majored in economics and minored in math. Prior to business school, Sam worked on the trading desk at JMP Securities in San Francisco, where he passed all three levels of the CFA Examination. Going forward, he plans to work for an investment management firm in either sustainability research or risk management.

Lucy Carmody is the executive director of Responsible Research, managing a team of twelve analysts who produce sectoral, thematic, and company research highlighting the sustainability performance of Asian-listed companies. Lucy also manages the Asian Sustainability Rating project. Prior to setting up Responsible Research, Lucy enjoyed over a decade of experience in Asian equity research and sales with top-tier banks, including Barclays Capital. Lucy is co-chair of the Asian Association of Independent Research

Providers, an advisory board member of Impact Exchange Asia, and an advisor to the Asian Water Project. She has consulted on projects for the International Finance Corporation, UNPRI, United Nations Conference on Trade and Development, and the Emerging Market Disclosure Project. Prior to Responsible Research she set up CSR Practice, an ethical investment and strategic corporate philanthropy consultancy. Lucy holds a Masters degree from St John's College, University of Cambridge.

Nancy Degnan is the executive director of the Center for Environmental Research and Conservation (CERC), an organization of the Earth Institute at Columbia University. CERC is a consortium of Columbia University, the American Museum of Natural History, the Wildlife Conservation Society, the New York Botanical Garden, and EcoHealth Alliance. Its mission is to build environmental leadership and solve complex environmental problems in pursuit of conservation of biodiversity. Nancy's research and writing has focused on community-based initiatives in education, sustainable development, and redevelopment as well as in microfinance and enterprise development. At CERC, Nancy spearheads initiatives and programming in education, training, and research in conservation science. The primary focus is to bridge the science and non-science communities with the goal of informing decisions and practices about environmental sustainability in corporations, nonprofit and public sector organizations.

Laura Dodge has worked in Asia since 1994 as a journalist, consultant, and an academic. She writes extensively on business and financial trends in Asia, with publications in the *McKinsey Quarterly*, Bloomberg, the Economist Intelligence Unit [EIU], CNN, and the U.S. China Business Council, among others. Laura has a doctorate in political science and has taught courses in Asia politics at Temple University in Japan and City University in Hong Kong. She currently teaches at Nanyang Technological University in Singapore.

Daniel C. Esty is the coauthor of the business bestseller *Green to Gold* and a recent follow-up *Green to Gold Business Playbook*, published by John Wiley & Sons in 2009 and 2011, respectively. He was environmental advisor to the Obama presidential campaign and transition team and, as of March 2011, commissioner for the newly formed Department of Energy and Environmental Protection in the State of Connecticut. He currently is on leave from Yale University, where he is Hillhouse professor and director of the Center for Business and the Environment. As a senior official at the U.S. Environmental Protection Agency, he helped to craft air and water pollution regulations and government policies affecting waste, food safety, and other issues, and was also the principal architect of the environmental provisions for the North American Free Trade Agreement.

Colm Fay is a student at the Erb Institute at the University of Michigan pursuing a dual MBA and MS in natural resources and the environment and will graduate in April 2012. He is interested in the overlap between business, environmental conservation, and social impact. He has six years of experience in financial services consulting and currently is working on academic projects focused on conservation finance and payments for ecosystem services. Colm hopes to pursue a career in impact investing focused on conservation and poverty alleviation in emerging markets.

Malte Griess-Nega has over 10 years of experience in entrepreneurial businesses. He currently is completing his executive MBA at the London Business School and works for Serengeti Capital spearheading its effort to raise a private equity fund focused on small and medium-size businesses in West Africa. Prior to this, he founded a management consultancy focused on branded consumer products. He started his career in Deutsche Bank's investment banking division.

Ashley Hamilton is a shareholder engagement expert that has worked with Canada's leading responsible investors in various consulting roles since 2005. She recently took on a new position as Shareholder Engagement Executive at Pensions & Investment Research Consultants (PIRC) in London, UK. Ashley has a Master of Arts degree from the University of British Columbia where she focused her research on responsible investment and corporate social responsibility. She has volunteered with a number of organizations, including the International Working Group of the US Social Investment Forum, the Responsible Investing Initiative at Carleton University, and the Vancouver Living Wage Campaign.

Paul Hawken is an environmentalist, entrepreneur, journalist, and author. Since the age of 20, he has dedicated his life to sustainability and changing the relationship between business and the environment. His practice has included starting and running ecological businesses, writing and teaching about the impact of commerce on living systems, and consulting with governments and corporations on economic development, industrial ecology, and environmental policy.

Sara Herald received her MBA from the University of Maryland's Smith School of Business in 2011. Originally from the Washington, DC, area, she graduated magna cum laude from Georgetown University in 2006 with a degree in Spanish and English. Prior to business school, she managed the Teach in Spain program in Seville, Spain, for the Council on International Educational Exchange, an educational nonprofit organization. Areas of interest include corporate social responsibility initiatives and shareholder advocacy campaigns.

Dr. Matthew J. Kiernan is founder and chief executive of Inflection Point Capital Management (IPCM). Prior to founding IPCM, he was the founder and chief executive of Innovest Strategic Value Advisors. He is the author of two books and numerous articles about nontraditional drivers of investment risk and return. His most recent book is *Investing in a Sustainable World* published by AMACOM in 2008. He holds advanced degrees in political science and environmental studies and a doctorate in strategic environmental management from the University of London.

Erika Kimball is a registered nurse and sustainable business professional dedicated to reducing the environmental footprint of the healthcare industry. The founder and cochair of the green team at California Pacific Medical Center in San Francisco, Erika completed received her MBA in sustainable management from Presidio Graduate School in December 2010. She now collaborates with organizations driving positive change in the health care industry.

Dana Krechowicz is research associate at Sustainable Prosperity. She has six years of international experience working at the intersection of business and environmental sustainability. Dana previously worked in the capital markets research team at the World Resources Institute (WRI) in Washington, DC. While there, she coauthored a series of reports examining the financial impacts of environmental risks on key sectors in South and Southeast Asia, working closely with HSBC's Climate Change Centre of Excellence. Prior to WRI, Dana worked as an equity analyst in the Paris and Toronto offices of Innovest, rating the exposure of companies in a variety of sectors to environmental, social, and corporate governance risks and opportunities. She holds an International MBA focused on sustainability from the Schulich School of Business in Toronto.

Amrita Vijay Kumar is a recent winner of the first annual scholarship of the Journal of Environmental Investing Scholarship Program (JEI SP) for her paper, "Challenges and Opportunities—Using Carbon Finance to Scale SMEs in West Africa." She is a strong proponent of using investment as a tool to enable social and environmental change, experiencing this firsthand through her work with Piper Jaffray's clean-tech banking area and with E+CO, a social venture fund that channels investment to energy businesses in emerging markets. She has also worked on pioneering carbon finance projects that have helped prevent deforestation in Indonesia and have scaled clean energy businesses in West Africa. Amrita has also consulted for the Environmental Defense Fund on nitrogen management strategies for U.S. agriculture and is the winner of the J.P. Morgan prize for Best Emerging Markets Portfolio in the 2011 Inaugural Impact Investing Competition. She is a fellow of the Erb Institute for Global Sustainable Enterprise and graduated from the University of Michigan in 2011 with an MBA and an M.Sc. in natural resources.

Lloyd Kurtz is chief investment officer at Nelson Capital Management, a money management firm based in Palo Alto, CA. He is also affiliated with the Center for Responsible Business, Haas School of Business, UC Berkeley, where he oversees the Moskowitz Prize, an annual award for the best quantitative research on social investing. He is a lecturer in investments at Santa Clara University and in 2010 served as faculty cochair for the Value of Values conference, presented by the Santa Clara Initiative for Financial Innovation and Risk Management. He is a chartered financial analyst.

Dr. David A. Lubin has more than 25 years of experience leading technology and consulting firms that have become world leaders in the field of corporate performance management. David currently serves as chairman of the Esty Sustainability Network, a research consortium led by him and Dan Esty. Before joining the Esty team, David served as chairman of the board of Palladium Group, a firm he founded with David Norton (the cocreator of Balanced Scorecard http://en.wikipedia.org/wiki/Balanced_scorecard) to advance the application of business analytics to measuring and improving corporate performance. He cofounded Renaissance Solutions in 1991, which became a publicly traded global information technology and management consultancy. Before beginning his career in business, David was a member of the faculties at both Tufts and Harvard universities.

Jenna Manheimer is currently pursuing a master's in public health with emphasis on environmental health policy at Columbia University. She is particularly interested in water resource management, conservation, and quality control, as well as sanitation systems in areas of limited resources. Holding an undergraduate degree in Spanish literature and biology, she has worked in disease control with the New York City Department of Health and in Mexico advocating for human rights, and Jenna will also participate in an internship with UNICEF in Madhya Pradesh, India, promoting hygiene and sanitation in a rural setting.

Dean Martucci is with Cogenra Solar, a Khosla Ventures funded start-up manufacturer of solar cogeneration systems, technology that is redefining solar efficiency and payback for the renewable distributed energy market. A partner with Environmental Entrepreneurs and member of the International Society of Sustainability Professionals, Dean completed his MBA in sustainability management at the Presidio Graduate School in December 2010.

J. Jason Mitchell rejoined GLG Partners in 2010 to launch and oversee the firm's sustainability investment strategies. Jason acts as advisor for the U.K. government's Commonwealth Business Council, presenting renewable energy solutions across sub-Saharan Africa, most recently in Ghana and the Niger Delta states. From 2009 to April 2010, Jason worked as chief operating officer of Hydrotech International, as advisor to the African Development Corp., and presented at the 2009 Copenhagen Climate Summit. His articles and comments frequently appear in the press, most recently in *Institutional Investor Magazine*, *Wall Street Journal*, *Global Times* (China), *Aftenposten* (Norway), and responsible-investor.com.

Thomas O. Murtha finances and develops sustainable businesses in energy and technology, as managing director for clean technology and environmental services at investment bank Enclave Capital LLC. Previously, Tom managed an alternative energy public equity and late-stage private equity portfolio for the Strategic Investment Group at Merrill Lynch. At T. Rowe Price in Baltimore, MD, Tom was a co–portfolio manager for the Global Technology Fund and International Stock Fund. Earlier in his career he worked in Tokyo, Hong Kong, London, and New York for the investment bank Robert Fleming/Jardine Fleming. Tom holds the chartered financial analyst credential and obtained an MPA degree in environmental science and policy from Columbia University as well as an MA in economics and a BS in mathematics from Ohio University.

Michael Musuraca was a managing director of Blue Wolf Capital Management, a private equity firm based in New York City, and Blue Wolf Capital Fund II, L.P. Michael currently is working as a consultant on pension and corporate governance issues. From 1996 to 2009, he served as the designated trustee to the New York City Employees Retirement System, a 300,000-plus member pension fund with assets of approximately $40 billion. He also served, from 1997 until 2009, as a trustee to the Cultural Institutions Retirement System, a $1 billion fund with members from the major cultural institutions and day care facilities in the New York City metropolitan area. Michael was also a member of the Principles for Responsible Investment board and was the labor representative to the Advisory Board of the New York City Independent Budget Office, and currently is serving on the board of the Shareholders Education Network, Sustainalytics, and Verité.

Thomas J. Nist serves as the director of Graduate Studies in the Donahue Graduate School of Business at Duquesne University in Pittsburgh, PA. In this role, Thomas is responsible for managing graduate business programs for their relevance in a rapidly evolving global marketplace. As Donahue chair in Investment Management, he is charged with building a nationally recognized program in investment management at Duquesne University, where his work also includes launching an investment fund with student-portfolio managers, advising the student Finance and Investment Management Association, coordinating the finance and investment advisory boards, and managing outreach and visibility with the corporate and professional investment community. He also teaches courses in corporate finance and commercial banking and is committed to the case method of instruction. Tom was recently named to the list of "25 Most Influential People Setting Global Trends in Cash Management" by the Institute of Financial Operations.

Simon Powell is head of sustainable research for CLSA in Hong Kong since 2009. CLSA is an independent Asian brokerage and investment group that has built a reputation for leading equity research and economic analysis, consistently voted best in Asia. CLSA was one of the first research houses in Asia to integrate environmental, social, and governance assessments into its securities coverage. CLSA is an active proponent of environmental awareness and action and was one of the first financial firms in Asia to write about pollution, carbon trading, and the "greening" of Asia, winning multiple awards for its research. Previously Simon was country head of Taiwan and head of utility research for CLSA, having joined in 2006 from his prior engagement as a director of consulting for Infosys.

Curtis Ravenel leads Bloomberg's global sustainability initiatives. This effort integrates sustainability considerations into all firm operations and leverages the Bloomberg terminal to evaluate sustainability-related investment risks and opportunities for its 300,000 customers. Curtis has worked for Bloomberg in multiple roles: He was the financial controller for Asia managing accounting, tax, treasury, and audit services for 23 legal entities, preceded by various roles in the capital planning and financial analysis groups. Curtis earned his MBA at Columbia Business School.

Nick Robins has over 20 years of experience in the policy, business, and investment dimensions of sustainable development. He currently heads HSBC's Climate Change Centre of Excellence and writes in a personal capacity. Prior to this, he was head of socially responsible investing funds at Henderson Global Investors, where he launched the world's first climate audit of an investment fund and designed the multithematic Industries of the Future sustainability fund. He is author of *The Corporation that Changed the World: How the East India Company Shaped the Modern Multinational* (Pluto Press, 2006) and coeditor (with Cary Krosinksi) of *Sustainable Investing: The Art of Long-Term Performance* (Routledge, 2008).

Dr. James Salo is senior vice president of strategy and research of Trucost. He is responsible for Trucost's research efforts in North America and coordinates Trucost's Advisory Panel. At Trucost, James has been the research lead for the *Newsweek* Green Rankings, Carbon Counts USA 2009 assessment of investment fund carbon exposure, and Carbon Risks and Opportunities in the S&P 500. James has earned a D.Phil. from Oxford University at the Oxford University Centre of the Environment on Environmental Impacts and also has a combined BA/MA degree in environmental science and policy from Clark University.

Sumantra Sen is a chartered wealth manager and a member of Chartered Institute for Securities and Investment with over 15 years of exposure to global capital markets and portfolio management. In recent assignments, he has been managing teams of analysts engaged in portfolio analytics, wealth structuring, and investment research at some of the leading global banking and financial service organizations. He is the founder of Responsible Investment Research Association, a not-for-profit organization with objectives to build a multi-stakeholder forum for responsible investment practice in India. His ongoing doctoral and independent research focuses on corporate governance and mainstreaming of environment, social, and governance factors into the investment management process.

Graham Sinclair is principal at SinCo, a boutique sustainable investment architecture firm with advisory engagements in frontier and emerging markets research. Since 2006, engagements have modeled investments integrating environmental, social, and governance factors into systems, strategy, and indexes for clients ranging from trillion-dollar investment managers to international organizations such as the International Finance Corporation, United Nations, and World Business Council for Sustainable Development, and include developing investor networks in emerging markets as project manager for the Principles for Responsible Investment and leading the Africa Sustainability Investment Forum project. Graham has nine years of specialist experience in sustainable investment globally after eight years in pensions consulting and investment banking in southern Africa. He has lectured at more than 25 business and graduate schools on four continents.

Bud Sturmak is managing director of RLP Wealth Advisors, a forward-thinking, independent wealth management firm providing retirement plan consulting, asset management, and financial planning services for individuals, families, nonprofit organizations, and corporations. Bud Sturmak helps lead RLP's cofiduciary retirement plan consulting program, which assists corporations and nonprofits in the prudent oversight of their plans. Additionally, he helped develop RLP's customized sustainable investment solutions for individuals and institutions that integrate environmental, social, and governance analysis. Bud received a BA from Dickinson College in 1995 and has been working in the investment business since 1996.

Dr. Rory Sullivan is strategic adviser at Ethix SRI Advisers and a senior research fellow at the University of Leeds. Previously he was head of responsible investment at Insight Investment, widely recognized as one of the world's leading responsible investment managers. He has written widely on investment, climate change, and development issues. His books include *Valuing Corporate Responsibility: How Do Investors Really Use Corporate Responsibility Information?* (Greenleaf, 2011) and with coeditor Craig McKenzie, the edited collection, *Responsible Investment* (Greenleaf, 2006).

N.A.J. Taylor researches and writes about morality and harm in world politics, particularly in relation to modern warfare. He has been published widely in academic journals and edited books, and regularly contributes to debates in news media, including ABC, Al Jazeera, SBS, and radio. In addition, he is a founding member of the United Nations Expert Group on Responsible Business and Investment in Conflict-Affected Areas, and casual lecturer at La Trobe University. He holds both a Bachelor of Economics in Economic History and Master of International Studies with honors from the University of Sydney, and is completing a doctorate in the School of Political Science and International Studies at the University of Queensland.

Mark L. Trevitt is an investment professional integrating sustainability into the capital markets and business. As a founding contributor to the Responsible Investment Academy, he designed and developed several lessons on analyzing the investment risk and opportunities presented by sustainability challenges. He has worked with the United Nation's Principles of Responsible Investment to evaluate and address systemic risks from environmental issues through collaborative engagement. An author for The Economics of Ecosystems and Biodiversity (TEEB) study, he contributed sections on the impacts and dependence of business on ecosystems. He also created an industry-leading analytical tool for assessing companies' risk from water scarcity.

Roger Urwin assumed the new post of Global Head of Investment Content in July 2008 after acting as the Global Head of the Watson Wyatt investment practice from 1995 to 2008. Roger joined Watson Wyatt in 1989 to start the firm's investment consulting practice and under his leadership the practice grew to a global team of 500. His prior career involved heading the Mercer investment practice and leading the business development and quantitative investment functions at Gartmore Investment Management.

Roger's current role includes work for some of Towers Watson's major investment clients both in the UK and internationally. He is also involved with the Watson Wyatt thought leadership group (Thinking Ahead Group). He is the author of a number of papers on asset allocation policy, manager selection, and governance. He is on the Board of the CFA Institute and an Advisory Director to MSCI Inc. Roger has a degree in Mathematics from Oxford University and a Masters in Applied Statistics also from Oxford. He qualified as a Fellow of the Institute of Actuaries in 1983.

Alexis van Gelder has over 15 years of leadership and management experience in the U.S. Air Force. In 2010, he completed his MBA in sustainable management from the Presidio Graduate School and currently is embarking on a new career as a product designer and sustainability consultant. His primary focus is on waste reduction and sustainable water management solutions.

Fernando Viana is a business consultant and advisor, investment banker, and private investor with over 20 years of experience in financial and managerial positions. After many years on Wall Street working as a finance specialist in diverse industries, such as media, telecommunications, and information technology, Fernando became a senior investment banker and managing director at a boutique mergers and acquisitions (M&A) and advisory firm focused on Latin America. He formed his own company in 2002 to advise private companies pursuing M&A, strategic, or capital-raising projects and, more recently, to consult and invest on projects related to renewable energy, clean technology, and sustainability. Among other projects, he wrote a master's thesis titled "Feedback Loops on Environment, Energy, and U.S. Foreign Policy," arguing that the United States should elevate climate change policy to a key variable in the conduct of foreign policy.

Dan Viederman is the chief executive officer of Verité, a global nongovernmental organization (NGO) committed to ensuring that people in factories and farms work under safe, fair and legal conditions. He has managed NGOs that work in developing countries since 1993, with most of his overseas experience occurring in China. Dan has been pleased to serve several world-class institutions in addition to Verité, including the World Wildlife Fund and Catholic Relief Services. For Dan's work with Verité he was named winner of the 2007 Skoll Foundation Award for Social Entrepreneurship and Schwab Foundation United States Social Entrepreneur of the Year for 2011.

Stephen Viederman has been involved in sustainable/impact investing since the early 1990s as president of the Jessie Smith Noyes Foundation. In addition to writing and speaking, he is on the advisory committees of Inflection Point Capital Management, Strategic Philanthropy, and Ethical Marketplace; he is on the finance committee of the Christopher Reynolds Foundation, is a fellow of the Governance and Sustainability Institute, and is a contributing editor of the *Journal of Sustainable Finance and Investment*.

Becky Weisberg completed two BA degrees, in English and psychology, from the University of Rochester, NY. She currently is completing her MBA degree with a concentration in sustainability from Duquesne University in Pittsburgh, PA. While receiving her MBA, she assisted in publishing two case studies and in writing a research paper. She also works with two companies on projects related to composting.

Alex Wood is the senior director of policy and markets at Sustainable Prosperity in Ottawa, Canada. Alex has extensive experience in the integration of economic and environmental issues in both the United States and Canada. He previously served as special advisor for corporate environmental affairs at TD Bank Financial Group. He also served as acting chief executive officer and president of the National Round Table on the Environment and the Economy (NRTEE). Before returning to Canada, Alex worked for 8 years at WWF International's Macroeconomics Program Office in Washington, DC.

Pavel Yakovlev is a professor of economics at Duquesne University in Pittsburgh, PA. He conducts research in public, international, and peace economics. He has written articles and book chapters on economic growth, arms trade, military spending, taxation, political institutions, torture, traffic fatalities, suicide, and battlefield deaths. Pavel earned his PhD and MA degrees in economics from West Virginia University and his BS in economics and business administration from Shepherd College.

Roselyne Yao is senior analyst at SinCo. She conducts sustainable investment research and analysis, such as the research study commissioned by the International Finance Corporation titled "Sustainable Investment in Sub-Saharan Africa" in 2010–2011. Through 2010 Roselyne was a research analyst for JPS Global Investments. She is a steering committee member at AfricaSIF.org, the Africa Sustainable Investment Forum. Roselyne received her MBA from the University of Illinois in 2009 and passed the CFA level I exam in June 2009.

Introduction

Cary Krosinsky

Most people would agree that we are entering a world of peak oil and rising energy prices. There are pending fresh water and food shortages in many parts of the world coupled with theoretically unsustainable yet inevitable increases in population. We further see soaring unsustainable debt as well as the ravages of climate change anticipated by science compounded by the pending effects of warming seas and a loss of vital coral reefs. There is a similarly critical loss of biodiversity, a shortage of arable land, and increasing inequity between the rich few and the many without. This is expected to lead to unrest from the many who don't have enough for themselves and their families, or any prospects of success, happiness, enrichment, and well-being, and may well continue to struggle from a lack of the classic definition of work, in a world of increasing automation.

Yet the majority of investors do not take such things into consideration in their traditional mainstream fund management strategies.

There can be danger as well within the so-called socially responsible investment (SRI) world, whose participants can get stuck focusing on narrow issues, at times equally if not less mindful of the trends now unfolding, regardless of a general intention to invest to a set of values. These sets of values sets vary widely. As the SIF Trends report of 2010 showed, while trillions of dollars are invested in a "socially responsible" manner, upward of 90% of that sum has been deployed over time using unsophisticated screens that arguably miss many of these risks and perhaps are especially not well positioned to harness the radical, transformational changes in technology and society that are developing to solve these problems of sustainability.

With sustainability risks and opportunities having become a global imperative and megatrend for business (see Chapter 1), it is now critically important that asset owners, their advisors, and fund managers build a connection to this reality within their investment strategies. In the United States alone, a majority of Americans have some portion of their retirement assets tied up in mainstream strategies that do not factor in the new realities before us.

Throughout the text, unless otherwise specified, $ are stated in U.S. dollars.

It is critical to point out that we are talking about a positive investment strategy that we see as the way forward—one that seeks the right opportunities while being equally mindful of macro trends and emerging risks from rapidly changing planetary conditions and the soaring wave of innovation and technology unfolding in university laboratories and elsewhere that will leave traditional business models behind.

A flat investment in the S&P 500 simply won't protect the average investor from the shifting seas. Taking a positive angle to investment and sustainability is critical—and equally critical is that this approach be adapted by the mainstream investment community to the point where this simply becomes an additional lens on top of existing practices, while the unsuccessful, negative approaches of the past are left behind.

The very good news is that large-capitalization companies aim to herald the way forward in a number of ways; such companies have clear risks now to their supply chains, and so they are already driving critical change—protecting their resources and business flows while innovating to ensure profitability. These companies are increasingly among the most efficient as well, and the correlation between the best-run companies and those being strategically mindful of their sustainability risks and opportunities is now becoming clear.

Perhaps most important, these companies are often flush with cash, well positioned with branding, and in a position to acquire innovation and bring it most efficiently and quickly to scale. These companies include those in the social media and technology spaces. A revolution is also under way to ensure that food, water, energy, and other basic needs are met in a world of shrinking resources and increasing mouths to feed. Every sector is affected by these trends. The clearest risk of all is to do nothing and be left behind. The best news of all perhaps is that markets need winners and losers in this regard as well.

The last two generations of fund managers have succeeded using strategies that have brought them great personal wealth. These strategies don't need to change at all. What is required is an additional lens of sustainability risks and opportunities to catch the predictable surprises of the future. In fact, the trends before us are now so clear that at some point in the not-too-distant future, advisors and fund managers could well be considered in breach of their fiduciary duty for not considering sustainability realities, as most today do not. Thus a sea change in practice is pending, which alone would guarantee further positive change.

The last decade saw a myriad of risks that were not black swans but rather inevitabilities that could have been prevented. From Enron to WorldCom, Adelphia to Tyco International, the tech bubble to the credit crunch and its abusers, rogue traders to Bernie Madoff and Allen Stanford: All of these variations of creative accounting, overvaluation, and looking the other way could have been foretold or easily avoided. The new predictable surprises before us are clearly emerging from environmental trends that may well be unstoppable, with related affects to the human condition. Investors can readily observe and consider the quality of management and operations, including the growing correlation between employee motivation and share price success. Innovation is harder to measure but critical to consider.

In this book we walk through the investment practices of those who believe that this sustainability megatrend has emerged already. We review practices regarding global fund managers who have factored sustainability risks and opportunities successfully into their considerations, or are in the process of converting fully in this direction.

Perhaps the most important thing we can stress is that politics needs to be fully removed from this equation. Too often, the mainstream investment community is biased toward the right, while the left is biased towards the SRI realm. There are few exceptions to this either way, with both camps potentially ignoring practical matters regarding unstoppable trends of sustainability. Investing to one's values is fine, if that's what one wants to do with one's money. Through our definition of sustainable investing, we separate the value we see in sustainability from the primarily negative screening values-based approach that tends to dominate SRI, especially in the United States.

Sustainable investing, then, sits neatly between the mainstream on the right, providing value opportunities that are sensible for any investor to pursue, and for investors on the left, who want to participate in an evolved, practical, positive perspective, that if taken to scale, can lead to the sustainable world they seek to aspire to.

Sustainable investing represents the practical center—where most investors and investment belongs. It is no different from how most political elections unwind, favoring the center, where the majority wants decisions to be taken. The same must be true for the aggregate goals of investment in general, aspiring to and protecting values of fairness, equity, and well-being while providing full incentives and opportunity, avoiding societal crash and burn in a rush to an unsustainable top.

Take a blinkered mainstream approach, without a sustainability lens, and you risk missing out on the crises that continue to affect markets globally, the clear trends toward innovation, and the companies that figure to deliver solutions going forward. Take a purely values-based approach, and you risk missing the very same practical opportunities in eco-efficiency and innovation, where the sustainability we require will come from.

The world and all of its various stakeholders need a sustainable investing dynamic to take hold, unless we are self-destructive as a species. I strongly suspect that we are not—and that the majority of the global population desires a world that is not unsustainable. As investors, then, the question arises: Are we best positioned for this inevitability, much as large global corporates, governments, cities, and countries also see themselves in an active, ongoing race to be the most sustainable, productive, educated, healthy, and prosperous possible?

And so let us now embark on a journey through the investors who fully integrate sustainability into their DNA, or intend to, and the metrics, data and regional considerations that are most relevant to get this right. This book in effect charts the history of SRI, while also observing the concurrent trends towards increased use of sustainability factors within investment decision making. It is exciting to witness the more positive, sustainability-minded, value-based investment philosophies, using values, coming out of the purely values-based approaches that have long predominated.

We observe the approaches of those who have been taking a more positive, opportunities-based approach successfully, and the longest, including the Jupiter Ecology Fund (Chapter 2), through others who attempt to embed these opportunities fully, including the Highwater Global Fund (Chapter 4) and Sustainable Asset Management (Chapter 6). We also observe how some of the longest U.S.-based SRI fund managers are now moving more in this direction, including Calvert (Chapter 8), and take an in-depth look at how Domini avoided BP (Chapter 7). Other long-standing fund managers who embed sustainability in North America in different ways are also discussed, including Winslow (Chapter 9), Portfolio 21 (Chapter 10), NEI Investments in Canada (Chapter 11), and Green Century (Chapter 12). European perspectives are also observed closely with looks at Pictet (Chapter 13), Aviva (Chapter 22), and Generation (Chapter 23), as well as Rory Sullivan's attempts to fully integrate sustainability at Insight (Chapter 24). Further regional perspectives are provided with three chapters on Asia (Chapters 25–27) as well as glimpses at Canada, Australia, Africa, and India (Chapters 28–31). Macro issues are also addressed, with analysis and use of environmental metrics (Chapters 15, 16, and 37), the lack of use of sustainability criteria and why (Chapters 17 –20), and Bloomberg's efforts in this area that attempt to bridge this gap (Chapter 21). Other macro issues include the potential for indexes (Chapter 32), private equity (Chapters 35–36), and performance (Chapter 34). Terminology is addressed at the end (Chapter 38) by Lloyd Kurtz, one of the longest-standing SRI researchers in the field.

You will also hear from many thought leaders in this book. They include those in the just-mentioned chapters as well as Roger Urwin on asset allocation considerations (Chapter 33) and noted author and entrepreneur Paul Hawken (Chapter 3). Let's start then with Dan Esty, author of the seminal work *Green to Gold* (John Wiley & Sons, 2009), and his partner David Lubin. The consistent message is that all organizations must seek sustainability as a strategic imperative to have the best chance of future success. The same is very much now true for global investors as well.

The Sustainability Imperative

David A. Lubin and Daniel C. Esty

Noted author, consultant, and educator Dan Esty returned to government in early 2011 as head of Energy and the Environment for the state of Connecticut. The public sector will benefit from the same toolkit and opportunity set he has provided to the corporate world via his seminal work *Green to Gold* (John Wiley & Sons, 2009) and related endeavors. Only through seizing the opportunities emerging from the megatrend of sustainability can corporations become the winners of tomorrow. There is a clear race to sustainability emerging between corporates and between countries and states. Investors likely cannot ignore these trends for much longer.

Our research into the forces that have shaped the competitive landscape in recent decades reveals that "business megatrends" have features and trajectories in common. Sustainability is an emerging megatrend, and thus its course is to some extent predictable. Understanding how firms won in prior megatrends can help executives craft the strategies and systems they will need to gain advantage in this one.

SUSTAINABILITY: A BUSINESS MEGATREND

The concept of megatrends is not new, of course. Businessman and author John Naisbitt popularized the term in his 1982 best seller of the same name,

---

Excerpted from a piece originally published in the *Harvard Business Review* (May 2010).

referring to incipient societal and economic shifts such as globalization, the rise of the information society, and the move from hierarchical organizations to networks.

Our focus is on business megatrends, which force fundamental and persistent shifts in how companies compete. Such transformations often arise from technological innovation or from new ways of doing business, and many factors can launch or magnify the process of change. Business megatrends may emerge from or be accelerated by many factors including financial crises, shifts in the social realities that define the marketplace, or the threat of conflict over resources. The geopolitics of the Cold War, for example, drove the innovations that launched both the space race and rapid developments in the field of microelectronics—ultimately unleashing the information technology megatrend. Electrification, the rise of mass production, and globalization were also megatrends, as was the quality movement of the 1970s and 1980s. The common thread among them is that they presented inescapable strategic imperatives for corporate leaders.

Why do we think sustainability qualifies as an emerging megatrend? Over the past ten years, environmental issues have steadily encroached on the capacity of businesses to create value for customers, shareholders, and other stakeholders. Globalized workforces and supply chains have created environmental pressures and attendant business liabilities. The rise of new world powers, notably China and India, has intensified competition for natural resources (especially oil) and added a geopolitical dimension to sustainability. "Externalities" such as carbon dioxide emissions and water use are fast becoming material—meaning that investors consider them central to a firm's performance and stakeholders expect companies to share information about them. These forces are magnified by escalating public and governmental concern about climate change, industrial pollution, food safety, and natural resource depletion, among other issues.

Consumers in many countries are seeking out sustainable products and services or leaning on companies to improve the sustainability of traditional ones. Governments are interceding with unprecedented levels of new regulation—from the recent Securities and Exchange Commission ruling that climate risk is material to investors to the Environmental Protection Agency's mandate that greenhouse gases be regulated as a pollutant. Further fueling this megatrend, thousands of companies are placing strategic bets on innovation in energy efficiency, renewable power, resource productivity, and pollution control. What this all adds up to is that managers can no longer afford to ignore sustainability as a central factor in the long-term competitiveness of their companies.

Megatrends require businesses to adapt and innovate or be swept aside. So what can businesses learn from previous megatrends? Consider the quality movement. The quality revolution was about innovation in the core set of tools and methods that companies used to manage much of what they do. Quality as a central element of strategy, rather than a tactical tool, smashed previous cost versus fitness for use barriers, which meant the table stakes were dramatically raised for all companies.

The information technology (IT) revolution was about tangible technology breakthroughs that fundamentally altered business capabilities and redefined how companies do much of what they do. Digital technologies deeply penetrated corporations in the 1980s and 1990s, and the trend accelerated as IT made its way into the daily lives of workers and consumers with the advent of desktop computing and the Internet. In both the IT and quality business megatrends—as in others we've studied—the market leaders evolved through four principal stages of megatrend driven value creation:

1. They focused on reducing cost, risks, and waste and delivering proof of value.
2. They redesigned selected products, processes, or business functions to optimize their performance—in essence, progressing from doing old things in new ways to doing new things in new ways.
3. They drove revenue growth by integrating innovative approaches into their core strategies.
4. They differentiated their value propositions through new business models that used these innovations like quality and IT to enhance corporate culture, brand leadership, and other intangibles to secure durable competitive advantage.

GETTING THE VISION RIGHT

Just as winners in previous megatrends outperformed competitors by following a staged evolution in strategy, so too must companies hoping to lead (or even compete) in the emerging sustainability wave.

Stage 1: Doing Old Things in New Ways

Firms focus on outperforming competitors on regulatory compliance and environment-related cost and risk management. In doing so, they develop proof cases for the value of eco-efficiency. At its inception 30 years ago, 3M's Pollution Prevention Pays (PPP) was just this kind of initiative. As of 2005, PPP had reduced 3M pollutants by more than 2.6 billion pounds and saved the company more than $1 billion. It also laid the foundation for the nearly completed Environmental Targets 2005–2010 program, which will reduce expenses related to energy usage, emissions, and waste by another 20%.

Stage 2: Doing New Things in New Ways

Firms engage in widespread redesign of products, processes, and whole systems to optimize natural resource efficiencies and risk management across their value chains. DuPont's "zero waste" commitment, for instance, increased the company's prioritization of eco-efficiency across operations. Its decision to shed businesses with big eco-footprints, such as carpets and nylon, was based on an analysis that the business and environmental risks would outweigh their potential contribution to future earnings.

Stage 3: Transforming the Core Business

As the vision expands further, sustainability innovations become the source of new revenues and growth. Dow's sweeping 2015 Sustainability Goals, designed to drive innovation across its many lines of business, yielded new products or technology breakthroughs in areas from solar roof shingles to hybrid batteries. The core business, which traditionally had relied on commodity chemicals, has shifted toward advanced materials and high-tech energy opportunities fully integrating sustainability into Dow's business strategy

Stage 4: New Business Model Creation and Differentiation

At the highest level, firms exploit the megatrend as a source of differentiation in business model, brand, employee engagement, and other intangibles, fundamentally repositioning the company and redefining its strategy for competitive advantage. For example, Unilever's recently announced Sustainable Living Plan would seem to qualify if executed fully. Unilever, the global consumer goods giant, has pledged that by the year 2020, it will halve the environmental footprint of its products and source all of its agricultural materials sustainably while helping 1 billion people with their health and well-being.[1]

GETTING THE EXECUTION RIGHT

Gaining advantage in a megatrend is not just about vision—it's also about execution in five critical areas: leadership, methods, strategy, management, and reporting. In each area, companies must transition from tactical, ad hoc, and siloed approaches to strategic, systematic and integrated ones.

Systematic Methods for Assessing Value

With a sustainability vision in place, the executive team must marshal specialized capabilities for weighing options and quantifying benefits and risks. Just as the quality and IT megatrends ushered in new skill sets and fresh perspectives, the sustainability megatrend will require firms to update traditional business tools—business case analysis, trend spotting, scenario planning, risk modeling, and even cost accounting—to encompass the specialized requirements of environmental sustainability.

Most current methods that companies use to track or project sustainability impacts generate inconsistent, incomplete, and imprecise data. Recognizing that if they can't measure it, they can't manage it, companies are developing better means of gauging costs and benefits related to corporate sustainability and of benchmarking performance. Fujitsu, for instance, employs a performance assessment scorecard—its "cost green index"—that assesses the potential cost, productivity, and environmental impacts of eco-efficiency initiatives across the firm.

Other companies are repurposing standardized tools and methods to bring a sustainability focus to all aspects of the business. For example, 3M, a longtime quality leader, is now applying lean Six Sigma methodologies originally aimed at improving operational efficiency and product quality to driving direct reductions in energy use, waste, and greenhouse gas emissions. To meet aggressive five-year sustainability targets, its Six Sigma leadership group has trained 55,000 employees in how to use these methods. As sustainability-related methods and tools mature, we expect training programs and certifications not unlike certified IT roles or black and green belts in the quality domain to emerge.

Developing Distinctive Strategies

Once firms have a solid base of analytical data, they will be positioned to develop distinctive sustainability strategies. Many aspects of strategy development will remain internal, but companies increasingly will adopt open-source approaches that engage outsiders. Perhaps more than any other company, Wal-Mart has pursued this approach. In 2006, then chief executive Lee Scott launched Sustainability 360, establishing explicit goals to purchase 100% renewable energy, create zero waste, slash greenhouse gas emissions, and sell products that sustain global resources and the environment. To this end, Wal-Mart created a dozen Sustainable Value Networks, each comprising Wal-Mart team members, nongovernmental organization experts, academics, government officials, and supplier representatives, all working under the direction of a Wal-Mart network captain. Each team focuses on a strategic issue targeted by the company's sustainability agenda—such as facilities, packaging, and logistics—and tries to develop new ways of doing business that support the company's sustainability goals. The payoffs are already showing up: One of the Sustainable Value Networks, tasked with fleet logistics, came up with a transportation strategy that improved efficiency by 38%, saving Wal-Mart more than $200 million annually and cutting its greenhouse gas emissions by 200,000 tons per year.

Integrating Objectives into Management

To capture the full benefits of the megatrend-driven strategy, firms must integrate sustainability objectives into day-to-day management. Leadership may come from headquarters, but responsibility for implementation lies in the field. Firms such as Dow have incorporated sustainability objectives into compensation models, reviews, and other management processes, including a requirement that all newly promoted business unit managers review their units' sustainability plans with senior management within 90 days. Managing sustainability strategy requires systems support as well. While many firms have invested in technology to record and report environmental events such as spills and waste disposal, others have gone much further.

Wayne Balta, head of Corporate Environmental Affairs at IBM, describes his company's environmental management system as the foundation for policy deployment, practice management, goal setting, decision-making, and data capture. IBM uses the technology to embed environmental strategies into all areas of the business, from research and development to operations to end-of-life product disposal.

BUILDING A SUSTAINABILITY PERFORMANCE SYSTEM

By joining a vision of sustainability value creation (the "what we must do") with evolving execution capabilities (the "how we must do it"), firms develop what we call a sustainability performance system. Depending on their sophistication in both realms and their desire to use sustainability as a competitive weapon, they will fall into one of the next four categories.

Category 1: Losers

As the sustainability megatrend accelerates, firms that have put in place only modest cost, risk, and waste initiatives and whose vision and strategies are vaguely conceived or disjointed will find it increasingly difficult to protect their position. It may be too early to see clear examples of firms that have lost their competitive position based on the failure to develop and execute sustainability strategies, but the casualties from other megatrends like quality and IT abound. GM's decline can be traced clearly to its earlier failure to understand how quality considerations would transform the auto industry. Likewise, Kodak's dominant position in photography eroded quickly as it missed or ignored the signals that digital technologies would displace film.

Category 2: Defenders

Some firms may choose a go-slow sustainability strategy for many reasons—the peculiarities of their industry sector or business processes, their environmental exposure, or other competitive considerations. Others will be content to make investments in the early-stage objectives of cost, risk, and waste management. This defensive posture can work, provided the gap between a go-slow company's market position and that of primary competitors does not grow too large and the company has execution capabilities commensurate with the complexity of its business. Maersk, the Danish shipping company, has focused its sustainability efforts on efficiency, slashing fuel costs and cutting carbon dioxide emissions through slow-speed shipping and other initiatives. As long as others in the shipping business do not pursue a more sweeping sustainability strategy, perhaps built on more efficient ship design, Maersk should be able to hold its position. Indeed, many companies may find that their best option is to play defense on sustainability and not try to make this the issue on which they differentiate themselves in the marketplace.

Category 3: Dreamers

When vision and ambition get too far ahead of the capacity to execute, companies face another set of issues. Those that seek first-mover advantages in the later stages of sustainability differentiation without having mapped out a clear strategy and mastered the fundamentals of execution may experience the same kinds of problems that plagued some aspiring pioneers in the quality and IT megatrends. For instance, the London Stock Exchange's vision of a paperless settlement system was a bold move and one that managers believed would catapult the organization ahead of its peers. Managers optimistically ballparked the cost at £6 million and jumped in with both feet. By the time the exchange acknowledged that it lacked the management and technical capabilities to execute this leading-edge IT project, in 1993, the tab had shot past £400 million, with no end in sight. Dreamers who try to ride the sustainability wave risk making sustainability promises they can't keep, inviting charges of greenwashing and the attendant reputational and financial harm. Some years ago, Ford Motor Company suffered from Bill Ford's attempts to green his business before his management team was ready. His unfulfilled commitments to improve SUV fuel economy and make Ford a leader in hybrid vehicles brought the wrath of environmental groups. His successor, Alan Mullaly, has moved Ford forward with new models that feature advanced materials, smart systems, and high efficiency, enabling the automaker to withstand the current downturn better than domestic competitors and positioning Ford for success.

Category 4: Winners

Although the sustainability landscape continues to shift, some early winners have emerged. GE's financial services business has lagged badly, but its Ecomagination product line has generated tens of billions of dollars in revenues and positioned the company as a leader in rapidly growing market segments such as energy infrastructure and high-efficiency appliances, jet engines, and locomotives.

The Ecomagination marketing campaign has also had a halo effect, helping GE transform its reputation from environmental bad actor to sustainability front-runner. Similarly, Clorox's Greenworks line of ecofriendly cleaning products has reframed the public's perception of the company—and generated billions of dollars of sales. Clorox's acquisition of Burt's Bees, a leader in natural personal care products, further convinced environmental stakeholders that the company's shift in strategy was both sincere and significant. Soon companies will have a clear sense of what it means to manage sustainability as a business megatrend. Best practices will emerge, and sustainability scorecards will allow companies to track cost and risk reduction as well as evaluate value-creation activities. As environmental data become richer and more accurate, companies will be able to chart their impacts in financial terms—making it easier for market analysts to identify the firms positioned to deliver an ecopremium. In this new world, the sustainability strategy imperative will be systematized and integrated into the day-to-day practices of firms of all sizes in all industries.

SUMMARY

Like the IT and quality megatrends, sustainability will touch every function, every business line, and every employee. On the way to this future, firms with a clear vision and the execution capabilities to navigate the megatrend will come out ahead. Those that don't will be left by the wayside.

NOTE

1. www.sustainable-living.unilever.com/

CHAPTER 2

Jupiter Ecology

Mark L. Trevitt

One fund has arguably been investing in sustainability as a positive driver of value and opportunities longer than any other: U.K.-based Jupiter Ecology. This fund has been a consistent outperformer over time, finding opportunities while being mindful of a full suite of environmental and social risks. It has done so with a consistent approach over the long term, with very low turnover in both companies invested in and personnel managing the fund, a clear sign of confidence and consistency.

For example, back in 2002, Jupiter Ecology's top two holdings were Vestas Wind Systems, the world's biggest wind energy provider, and Cranswick plc, a food producer. In 2010, these two companies remained the fund's largest holdings, and Cranswick was still its largest position as of this writing.

Jupiter Ecology's story is an ideal place to begin our journey.

ROOTS OF THE FUND

The word "ecology" is derived from two Greek words: *oikos*, which means "house" or "household," and *logia*, which means "the study of." At its

---

With input from Mark Campanale (email correspondence, December 3, 2010), Emma Howard Boyd and Charlie Thomas (interviewed on November 15, 2010 at Jupiter's offices), and Tessa Tennant (email correspondence, March 14, 2011). Nick Robins assisted in editing the final draft.

essence, ecology is the study of Earth and its relationships with organisms and the environment, as well as how those relationships affect the planet. The concept of sustainability emerges from this study of human activity and its onward effects on Earth's ability to support life.

The Brundtland Commission's famous report of 1987 sought a definition of sustainability, calling for a need to find a way to satisfy our present needs without jeopardizing future generations' ability to do the same.[1] The Jupiter Ecology Fund has aimed to demonstrate that by investing with sustainable principles in mind, one can hasten the day when economy and ecology are no longer at odds but are aligned.

JUPITER ECOLOGY'S INVESTMENT PROCESS

Jupiter's philosophy is predicated on the belief that investment success is based on conducting extensive proprietary company analysis and research. Strict stock-selection criteria are combined with a thematic investment strategy: investing in companies benefiting from green growth. A company's eligibility for investment is determined by research conducted through meetings with management, on-site visits, and desk-based research along with analyzing additional information received from other interested stakeholders, including campaign groups, financial analysts, and trade bodies. Currently Jupiter has eight dedicated analysts and portfolio managers, which enables frequent meetings with the management of companies in which they invest or are considering.

When analyzing core holdings following results, Jupiter's socially responsible investment (SRI) and governance team meets with the chief executive and/or chief financial officer and also seeks to meet with the head of sustainability. This approach allows Jupiter to gain additional insight, as sustainability issues are discussed in light of the company's long-term strategic direction. It is also of importance to Jupiter to understand the chair and board roles from a governance standpoint: how they foresee environmental and social trends shaping the company's business outlook longer term as well as their transparency around management and reporting of these issues. Through this process, Jupiter's team members gauge to what extent sustainability is engrained in the company's operational DNA.

Jupiter Ecology takes a systematic approach to integrating environmental and social factors, backed by its extensive research. A company's environmental and social performance and financial prospects are considered separately by the Jupiter SRI and governance team and the specialist Jupiter SRI Fund management team respectively. Only once companies meet both financial and social/environmental criteria will the fund consider investing.

Jupiter believes that this approach not only benefits Jupiter's Green Funds but also the wider sustainable development process.

Two-Pronged Strategy

The Jupiter Ecology fund combines strict "dark green" ethical criteria with a positive selection focused on green growth opportunities.

First, companies are evaluated against a set of predefined ethical criteria. When researching companies, the fund leverages the expertise and abilities of the SRI and governance team to uncover whether companies are involved in activities that conflict with the fund's environmental, social, and ethical objectives. To assist in the evaluation of how companies are managing their social and environmental impact, ratings research is used from what is now MSCI ESG Research (originally Innovest; see Chapter 17.) If team members are concerned about a company's involvement in particular activities, they will not invest in it.

Such activities include:

- *Armaments*. Companies that manufacture or sell armaments
- *Alcoholic drinks*. Companies that manufacture or sell alcoholic drinks
- *Tobacco*. Companies that manufacture or sell tobacco products
- *Pornography*. Companies that publish, print, or distribute pornography
- *Nuclear power*. Companies that generate nuclear power or build nuclear power plants
- *Gambling*. Companies that operate betting or gambling facilities

Companies that are marginally involved in any of these areas (e.g., if they derive less than 10% of turnover from any one of these activities) may be invested in if they demonstrate strong environmental and social performance in other respects.

In addition, team members avoid companies that conduct or commission animal testing for cosmetic or toiletry purposes. They also pay particular attention to issues such as sustainable sourcing of food and biotechnologies.

Second, the fund is then tilted toward those companies providing solutions to environmental and social problems. Jupiter Ecology's aim is to benefit from a shift toward sustainable development, notably: renewable energy companies, environmental control systems, organic foods and cosmetics, water treatment technologies, and recycling. Initially four investment themes were developed that the fund would focus on, with later additions bringing the total to six. Today many of these themes are followed by other sustainability fund managers, but Jupiter Ecology was among the very first funds to do so.

Water Management   Water is one of the world's most critical resources, and it is believed that economic growth, population shifts, and climate change will contribute to severe shortages and degradation of global water supplies. Global demand for water is rising dramatically with annual global water withdrawal expected to grow to approximately 6.9 trillion cubic meters by 2030, while the quality of available water continues to deteriorate.[2] As an international water crisis edges closer, governments and businesses are taking action, creating a range of opportunities. (See Chapter 16.) In developed countries, this trend is forcing the replacement and upgrading of aging infrastructure; developing countries, however, require new infrastructure to support growth. Jupiter invests across the spectrum of the global water industry, from established utilities engaged in water and wastewater services, including sewerage and treatment infrastructure, to the high-tech players involved in innovative technology-based solutions, such as membranes and ultraviolet disinfection. Jupiter notes that the sector is not without its pitfalls, as ensuring adequate supplies of clean water is an emotive and highly politically sensitive issue, creating uncertainty and risk.

Clean Energy   The world's demand for energy is immense and expected to grow. The International Energy Agency, for example, says that global energy demand is expected to rise by more than 50% by 2030. A primary driver is the rapid industrialization of developing countries, such as China and India, which is placing increasing pressure on energy supplies. Two principal and related problems are changing the energy landscape:

1. The looming threat of peak oil and concerns over the security and supply of fossils is causing prices to escalate.
2. The global threat of climate change means the transition to alternatives over fossil fuels is accelerating.

Bloomberg New Energy Finance estimates that the total worldwide new investment in clean energy industry in 2010 was $243 billion.[3] HSBC also forecasts a tripling of the low-carbon energy market between now and 2020 based on three key drivers: climate change concern, energy/resource security, and innovation.[4] Jupiter focuses its investment in technologies, such as wind, solar, and fuel cells, as well as emissions reduction and energy efficiency.

Waste Management   Across the globe, levels of waste have breached the capacity for environmentally sound management. This situation is driven in a large part by urbanization, as city dwellers produce up to three times as much waste as those in rural areas. In industrialized nations where a larger portion of the population is concentrated in cities, waste per capita is higher. Jupiter Ecology took notice of this trend early, realizing that one person's trash is another's treasure, and it started looking for companies that were adapting to the needs of a closed-loop economy. In an effort to curb this trend, governments are implementing policies incorporating four key tenets: reduce, reuse, recycle, and energy recovery, policies that are creating an array of investment opportunities. Reducing waste is catching on with corporations, which are now striving to remove unnecessary packaging from their products while achieving cost reductions along the way. Wal-Mart, for example, has set a target to reduce its packaging by 5% by 2013, hoping it will save the company over $3 billion.[5] The fund sees three principal drivers accelerating the take-up of recycling.

1. As resources scarcity begins to take its bite it will become imperative to recover valuable materials.
2. The economics of recycling become more attractive as the price of oil rises.
3. It is now recognized that for a range of materials, such as aluminum, recycling reduces greenhouse gas emissions. The pressure to reduce greenhouse gas (GHG) emissions from waste fermentation and incineration is also sparking interest in biogas capture, energy recovery, and composting technologies.

Environmental Services   When Jupiter started looking into the environmental services sector, many companies were offshoots from engineering firms and academic institutions, but this sector has grown into a market in its own right. As sustainability has become entrenched in public policy, it has found prominence in boardrooms. Corporations are now considering sustainability against the backdrop of their strategic direction and employing consultants to examine it through the lens of corporate liability and risk. Companies have realized that the public is more than ever concerned about environmental issues and are taking measures to improve their image. Environmental consultants are increasingly drawn on to provide services related to a company's corporate responsibility program, considering both its direct impacts and those of its suppliers. Jupiter looks for opportunities in companies directly benefiting from increased environmental and safety legislation, whose goods and services facilitate sustainable management of environmental resources and pollution control technology.

Green Transport   The transport sector faces the challenge of reducing fossil fuel use, both to ensure energy security and to contribute toward efforts to reduce GHG emissions. Transport accounts for nearly a quarter of global GHG emissions, an amount that is expected to rise rapidly as motorization spreads across developing countries.[6] Measures are being taken globally to reduce the environmental, social, and economic costs of transport through development of cleaner fuels, promoting low-carbon vehicle technologies, and changing consumer consumptions patterns. Jupiter looks for innovative companies providing public transport services and vehicle emissions and energy-efficiency control systems.

Sustainable Living   Living standards are on the rise globally, and an aging population is creating two major demographic trends: People are living longer, and there are more people aged 60-plus as proportion of the total population. According to the United Nations, the proportion of the global population age 60-plus is projected to reach 21% by 2050.[7] This aging population is creating a greater need for better long-term healthcare and medicines. People are now more focused on their well-being, having an active healthy lifestyle, and eating a more nutritious diet, which stems from concerns over the growing incidence of obesity. Consumers are increasingly worried about food safety and quality following food-related crises, such as avian flu and the presence of pesticide residues on imported foods. Farming practices are also under more scrutiny as pressure mounts to switch to sustainable agricultural practices to reduce the loss of biodiversity and soil and water degradation from the large-scale use of synthetic fertilizers and pesticides. While this theme started off as a niche market, it has expanded into a mass market, as recent trends have created opportunities in organic and natural food, complementary medicines, and bioanalytical and safety testing.

GOOD GOVERNANCE

The fund also has the option to invest in companies outside these six themes if they meet one of three criteria.

1. *Leading company.* Companies that demonstrate leading practice among their industry peers
2. *Limited impact company.* Companies that have relatively low environmental impact and therefore can manage these appropriately using a light-touch approach
3. *Small company.* Companies whose management has a commitment to improve performance and can demonstrate that key social and environmental risks are managed well

As the strategy of the fund has progressed, there has been a deemphasis on this element, falling from up to 25% to less than 1%. This reduction reflects the growing availability of stocks corresponding to the thematic approach.

BUILDING A FOLLOWING

Jupiter's long-standing green heritage has been vital to its sustained success.[8] In 1987, Tessa Tennant and Francis Miller, with the backing of Derek Childs (then a director of Warburg Pincus and fund manager at Mercury Asset Management), founded Merlin Fund Management. In April 1988, they launched the first green fund in Europe, Merlin Ecology. Jupiter acquired Merlin Fund Management in a merger in 1989, and the fund became known as the Jupiter Ecology Fund. The fund has the unique position of having over 20 years of experience in the field of opportunities-focused sustainable investing.

Jupiter Ecology pioneered the inclusion of sustainable development goals alongside ethical factors within its investment philosophy. It also helped stimulate thought leadership and collective action to move the agenda forward. One of the first initiatives came through Mark Campanale, working as an investment analyst under the head of research, Tennant. Campanale encouraged Jupiter's involvement as cofounder of the industry investment body known as the UK Social Investment Forum, and Jupiter has stayed heavily involved in this group ever since.

Jupiter Ecology played a pivotal role in helping submit the Rio Resolution at the 1992 Earth Summit, highlighting the role SRI can play in incorporating sustainability within the mechanics of global capital markets.[9] It was a natural inclination for Jupiter to produce and encourage thought leadership, but it also served the additional purpose of attracting interested investors to its way of thinking. Jupiter also wrote the first set of investment guidelines for sustainable investing, called the "Investment Process for Green Investment," launched by the Association of Chartered Certified Accountants in 1992, which established criteria for assessing products, processes, and practices. These concepts set the groundwork for beginning to study a more diverse range of businesses on corporate performance, focusing on industries of the future and utilizing the approach of best-in-class and shareholder engagement.

With a focus on sustainability, Jupiter Ecology's primary objective was to invest in companies on a global basis that addressed the challenges of environmental degradation and to make a positive commitment to societal well-being. Childs's logic was straightforward: Invest in great companies that provide these solutions, with the idea that the fund would benefit from the transition to sustainability. The potential for climate change meant the fund went looking for renewable energy companies; resource conservation meant recycling businesses; and water scarcity meant finding innovative water treatment firms.

Childs's insight drove Jupiter Ecology's focus to a number of encouraging green enterprises at an early stage in its development. The inclusion of nonlisted investments (in effect, private equity) was a dramatic break from convention. Some of the businesses the fund invested in during the early 1990s have gone on to become industry leaders, such as Fuel Tech Inc., a company in the field of energy-efficiency technologies.

In the fund's earliest days, many of Jupiter Ecology's investors were individuals who believed in what they were trying to accomplish and wanted to influence businesses to do the right thing. Tennant recalled an early memory of a man in biker gear turning up at the office and writing out a check for $16,500 shortly after the fund was launched.[10] He said that this was "all his savings," and he believed in the fund's mission and wanted to back it as fully as he could. It is therefore not surprising that many of the fund's investors have literally stayed with Jupiter over its more than 20-year life.

Although there were those who passionately supported Jupiter Ecology in its infancy, Campanale recalls that one of the greatest challenges was the distribution of the fund itself. Most mainstream investment advisors or wealth managers were skeptical. However, the public started taking notice of the strong performance under fund manager Clare Brook, whose investment acumen had been honed under Childs's previous leadership as investment manager. Tennant supported this with her ideas. The story of Jupiter Ecology started to resonate with the U.K. media, and investors started buying into the fund's approach.

BUILDING ON FIRM FOUNDATIONS

Today, the Jupiter Ecology Fund, managed by Charlie Thomas with the SRI and governance team headed by Emma Howard Boyd, has $654 million in assets invested across the globe. Howard Boyd notes:

> *Interest in climate change is now coming from right across the board, particularly from those with a long-term focus, and in particular, from pension fund trustees who by definition need to take a longer-term view. These trustees know they need to start considering the possibility of longer term environmental change, and are considering ways to increase exposure to this in their underlying portfolios.*[11]

She says that climate change is now perceived as an investment theme in itself with trustees in some cases allocating upward of 5% to 15% to such strategies.

The same values that were ingrained in Jupiter Ecology a generation earlier are instilled in current managers, while other investors have begun to catch up to their way of thinking. Jupiter sees this increased awareness translating into continued growth, stemming from three key drivers:

- Legislative and government support on a global basis
- Corporate commitments
- Longer-term consumer purchasing trends

These pillars of growth create a virtuous circle, where government, companies, and consumers are all making positive contributions to change.

Increasing global legislation is helping drive international corporate commitment. These efforts include the reduction of the environmental impacts of company operations and of the products they sell, to conform to national and international standards. Consumers' awareness of sustainability is also becoming a major secular trend that is motivating corporations to commit to greening their operations. This change is also being supported by mounting pressure from nongovernmental organizations campaigns and stakeholder activism. Additional capital spending is driving demand from small to mid-cap companies for new and cleaner technologies. Furthermore, consumer awareness is translating into shifts in consumption patterns as individuals become more concerned about environmental issues when making purchases. Historically, green consumers have represented 6% to 8% of the market, but this segment of the economy is steadily rising.[12] There has also been a proliferation of new products catering to these consumers, such as fair trade coffee, hybrid cars, and energy-saving lighting.

Business practices are shifting to adapt to changing consumer preferences and to develop a competitive edge in new and innovative markets. Investors are also another factor shaping business attitudes toward the environment, as a company's performance on environmental issues is increasingly seen as proxy for management quality. Although these trends are gaining momentum, Thomas believes that many of the sustainability issues that Jupiter takes into consideration have yet to be fully factored into valuations, particularly for small to mid-cap companies. As result, Jupiter Ecology has developed a natural bias toward this area of the market, where it typically finds innovative business models with novel technologies.

ASSESSING COMPANIES FOR THE LONG TERM

The specialist SRI fund management team at Jupiter takes a rigorous approach to company selection by emphasizing fundamental bottom-up stock picking. The team looks for three essential elements that are core to long-term small and mid-cap investing:

1. The company must have a leading technology or be providing a leading solution.
2. It is paramount that management has the skill set to deliver on the business model.
3. It is critical for the investment horizon considered—three to five years typically—that these companies can generate long-term returns.

Another aspect of the fund that reflects its long-term commitment is its low portfolio turnover. Thomas himself is a testament to this. On the first day Thomas joined Jupiter in 1994, Simon Baker, the fund manager who had taken over from Brook, passed off his company valuations to him. Meeting with Thomas in Jupiter's offices overlooking Hyde Park, he still has the original paper, from which he read off 12 stocks from the portfolio in 1994 that are still held today. According to Thomas, "The annual turnover for Jupiter Ecology is 20%–25%, while the average of most funds in the U.K. is 125%."[13] The reason for this, Thomas says, is that Jupiter scrutinizes companies from both the environmental/social and the financial angle intensely and takes time to consider carefully whether to invest. While many investors seek to buy in at the early-stages of a company's development, Thomas believes this is risky and that it is more sensible to invest in companies that are already profitable and whose hype has not gotten ahead of reality. Thomas mentions that some of the best risk-adjusted returns often are found in those companies that employ and use existing technologies.[14] When they do invest, they typically initially take a small position and increase it over time as they become more confident in the company's ability to deliver.[15] For these reasons, they try to avoid blue-sky companies and rarely participate in the latest hot initial public offering. Instead they prefer gradually to get to know a company to ensure that risks and potential are identified and managed.

VOTING AND ENGAGEMENT: PARTICIPATING IN THE PROCESS OF CHANGE

Since the beginning, Jupiter took a holistic view to research and analysis, with a triple-bottom-line approach, reflecting an integrated understanding of business performance in which social, environmental, and economic bottom lines are interdependent. At Jupiter, engagement is effectively working from the inside, using its vital role as shareholders to encourage a higher level of corporate performance and appropriate culture to enhance long-term shareholder value through the adoption of best practices on environmental, social, and governance matters. Motivated to change business behavior, one of Jupiter's earliest engagement tactics was to write regularly to the Hundred Group, that represent the Finance Directors of U.K.'s largest companies, requesting disclosure on environmental issues. They weren't afraid to ruffle a feather or two, engaging with listed companies they didn't hold and leveraging the Jupiter brand to have their ideas heard by the boards of companies.

Jupiter's SRI and governance team—now overseen by Howard Boyd—is responsible for engaging and voting on a wide range of issues, such as remuneration, business strategy, capital raising, risk management, and relevant sustainability issues in accordance with Jupiter's Corporate Governance and Voting Policy.[16] Across Jupiter's funds in the six months prior to June 30, 2010, the team held 89 meetings with companies and sent 117 letters to companies on sustainability issues.[17]

FINDING GREAT GREEN COMPANIES

In the early days, the greatest challenge the fund faced was finding enough pure-play green companies that were aligned with its philosophy. Analysts searched through stock exchanges and published documents for innovative green businesses around the world. Although there were plenty of service agencies attempting to cater to the needs of the ethical investor, those agencies were structured to screen companies against simple environmental norms. Jupiter Ecology needed to pull out the micro-cap pure-play companies; these agencies weren't able to fill that requirement.

The sector has since matured and become more diverse. Large businesses are increasingly greening their existing products or entering new markets to provide solutions to the challenges faced. They range from the smallest start-up companies to some of the world's biggest enterprises. Jupiter sees the 2005 launch of GE's Ecomagination campaign as a watershed moment. As GE seeks to capitalize on the demand for environmental products, the campaign has spurred innovation and growth. Boyd says that revenues from Ecomagination products are growing at nearly twice the company average. In June 2010, the company announced a further $10 billion investment in the strategy by 2015.[18] While today around a quarter of the fund is invested in small-cap companies, this figure used to be much higher.[19] This change reflects many of the fund's early small-cap investments growing into larger companies, along with the emergence of more large-cap companies that finally satisfy Jupiter Ecology's criteria. While there are many great green ideas, there are fewer great green companies, and this is where Jupiter's emphasis on extensive firsthand research has proven a decisive element in its success.

Cranswick Plc

One of the first pieces of sell-side investment research on environmental opportunities alerted the Jupiter team to a potential fund holding. "The James Capel Green Book," produced by Roger Hardman and Tim Steer in 1991, profiled a pig-meat processor that had decided to develop "high-welfare" pig products based on traditional methods that would provide better standards of living for the animals. The company was Cranswick plc, which immediately sparked the interest of then analyst Mark Campanale, who recalls its initial appeal: "avoiding tethering, clipping of tails; giving plenty of access out of doors for roaming and even giving the highly intelligent pigs footballs to play with when indoors."[20] Today, the company is involved in all aspects of the high-welfare pork business from processing and packing to the production of sausages and cooked meats. The organic approach is designed to deliver positive health throughout soils, plants, and crops through to the animal, avoiding the need for agrochemicals and routine antibiotics and contributing positively to the environment and wildlife.

Jupiter Ecology anticipated a shift to organics and high-welfare animal products, driven by increasing concerns over welfare and the impact of intensive farming. Demand for organic food is also increasingly stimulated by a growing public concern around food safety, health, and nutrition. The U.K. organic market has grown at around 10% a year since 1993, reaching $2.8 billion in total sales in 2010.[21] Although sales have slowed during the economic downturn, the Soil Association sees positive signs of resilience and recovery for the organic sector overall. (See Figure 2.1.)

However, it wasn't just sustainability and the macro story that attracted Jupiter to Cranswick. The fundamentals of the company were also compelling. Cranswick had excellent company management with a track record in generating positive cash flows and delivering on their business strategy. While the average food processing company in the United Kingdom was experiencing 1% to 2% growth a year, Cranswick was bringing home the bacon, growing by more than 10% a year, as the demand for organic food escalated.[22] As low-cost importers dominated the cheap end of the market, high-welfare producers such as Cranswick were able to attract affluent customers and protect margins. The company itself mirrors Jupiter's long-term commitment, as its then chief executive is now chair of the board.

As of this writing, Cranswick constitutes the fund's largest holding at 3.1% (Sustainable Living), having remained in the fund since first

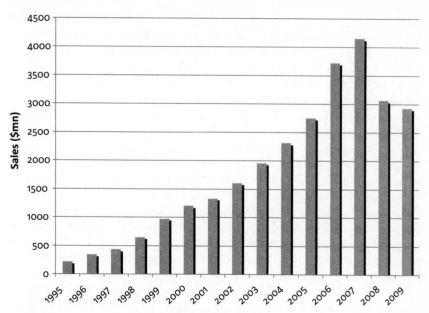

FIGURE 2.1   U.K. Organic Sales, 1995 to 2010
Source: Soil Association Organic Market Report 2011, www.soilassociation.org

investing.[23] The company has developed a prominent position in the high-quality and organic food markets as one of the United Kingdom's biggest suppliers of organic pork to supermarkets. Jupiter also actively engaged with the board of Cranswick from the outset to reduce the company's impact on the environment. Environmental considerations are now core to the business, with Cranswick coordinating the group's approach to environmental management into a project known as Green Thinking.[24]

RPS (Previously Rural Planning Services Ltd.)

In the early years, there weren't many companies that fit the Jupiter Ecology mold. One the first pure-play green companies emerging at the time was Rural Planning Services Ltd. (RPS), founded in 1970 as the United Kingdom's first environmental consultancy. It was listed on the London Stock Exchange in 1995, and the ecology fund bought shares at the initial public offering.

Over the years, the company has grown through acquisitions to become a multidisciplinary consultancy. It provides advisory services to the public and private sector in the development of land, property, and infrastructure, the exploration and production of energy and other natural resources, the management of the environment, and the health and safety of people. RPS has also increased its geographical reach and now has 60 offices throughout the United Kingdom and 31 international offices in Europe, North America, and the Far East. It has proven to be a huge success story in the United Kingdom, growing at an average rate of 27.4% per annum over the past decade. Currently, RPS is working with Centrica Renewables on the development, engineering, and construction of the largest wind farm under construction in U.K. waters.[25] It also recently aided Scottish Power in developing Scotland's largest dedicated biomass-fired energy plant, through extensive air quality, health risk, and ecological studies. RPS sees the long-term paradigm shift toward sustainability required to address the challenges of the twenty-first century taking center stage once problems associated with the financial sector are resolved and has positioned itself accordingly. The company has built up a dedicated unit that advises on the opportunities and threats arising from climate change. RPS is also serious about tackling this issue itself and has set a target to reduce per capita energy consumption by 5% each year from a 2007 base.[26] If achieved, this would halve the RPS per capita energy use by 2020. Currently, the fund has a 1.45% stake in RPS (Environmental Services); RPS has long been one of the fund's top ten holdings.[27]

FUND PERFORMANCE

More than 20 years on, Jupiter Ecology's long-term outperformance and lateral thinking has garnered it a respected reputation among both its SRI and traditional peers. The fund has consistently outperformed its U.K. benchmark index (the Investment Management Association (IMA) Global Growth index) in each of the past five difficult years (2006–2011) returning +34% versus benchmark 31% and sector average fund return of 21%. It has also held up well against its nonethical peers, having achieved a top-quartile five-year return to January 31, 2011, making it thirtieth out of 154 global growth funds. Thomas's direction has been crucial. Following his appointment in August 2003, he implemented more stringent risk controls by diversifying and deconcentrating the portfolio. The top 10 stocks went from being 50% of the fund to less than 30%, and he also imposed a 5% maximum limit on any one holding.[28] Over a longer time frame, Jupiter Ecology has increased by over 460% since its inception.

Jupiter Ecology's great track record, long-standing ability to find novel opportunities, and commitment to investing for the long term have bridged the gap in pushing its version of sustainable investing into the mainstream. (See Figure 2.2.)

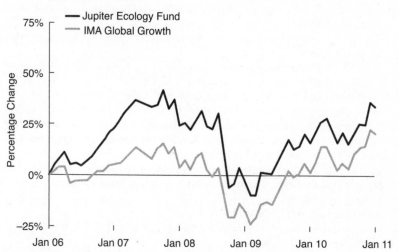

% Growth over 5 years

FIGURE 2.2 Jupiter Ecology Performance
Source: Jupiter.

Charlie Thomas and Emma Howard Boyd are optimistic for the outlook of green investment; an increasing awareness of environmental issues in the political, corporate, and social mainstream, resource scarcity, and shifting demographics strengthen their investment thesis. They see environmental and social issues staying firmly at the top of the political agenda, whether it is climate change, energy security, or food and water scarcity. Importantly, though, they believe that all fund managers, irrespective of whether they invest in this field, will have to consider the impact of these trends on their investments.

NOTES

1. www.un.org/esa/sustdev/csd/csd15/media/backgrounder_brundtland.pdf
2. www.mckinsey.com/App_Media/Reports/Water/Charting_Our_Water_Future _Full_Report_001.pdf
3. http://bnef.com/Presentations/download/60
4. www.reuters.com/article/2010/09/06/energy-carbon-idUSLDE68511 K20100906
5. www.awarenessintoaction.com/whitepapers/Wal-Mart-Supply-Chain-Packaging-Scorecard-sustainability.html

6. International Energy Agency, CO2 Emissions from Fuel Combustion, International Energy Agency, Paris, France 2010.www.iea.org/co2highlights/co2highlights.pdf

7. UN Department of Economic and Social Affairs, World Population Ageing, 1950–2050, 2002.

8. In 1985, John Duffield established Jupiter Asset Management as a specialist boutique; then he sold it to Commerzbank, a leading German bank. In 2007, the current chief executive of Jupiter, Edward Bonham Carter, led a management buyout back from Commerzbank. Over the years, Jupiter's success has allowed the company to attract significant fund manager talent. This has led Jupiter to become one of the United Kingdom's most successful investment houses currently managing over $39.3 billion.

9. This was further put forth in the capital markets chapter of the Business Council for Sustainable Development input into the same Rio summit in 1992 called "Changing Course."

10. www.gaeia.co.uk/TT001.HTM.

11. www.investmentweek.co.uk/investment-week/feature/1403798/the-future green#ixzz1GEp3MuGw

12. Jupiter, "Green Investing: An In-Depth Analysis," March 31, 2008. www.jupiterinternational.com/ApplicationFiles/GetFile.pdf?docId=893]

13. Author interview with Charlie Thomas and Emma Howard Boyd, November 15, 2010.

14. www.investorschronicle.co.uk/InvestmentGuides/Funds/article/20091201/ e3207d3e-ddaf-11de-a6d5-00144f2af8e8/Jupiters-green-heritage.jsp

15. www.iii.co.uk/articles/articledisplay.jsp?article_id=7922384§=Funds

16. Jupiter, Corporate Governance and Voting Policy, January 2011. www.jupiteronline.co.uk/ApplicationFiles/GetFile.pdf?docId=1256

17. Jupiter, Voting and Engagement Report, January 1, 2010–June 30, 2010, No. 12. www.jupiteronline.co.uk/ApplicationFiles/GetFile.pdf?docId=701]

18. www.ecomagination.com/about/fact-sheet

19. Jupiter, "Green Investing."

20. Author interview with Mark Campanale, December 3, 2010.

21. Soil Association Organic Market Report 2010. www.soilassociation.org

22. www.fundstrategy.co.uk/jupiter-takes-green-funds-mainstream/133857.article

23. Jupiter Ecology Fund Factsheet, March, 2011.

24. www.cranswick.plc.uk/greenthinking/greenthinking_index.html

25. www.rpsgroup.com/getdoc/2389ca45-7b56-4f14-bf42-f2dbbd004696/BTE_ Profile_RPS_Group.aspx

26. RPS Group, Report and Accounts 2009, 2010. www.rpsgroup.com/getdoc/ 3be6551e-9235-4780-a422-f693602f9557/Report-and-Accounts-2009.aspx]

27. Jupiter, "Jupiter Ecology Fund Report and Accounts," September 30, 2010.

28. www.fundweb.co.uk/jupiter-takes-green-funds-mainstream/133857.article

CHAPTER 3

A Predictor of Performance

Paul Hawken

Paul Hawken, leading entrepreneur and author of *Natural Capitalism*: Creating the Next Industrial Revolution (Back Bay, 2008), has at times been intrigued and frustrated by the state of socially responsible investing. His landmark Natural Capital Institute report of 2004 (www. naturalcapital.org/docs/SRI%20Report%2010-04_word.pdf) regarding the state of socially responsible investing remains a landmark piece well worth reading. His analysis indicates how institutional ownership, if steered into a positive dynamic, could help encourage companies to be more efficient and innovate their ways out of problems or, in effect, not be owned by investors. Hawken's frustration with the field of socially responsible investing as practiced at the time led him to help launch Highwater Research, putting his concepts into action through the Highwater Global Fund. This chapter offers his perspective in his own words.

Environmentally sound practices, intelligently done, typically cost less and return higher profits than destructive ones; companies of the future understand this and are prospering; those that don't often struggle.

INVESTMENT IN *NATURAL CAPITALISM*

The original definition of "investment" is to devote time, effort, and energy in an undertaking with the expectation that it will yield a worthwhile result. Today, "investment" means to place money for profit and material gain. We try to unite both meanings. We believe that rigorous social and environmental evaluation combined with exacting financial analysis yields superior monetary returns. The dichotomy between conventional equity funds and socially directed equity funds is becoming increasingly irrelevant. Companies that will prosper in the future direct their research and development to products and services that become more valuable over time. In short, they have a clear sense of current global trends and future societal needs. A company that does not address the clear and present challenges facing society and the environment will be at a disadvantage.

We see clouds ahead, dark and light, a world of significant restrictions and commensurate opportunity, each being the mirror of the other. These constraints can be either limiting factors to economic prosperity or gateways to new industries and products. Limiting factors include climate change, shortage of water, declining production of oil, hunger combined with an agricultural system heavily reliant on fossil fuels, growing poverty, deforestation, a broken allopathic-based healthcare system (treating symptoms instead of preventing causes), income polarization, the digital divide, and social inequity. Companies that ignore or only pay lip service to these factors are placing shareholder assets at risk.

This conclusion became particularly evident when I was researching and writing *Natural Capitalism*, which was published in 1999. I looked at economies and companies with respect to limiting factors at critical periods in their evolution. Over and again, I saw a pattern wherein companies that looked farther ahead and embraced social and environmental constraints outperformed companies that favored the status quo. Longer-value strategies produced more robust earnings outcomes. Today, the limiting factor to human well-being is natural capital, the resource base of the world that includes water, soil, oceans, carbon sinks, and more. When a limiting factor arises, the intelligent company works toward minimizing the use of what is limited.

Radical resource productivity, which would not have been possible at the outset of the Industrial Revolution, is critical today, even in advance of actual shortages. Companies that embrace scientific and economic realities with respect to resource constraints produce the greatest amount of innovation and breakthrough technology.

DISCOVERING OPPORTUNITIES

From this historical perspective arise four principles that can guide us through the century-long era of constraints that is upon us:

1. *Radical resource productivity* wrings more work out of less stuff, from extraction to end use. It uses fuels, minerals, water, and other resources

4, 10, and even 100 times more productively and dematerializes products and make them last longer. It comprehensively reduces the extractive flow needed to maintain the stock of physical goods and the flow of services required by society.

2. *Biomimetic production* closes the loops in extraction and manufacturing and designs waste so that it has ongoing value. By employing green chemistry, it eliminates toxicity so the flow of materials back into nature does no harm.

3. The *solutions economy* rewards both these shifts: The fewer material resources a provider needs to deliver a service or goods the service is designed to provide, the more money producers make and customers save. For example, this fixed/improved can come about when a manufacturer is paid for the service of product rather than selling the product itself, which provides the maker with powerful incentives for durability, safety, quality, and reuse.

4. *Reinvestment in nature* restores and enhances nature's fecundity, boosting the ability of ecosystems to provide more food, fiber, and ecological services to enhance life for all beings.

The flow of energy and materials into the global economy reveals a wealth of opportunity that remains largely untapped. For example, in the United States:

- We mine or grow or harvest materials whose daily flow per person averages 20 times that person's weight—counting only water returned dirty, not water returned clean.
- Ninety-eight percent of this mass flow is lost in extraction and manufacturing; only 2% gets into products.
- Six-sevenths of that 2% are consumer goods that are thrown away after one or no uses. Thus only 0.28% of the original mass is retained in durable products.
- Of the material in those durable products, only about 1/50th later returns to produce more value from recycling and remanufacturing.
- Thus, the flow of molecules in the U.S. economy is about 99.99% pure waste. Correcting this is an unparalleled business opportunity.
- Moreover, much of the waste is toxic. Its disposal erodes nature's ability to maintain production of the food, fiber, clean water, and many ecological services.

Other industrial countries differ in the data, but by less than one might expect.

Companies that adopt the four principles, regardless of what they name them or where they get their inspiration, are more resilient and adaptive, less likely to experience market failure, and more likely to be ahead of the curve. If a company is not addressing these factors, essentially it is operating on relatively short timelines that do not cumulate into a long-term plan or earnings stability.

Together, these principles, when applied to an enterprise, reduce costs and increase customer satisfaction and loyalty. They yield processes and economies that surpass conventional business practice while also fulfilling the business goal of Interface carpet company founder Ray Anderson to take nothing, waste nothing, do no harm, and do well by doing good, at the expense not of the planet but of less alert competitors. Environmentally sound practices, intelligently done, typically cost less and return higher profits than destructive ones. Firms that understand this are prospering; those that don't can find their costs and earnings negatively impacted by unanticipated externalities. Integrative environmental design and engineering that employs these principles has been shown repeatedly—in thousands of buildings, diverse vehicle designs, and scores of factories—to reduce capital and operating costs. Why all companies do not yet employ these sorts of approaches we leave to cultural historians to analyze. Our goal is to find the companies that do, and do it well.

IDENTIFYING THE COMPANIES OF THE FUTURE

At Natural Capital Institute, in 2004 we created a database of 600 socially responsible investment mutual funds in the world. With the cumulative portfolio of 600 fund managers located in the United States, Canada, Europe, Australia, Japan, Hong Kong, and South Africa, we had a comprehensive list of companies that met negative and/or positive screens. Additionally, we invited over 400 colleagues who study, write about, consult with, or operate socially responsible businesses to nominate companies that they thought most exemplified the values and needs of the future. From the two lists, we compiled a list of over 6,000 companies to sift and sort through.

We learned that great companies are located throughout the world; they're geographically and culturally diverse, both new and old, and reflect business models that improve the lives of the people they serve and the places they live through innovative products, services, or technologies.

Many people view the term "sustainability" as a catchall that covers a wide variety of interpretations and has come to mean less than it could and more than it should. We also use the word, but we believe that sustainability is a scientific concept, not a feel-good term. It is rooted in biology and physics, and describes the limits within which society can grow and prosper over time. Those limits, when understood and applied, provide an invaluable metric to parse company activity. We reverse traditional perspectives and weigh companies heavily on what they do, not what they say they do.

To identify the companies that have long-term value with respect to practices and strategies, we employ a variety of research methods, most of which differ from those of other funds. What we have in common with other funds is knockout categories: activities or practices that immediately disqualify a company from further analysis. These include human rights violations, hazardous waste generation, industrial agriculture, animal cruelty, nuclear power, unethical conduct or corruption, gambling, and so on. Simply stated, we get rid of the chaff.

Determining a Company's Type

We recognize three types of companies: Innovators, Shifters, and Neutrally Good. Innovators are companies whose whole purpose is to address social and environmental problems with advanced research, technology, and services. Vestas, which pioneered large-scale wind turbines, is such a company. Shifters are companies that are successful in their business pursuit but realized that their product, manufacturing methods, and materials were harming people and the environment and are now making a determined effort to reverse their course. The classic example would be Interface carpet company, but there are also large-cap companies, such as Canon. The Neutrally Good category includes companies that set out to provide a product or service and, without an original intention, address a key or pressing issue by default. For example, eBay and Amazon are the antithesis of big-box retailers and enfranchise small businesses and industries that could otherwise not compete. Google is both an Innovator and Neutrally Good. It wants to make all information available to all people for free, which is the Innovator category. Through its placement ads in search, it empowers small-scale, local vendors that otherwise would be unable to achieve sufficient critical mass to survive in the marketplace. This is Neutrally Good.

Examining the Company's Intention/Business Model

We then examine the intention and business model of each company, which is the most important Qualifying Screen. The intention of a company is supposed to be expressed in its mission or values statement. Most funds accept a company's business model and then grade the company on how well it performs within its chosen mission. However, we are not interested in best of class or relativism. We reverse this perspective and weight the company heavily on what it *does*, not what it says it does. Our main question is straightforward: Are the company's products or services helpful? The reasoning here is simple: If a company is heading down a path that does not serve society forward into the future, it matters little how it gets there. For example, the values statement at Kellogg's has lofty goals. However, at no point does it mention children or health. There is a children's health crisis in the United States due to obesity and type 2 diabetes. Advertising and promoting Cookie Crunch, Frosted Flakes, and Star Trek cereals, all of which contain more than one-third simple sugars, during Saturday morning cartoons, belies Kellogg's values statement. At Ford Motor Co., there is a vestigial mission statement about being the "world's leading consumer company of automotive products and services." This is not helpful either. However, Ford's operative intention today is to become the greenest, most efficient transport company in the world. First Solar's mission is to "enable a world powered by clean, affordable solar electricity." And that is exactly what it does. Ford and First Solar pass; Kellogg's does not.

We evaluate the mission and business model of companies within the system of five attributes drawn from the work of *Natural Capitalism*. They are:

1. Provides innovative services and products that address the current and future needs of people and Earth
2. Addresses climate change and carbon emissions (internal energy use, energy sourcing, external product impact)
3. Works proactively to minimize natural resource use through resource productivity (material sourcing, raw material use, recycled content)
4. Facilitates a shift from an economy of consumption to an economy of well-being (ecological economics: scale, distribution, allocation)
5. Integrates and demonstrates a social and environmental commitment in corporate values and stated objectives

If the prospective company passes the Qualifying Screen, we then move to the next stage of the analytical process: elaborate evaluative criteria consisting of over 200 categories. By employing intention or business model as the overriding criterion, we can eliminate many companies, avoid lengthy and expensive screening procedures, and concentrate on those companies that we feel have the best chance of excellent performance on all levels.

SUMMARY

We believe our method is conservative, not sentimental. In other words, we do not hold truck with the idea that investing with a social and environmental framework sacrifices return. For example, at the outset of the Highwater

Global Fund, we spurned money center banks because of social issues including liar loans, teaser rates, and usurious interest on rampant consumer credit. At that time, their soaring earnings growth seemed to mock our refusal to qualify the sector. Similarly, no large-scale pharmaceutical company except Novo Nordisk met our social or environmental screens. Pharma cratered before the panic of 2008, and the banking sector *was* the panic of 2008.

We are cautious about the companies we recommend to invest in, and we are equally vigilant on a sector and macroeconomic level. We invest with the conviction that companies that address the future in a realistic and intelligent manner offer investors a secure, long-term return.

CHAPTER 4

Highwater Global

Alexis van Gelder, Dean Martucci, and Erika Kimball

The Highwater Global Fund represents the evolution of an ongoing relationship between Paul Hawken and the investment firm Baldwin Brothers Inc.

Collectively, they see sustainable investing as nothing more than simple prudent fund management, given ongoing macroeconomic trends. Michael Baldwin warns that, if humans stay on the current trajectory of growth at the expense of social and natural capital, it will kill the planet. Highwater therefore attempts to solely invest solely in high-impact public companies that provide a framework, or solutions, for dealing with environmental and social challenges while setting an example for others in their sectors.

Ultimately, Hawken and Baldwin believe that many companies that exhibit these higher standards will see benefits that translate into better financial performance.

This fundamental observation has been validated by the strategy's performance. Highwater has remained at the top of the socially responsible investing world, performing at the apex of social investment funds and indexes, outperforming the MSCI World Index by a cumulative 39%, net of fees, since its inception in September 2005 until December 2010.

The authors wish to thank Paul Hawken and Holly Coleman of Highwater Research, as well as Michael Baldwin, Chris de Roetth, and Bill Marvel of Baldwin Brothers, for their gracious time and support. Unattributed quotes are based on personal communications in late 2010.

These results are consistent with the fund's premise that investors no longer need to classify socially directed and conventional funds as inherently different investment strategies. Superior monetary gains can be found through a combination of rigorous social, environmental, and financial analysis of investible companies.

The evolution of Paul Hawken's involvement in equity investing, specifically with investment firm Baldwin Brothers, has been particularly interesting to watch. Since its early years, sustainability and investing had been something of a niche for Massachusetts-based Baldwin Brothers, mostly through community-focused and venture capital investments, but its clients were looking for more options. Michael Baldwin and partner Ellen Stone spent a good amount of time vetting externally managed sustainability-focused equity portfolios for Baldwin Brothers' private wealth management clients, describing the potential and available choices at the time as "an absolute disappointment."

In 1991, Michael Baldwin and his wife, Margie, founded the Marion Institute with the goal of creating positive change by uncovering and addressing the root causes of societal problems. Initially focusing on problems in education, healthcare, and community building, the institute became increasingly concerned with environmental issues. One day, Baldwin called Paul Hawken cold turkey and invited him to speak at a conference. Hawken accepted on the condition that he could give two speeches, with one being on the subject of the Natural Step, a Swedish organization that created a science-based definition and process of attaining sustainability.

Hawken had just published *Natural Capitalism* (Back Bay, 2008) and was a key figure in establishing the Natural Step in the United States. He returned to the Marion Institute three times for conferences, during which time Baldwin and Hawken gradually developed a close friendship. Meanwhile, Baldwin says with a laugh, "The Marion Institute conferences were being hosted in Baldwin Brothers [BBI] offices. People just assumed we were SRI [socially responsible investment] fund managers." Baldwin fondly recalls the evolution of the Marion Institute meetings. "There was one particular conference with Paul when we shifted from simply learning [about sustainability] to starting to do something about it."

HAWKEN TAKES ON DOMINI

Hawken notes the catalyst that led to his involvement in the SRI world was a talk that he gave in 2004 at the Bioneers Conference in San Rafael, California where he said that he didn't understand SRI screening or why Domini Asset Management specifically could be such a big shareholder in McDonald's. Hawken took exception to McDonald's marketing of unhealthy food to children, describing the company's business model as unsustainable. After the Bioneers talk, he received many inquiries about where people should invest their money, and he said he didn't know in terms of existing funds. Soon thereafter, Baldwin called Hawken with a proposition to fund a more thorough research project at the Natural Capital Institute on SRI investing.

Hawken spent the next two years conducting an in-depth analysis of SRI, concluding that the lack of transparency, combined with the absence of rigorous analysis of company sustainability claims, had resulted in a situation where the holdings of many SRI funds were nearly identical to those of conventional funds. Hawken's findings concluded that 90% of Fortune 500 companies were represented in the portfolios of ostensible SRI funds, and those funds' top North American holdings were virtually identical with the Dow Jones Industrials. Hawken's first concern for sustainable investing is the core intention of the company. "If the business model is corrupt, it hardly matters if the company uses recycled paper or provides daycare," he says.[1] At some point as the research was concluding, Baldwin and Hawken wondered if Baldwin Brothers should set up a fund to practice what Hawken was preaching in his SRI recommendations, and that is how the Highwater Global Fund was born.

On September 1, 2005, the Highwater strategy was launched, combining a team of environmental, social, and financial research experts to create an alpha-driven risk-adjusted public equity fund. Besides using his SRI analysis, Hawken invited 400 thought leaders from all disciplines to nominate companies they felt exemplified and acted on the values needed for a better future. Since that initial foray, the Highwater Research (HWR) team has reviewed approximately 2,600 companies. Of these, 2,300 have failed the HWR environmental and social analysis, and 320 have passed. Currently, the Highwater Research company universe is made up of 300 companies representing close to $2 trillion in market capitalization.

Baldwin recalls that the biggest risks to the fund at inception were lack of a track record and a portfolio populated by many companies then unfamiliar to investors. In spite of these detractions, the Highwater Global Fund was successful in initially attracting investors and is now in its sixth year of operation with five people on the investment team at Baldwin Brothers and three on the environmental and social research team at Highwater Research.

Baldwin and Hawken attribute the consistently high sustainability standards and impressive fund performance to the fact that the two teams work well together and respect each other's research. Environmental and social analysis is done on "one side of the fence" by Hawken's HWR team, and investing is conducted "on the other side" through Baldwin Brothers'

Highwater Global Fund investment team. While communication is frequent and forthcoming, Hawken has no influence, aside from passing or failing a company on sustainability, over what companies Baldwin Brothers invests in. Likewise, the investment team has no involvement with setting the sustainability standards.

FUND DRIVERS BASED ON GLOBAL SUSTAINABLE THEMES

At its simplest, the Highwater Global Fund team at Baldwin Brothers identifies companies, industries, and markets that inherently operate with sustainability principles as core tenets. The rationality of an equity evaluation screen based on sustainability principles is considered *vera causa* with today's macro drivers, such as:

- Global population explosion
- Rapid economic growth in developing nations
- Growing global energy demand
- Resource constraints
- Climate change
- Carbon emission reduction goals
- Loss of ecosystem services

As Baldwin says: "If you look at current growth trends, you see only one world and that equates to shortage: shortage of energy, food, and water." He also notes that the three macroeconomic forces that pose the greatest threat to our future are economic collapse, environmental degradation, and peak oil. The Highwater Global Fund invests in companies that are working to address these threats and others.

FINDING INVESTMENT OPPORTUNITIES

The Highwater Global Fund team at Baldwin Brothers sees significant opportunities based on intelligent growth and has identified several key sectors and industries. (See Table 4.1.)

Clearly, the energy sector is a primary focus; it includes renewables, energy efficiency, smart grid, and battery and storage technologies. Some tech sector plays include companies encouraging digital connectivity for all as well as green building advancements. Health, community, sustainably produced food, and companies that conserve natural resources are all considered

TABLE 4.1 Themes

Investment Theme	Weighting
Air, Water, and Soil	12%
Bridging Digital Divide	22%
Cash Strategies	16%
Community Investment	4%
Energy Efficiency	14%
Finance	6%
Food	2%
Human Health	5%
Mobility	11%
Renewable Energy	8%

Source: Highwater Global Fund Fact Sheet, December 2010. Baldwin Brothers Inc.

solid investments for the fund. The challenge is to find excellent companies with visionary and capable management that are leveraging these areas of opportunity.

Looking for long-term growth and new innovation along Hawken's principles might seem to be a conflict of stability versus volatility. Initially, the fund found it challenging to develop a blend of holdings with adequate diversification to maximize financial gain and mitigate risk.

While Baldwin and Hawken found common ground in their desire to create a quality sustainable equity fund that truly contributed to sustainability, reconciling the details of their respective worldviews on sustainable investing took some time and effort. Hawken recalls concern early on from the investment team that HWR had broadly excluded banking and pharmaceutical companies from the universe. Yet Hawken couldn't find any candidates in these sectors that passed his analysis. Eventually, some financial and healthcare companies were discovered that met HWR's criteria. Hawken and Baldwin attribute the success of the fund to the combination of individual core values and effective ongoing communication between the research and investment arms of Highwater Research and Baldwin Brothers Inc.

Interestingly enough, a number of large companies, including Ford and Cisco, easily fit into the innovative and responsible themes that excite the Highwater Global Fund team. Additionally, in light of the multiple bank failures during the 2008 economic downturn and the instability of the nation's current healthcare system, Hawken's far-reaching exclusion of most companies in these industries validates the sustainability premise of the fund.

Highwater Environmental and Social Methodology: A Two-Step Evaluation Process

The mission of the environmental and social team at Highwater Research is to create global standards for responsible and sustainable business practices and evaluate companies based on these benchmarks so that innovative businesses receive the recognition and investment they deserve for serving society's best interests through the promotion of social equity, environmental restoration, and sustainable economic development.

HWR has a two-step company evaluation process that looks at a system of attributes, which include product innovation, climate change response, natural resource conservation, economic well-being, and demonstrated commitment to social and environmental values.

Step 1: Qualification Assessment   Holly Coleman, managing director and head of research at HWR, explains that the first step in qualifying a potential company is the application of a pass/fail screen based on "management-articulated positive intention. We look at a company's intentions but also verify that companies are walking the walk and showing results."

Coleman points out that the company selection process is very much a "bottom-up approach," though HWR will give some industry sectors an immediate fail. Industrial agriculture, nuclear power, tobacco products, gambling, and hazardous waste generators are the usual suspects; but pharmaceuticals and healthcare are also generally eliminated. As previously mentioned, in the early days of the fund, Baldwin felt that healthcare offered avenues toward balancing the portfolio, but Hawken vetoed that move, based on the toxic and excessive waste streams endemic in healthcare, the revolving-door policy with the Food and Drug Administration and pharmaceutical executives, among other questionable practices. His position that many healthcare companies are on an unsustainable track and therefore destined for a major transformation leaves the door open for future industry plays.

Further, companies or management found guilty of human rights violations, animal cruelty, unethical conduct, or corruption are all disqualified. This pass/fail screen is not unique. In fact, negative screening can be the sole assessment for some investment managers.[2] Hawken acknowledges this point and uses it as a quick and effective way to narrow the focus for deeper evaluation.

A point of accountability for the Highwater Research–approved company universe is that Hawken has the final say on whether any company should be added to the universe of Highwater candidates. This also leads to many interesting internal dialogs when the pass/fail line is gray. For example, while Hawken chooses not to invest in sugar as a nutritional product, because of its potentially detrimental health effects, he may pass sustainably grown sugar for use as a plastic alternative. Plastics made from food crops are not acceptable, but sugar is not considered a food crop. Here is where intent becomes a meaningful metric of assessment.

Selected companies are classified as Innovators, Shifters, or Neutrally Good—a reflection of the manner in which their business activities benefit society and the environment. Innovators are dedicated to discovering and monetizing sustainable solutions through new products and services. Shifters are mature companies that have recognized that their prior practices were unsustainable and are now taking tangible steps to improve. Coleman describes Neutrally Good companies as "companies whose products or services are helpful to society, although the company may not have a stated policy or intention that speaks to this."

Step 2: Scoring Assessment If a company passes the qualification assessment, it then moves into a queue for the second part of the evaluation process. At this stage, HWR performs an exhaustive analysis, using over 200 evaluation criteria to determine whether a company is "walking the walk" and if actual performance is true to management intentions. To find factual evidence necessary for assessment, Coleman explains that HWR reviews corporate social responsibility reports, company Web sites, credible nongovernmental and governmental organizations, as well as reporting databases, such as TruCost and the Carbon Disclosure Project. Transparency is valued and indicative of management intention, but the reports themselves are not deciding factors. For example, smaller companies may not have the time and resources for reporting. Also, the level at which a company reports on greenhouse gas emissions is not standardized. HWR digs deeper: "We want to see metrics, an historical record, goals and tracking," Coleman explains.

Such an extensive list of metrics places a high bar for inclusion in the Highwater Research universe of passed companies. Even companies with stellar sustainability records may not report on every single criterion. Environmental metrics have a longer history and more widely available data than other categories, such as job quality and employee wellness. When clarification is needed, HWR will seek a direct response from the company's investment liaison officer and management. A full company evaluation includes a quantified numerical rating based on sustainability performance and a confidence rating based on transparency.

An important aspect is HWR's ongoing assessment of passed companies. If a company in the portfolio fails, the portfolio manager has 90 days to divest the holdings. This is not a common occurrence; rarely does a company that originally passed the assessment make such a dramatic alteration in course to later fail, but it has happened. For example, Chaoda Modern Agriculture (CMA) is a leading grower and exporter of organic vegetables and fruit in China. HWR decided to remove it when CMA announced a significant shift to frozen vegetables that were already abundant in its export markets. The embedded carbon for shipping was the deciding factor.

Stateside, Ford, and Apple are examples of companies that the fund has grown to like. Ford was "an early fail, but has redeemed itself with product and manufacturing innovations. Ford is beginning to use more recycled materials, shifting to nontoxic paint and has begun to implement compelling supply chain policies," according to Chris de Roetth, fund manager at Baldwin Brothers Inc. "Where they are going gives us a lot of hope and is a good example of what we consider a Shifter," he explains.

Another illustrative example is Apple, which fits uneasily into the portfolio. Apple was late to the table with respect to environmental initiatives, arrogant about it sometime back, and not transparent. However, Apple actually walks the path to some degree while failing to be fully open and transparent.

Highwater Investment Process

Chris de Roetth, portfolio manager at Baldwin Brothers, brought the investment strategy behind the fund into perspective by discussing the investment process, portfolio management, and risk management. The fund is a global all-capitalization public equity strategy. Investments are made opportunistically combining a top-down thematic approach with fundamental bottom-up analysis. The investment strategy is to look top down at "the macro picture" and allocate the investments based on various medium- and long-term themes and scenarios. These themes are populated by companies only after the investment team performs an exhaustive bottom-up financial analysis. Companies are modeled based on typical value and growth investing concepts, management teams are visited, and additional qualitative factors are taken into account, including the research performed by Highwater Research.

Typically, a new public equity investment will enter the portfolio at 1.5% to 2% of total assets. Current long-term holdings are averaging from 3% to 4.25%, and the fund takes profits when a stock appreciates above 5% of total assets. This was the case with Ford Motor in the first half of 2010 and SSL International subsequently. Within each theme and sector, the fund has a maximum limit of 25% of assets. Typically, the maximum exposure to each theme sector is closer to 15%. From a liquidity perspective, the holding has to be less than 25% of the volume over three trading days. Investments are sold when a stock has become overvalued to its financial model, the thesis changes, and/or the view of management has changed.

The strategy remains long term, but scenario planning and tactical quarterly adjustments keep the fund nimble. For example, in 2010, Highwater reduced its holdings in wind energy and increased solar. Reacting to geopolitical events, de Roetth eliminated German solar positions, because of the recent expiration of German solar subsidies, and added two Chinese solar names. Further solar movement included buying more First Solar and later taking profits as the position approached its valuation target. In other words, de Roetth explains, "The tactical perspective is driven by events and valuations, but tactical adjustments typically play a small role in the overall management of the strategy."

In closing, de Roetth shared thoughts on where Highwater is looking for new breakout opportunities:

> *We're paying a lot of attention to smart grid technology and energy efficiency. . . . We're interested in consumer nondurables, Chipotle Mexican Grill here in the States, Vivo Participacoes in Brazil. . . . We're still bullish on emerging markets, neutral on tech as a sector. Wind energy remains too capital intensive at this time; we have had investments in low-cost Chinese solar companies.*

Highwater's Portfolio Profile

In November 2010, de Roetth and Bill Marvel, head of business development at Baldwin Brothers, discussed the fund's portfolio characteristics. Marvel explains that the portfolio is a blend of 30 to 40 equities, diversified across industry sectors, market capitalization, and geography. Positions are taken with a low turnover and mid- to long-term investment horizon expectation. Currently, three years is not an unusual time to hold an equity investment. Table 4.2 shows a diversification snapshot for Highwater as of December 2010.

Long-term fund performance is a solid endorsement of the screening and investment process, overall strategy, and tactics. According to the Highwater Global Fund Fact Sheet (December 2010), Highwater has outperformed the MSCI World Index by a cumulative 39% since inception and net of fees. Over the past five years (as of December 2010, annualized), the fund's annualized return stands at 6.4%, compared to 0.1% for both the Dow Jones World Sustainability Index and 0.4% for the MCSI World Index for the same period. The fund has remained at the top of the socially responsible investment universe.

TABLE 4.2 Diversification Snapshot

Equity Holdings by Region	
North America	46%
Asia	20%
European Union	19%
Latin America	15%
Market Capitalization Distribution	
<$1 BN	9%
$1B–$10 BN	42%
$10–$25 BN	12%
>$25 BN	37%

Source: Highwater Global Fund Fact Sheet, December 2010.

SUSTAINABLE INVESTING IS RESPONSIBLE INVESTING

Baldwin is not your typical investment firm president. He knows firsthand that there is huge interest in socially responsible or sustainable investing, and he believes that the key to success in the investment world is "doing what the client wants to do, not what we want to do." Investing is a highly personal experience for each client, and, therefore, sustainable investing is an individual judgment call. He adds that an astute investor doesn't simply write a check to a company without first "going down to kick the tires." Baldwin's efforts to do just that have found him traveling to the Amazon and witnessing the detrimental effects that large corporations, some of which bill themselves as sustainable, have had on the culture and environment of indigenous peoples. Baldwin believes that many companies are beginning to realize that successful business isn't just about being "lean and mean and delivering increasing profits." He states that if anyone does the math, there simply aren't enough natural resources to support growth as we know it.

Baldwin's investing strategies for his firm's private wealth management clientele include investment in the Highwater Global Fund or incorporation of specific sustainable equity holdings into their personalized portfolios. "There are a lot of gray areas," Baldwin notes. "For example, Baldwin Brothers is a strong believer in precious metals because we think we are headed for inflation and currency debasement." However, precious metals would never be considered sustainable; therefore, they are not included in Highwater Global Fund. But for an individual investor interested in full diversification of his or her investment portfolio, holding precious metals and Highwater among other investment strategies would make sense.

Future of SRI

Baldwin and Hawken both agree on the impetus behind the creation of the Highwater Global Fund. "Our idea," Baldwin humbly explains, "maybe it's grandiose, but if we can increase the assets in the strategy into the hundreds of millions and show superior returns, this is a game changer." Hawken echoes the convictions of his friend and business partner, commenting "The whole reason I went into this is to make a difference, not to make money." Hawken feels that the way to make a difference may be to have a nonprofit performing rigorous analysis of companies. "Once you find correlations between sustainable practices and stock performance, then you get feedback. Once you have that feedback, then you start to engender change." Acting on this belief, HWR shared its investment screen, arguably the most intensive and stringent sustainability screen in the industry, with B Corp in efforts to contribute to development of quality, uniform SRI standards.

Hawken supports the creation of universally high industry standards and total transparency in the SRI universe, commenting that without these developments, sustainable investing has little ability to move markets. Unfortunately, he has seen no real improvement in SRI standards in the corporate community because many large corporations are heavily invested in maintaining business as usual.

Baldwin takes a slightly more optimistic approach to the evolution of SRI, noting that "it's a slog, but it's catching on." He points out that even Goldman Sachs thinks SRI is a hot new area for investment and that more major foundations are beginning to check whether their financial investments are congruent with their organizational missions. "SRI is an attractive area to go into. However, it's incredibly compromised when you go into it. There is only so much new product to invest in." The Highwater Global Fund, therefore, invests in innovative sustainable growth companies as well as large shifting corporations that currently are working hard to establish sustainable practices and products.

SUMMARY

The performance of Highwater has demonstrated to the investment community that sustainability can make for a solid long-term investment and a better world at the same time. Unfortunately, this strategy is available only to high-net-worth investors. It would be exciting to see a strategy like this become available to the general public.

NOTES

1. P. Hawken and A. Domini, letter to the editor (and responses) featuring Paul Hawken and Amy Domini. *Green Money Journal* (2003). www.greenmoneyjournal.com/article.mpl?newsletterid=23andarticleid=229
2. Good Money Web site, "A Brief History of Socially Responsible Investing," February 1, 2007. www.goodmoney.com/srihist.htm

CHAPTER 5

Further Context

Cary Krosinsky

Now that we have reviewed a few funds and their practices, we need to look a bit further into measurement and intention within a context of sustainability.

As my colleague Nick Robins, head of Climate Change for HSBC, wrote in our PRI Academic Network paper:

> [W]e believe one of the key distinguishing features of sustainable investing is its forward-looking, prospective methodology which we argue will systematically add value over time. Our hypothesis rests on two assumptions:
>
> The first is that the best way of generating returns in the 21st century, both risk-adjusted and opportunity-directed, is to acknowledge long-term economic, social and environmental realities and integrate these into investment and ownership decision making ("the reasonable investor hypothesis").
>
> The second is that capital markets themselves need to be recast to confront the risks of financial collapse posed by long-term economic, social and environmental realities ("the market resilience hypothesis").
>
> If the first assumption above speaks the language of financial value at the micro-level, the second refers to the imperative of structural reform at the macro-dimension. Sustainable investing thus provides an agenda for action for purely financially motivated investors eager to mitigate risk and benefit from upside opportunities, as well as for governments seeking long-run economic development and civil society organizations aiming to achieve social and environmental progress.[1]

And so, the agenda is clear for investors. There is also a context for which companies can be measured in this regard, as I wrote for Green-Biz.com in August 2009.[2] For companies to succeed during these times of change, they'll need to define and embrace a rigorous framework for sustainability—something that goes beyond well-intentioned but overarching statements and builds a foundation that helps firms achieve their sustainability and business goals.

STARTING POINT FOR MEASURING SUSTAINABILITY

The starting point for any measurement of the sustainability of companies should be the work of the aforementioned Brundtland Commission of a generation ago, which in effect held that we need to find a way to meet the needs of the current generation without jeopardizing the ability of future generations to meet their needs. The commission's work came as the world was said to have passed the point of consuming an amount of resources per person that ultimately would be sustainable for the planet, so equity and fairness are also implied in the definition.

Ultimately, then, sustainability is a risk factor, and an all-encompassing one at that. Some companies and their business practices, as well as many traditional investors, likely will have no chance of succeeding in this new reality without evolving, as we move to an inevitable situation of rectifying overconsumption on a global basis.

Further, during this current economic downturn, we have witnessed the coalescing of the meaning of sustainability as pertaining both to the outright survivability of companies (let alone those that will be most profitable) and to those that survive environmental, social, governance (ESG) scrutiny.

To measure true sustainability, therefore, a framework is required that also encompasses mainstream factors—the usual ones that financial analysts use to measure profitability and valuation, such as return on capital, stock price to earnings, cash flow, and the like. At the same time, this framework needs to judge companies looking to succeed in a changing world while positioning themselves best from a risk standpoint with ESG factors in mind.

We suggest that companies need to be measured on a sliding scale of relative sustainability from an overall ideal score of 1 down to zero, where 1 represents the most sustainable company in the world (it is almost certain that no company currently is a 1) and zero denotes companies that have no hope of surviving.

Key to this all-encompassing framework is that failure in any one factor is in and of itself disqualifying. Thus, ESG and mainstream factors act in an independent, parallel fashion in this risk assessment, as opposed to being percentage factors in a score.

Any or all ESGFQ (environment, social, governance, financial, quality of management) factors can bring a company down to zero. It's assumed that many or most companies would score between 0.1 and 0.9, with a majority skewed between 0.1 and 0.5, and that this score could even be used as something of a coefficient for investment. Because failure on any one factor is disqualifying, there is no room for the sort of calculation that would enable a company to score 30% for its E factor, 40% for S, and 30% for G to equal 100% or a similarly deceptive "strong" score. A company that fails on any one of these factors may well fail completely as a business, so why give any of these factors less than 100% weight? Furthermore, these are potentially disqualifying factors for companies that are looking to avoid risk as they evolve with the changing world, instead of embracing the concept that excellence can be achieved only by across-the-board outperformance. For example, a company that has multiple operational disasters can completely negate any benefit they might see from social efforts they might make elsewhere.

SUSTAINABILITY 2.0'S FIVE FACTORS

This proposed method is overarching and of equal relevance to mainstream and socially responsible investing. Investors and asset owners who ignore it would do so at their peril. Call this method Sustainability 2.0.

Sustainability factors often are referred to as covering perhaps only the classic categories of E, S, and G: environment, social and governance. Each of these is an umbrella term unto itself, deserving of individual consideration, and we also see two other categories as crucial to this equation.

To break down these factors a bit further:

> E. *Environmental impacts, risks, and opportunities.* For example, Trucost impacts data showing companies with the largest environmental damage costs per dollar of profit or revenue, and the HSBC climate change index looks at companies best attempting to find innovative environmental solutions.
>
> S. *Social risks and opportunities.* Arguably, social metrics are the hardest to quantify, but firms like KLD take a stab at doing so, reviewing issues such as employee relations, human rights, diversity, and product safety among many others. Any company failing to perform well on these issues runs the risk of not attracting or retaining the

best and the brightest employees; of not retaining shareholders who focus on specific issues, such as involvement in Sudan; and of not retaining customers who focus on lifestyle choices and their consumer patterns accordingly. On the plus side, plans have been forwarded for establishing the prototype of a Social Stock Exchange, as previously funded by the Rockefeller Foundation, whereby companies would need to demonstrate best social attributes to retain exchange membership. This sort of "exchange plus" is already in place in Brazil and South Africa and has been successful. It would be useful if more investors, including the pension funds of unions such as those administered by the likes of the AFL-CIO, insisted on minimum sustainability standards for investment. Such an increased investor dynamic would create its own risks and opportunities accordingly.

G. *True governance risk.* The Corporate Library highlights situations of overcompensation, board composition, and related conflicts of interest. For example, well before the 2008 financial crisis, the Corporate Library had flagged Bear Stearns and Lehman Brothers as Ds and Fs in its scoring system; if its system had been part of an overall true sustainability risk system, as proposed, investors would have been protected from the collapse of these companies. On the positive side, companies that reward all employees, shareholders, and investors equally and have in place full checks, balances, and incentives arguably represent an ideal that few firms achieve—but those that come closest may well outperform. Private equity firms increasingly recognize that to best maximize their assets, they need to be top performers in these areas; increasingly creative and thoughtful short-term investors also see that this is the way forward.

F. *Traditional financial criteria.* Among too many examples these days, GM would have been an automatic zero over the last few years, although it is owned widely by passive investors. If you hold a flat index that had GM as a constituent, that portion of your assets was doomed. Hence even for passive investors, sustainability risk is essential to consider. And it should go without saying that combining positive financial criteria (value plays from traditional Ben Graham/David Swensen approaches, etc.) with sustainability risk should offer the best of all possible worlds.

Q. *Quality of management.* Quality of management is something that can be achieved only by direct interaction and investor judgment. Hence, sustainability inevitably needs human interaction, face-to-face dialogue, and understanding that management is committed to full integration of sustainability—walking the walk, not just talking the good talk.

SUMMARY

Investing and measuring without the framework offered in this chapter inevitably ignores some or all the risks that are critical to a company's success. Wal-Mart's recently announced effort to build a sustainability consortium and related index of products, for example, falls short of what many investors require in a larger framework that includes judgments on management and other factors of direct relevance.

Ultimately, true sustainability may well be a holy grail—something that is strived for, as opposed to something that can be pinned down completely. This is likely a good thing, as markets need winners and losers, and those who get this right through sound judgment, creativity, and innovation should win in the end.

NOTES

1. Paper presented in 2009 at Carleton University in Ottawa. www.unpri.org/files/Robins_Krosinsky_Viederman_PRI2009.pdf
2. www.greenbiz.com/blog/2009/08/14/how-build-framework-sustainability-20

CHAPTER 6

Sustainable Asset Management

Thomas O. Murtha and Ashley Hamilton

Perhaps the world's largest fund manager attempting to use sustainability as a lens is Zurich-based Sustainable Asset Management, whose information is used in the creation of the high-profile Dow Jones Sustainability Indexes. Thus, this profile will be more in depth than others.

The firm had a number of issues in 2010. It heralded BP as a leader prior to the Deepwater Horizon incident, then dropped the company and replaced it with Halliburton. Subsequently SAM announced an off-schedule rebasing late in the year due to a "software fault." But it is moving on, challenges and all, trying to maintain its leadership position in the industry.

There is a significant market for passive investment in general, and SAM and others have an opportunity to capture it within the realm of sustainable investing. The challenge for any firm like SAM is rooted deeply in the active versus passive debate: Can any firm completely quantify all the necessary factors, or, at the end of the day, is some subjectivity in effect a requirement?

A s one of the oldest pure-play sustainable investing practitioners, Sustainable Asset Management (SAM) is an interesting case study. Unlike many investment managers that have adapted their traditional mandates to sell sustainability-related products, SAM was founded on these principles. SAM's mission is to "to translate sustainability foresight into outstanding investment results."[1] To this end, it has developed a sophisticated system to evaluate sustainability performance and choose stocks on both fully integrated financial and sustainability criteria.

For early adopters of sustainability investing like SAM, promising developments in academic research are beginning to confirm the long-held belief that sustainability pays.[2] however, the question has not yet been put to rest. (See Chapter 38 for more on sustainable investing performance.)

SAM has a first-mover advantage and is arguably ahead of the game in terms of developing a sophisticated understanding of the nexus between sustainability and financial performance. It has been developing its expertise in the art and science of sustainability integration since 1995. Given SAM's position as a pioneer, the firm is about a decade ahead of many other asset managers, many of which are only now scrambling to put together sustainability analyst teams.

SAM attempts to distinguish itself with an investment process that draws on a proprietary database of corporate sustainability metrics. As of early 2011, SAM actively managed about $7 billion across various public equity strategies focused on sustainability themes including climate change, water scarcity, smart materials, healthy living, smart energy, and agriculture as well as a diversified global equity strategy. The remainder of SAM's fee-based income is comprised of a $1 billion clean-tech private equity portfolio and $8 billion in assets associated with a family of sustainability equity indexes in a joint venture with Dow Jones Indexes.

The group's central business premise is that "sustainability is a company's capacity to prosper in a competitive and changing global business environment by anticipating and measuring current and future economic, environmental, and social opportunities and risks by focusing on quality innovation, and productivity to create stakeholder value."[3] SAM's business model relies on the assumptions that sustainability metrics will have financial materiality and that integrating sustainability factors into stock valuation and momentum analysis can generate superior long-term investment results.

What distinguishes SAM in the increasingly competitive field of sustainable investing? How does SAM's sustainability analysis assist it in picking stocks, constructing portfolios, and encouraging improvements in company sustainability performance? This chapter explores these questions, highlighting what makes SAM stand out from the crowd and what challenges it might face in the future.

SAM'S ORIGINS AND EVOLUTION

Reto Ringger, a soft-spoken Swiss fund manager and investment banker, founded SAM in 1995 with early backing from Swiss Re and the Volkart brothers. Ringger recognized a problem in the way pension assets were traditionally managed: There was a growing gap between the time horizons of many pension funds (20 to 30 years) and the time horizons of the investment management industry (less than 1 year). It was an unsustainable investment model, according to Ringger, and no one at the time was offering investment products that took a longer-term approach.[4] Long-term risks, such as climate change, environmental regulation, and innovation, were not factored into investment decision making. Ringger set out to craft investment products that incorporated these longer-term risk factors as a basis for delivering superior risk-adjusted returns.

Ringger's business proposition was somewhat radical in 1995: The more sustainable a company is, the more valuable it will become over time, and at that point, the market perception of business value and sustainability was exactly the opposite. Ringger's self-described naiveté helped him persevere despite this challenge.[5] He and his partners decided to develop a prototype to demonstrate that this proposition was viable. With an initial investment by Swiss Re, Ringger initiated a project to build an index of companies with superior sustainability performance. The index would allow SAM to monitor and track the price performance of sustainable companies over time and either prove or disprove its key assumption. SAM successfully struck a deal with Dow Jones in 1999 to launch the Dow Jones Sustainability Index (DJSI). In the same year, SAM also launched its first investment fund based on the DJSI.[6]

The DJSI was launched as a joint venture between SAM and what has now become Dow Jones Indexes, a joint venture company owned 90% by the CME Group Inc. and 10% by Dow Jones and Company, Inc. (a subsidiary of Rupert Murdoch's News Corp). After a few years, Ringger and his team were able to demonstrate that his initial proposition was true: Companies that were more sustainable (according to SAM's own environmental, social, and governance [ESG] research) were outperforming companies that were deemed to be less sustainable. From these beginnings, and with this evidence, SAM grew to become a well-respected asset manager, featuring a team of analysts and portfolio managers committed to forging a new approach to investing.

In 2006, Ringger sold a majority interest in SAM to Dutch asset manager Robeco for an undisclosed amount and left in February 2009 to pursue new interests. The top job at SAM was taken over by Sander van Eijkern, a Robeco veteran, who had spent eight years in the parent company's Alternative Investments group. Further restructuring and integration with Robeco continues. In addition to moving its clean tech private equity division over to SAM in 2009, Robeco has assigned SAM responsibility for managing two additional sustainability-themed equity strategies, the SAM Agribusiness Equities Fund and the SAM Sustainable European Equities Fund.[7]

However, it appears there is some unrest, as SAM has since seen a number of high-profile staff members leave the company. Van Eijkern left one year into the job, citing a disagreement over SAM's future strategy.[8] Michael Baldinger, SAM's global head of clients and marketing, was later named van Eijkern's replacement in December 2010 after serving as interim co–chief executive officer with the chief investment officer, Stephanie Feigt. Following his appointment, Baldinger made a number of significant changes to the management team at SAM, which led to the departure of Feigt and Pierin Menzli, SAM's head of research, in February 2011.

Whatever the reasons for the changes, SAM is under pressure to achieve superior returns as investors facing a new set of risks and opportunities following the rebound in equity markets in 2009 and 2010. SAM's new management is under pressure to demonstrate that its business can achieve the same high returns on invested capital expected of other leading companies in the financial services sector.

BUILDING A SUSTAINABLE INVESTING PRACTICE: BASIC BUSINESS SEGMENTS

Even with the provision of sustainability index products in partnership with Dow Jones Indexes, SAM's primary focus remains active asset management. SAM offers two types of actively managed investment products: Theme and Core strategies. SAM's Sustainability Theme strategies target companies operating in sustainability industries: Sustainable Water, Smart Energy, Smart Materials, Healthy Living, Sustainable Climate, Sustainable Agribusiness Equities, and a Multi-Theme strategy. The Theme strategies are future oriented, seeking to invest in small and midsize companies that are positioned to benefit from emerging sustainability trends. The Core strategies are multi-sector, constructed from the MSCI World universe plus companies in SAM's Sustainability Theme strategies.

SAM is also developing a private equity business focused on the clean-tech sector. In 2009, parent company Robeco moved its Clean Tech Private Equity fund to SAM. SAM's private equity team attempts to invest in unlisted companies operating businesses with potential for superior financial performance, including those involved with alternative energy generation and storage, transportation, water, materials, agriculture, and waste management.

Finally, SAM continues to operate SAM Indexes, which participates in the construction and operation of the DJSI. The flagship Dow Jones Sustainability World Index is composed of global sustainability leaders as identified by SAM's annual Corporate Sustainability Assessment (discussed later). The top-scoring 10% of the largest 2,500 companies in the Dow Jones Global Total Stock Market Index are eligible for the Sustainable World Index based on economic, environmental, and social criteria.[9]

Since its establishment in 1999, the DJSI has spawned a family of indexes that have become popular with both mainstream and responsible investment managers. More than 70 investment managers in 19 countries are now licensed to offer investment products based on the DJSI performance and methodology. In just over ten years, global assets invested according to the DJSI have increased from less than $500 million in 1999, to over $8 billion in 2010. Over the same period, the index offerings have grown to include 18 world and regional indexes. DJSI have also created indexes for investors that choose to screen out certain "sin" stocks, such as tobacco, nuclear, alcohol, and pornography. The indexes' most recent launch included a World Enlarged Index of 513 companies as well as the Northern Europe index.

MEASURING INTANGIBLES: SUSTAINABILITY RESEARCH METHODOLOGY

Sustainability analysis at SAM follows a structured five-step evaluation process:

1. A high-level global analysis of relevant economic, environmental, and social trends
2. A sustainability questionnaire
3. Evaluation of company public disclosure and performance
4. Media and stakeholder analysis
5. Contact and engagement with company representatives

The global analysis is undertaken each year to survey the sustainability landscape for emerging sustainability issues, both globally and at the sector level. SAM draws on expertise from a selection of experts each year, the SAM faculty, which often includes academics and industry practitioners.

SAM's analysts are trained to examine both the sustainability and the financial dimensions of each company. According to Neil Johnson, SAM's head of global clients and marketing, "We focus on ESG issues that are material to the companies' respective industries, are long-term in nature, and are under-researched in traditional financial analysis."[10] Many of the analysts have previous work experience in the sector they are covering, which SAM believes gives them an edge over the competition in identifying potential sustainability risks and opportunities. The pairing of SAM's financial analysis with its sustainability analysis ensures that the company takes a true "ESG integration" approach.

Measure by Measure: SAM's Sustainability Assessment Questionnaire

The annual questionnaire is the cornerstone of SAM's Corporate Sustainability Assessment and provides the research platform for the DJSI. The questionnaire is comprised of approximately 100 questions regarding company sustainability policies, practices, and performance. Questions are in a multiple-choice format in order to limit qualitative responses, and companies are expected to provide public documentation to support their answers.

SAM takes care to select each sustainability indicator and survey question. New criteria and questions are added every year to reflect SAM's evaluation of global sustainability drivers, and new and emerging issues in each sector. A meeting of senior analysts determines which new criteria are added. When deciding what to include, the analysts base their decisions on the relevance and expected long-term material financial impact of each issue on the sector in question. They are careful not to make excessive changes to the questions asked of companies each year, because, according to SAM, many companies base their internal processes and evaluations on the questionnaire, and significant change can be disruptive. For this reason, analysts aim to change less than 10% to 20% of the questions each year.[11]

The evaluation metrics used by SAM to assess company performance and assign an overall sustainability score (see Table 6.1) are divided into 3 broad dimensions, 12 criteria and 123 indicators across all 58 sectors.[12]

How to assign value and importance to each issue set or criteria is a significant challenge for all investors undertaking a best-of-sector approach. When are environmental factors more important and material than health and safety performance? Do employee turnover metrics trump biodiversity efforts? These are complicated questions that are difficult to answer. And yet they are vital; how you weight the criteria has direct effect on the ultimate sustainability performance score or ranking for each company and each sector.

Assigning weights is more of an art than a science. For SAM, the weighting of the criteria and indicators in the questionnaire is intended to reflect each sector analyst's best determination regarding the material financial significance of the issue for each industry. For example, questions related to ecological biodiversity would have a greater weighting for the mining sector than they would for the information technology sector. The analysts at SAM base their criteria weighting decisions on their knowledge of the

TABLE 6.1 Evaluation Metrics

Dimension	Criteria	Weighting (%)[a]
Economic	Codes of Conduct/Compliance/Corruption and Bribery	6.0
	Corporate Governance	6.0
	Risk and Crisis Management	6.0
	Industry-Specific Criteria	Depends on industry
Environment	Environmental Reporting[b]	3.0
	Industry-Specific Criteria	Depends on industry
Social	Corporate Citizenship/Philanthropy	3.0
	Labor Practice Indicators	5.0
	Human Capital Development	5.5
	Social Reporting[b]	3.0
	Talent Attraction and Retention	5.5
	Industry-Specific Criteria	Depends on industry

[a]Can vary over time and by industry.
[b]Criteria assessed based on publicly available information only.
Source: Adapted from "SAM European SRI Transparency Guidelines," September 2010.

industry, current company best practices, and their evaluation of the potential material financial impact of the issue.

Each of the 58 sectors evaluated by SAM receives its own customized questionnaire. SAM's criteria include indicators that are considered broadly applicable to companies in all sectors while leaving significant room for industry-specific evaluation criteria. Over time, SAM has put increasing importance on sector-specific data. In 2009, approximately 57% of the indicators on the questionnaire were specific to each company's sector, which is a significant increase from 1999, when only 30% of the indicators were industry-specific.[13]

The nature and emphasis of the questions have also evolved over time. For example, when SAM first initiated its sustainability assessments, a significant differentiating factor was its ability to identify and evaluate the effect of corporate governance issues on long-term financial performance. Now corporate governance analysis is nearly ubiquitous. SAM has since branched out into new evaluation criteria, such as innovation management, talent attraction and retention, and water risks. Indeed, SAM's value proposition as an asset manager relies on the ability to identify new and emerging sustainability issues before the mainstream market fully understands and quantifies the impact. The ability to foresee the financial impact of key sustainability issues is critical to SAM's future success.

Since the questionnaire is the centerpiece of the SAM process, how and indeed *whether* companies respond becomes of vital importance. SAM uses the detailed company responses to the survey to help evaluate whether a company should be eligible for the core portfolio strategies. Companies can be included in the thematic strategy portfolios without SAM conducting a formal Corporate Sustainability Assessment. Companies that do not answer the questionnaire, for whatever reason, are evaluated by SAM using the best available public documentation. The questionnaire is voluntary and is just one of dozens sent to companies by various organizations each year. Understandably, companies have limited resources to respond to all requests. While SAM boasts relatively good survey response rates (~32% responses from 1,962 corporations surveyed in 2009 and ~27% from 2,617 surveyed in 2010), the ability to evaluate unresponsive companies at the same level of depth as those that take the time to fill out the survey is limited. Concerns about falling into a trap of "responsiveness trumps performance," as expressed by think tank SustainAbility, are not unfounded.

What Others Are Saying: Media and Stakeholder Analysis

Further stakeholder and media analysis is used to help augment the analyst's view of a company. Unlike the questionnaire, which is structured and methodical, SAM's stakeholder analysis is more fluid and open to interpretation and judgment. Analysts rely on data from the Web-based platform provided by supplier RepRisk. They also scan media reports and information gathered by other stakeholders, including nongovernmental organizations (NGOs), community groups, academia, industry groups, and government. The analysts use this process to look for additional information regarding controversial business activities and critical incidents affecting financial performance and any concerns regarding environmental and social performance.

The media and stakeholder analysis can affect the score for each weighted criteria by up to 50%, and can influence the overall score of a company by up to 19%.[14] This analysis is one of the tools available to SAM to identify critical incidents that are potential "canaries in the coal mine." However, as any analyst knows, the real skill here is in wading through all the noise and identifying what issues have the potential to affect corporate reputation or financial performance.

SAM's New Alchemy: Scoring and Valuation

SAM's analysts verify and quantify the sustainability performance data of each company and assign an absolute sustainability score based on a

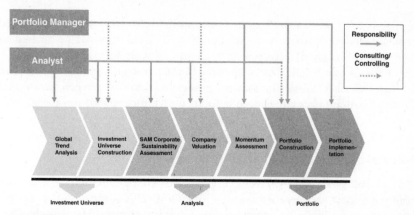

FIGURE 6.1 SAM Sustainability Analysis and Portfolio Construction Process
Source: SAM, 2011. Written correspondence Francois Vetri, SAM, January 24, 2011.

predefined formula for each industry. This score is then translated into a measure of relative performance, based on a peer group comparison. The analysts then evaluate companies based on:

- Each company's understanding and awareness of the sustainability issues
- The quality of the company's management systems and business models
- Its ability to address the issue or implement a sustainability strategy
- The company's actual performance or results

The sustainability scores are then used in SAM's asset selection process and for the construction of the DJSI (see Figure 6.1). In the asset selection process, the sustainability score is integrated into SAM's equity economic value-added model, which is used to determine the fair value of each company. Analysts also use the sustainability information they gather when conducting company forecasting. The ultimate goal is to identify companies that are attractive financial investments and can demonstrate they have what it takes to proactively manage sustainability issues.

SUSTAINABILITY LENS: ACTIVE PORTFOLIO MANAGEMENT

In early 2011, SAM had six actively managed strategies based on sustainability themes such as water, energy, smart materials, climate change, agribusiness, and healthy living. These thematic strategies each have concentrated portfolios of 30 to 60 companies. SAM also offers diversified European and global investment strategies as well as discretionary mandates for institutional clients, mutual funds, private-label strategies, and advisory services. SAM's investment process focuses on idea generation and fundamental analysis to create portfolios with concentrated positions.

Roles of Analysts and Portfolio Managers

One of the goals of SAM is to use the lens of sustainability to identify companies that will prosper over the long term. This is a structured process but with an emphasis on communication and interaction. The Zürich office is an open-space bullpen that facilitates frequent dialog between analysts and portfolio managers. Even though they travel frequently to visit companies and attend conferences and trade shows, analysts and portfolio managers maintain an ongoing dialog to formulate, substantiate, and revise what they believe are significant secular growth themes based on global sustainability trends. Development of long-term investment themes is based on talking to companies, trade literature, and, most important, analyzing responses to SAM's Corporate Sustainability Assessment that is sent out to 2,500 companies annually.

Analysts and portfolio managers together formulate the Core and Theme investment strategies. As mentioned, the Core sustainability strategies cut across all sectors and geographies and reflect how environmental, economic, and social challenges currently impact regions, sectors, and companies. Analysts translate these sustainability challenges into assessment criteria, representing a risk or opportunity, and sometimes a combination of both, leading to the creation of the aforementioned quantitative sustainability score for each company assessed. These scores are then added into SAM's equity valuation model. SAM's fair value for each company is based on an estimated valuation derived from an economic value-added analysis, and analysts' earnings projections for the company.

This Core sustainability strategy aims to generate outperformance by identifying the best-positioned and most attractively valued companies in each global sector.

By identifying undervalued companies that are well positioned to adapt to the risks and opportunities of a changing business environment, SAM's Core strategy managers create concentrated portfolios of companies that have the ability to create long-term shareholder value. The Core strategy stocks tend to have a large capitalization bias because the sustainability survey sample set is the largest 2,500 global companies by market capitalization.

Investment Universe Construction

The use of nonexclusionary positive investment screens distinguishes sustainable investing from ethical investing and socially responsible investing (SRI), which often use negative screens to exclude certain companies and industries. In contrast, SAM favors a large investment universe to enable construction of well-diversified portfolios from the broadest possible opportunity set. For example, the investment universe for the SAM Global Active Strategy includes 80% of the companies in the MSCI World that have been assigned a sustainability score. This universe is broadened to include any companies with exposure to one or more of SAM's sustainability themes. Many of these companies with attractive exposure to sustainability themes are smaller-capitalization and fast-growing companies. The net result is an investment universe that contains approximately 1,800 global and theme stocks, all of which have a set of sustainability data that enables further analysis and ranking by sector and geography. (See Figure 6.2.)

To supplement the Core strategies, the analysts develop separate sustainability Theme strategies for the portfolios that address global sustainability trends such as water, clean energy, smart materials, climate change, agriculture, and healthy living. These strategies are translated into single and multithematic portfolios and aim to maximize investment in attractively valued small- and mid-size companies. These smaller, often more agile, companies have the potential to develop innovative products and services and the possibility of experiencing high rates of earnings growth for an extended time.

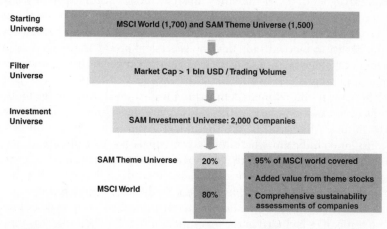

FIGURE 6.2 SAM Global Active Portfolio Construction
Source: SAM, 2011. Written correspondence Francois Vetri, SAM, January 24, 2011.

The thematic portfolios are aimed at capturing exposure to new sectors that are expected to experience above-average growth and offer superior reward potential.

SAM AND PERFORMANCE

SAM conducts a wide variety of empirical studies on materiality and encourages academics to conduct studies using SAM's data. In 2010, SAM published a white paper titled "Alpha from Sustainability" that argued sustainability criteria enable a firm's intangible assets to be valued. By comparing the SAM sustainability leaders to laggards, SAM claims a 1.48% annualized outperformance over an eight-year period from 2001 to 2008. As a leading practitioner of sustainable investing, SAM's ultimate goal is to turn sustainability into alpha by making a nonfinancial factor a key component of valuation.

The SAM valuation model incorporates sustainability factors in two phases. The first phase reflects a fundamental analysis of the company's ability to generate economic profits based on assumptions about competitive financial performance, including sales growth, operating margins, tax rates, changes in invested capital, and the weighted average cost of capital. In this first phase of the model, sustainability factors may affect the company's ability to achieve above- or below-average returns on invested capital. The analyst may incorporate assumptions about the company achieving returns on capital higher or lower than the industry average. A company with a high relative sustainability score for a particular industry may, for example, have higher returns than its competitors because of greater resource efficiency, a greater ability to innovate and develop successful products and services, and better stakeholder relationships that promote a stronger brand and enable premium pricing.

The SAM model assumes competition will cause above-average industry returns to normalize or fade to the industry average within the first ten years of the model. After year 10 on, the model assumes that return on capital fades to an equilibrium where the return equals the cost of capital. In the second phase, SAM assumes that companies with more sustainable business models will see their competitive advantage erode at a slower rate than a company with a less sustainable business model. (See Figure 6.3.)

The 22 analysts at SAM cannot actively follow, score, model, and value all the companies included in the investment universe. Therefore, to complement the fundamental analysis of the research analysts, portfolio managers perform a systematic valuation of the full investment universe using a multifactor regression model to estimate each company's fair value and to identify

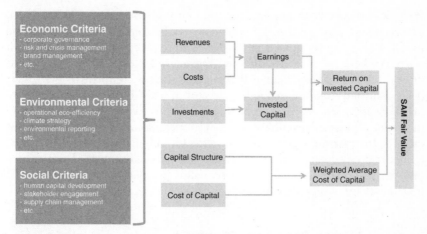

FIGURE 6.3 SAM's Fair Value Model
Source: SAM, 2011. Written correspondence Francois Vetri, SAM, January 24, 2011.

companies that are mispriced by the market compared to companies with similar characteristics in the same sector. Importantly, this systematic valuation process integrates sustainability scores into the expanded investment universe.

Portfolio Construction and Risk Management

For the Core products, SAM uses a disciplined process for constructing and managing portfolios. The weightings for portfolio holdings are determined based on expected returns, the sustainability score, the fundamental valuation, and a momentum score. The result is a portfolio that is optimized for estimated risk factors and expected alpha estimated by the portfolio management team. The goal of portfolio construction at SAM is to have security selection as the main source of risk. The result is portfolios with moderately concentrated positions. Risk management includes monitoring the portfolio risk parameters and rebalancing as required. An important part of risk management and alpha generation is that stocks with an attractive valuation relative to estimated fair value are bought and stocks that are close to or over fair value are sold.

Over the past decade, SAM's portfolio managers have achieved a respectable performance record. Many of the thematic portfolios have consistently outperformed the MSCI World Index since inception. The Water and Smart Energy strategies stand out for outperforming their benchmarks without excessive volatility during a tumultuous period from 2003 to 2010. The relatively new Sustainable Global Active Strategy underperformed the MSCI World slightly in its first two years since inception in early 2009. In a world where the majority of active managers underperform their benchmarks, SAM's actively managed strategies remain competitive with their peers. Rodrigo Amandi, managing director of SAM Indexes, sees corporate business practices evolving in a predictably positive direction. "As more companies invest in sustainability, costs are recognized before benefits but over the long term the cumulative benefits should increase competitiveness, reduce risk and create opportunities that far exceeds the costs. This suggests that the sustainability leaders in each sector are putting in place essential ingredients for competitive advantage."[15]

SAM'S EXTENDED FAMILY: DOW JONES SUSTAINABILITY INDEXES

SAM's flagship index product is the Dow Jones Sustainability World Index. The DJSI selects index constituents according to a nonexclusionary best-in-class approach. Across the $8 billion of assets using SAM's index families, approximately three-quarters are passive managers and the other quarter are active managers.[16] SAM also constructs custom indexes for clients that choose to exclude certain companies on the basis of ethical, religious, or social value strictures.

Dow Jones Indexes are responsible for all index calculations and jointly markets and distributes the DJSI family with SAM. SAM is solely responsible for general operations and the evaluation and ranking of companies based on sustainability criteria. An index design committee is comprised of two members each from SAM and Dow Jones Indexes, plus an independent member, Richard Sandor, chief executive and founder of Environmental Financial Products, LLC. The committee is responsible for all decisions regarding index composition, methodology, and company exclusions. The best-in-class approach is a key strategy of the DJSI. SAM's investment professionals are adamant about the importance of a nonexclusionary process. Amandi points out: "The best-in-class approach is an economic concept. We do not see ourselves as moral judges who decide what is acceptable and what isn't."[17]

The SAM Corporate Sustainability Assessment provides a sector relative score for every company, which is used to select the constituents of the DJSI. This means that companies in high-impact sectors, such as the oil and gas, mining, and tobacco sectors, are still eligible for inclusion in the DJSI index family. The only time the DJSI will exclude an entire sector is if the best-performing company in the sector scores less than one-fifth of the

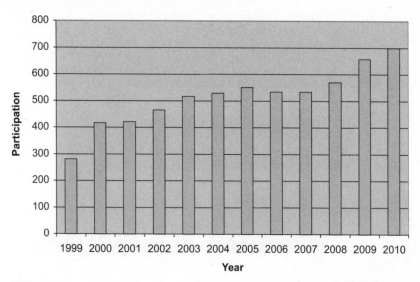

FIGURE 6.4 SAM Corporate Sustainability Assessment Participation Rates
Source: SAM.

maximum available score.[18] Amandi argues that no sectors are purposely excluded from the sustainability indexes because "looking the other way doesn't solve the problems of any sector, industry, or company." Instead, SAM's best-in-class approach "gives us an opportunity to conduct a dialogue with companies from all sectors and thereby promote incremental improvement in companies' sustainability performance."[19] This approach can result in the inclusion in the index of some companies recognized as unsustainable or even unethical by some socially responsible or ethical investors (e.g., tobacco, weapons, or nuclear companies) if they are deemed to be sustainability leaders within their sector. For example, Reynolds American Inc., a major supplier of cigarettes and other nicotine products, was designated a "SAM Sector mover" in the 2010 Sustainability Yearbook.[20] (See Figure 6.4.)

Index Construction and Performance

Using SAM's annual sustainability survey results, the index construction process is straightforward. Using the DJSI World product as an example, SAM selects 2,500 of the largest companies on the Dow Jones Global Total Stock Market Index, calculated by free-floating market capitalization, for its annual sustainability assessment.[21] SAM's sustainability scoring process

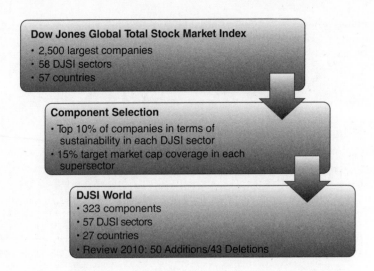

FIGURE 6.5   Construction of the DJSI
Source: Dow Jones Sustainability Indexes, 2010. "Presentation 2010 DJSI Review." Available at www.sustainability-index.com/ djsi_pdf/publications/Presentations/SAM_Presentation_101104 _Review10_1.pdf

is then applied to the universe, and the highest-scoring 10% of companies in each sector are added to the DJSI World. (See Figure 6.5.) Scores are sector relative so care is taken to double-check categorization according to the Industrial Classification Benchmark. The resulting indexes are a representative set of global sustainability leaders according to SAM's sustainability evaluation.

Methodologies underlying sustainability index construction are complex by nature, boiling down a comparison of a wide cross-section of sectors, firm sizes, and regulatory regimes into a simplistic weighted average score of relative performance. Selecting indicators of global sustainability performance and then constructing indexes representing diverse regions or countries is a further challenge. Quality of data is also a significant challenge. Researchers note that all data must be of equally high quality; otherwise, the analyst is left to make a judgment call regarding the relevance of the information.

As discussed, there is no simple way of assigning weights to the indicators without including a high degree of subjectivity and arguably even arbitrariness. Researchers examining the DJSI have found a greater emphasis on economic indicators (comprising 30.6% of weighting) and only a nominal weighting for environmental factors (9.2%), which raises questions about what criteria and judgments are used to set the weightings.[22] Some academics have asked what would happen if the assumptions underlying either the set of indicators or the weightings of indicators were altered—would a significantly different list of companies make the cut?[23]

A review of the DJSI selection process also found some bias in selection due largely to response patterns, region, and market capitalization.[24] European companies, for example, are featured prominently in the indexes, likely because they have a greater tendency than companies from other regions to respond to SAM's survey and because they tend to have a greater awareness of sustainability issues. Asian companies are underrepresented, perhaps due to language barriers. Few emerging market companies are included in the DJSI because corporate sustainability practices are at a nascent stage in many of those countries and generally firm market capitalization is much lower. However, extended high-growth trajectories inevitably put emerging market companies on a collision course with sustainability issues. We would expect a growing number of these companies to be included in the DJSI as they further improve their corporate sustainability practices.

Compared to the popular MSCI World benchmark (in Figure 6.6), the DJSI World's total returns are not significantly different over the last ten years. Perhaps more interestingly, the DJSI World Sustainability Leaders, an index of 80 of the best-performing companies weighted according to sustainability scores, outperformed the MSCI World Developed index over the same period. (See Figure 6.7.)

Ongoing Monitoring and Delisting of Companies

Following the Deepwater Horizon oil spill in April 2010, BP became the first company to be excluded from the DJSI due to a "critical incident." The decision to remove BP flowed from SAM's monitoring process, which involves an ongoing review of company performance to ensure that companies in the DJSI continue to meet SAM's sustainability criteria for inclusion. According to SAM, a company may become ineligible for the DJSI if analysts find evidence of questionable commercial practices, human rights abuses, labor disputes, or significant disasters or accidents.

If a company is found in breach of best practice, the Index Design Committee is responsible for deciding if a company should be excluded. When a critical incident is deemed severe enough, the committee can exclude the company from the indexes, regardless of the company's annual sustainability assessment score. Once a company is removed from an index, the next highest-scoring company from within the same sector is added to rebalance the index.

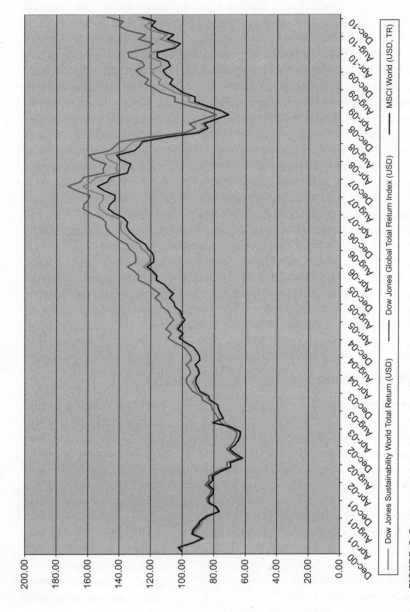

FIGURE 6.6 Financial Performance of MSCI World versus DJSI World 80 Index

Source: Dow Jones Sustainability Indexes.

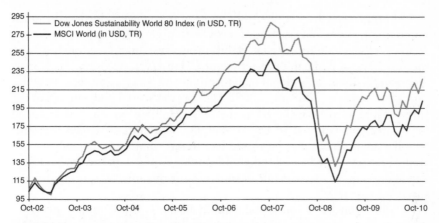

FIGURE 6.7   MSCI World versus DJSI Sustainability Leaders 80
Source: Dow Jones Sustainability Indexes.

The fact that BP was the first company to be removed from the DJSI due to a critical incident is notable. All other companies removed from the indexes to date had been bumped due to changes in the annual sector sustainability scores and not due to critical incidents. According to Amandi, BP's transparency relative to other companies in the oil and gas sector was good. Interestingly, BP was a company that did *not* actively engage with SAM or seek feedback on its sustainability performance, yet it scored well enough to be included in the index. Amandi points out, "Looking at BP post spill it is easy to zero in on the deteriorating safety record but the fact is that BP still had a high enough relative score to qualify as a sustainability index constituent."[25] As a result of the BP experience, SAM has started assigning a higher level of importance to risk and crisis management issues for the oil and gas sector in the annual assessment process.

In a move that some believe added insult to injury, SAM Indexes added Halliburton as a new DJSI World Index constituent in September 2010, just months after BP was expelled. Halliburton, a blue-chip oil services company, qualified as one of the top 10% sustainable companies within the oil equipment and services sector, according to SAM's 2010 survey results. While SAM insists that Halliburton did not directly replace BP on the index, it was a surprising move, considering that the U.S. government had accused the company of being partially responsible for BP's Deepwater Horizon oil spill. Halliburton also has a checkered past. As one commentator pointed out: "When we think of companies that stand out as role models of exceptionally responsible behavior in the realm of sustainability, Halliburton is hardly one of the first to spring to mind."[26]

SAM claims it did not block Halliburton from being added to the index because it remains unclear and unproven that Halliburton was negligent. Moreover, SAM points out that Halliburton's sustainability score puts it in the top 10% of companies in its sector.[27] However, according to Robert Sherman, Halliburton's global manager of health, safety, and sustainability, "In previous years [2008 and 2009], Halliburton scored high enough in the survey ranking to be included in the DJSI. Halliburton was not included on the recommendation of the DJSI design committee." Going forward, Sherman commented that he would like to see "more transparency associated with SAM's media and stakeholder analysis and with the Index Design Committees' power to overrule or overturn the quantitative scoring that the survey provides.[28]

Halliburton has a valid point about fairness. If a company plays by the rules and wins, it should receive the winner's award. To the Index Design Committee's credit, it treated Halliburton fairly in the 2010 and 2011 rankings. Nevertheless, given Halliburton's controversial history, one wonders if SAM's media and stakeholder analysis should play a more prominent role in how it evaluates the company's sustainability performance in the future. Should SAM disclose more useful information to both companies and investors about the evaluation process, and the media and stakeholder analysis in particular? According to SAM, companies are welcome to fully disclose the content of their Sustainability Assessment Score. However, SAM does not disclose the scores directly because it would make many companies reluctant to participate in the survey. A few companies, such as Nestlé, disclose the results of their SAM assessment on their Web sites.

To SAM's credit, companies have come to value the DJSI sustainability rankings and prominently display their sector leadership status on their Web sites and in presentations to investors. According to Ralf Pitzner, of Siemens Sustainability Office, Siemens, Europe's largest company in the diversified industrial sector, sees ongoing inclusion as a sector leader in the DJSI as validation of a successful sustainability strategy.[29] Companies frequently refer to their inclusion in the DJSI to help ward off attacks from opponents. For example, Kimberly Clark and Philips both have cited their DJSI status in an attempt to rebut criticism from Greenpeace. Arguably the most significant corporate endorsements of SAM's sustainability survey have come from Royal Dutch Shell and AkzoNobel, SAM sustainability leaders in 2010. Both companies adopted executive compensation practices based on the scores obtained in the SAM assessment. While SAM does not endorse or encourage this practice, it will be interesting to note how many companies adopt a similar practice, particularly as shareholders increasingly ask for corporate financial incentives to be tied to environmental and social outcomes. Royal Dutch Shell has since announced it would no longer link executive pay to the company's SAM score.

Behind the Mask: Summary Sustainability Scores and Systemic Risk

The oil spill debacle in 2010 may have been a low-water mark for BP, a 2010 constituent of SAM's top 10% sustainable companies in the oil and gas sector. The incident highlights an important issue for sustainability scoring methodologies: namely, that there is potential for sustainability ranking methodologies to mask systemic risk, since the scores are constructed using a set of diverse indicators aggregated to produce a final score.[30] The analysts at SAM carefully analyzed BP on the basis of a set of economic, environmental, and social sustainability scores that provided a comprehensive overview but not a detailed picture of risk at the company. In this case, the aggregate sustainability score indicated that BP was a standout in the oil and gas sector, perhaps due to excellent scores on its transparency and renewable energy commitments, but this overall score obscured BP's poor health and safety record. Certainly SAM was not the only sustainable investing firm that faced this problem. Many SRI funds in the United States owned BP at the time of the spill. And many have since scrambled to tweak their processes to take better stock of systemic risks that lurk beneath the aggregate scores assigned to companies.

  Transparency of methodology is therefore essential. Comprehensive disclosure of sustainability survey methodologies and results can provide assurance to stakeholders and clients and help demonstrate how SAM arrives at its scores. It also can highlight where a company may be underperforming, acting as a red flag for SAM, its stakeholders, and the third-party investment managers that rely on its methodologies. Given the importance of these data to SAM, it is somewhat understandable that it considers the data a trade secret and limit disclosure. However, calls for more transparency from sustainability rating companies are becoming louder.[31] Like many others in the sustainability ratings business, there is some inconsistency in SAM's objective of helping companies improve their performance and disclosure and its own need for greater transparency, as per Halliburton's comments.[32]

  SAM has the opportunity to strengthen its brand by disclosing more data. Improved disclosure may also provide add-on benefits of opening up a more public discussion about the various aspects of company performance and assist SAM in expanding the reach of its sustainability advocacy strategies.

SUSTAINABILITY ADVOCACY AND COMPANY ENGAGEMENT

A key component of SAM's value proposition is its interaction with companies and the role it plays in stimulating them to do better. The company's direct engagement approach is inspired by the philosophy that in order to move capital markets toward more sustainable practices, investors must encourage *and reward* good corporate environmental and social performance.

SAM uses its annual Corporate Sustainability Assessment as its primary engagement tool. Typical shareholder engagement processes, whether conducted internally by an investor or externally by an engagement service provider, often focus time and attention on achieving a specific and measurable sustainability outcome at one or more companies over a period of time.

The questionnaire is SAM's way of engaging with companies and communicating expectations of sustainability performance. This more passive approach is interesting and unique in that it is scalable and has broad reach. For example, in 2010, SAM sent out questionnaires to 2,617 global companies and received 698 responses. Because engagement is used as a tool to select and evaluate stocks, SAM does not actively pursue discussions with companies that display poor sustainability performance in order to initiate improvement at those companies.[33] SAM relies mostly on companies' own initiatives to reach out and seek additional feedback on how to improve performance.[34] SAM reports that it conducts between 80 and 100 one-on-one dialogs with companies that ask for more feedback each year. According to SAM, this interaction has significant value for both the analyst and the company and can lead to better understanding of company strategy and value. The interaction also can help improve a company's sustainability performance the following year.[35]

However, not all companies may choose to interact with SAM, and SAM has no process for proactively reaching out to laggard companies, except in extraordinary circumstances where a critical incident has occurred. SAM's ability to engage is limited by the number of companies participating in the survey each year. Indeed, the majority of companies (approximately 73%) contacted by SAM in 2010 did not reply to its annual questionnaire. Reto Ringger acknowledges that getting companies to participate in the survey has always been one of SAM's major challenges.[36] Once SAM's analysis is complete, each company receives a copy of its scorecard comparing its score to those of peers, but there is no guarantee that management reads or takes seriously the scorecard.

Despite its passive nature, peer pressure is powerful, and SAM uses this by creating comparative company sustainability scores. The goal is to entice firms to outpace (or at least match) the sustainability performance of their peers within their sector. There are clear indications that SAM is having some level of success. It reported that 77% of the companies it evaluated improved their sustainability scores between 2008 and 2009.[37] The number of companies responding to the questionnaire has also risen over time as companies begin to recognize the value of sustainability and understand the rationale behind SAM's annual request. SAM has seen significant improvement in corporate disclosure more generally over the past ten years,[38] and recently noted marked improvements in disclosure of water-related risks and greenhouse gas emissions.[39]

It is likely that these improvements are not solely attributed to SAM but the product of SAM and countless other organizations gathering data and campaigning to improve corporate practices. Many shareholders have been mobilizing around many of the same key issues over the past ten years. SAM and Robeco were 2 of 16 investors that initiated a series of discussions with companies about water risk management in support of the CEO Water Mandate.[40] Similarly, $71 trillion of investment dollars now back the Carbon Disclosure Project, which asks companies to disclose their greenhouse gas emissions and management plans. Both of these initiatives, and dozens more like them, have had significant effects on how companies manage, track, and report on their sustainability impact.

However, as one of the first movers in the market, it is clear that SAM has been instrumental in helping shape the "what" and "how" of corporate sustainability measurement and reporting. In addition, many major companies have accepted and even embraced aspects of SAM's methodology, using it for their own internal sustainability management systems.[41] As mentioned, some companies have integrated their annual sustainability score into staff incentives.

This growth in interest from companies has also been good for business. Over the years, SAM's evaluations have led to increasing demand from companies for greater interaction with analysts as well as more in-depth information on companies' comparative performance. This growing demand has led SAM to offer additional fee-for-service benchmarking services to companies. This benchmarking service, which enjoys increasing annual revenue, provides companies with an in-depth report comparing corporate sustainability performance with peer performance and industry best practice on a question-by-question basis.[42] Companies using this service can choose to hold follow-up meetings with analysts to discuss their results and get further information about SAM's assessment process and sustainability expectations.

SAM is careful to note that it stops short of providing consulting services to companies.[43] This is an important line to draw. Providing advice to paying companies about how to improve their sustainability scores could be viewed as compromising SAM's methodology for objectively selecting DJSI sustainability leaders. It could also lead to the perception of "payer takes all." However, despite these cautions, growing demand from companies for SAM's feedback is a positive indication that SAM has played a role in improving awareness of sustainability issues within the upper reaches of the executive suite. It is also perhaps an endorsement of SAM's robust research and analysis process and of Reto Ringger's vision of sustainable investing.

SUMMARY

Separating out sustainability from other drivers of financial success may be impossible since many company success factors, such as innovation, product life cycles, and management quality, are inextricably linked to each other and to sustainability. There is some evidence that sustainability may help lower the cost of capital and provide higher returns on invested capital among large-capitalization blue chips in Europe and North America,[44] but valuing sustainability continues to be tricky. The sustainability paradigm shift promoted by SAM and many other sustainable investment advocates may be slow to materialize in the short term, yet there continues to be significant room for optimism.

It will also be increasingly important for SAM to demonstrate to outside stakeholders that its methodology is sound. The recent controversies surrounding BP and Halliburton ignited suspicion and concern. The DJSI has significant brand recognition, and care needs to be taken to ensure that companies are not given an unwarranted stamp of approval. Staying focused on improving sustainability practices will be vital.

For SAM, corporate sustainability performance serves as a proxy for good corporate management and provides a window into the murky world of valuing intangible drivers of success. SAM's challenge is to improve the effectiveness of its corporate sustainability analysis ahead of competitors and to use that information to generate superior long-term investment returns. In the meantime, institutional competitors continue to develop and refine their own approaches to sustainability that could eclipse SAM's early success as an innovative pioneer in sustainable investing. As competitors catch up, SAM increasingly will have to differentiate itself based on the quality and comprehensiveness of its sustainability analysis. Meeting this challenge could take SAM into the major league of equity asset management and help legitimize sustainability for mainstream investors as well.

NOTES

1. "European SRI Transparency Guidelines," SAM, September 2010. www.sam-group.com/.../European_SRI%20_Transparency_Guidelines_SAM_FINAL.pdf
2. A useful survey of academic research on the materiality of sustainability is found in Mercer, "Shedding Light on Responsible Investment: Approaches, Returns and Impacts," November 2009. www.mercer.com/surveys/1363935
3. Author correspondence with Neil Johnson, SAM January 24, 2011.
4. Reto Ringger, "Reto Ringger Explains How He Builds a Sustainable Bank," Presentation at TEDxZürich. Available at www.youtube.com/watch?v=hw5fk-ko-k4
5. Ibid.
6. "SAM Corporate Sustainability Assessment—The Review: 10 Years 1999–2009." www.sam-group.com/htmle/yearbook/?CFID=2901953andCFTOKEN=20ff8faa1b918501-82832EBF-A610-C3E6-5D633D07A01D9484
7. Daniel Brooksbank, "SAM Gets €800m Asset Boost as Parent Robeco Transfers Funds," Responsible-Investor.com, January 20, 2011. www.responsible-investor.com/home/article/sam_gets_800m_asset_boost_as_parent_robeco_transfers_funds/
8. Hugh Wheelan, "SAM Chief Executive Steps Down over Robeco Strategy Dispute after Just a Year in Top Job," Responsible-Investor.com, February 3, 2010. www.responsible-investor.com/home/article/sam_chief_executive_steps_down_over_robeco_strategy_dispute_after_just_a_ye/
9. "Dow Jones Sustainability World Index Fact Sheet," December 2010. www.sustainability-index.com/.../Factsheets/SAM_IndexesMonthly_DJSIWorld.pdf
10. "PRI Reporting and Assessment Survey: SAM Sustainable Asset Management AG," SAM, 2010. www.unpri.org/report10/
11. Author interview with Neil Johnson and Daniel Wild, SAM, January 25, 2011.
12. Author personal communication with Neil Johnson, January 26, 2011.
13. "The Sustainability Yearbook," SAM, 2010. www.sam-group.com/yearbook/
14. Author interview with Johnson and Wild.
15. Dow Jones Sustainability Indexes, 2011. Interview by Tom Murtha with John Prestbo and Rodrigo Amandi, January 4, 2011.
16. Ibid.
17. Ibid.
18. "DJSI World—Methodology," Dow Jones Sustainability Indexes, 2010. www.sustainability-index.com/07_htmle/indexes/djsiworld_methodology.html
19. Author interview with Rainer Baumann and Neil Johnson, SAM, February 3, 2011.
20. SAM, "The Sustainability Yearbook," 2010, p. 92. www.sam-group.com/yearbook/ The author would like to acknowledge the work of Cecile Churet,

SAM, and her help explaining ESG factor integration and the corporate engagement process.

21. Only the most liquid stock of each company is eligible for consideration by the DJSI. "DJSI World Guidebook." www.sustainability-index.com/djsi.../DJSI_World_Guidebook_11_5.pdf

22. Stephen J. Fowler, and C. Hope, "Critical Review of Sustainable Business Indices and Their Impact," *Journal of Business Ethics* 76 (2007): 243–252. Note: Exact weightings vary depending on the sector.

23. Ibid.

24. Andreas Zielger and Michael Schröder, "What Determines the Inclusion in a Sustainability Stock Index? A Panel Data Analysis for European Firms," *Ecological Economics* 69 (2010): 848–856.

25. Dow Jones Sustainability Indexes, 2011. Interview by Tom Murtha with Prestbo and Amandi.

26. R. P. Siegel, "When Pigs Fly: Halliburton Makes the Dow Jones Sustainability Index," *Triple Pundit*, September 24, 2010. www.triplepundit.com/2010/09/when-pigs-fly-halliburton-makes-the-dow-jones-sustainability-index/

27. Author interview with Johnson and Wild.

28. Author personal communication with Robert Sherman, January 27, 2011.

29. Author personal communication with Ralf Pitzner, January 20, 2011

30. In its February 2011 newsletter, NEI Investments discusses lessons from BP's catastrophic oil spill in the context of material risk analysis and advises caution on the use of aggregate scores. See "ESG Valuations: Less Is More." www.neiinvestments.com/NEIFiles/PDFs/5.1.4%20Sustainable%20Investing%20Update/ESG%20Newsletter%202011/ESG_02_11_EN_WEB.html

31. SustainAbility, "Rate the Raters, Phase Three, Uncovering Best Practices,", February 2011. www.sustainability.com/library/rate-the-raters-phase-three

32. The consultancy SustainAbility provides an excellent discussion of these issues. Ibid.

33. SAM, "European SRI Transparency Guidelines," September 2010. www.sam-group.com/.../European_SRI%20_Transparency_Guidelines_SAM_FINAL.pdf

34. For example, when companies receive a copy of their annual SAM scorecard each year, they are invited to provide feedback, clarification, or corrections where necessary. Firms also can ask questions and engage with SAM analysts in a discussion about their sustainability performance, if they choose.

35. Author interview with Neil Johnson and Daniel Wild.

36. Telephone interview with Reto Ringger, February 10, 2011.

37. SAM, "PRI Reporting and Assessment Survey: SAM Sustainable Asset Management AG," 2010. www.unpri.org/report10/

38. SAM, "European SRI Transparency Guidelines," September 2010.

39. SAM, "The Sustainability Yearbook."

40. CEOs who endorse the Water Mandate recognize the impact of business operations on water resources and agree to make managing water risks a priority for their organization.

41. Author interview with Johnson and Wild.

42. Ibid.
43. Ibid. For firms seeking more detailed guidance on how to implement changes, SAM directs them to their consulting partners, PricewaterhouseCoopers and Brugger and Partner AG. The consulting partners are familiar with the SAM assessment process and provide guidance to companies on the nuts and bolts of improving their sustainability management practice and ultimately their sustainability assessment score.
44. Mercer Group, "Shedding Light on Responsible Investment: Approaches, Returns, Impacts," November 2009.

CHAPTER 7

Domini and BP

Colm Fay

A seminal moment in the history of investing was arguably the Deepwater Horizon explosion in the Gulf of Mexico of 2010. Many socially responsible investors heralded BP as an industry leader, and the company was considered as such by the Dow Jones Sustainability Index until after the spill. As the definition of what constitutes a sustainable company evolves, here's the tale of how one well-established socially responsible investment (SRI) firm, Domini Social Investments, used quality and safety as an important lens well in advance of the incident. Domini is a firm firmly rooted in the origins of SRI, but this investment decision was clearly a case of using sustainability risk as a way of getting ahead of what would become a serious problem for many investors. It will be interesting to see whether Domini uses this specific example as a driver to look more fully at opportunities emerging from sustainability going forward. One could argue that Domini reduced risk for its shareholders by considering the operational practices of a company like BP, even though, as of this writing, BP's share price has largely recovered.

BP had humble beginnings in 1908 as Anglo-Persian, a company formed by William D'Arcy and George Reynolds after seven years of exploration in the Persian desert resulted in the discovery of significant oil fields. What followed was a massive operation to build the necessary infrastructure to bring this resource effectively to market. At the time, when cars were not yet providing a mass market for fuel, Anglo-Persian spent much of the next seven years struggling to find a market for its products. The company's saving grace was the foresight of Winston Churchill, who recognized the need for Britain to secure a reliable supply of oil with a world war shortly at hand. The government purchased a key stake, which positioned Anglo-Persian for success as the automotive revolution followed the war.

In 1935 Persia became Iran, and Anglo-Persian became Anglo-Iranian. During this period, the company started to use the BP brand to market its gasoline products in the United Kingdom. The Anglo-Iranian name lasted for almost 20 years before nationalist concerns in Iran convinced its parliament to take control of the country's oil operations. While this decision ultimately was reversed, Anglo-Iranian became British Petroleum in 1954.

During the 1960s, BP expanded its operations to include exploration in the English Channel and the North Sea, which led to much wealth generation for the region for the next two generations. And in 1969, the company made the largest oil discovery in North America at Prudhoe Bay, Alaska. Against the backdrop of the first Earth Day in 1970 and the groundbreaking Clean Air and Clean Water Acts that would soon be enacted by the Nixon administration, the risks of undertaking oil exploration in such an environmentally sensitive area were high on the public agenda for the first time. As a result, BP was subjected to an extended legal process with federal and state authorities over its planned operations on the North Slope and the 745-mile pipeline that was required to transport oil out of the region through areas that were both environmentally and culturally sensitive. The dispute was resolved when President Nixon signed the Trans-Alaska Pipeline Authorization Act 1973, which halted all legal challenges brought against the pipeline's construction under the National Environmental Protection Act 1970 (NEPA) and the Mineral Leasing Act 1920 (MLA). It is this pipeline that proved problematic for the company in later years.

Toward the end of the twentieth century and under the stewardship of chief executive Lord Browne, BP appeared to begin to embrace the energy challenges of the future. The company's new philosophy to explore alternative and renewable energy options were summed up in the rebranding of the company with a new, greener image. The tagline for this new identity became the well-known "Beyond Petroleum," which shaped activities that attempted to position BP as the sector's leader in sustainability and transparency. BP was the first of the major oil companies to publicly recognize the causal link between increasing carbon dioxide emissions and global warming.[1] The company embraced new sustainability reporting standards developed by the Global Reporting Initiative and won awards for its sustainability reporting, being ranked number one by *Fortune* magazine in its most accountable companies in 2005 and most responsible company by the same publication in 2008.[2] However, despite this seeming transparency, there were warning signs that the culture of disclosure and the actuality of practice were significantly divergent. The green marketing which the company's sustainability reporting was communicating publicly hid significant shortcomings, specifically with respect to the safety culture within the company and a fear of being reprimanded that prevented employees from disclosing safety concerns.

DOMINI SOCIAL INVESTMENTS

Amy Domini spent most of the 1980s working as a traditional stockbroker. During this time, she noticed an increasing amount of client interest in investment options that aligned with their ethical values. Domini realized that investors needed a benchmark to determine investment performance with respect to the market as a whole and to test whether socially responsible investing was a good financial proposition and a solid ethical concept. In 1990, Domini, along with partners Steve Lydenberg and Peter Kinder, launched the Domini 400 Social Index to address this information gap.[3] The index included 400 large-cap U.S. corporations chosen based on their social and environmental credentials. A year later, the Domini Social Equity Fund was launched, initially as an index fund.[4] It transitioned to active management in 2006, based on the belief that the use of social and environmental standards could produce equal or better long-term financial performance.

The fund launched amid skepticism from Wall Street that imposing social and environmental criteria on investment decision-making would limit the universe of corporations that could form part of a portfolio and therefore limit potential profitability. However, over the long term, the Domini 400 Social Index has demonstrated strong individual stock selection and at minimum benchmark returns for investors committed to long-term capital growth.

In October 2005, Domini was set to launch its first non-U.S. fund designed to give investors the opportunity to achieve impact on an international scale through their investments. As the investment committee was assessing stocks for inclusion in the fund, a key question was whether to include BP in the portfolio. Despite BP's award winning accountability credentials,[5] its "Beyond Petroleum" strategy and 1999 acquisition of Amoco, which had been part of Domini's domestic portfolio, this was the investment team's first opportunity to take a hard look at BP's operations to identify any risks that might indicate future problems and to determine the company's alignment with fund objectives and investors goals.

SAFETY, ENVIRONMENTAL, AND ETHICAL CONCERNS

The year 2005 was not a good one for BP. In March, a massive explosion at the company's Texas City oil refinery resulted in the deaths of 15 employees and serious injuries to an additional 180.[6] Subsequent investigations found systemic problems within BP's Texas City operations and management relating to accountability, communications, performance management, clarity of roles and responsibilities, training and the lack of early warning when problems were identified.[7] As such, a significant number of safety improvements were instituted. Despite BP's efforts and $1 billion investment in improved safety, the Texas City facility has seen three additional fatalities since the 2005 explosion, making it the deadliest refinery in the United States.[8]

In the wake of the disaster, BP reached out to many socially responsible investors, including Domini, to reassure them that this was an isolated incident. Most fund managers met this outreach with caution, and many chose not to drop BP from their portfolios. Domini, however, chose to dig a little deeper in order to justify including BP in its portfolio after such a high-profile incident. In the end, Domini chose to exclude BP. Another catastrophe in March 2006 raised further concerns regarding BP's technical capabilities. A faulty pipeline at the company's Prudhoe Bay facility in Alaska resulted in a spill of 200,000 gallons, the largest oil spill in the history of the state's North Slope area.

Although these incidents attracted modest fines of $50 million for the Texas City disaster and $20 million for a single violation of the Clean Water Act for the Prudhoe Bay spill, these fines were dwarfed by a $303 million settlement with the Department of Justice in an antitrust suit taken against BP for price-fixing activities in its propane, gas, and crude oil trading businesses. What concerned the investment team at Domini, however, was not just the impact of these events, or the magnitude of the fines, but what they indicated about the culture within BP's operations. Despite its reputation as a leader in sustainability reporting and its green credentials, the Domini investment team had a lot to consider as it analyzed BP's operations and the fallout of recent safety issues to determine the company's alignment with the fund's goals, objectives, and investment philosophy.

DOMINI INVESTMENT PHILOSOPHY

Domini's investment methodology assesses each company according to its core business model and the strength of its relationships with its stakeholders as indicators of that company's long-term value proposition for society.

Consideration along both of these axes creates an "approved universe" of stocks that are candidates for the portfolio. Starting with the Russell 1000 and the Standard & Poor's 500, the investment committee makes eligibility decisions based on a methodology informed by social and environmental research, with attempts to capture sources of risk and opportunity that would be overlooked by traditional analysis. It is believed that these indicators constitute an excellent proxy for the quality of management at such companies.

Stakeholder Relations

The core belief of the Domini strategy is that environmental sustainability and universal human dignity do not have to be attained at the expense of financial sustainability. Since there is often mutual interdependence between companies and their key stakeholders, the development and enrichment of partnerships is a strong indicator of long-term value creation. While effectively managing these relationships provides an opportunity for improved returns, the failure to manage them externalizes costs and erodes both social and natural capital resulting in significant financial, social, and environmental risk.

As part of the determination of eligibility,[9] companies are assessed on the strength of their relationships with these key stakeholder groups:

- Communities
- Customers
- Ecosystems
- Employees
- Investors
- Suppliers

Stakeholder relationships are classified as:

- Strong
- Occasionally strong
- Neutral or mixed
- Occasionally weak
- Weak

BUSINESS MODEL ANALYSIS: KEY PERFORMANCE INDICATOR ALIGNMENT MODEL

Domini believes that certain companies are fundamentally misaligned with its investment strategy due to their negative environmental or social impact.

Therefore, Domini seeks to exclude those companies that have significant involvement in or derive significant revenue from these activities:

Tobacco and alcohol manufacturing

Gambling

Nuclear power production

Weapons manufacturing

As companies move along the spectrum from aligned to misaligned, there is an increasingly higher hurdle required for inclusion in terms of stakeholder relationship management. This balance ensures that the process is grounded in the company's core business model and takes into account the key sustainability challenges it faces.

Alignment with Domini's investment standards is categorized in this way:

- Fundamental alignment
  - Pioneer innovative products that address the most pressing problems of our times (e.g., non–fossil fuel energy, pollution prevention equipment, disease prevention, and accident risk mitigation).
  - Pioneer access to wealth-creating, sustainable products for underserved sectors of society or the environment (e.g., mobile telephones, Internet access, and microfinance).
- Partial alignment
  - Businesses that contribute value to society and the environment as long as stakeholder relations are appropriately managed. The majority of businesses fall in this classification.
- Partial misalignment
  - Pose substantial, avoidable threats to the environment (e.g., pesticide manufacturers, gold and diamond mining companies).
  - Are large contributors to global warming (e.g., oil and coal companies, automobile and truck manufacturers, electric utilities).
  - Undercut the provision of basic public goods. These include, for example, for-profit companies in the fields of primary school education, prisons, and security.
- Fundamental misalignment
  - Cause severe harm to customers by, for example, producing addictive and harmful products and services. These include tobacco and alcohol manufacturers and gambling companies.
  - Threaten geopolitical stability. These include nuclear weapons manufacturers, international arms dealers, uranium mining companies, and nuclear power utilities.

Fundamentally misaligned companies are not eligible for inclusion in the Domini funds.

INTEGRATING BUSINESS MODEL ALIGNMENT AND STAKEHOLDER RELATIONSHIP STRENGTH

Domini's approach to integrating business model alignment and stakeholder relations is illustrated in Figure 7.1. Depending on business alignment, Domini sets corresponding thresholds for the company's relationships with its key stakeholders. A company that is fundamentally aligned with its standards will have a lower stakeholder relations threshold to cross than one that is partially misaligned. For example, a solar cell manufacturer is considered fundamentally aligned with Domini's standards due to the ecological benefits provided by its core business model. Without severe stakeholder relations challenges, it probably would qualify for inclusion in Domini's portfolios. In comparison, nuclear power operators or coal-burning utilities are fundamentally misaligned businesses and would be excluded from the Domini portfolios.

Most companies fall in the middle of the spectrum, in which case stakeholder relations play a key role in determining its eligibility. Domini is not looking for "perfect" companies. Rather, it is seeking to identify the key sustainability challenges and rewards for each company and then to assess whether that company is, on balance, responsibly acknowledging and addressing them.

Industry-Specific KPIs

The first step in making the determination of whether to invest is to assess the company based on industry specific key performance indicators (KPIs). BP is classified as Integrated Oil/Supermajors within the energy sector, a category that consists of companies that generate significant portions of

	Fundamental Industry Alignment	Partial Industry Alignment	Partial Industry Misalignment	Fundamental Industry Misalignment
Pattern of strong stakeholder relations	✔	✔	✔	✘
Occasionally strong stakeholder relations	✔	✔	★	✘
Mixed or neutral stakeholder relations	✔	★	★	✘
Occasionally weak stakeholder relations	✔	★	✘	✘
Pattern of weak stakeholder relations	★	✘	✘	✘

FIGURE 7.1 Integrating Business Alignment and Stakeholder Relations

their revenues from exploration and production, refining, basic chemical production, transportation, and marketing. Companies in this category tend to be mega-caps with a global diversified presence. Domini classifies each subindustry category according to its alignment with the fund's goals for energy production, which supports the generation of energy from sustainable natural resources (wind, solar, etc.).

Classification within the Integrated Oil/Supermajors category implies partial misalignment with Domini's goals due to the large-scale nature of these businesses and the tendency for companies to be involved in business lines such as unconventional oil and gas production techniques (tar sands, shale etc.) or concentration on developing countries. These large companies tend to take highly visible positions on matters of public policy, which magnifies the impact of both their positive and their negative actions within the industry. Key stakeholder management issues for this subindustry include:

- Corporate climate change policy
- Workplace and community safety (especially controversies related to spills or leaks)
- Relationship with regulatory bodies and history of fines or other punitive actions
- Environmental management systems
- Human rights record

While many indicators are taken into account when assessing companies for inclusion in the fund, rather than assessing a company based on an average of its performance in all possible areas related to environmental and social responsibility, the specific indicators that are deemed particularly relevant for each industry subgroup are given significant weighting. Given the strong focus on safety and relationships with regulatory bodies, the disasters at Texas City and Prudhoe Bay were central to the investment committee's ultimate decision regarding BP.

Assessment of BP's Eligibility

After an assessment of BP's record, with a focus on the company's alarming safety violations, Domini's investment committee decided against including BP in its funds. Since the inauguration of Domini's first non-U.S. fund, this decision has been reevaluated at least every 18 months, as per Domini's standard review process. The investment team has continued to determine that the stock should not be included due to ongoing concerns, as described next.

Health and Safety Record   The Texas City and Prudhoe Bay disasters were seen to be evidence of systemic safety problems. The committee had major concerns over the safety culture in BP, which presented the risk that additional environmental and safety issues could be raised in the future.

Ongoing Regulatory Issues   The company has been penalized for a number of high-profile incidents and continues to attract punitive actions for repeated health, safety, and environmental infractions and for the failure to implement recommended improvements. A 2009 inspection by the Occupational Safety and Health Administration would determine that a huge number of the improvements to safety processes and protocols recommended after the Texas City Refinery disaster had not been implemented in the more than three years since the recommendations had been made.[10] In some cases, BP were still assessing the implementation challenges; however, in other cases the company had failed to take any action on the issue.

Unconventional Resource Plays   After Lord Browne sold off BP's Canadian tar sands interests in 1999,[11] the company has reversed its policy and is once again investing significant effort to pursue this unconventional bitumen extraction process, which has the potential to have a large negative impact on the environment. Tar sand production requires large amounts of water and energy with potential negative impacts on air and water quality and has one of the lowest energy return on investment ratios of any fossil fuel at less than 10:1.[12] This results in significantly higher carbon dioxide emissions per unit of energy—almost 50% more than traditional hydrocarbons when the combustion of products extracted in this way is included in the carbon footprint.

Beyond Petroleum Positioning   BP has stepped back from some of the positions it took as part of the "Beyond Petroleum" strategy, most notably in the wake of Tony Hayward taking over as chief executive from Lord Browne in 2007. Hayward focused on stripping down the organization and improving efficiency, including a restructuring effort that shifted focus from investment in renewable and alternative energies, to driving maximum profitability from its fossil fuel business segments. Explaining this change in strategy in a lecture to the Stanford Business School, Hayward stated that in his view "we had too many people that were working to save the world" and that the company had forgotten that its "primary purpose was to create value for our shareholders."[13]

Conclusion   Domini's systematic approach to determining a stock's eligibility for inclusion allowed the investment committee to see beyond BP's sustainability marketing and reporting efforts to identify genuine business risk within the organization. By analyzing both BP's business model and their stakeholder relations the investment committee compiled an integrated view of the company's operations, which uncovered systemic safety issues that would lead to future high profile incidents that would not only have a damaging effect on the environment, but ultimately would erode shareholder value and negatively impact investor returns.

NOTES

1. http://dieoff.org/page106.htm
2. www.csrwire.com/press_releases/14277-Accountability-Rating-of-World-s-Biggest-Companies-Released; www.energy-pedia.com/article.aspx?articleid=126907
3. www.kld.com/indexes/ds400index/index.html
4. www.domini.com/domini-funds/Domini-Social-Equity-Fund/index.htm
5. www.csrwire.com/press_releases/14277-Accountability-Rating-of-World-s-Biggest-Companies-Released
6. www.csb.gov/newsroom/detail.aspx?nid=205
7. www.bp.com/liveassets/bp_internet/us/bp_us_english/STAGING/local_assets/downloads/t/final_report.pdf
8. www.txattorneys.com/news-105.html
9. www.domini.com/GlobInvStd/index.htm
10. www.osha.gov/dep/bp/Fact_Sheet-BP_2009_Monitoring_Inspection.html
11. www.independent.co.uk/environment/the-biggest-environmental-crime-in-history-764102.html
12. For each 10 units of energy extracted, 1 unit of energy is expended on the extraction process. As a comparison, the first oil wells produced an energy return on investment of approximately 100:1.
13. www.vpr.net/npr/127884525/

CHAPTER 8

The Story of Calvert

Sam Brownell and Sara Herald

Like Domini, Calvert Investments has been around as long as any investor in the socially responsible investing space, from the very first waves of the field. They continue to be strong advocates for change and the values it believes in. Calvert's ongoing evolution towards integrating sustainability and all its aspects fully into what the company does has been interesting to watch, as is their storied history.

Calvert Investments, the largest socially responsible investment (SRI) fund manager in the United States,[1] has a long history, and its evolution toward sustainability has been fascinating to observe. The firm was founded in 1976 by D. Wayne Silby and John G. Guffey Jr. in Washington, DC, as a relatively straightforward money market fund. Silby and Guffey, both graduates of the Wharton School at the University of Pennsylvania, joined together to start the First Variable Rate Fund for Government Income, one of the first funds in the country to combine "an innovative mix of short-term, fixed-rate securities with long-term, variable-rate securities to provide attractive yields, as well as a strong measure of safety."

UNCONVENTIONAL HISTORY

The firm's culture was anything but traditional: Everyone worked from Silby's town house, employees were encouraged to meditate in a float tank

---

Unless otherwise indicated, details about Calvert Investments are available at the company site, www.calvert.com.

located in the kitchen, and dress was casual. Silby's business cards read "Chief Daydreamer," and early employees remarked that "being weird was a good thing." According to Bill Baue, at the time with SocialFunds.com, the fund "achieved the highest yield of all money market funds for a number of years,"[2] but the founders weren't satisfied with the company's early success. After attending a Buddhist retreat, Silby was inspired to connect the company with the values he attributes to growing up in the 1960s, such as respect for human rights, environmentalism, and equality. And so in 1982, the firm's founders joined with Robert Zevin of U.S. Trust to create the Calvert Social Investment Fund, "a group of portfolios that incorporated environmental, social and governance criteria into their investment-selection process." One of that fund's first steps was to take a public stance against apartheid and divest holdings of companies doing business in South Africa.

In the 1990s the company expanded its socially responsible investment equity offerings, although the fixed-income side of the business remained the primary source of the firm's revenue. The High Social Impact Investments fund was created in 1990, targeting 1% of investments toward community development. In 1992, both the Special Equities program, which invested in early-stage companies with social missions, and the Calvert World Values International Equity Fund, the first international socially responsible fund, were created. Throughout the rest of the decade, the firm continued to grow and diversify its offerings, serving both individual and institutional investors, and by 1997, the firm had over $6 billion of assets under management.

In 2006, the firm's leadership began to contemplate adjusting the traditional SRI approach. Bennett Freeman, senior vice president of sustainability research and policy, notes that "in the mid-2000s, the corporate social responsibility and sustainability landscape had changed, and these issues had become more mainstream." Calvert's analysts had noticed that "leadership and innovation around sustainability [was emerging] from companies that did not meet the criteria for the SRI funds, [such as] General Electric, DuPont, and Shell," and the firm wanted to "develop new strategies that would provide Calvert new investors, SRI or mainstream, the choice to walk down different paths that would be innovative but show returns." The company created three SRI categories—Signature, Solution, and SAGE (Sustainability Achieved through Greater Engagement)—and began launching funds in 2007 that reflected these new strategies. Today, Calvert Group manages over $14.5 billion in assets and has evolved from a small, counterculture bond fund to a mainstream player in the financial services industry.

In 1988, Calvert also launched the Calvert Foundation, founded with the Ford, MacArthur, and Mott foundations. It is now a completely separate and distinct philanthropic arm. The foundation's "mission is to maximize the flow of capital to disadvantaged communities in order to create a more equitable and sustainable society."[3] The foundation collects capital from interested investors as well as from the Calvert Fund, and gives low-interest loans to qualified organizations trying to make a social impact. Through 2010, Calvert Foundation had invested approximately $200 million in 250 organizations. In 1995, the foundation expanded to include the Giving Fund, a strategic philanthropy vehicle focused on making grants to further community investment.

CALVERT'S PEOPLE

Calvert, now located in Bethesda, MD, currently employs over 150 people. The company's chief executive officer (CEO), Barbara Krumsiek, joined the firm in 1997. Previously a managing director at Alliance Capital Management in New York, her arrival marked a significant shift for the firm. She was the first hire with a conventional investment management background, bringing over two decades of Wall Street experience to the company. Krumsiek notes that on being approached about the position, she "was surprised by Calvert's small size. [Her] experience up to that point had been in the mutual funds 401k arena, and Calvert's name had always come up, so [she] thought the firm would be larger." Ultimately, she decided to join the company because Calvert's model was a "better way to invest." Rather than focusing solely on financial performance, Calvert's analysts and portfolio managers were "assessing quality of management and workplace practices," essential components to long-term performance. Furthermore, Krumsiek felt that joining Calvert would allow her to connect her professional and personal interests, particularly in regard to finding ways to advance women's leadership opportunities.

Upon taking over as CEO, Krumsiek's two goals were to "help the firm [grow and] succeed in a business sense without losing its principles," and to "make a real difference in corporate behavior [as a] leader in sustainability policy." She noticed that the prevailing attitude at the firm was one of a niche player, as Calvert employees "seemed to feel that there [was] a limited number of people interested in [the firm's products]." The focus up to that point had been on the very socially conscious group of investors that "embraced all of the Calvert principles."

However, it had become clear that those investors also were investing elsewhere, as "returns still mattered to them, and they invested in other options if they weren't getting satisfaction from Calvert or other socially responsible portfolios." Krumsiek also realized that the firm lacked a sales culture. Although there were over 2,000 selling agreements already in place with distribution outlets, the focus was not out actively selling the firm's products. Therefore, she launched the "Ambassador Program" to create that missing sales culture and rethink how the company presented itself. The program was successful in its first year, and the image of the Calvert investor started to shift away from that of the older hippie to one of "average folks who go to work every day" and invest with Calvert via their 401(k)'s.

However, one key obstacle to reaching these average folks and their 401(k) dollars remained: the argument that the socially responsible investing model was in violation of fiduciary duty. Some money managers and financial institutions felt that restricting the universe of companies in which they could invest their clients' money went 'against their commitment to act in those clients' best interests. Calvert's legal team petitioned the U.S. Department of Labor to define and explain the issue, and the government responded with a letter (now often referred to as the "Calvert Letter") that found that the socially responsible investing model was not in violation of fiduciary duty. With that legal clarification, the company was able to pursue 401(k) investors more aggressively, and Calvert's products are now offered on nine out of every ten investment platforms.

Looking forward, Krumsiek remains focused on growth. Assets under management have grown from $6 billion to over $14 billion under her leadership, but she wants the firm to be "double or triple" its current size in order to make a bigger impact. For Krumsiek, the sky is the limit, as SRI "should not involve any [decrease] in returns. Managers shouldn't enter into the process [thinking SRI returns are lower than nonscreened ones]. These investments should perform at or above benchmark averages." On a policy level, she recognizes the need to develop "better metrics around advocacy and engagement." The company can boast of several policy achievements during Krumsiek's tenure, namely the creation of the Calvert Women's Principles in 2005, which have since been adopted by UN Women; a board diversity initiative that has resulted in more companies "committing to interview women and minorities for open board positions"; and Apple Computer's first-ever appointment of a woman to its board of directors in 2008. While proud of those achievements, Krumsiek isn't satisfied. She feels that "new initiatives are necessary every five to seven years" in order to keep companies engaged and continue to make progress on the principles Calvert stands for.

In 2006, Bennett Freeman joined Calvert after previous stints as the head of Buston-Marstellar's Global Corporate Social responsibility practice from 2001 to 2003 and as deputy assistant secretary for Democracy, Human Rights and Labor from 1999 to 2001 under the Clinton administration. At Calvert, Freeman oversees the sustainability research department as well as the firm's advocacy work conducted through its SAGE funds.

Soon after he was hired, Freeman began to look at whether Calvert needed to differentiate and broaden the framework for its sustainable funds, although "not due to performance problems, [as they were] experiencing record sales growth." Freeman saw the need for a "fresh approach." He was struck by how much the world had changed from the mid-1990s to 2006, especially after the release of Al Gore's film *An Inconvenient Truth*, which helped move climate change awareness from the margins into the mainstream. In this new environment, Calvert's leadership began thinking about new ways to approach SRI and keep Calvert in line with what was important to its investors.

The executive team made the decision to restructure Calvert's approach to SRI, retaining the "core rubric" of five industry exclusions and the seven environmental, social, and governance (ESG) criteria under the name "Calvert Signature Funds." These Signature Funds would reflect the more traditional approach to SRI and represent the majority of Calvert's equity holdings. The next step was to "develop new strategies that provided all of Calvert's investors the choice to walk down different paths that would be innovative while focused on returns for both retail and institutional investors, which is how the Solution and SAGE funds were born." The Solution Funds would invest only in firms addressing specific environmental issues, and the SAGE Funds would broaden their universe, allowing Calvert to work with specific companies that didn't pass Signature criteria to make progress on sustainability initiatives.

More recently, Freeman has been working to update two areas in Calvert's list of exclusions, nuclear power and weapons. Nuclear power had been on the list of exclusions long before Freeman joined the firm, but with the launch of the Alternative Energy Solution Fund, which focuses investment on companies working to counteract global warming, Calvert faced a decision about its stance on nuclear power. Eventually, Freeman and the other executives decided that they were going to "have to make tough decisions about climate change" and that they could "invest in nuclear if a certain threshold for alternative revenue was met" and if the company was not planning on adding nuclear power facilities. This decision, which applied only to Solution and SAGE funds, opened up the opportunity to invest in companies such as Florida Power and Light, which has a legacy nuclear power plant but separately met Calvert's minimum requirement for revenue from alternative energy.

After tackling nuclear power, Freeman moved on to weaponry. Prior to his arrival, the company had been prohibited from investing "in companies with greater than 10% of their revenue from the design, manufacture, and sales of weapons." Through discussions over the crisis in Darfur, Calvert came to the realization that a company could manufacture cluster bombs and land mines with as little as 1% of its revenue; therefore, any investment in weapons would be unacceptable to the firm. Currently, Calvert looks at two criteria to determine whether to invest in a company that manufactures weapons: "precedent set by international humanitarian law and no inherently offensive weapons." Moving forward, Freeman wants to use the weapons decision as a springboard to growth by continuing to strike a "balance between who we are and current trends and opportunities."

CALVERT'S METHODOLOGIES: SIGNATURE, SOLUTION, AND SAGE

Since the company's beginnings as a money market fund, it has expanded to offer three distinct SRI products: Calvert Signature, Calvert Solution, and Calvert SAGE strategies. Each category has specific investment criteria and exclusions, but companies in the tobacco and weapon industries, as well as companies that violate human rights criteria, never form part of any of these portfolios. The Signature Funds are the traditional SRI vehicles: Companies that are part of Signature Funds must meet or exceed baseline criteria in seven areas commonly associated with responsible investing, such as environmental stewardship, transparent and ethical governance practices, and a focus on product safety. Solution portfolios are designed to promote investment in companies working to address the world's "most pressing environmental topics." The first Solution Fund, focusing on alternative energy, was launched in June 2007. The second Solution Fund was launched in October 2008 and focused on investments in water resource companies, such as Severn Trent PLC, a British-based company that focuses on water treatment, distribution, and wastewater removal.[4]

Two months later Calvert launched its first SAGE Fund, which according to Freeman was "unprecedented for Calvert and a bold move for the SRI community" as a whole. SAGE funds promote engagement around ESG issues with companies in particularly extractive or potentially damaging industries, such as oil and gas, chemicals, and manufacturing. That structure allows those companies that do not pass traditional screens to be held in a portfolio and targeted for specific advocacy goals. In 2010, companies in the SAGE fund included ExxonMobil, Duke Energy, and Wal-Mart Stores Inc. Calvert's analysts identify these companies as good targets for "enhanced engagement" and work with each company's leadership to make progress on specific sustainability goals. Calvert also offers financial products outside of the SRI realm, including traditional mutual funds and variable insurance products.

Signature Funds

The Signature Funds are the bedrock of the Calvert investment philosophy. As the company Web site states, "At the core of Calvert's SRI investment philosophy is a belief that, over time, responsible corporate conduct and solid investment returns go hand in hand." The Signature Funds have remained the same, in both investment criteria and exclusions, since launching in the 1980s. Each company that is bought for a Signature portfolio must meet specific standards in each of seven categories:

1. Governance and ethics
2. Workplace
3. Environment
4. Product safety and impact
5. International operations and human rights
6. Indigenous people's rights
7. Community relations

Along with these seven criteria for screening companies, Calvert also has five exclusions that it uses to filter prospective investments. Companies in the weapons, alcohol, tobacco, gambling, or nuclear power industries are barred from inclusion in any Signature portfolio. Although this limits the universe of companies that Calvert portfolio managers can invest in, the company still believes that, over the long run, it can produce returns to match any traditional mutual fund.

However, the Signature Funds will always be defined by the screen criteria. Freeman oversees 18 sustainability analysts who "spend anywhere from 12 to 24 hours [researching] a normal company and more for a large and complex company." Calvert's sustainability analysts are constantly monitoring the seven areas to make sure current holdings are in compliance and to look for new opportunities. In governance and ethics, analysts continually monitor "disclosure of policies and procedures, board independence and diversity, executive compensation, and attention to stakeholder concerns." Calvert will not invest in companies that have poor governance structures or a track record of questionable activities. Workplace screens look at three areas of a company: "diversity, labor relations, and employee health and safety." When looking at the environmental impact of a firm, Calvert analysts' due diligence includes looking for companies "that find opportunities to mitigate their environmental footprint, have better-than-average environmental records relative to their industry peers, and are responsive to stakeholders." Product safety and impact includes not investing in companies that make products that are detrimental to human health (such as tobacco) and investing in those that respond to safety violations and show accountability and honesty in their advertising. Calvert feels that companies that do not adopt a code of conduct to "cover their entire scope of operations" and that do not have specific human rights standards are not practicing sustainability and therefore are not going to be strong long-run performers. Likewise, Calvert believes that companies that do not respect indigenous people's land, legal rights, and/or human rights do not belong in a sustainable portfolio. Finally, Calvert analysts look for companies that give back to the communities in which they operate through initiatives such as fair lending, "corporate philanthropy, employee volunteerism, and support of women- and minority-owned businesses." A company that does not meet even one of these criteria is eliminated as a potential holding for Calvert's Signature Funds. While these standards are stringent, many companies operate in accordance with these criteria and have been long-term holdings in Signature funds, such as Gap and Hewlett Packard.

Calvert currently has 12 Signature Funds (with multiple classes of shares in each fund), including both domestic and international. These funds range from Large-Cap Growth Funds, to Mid-Cap Accumulation Funds, to a Social Index Fund. As with any mutual fund company, Calvert's funds have experienced varying degrees of success over the years. For example, their Large-Cap Growth Fund has returned a positive 7.92% since inception; based on the past 10 years of return data, the fund slightly trails its benchmark as of December 31, 2010. Holdings of the fund include Apple, Cameron International (a maker of blowout preventers), Carmax, McKesson, and Genworth Financial. Portfolio manager John Montgomery continues "to be overweight to the Information Technology sector relative to the S&P 500 Index . . . primarily due to the significant representation of IT stocks on the growth side of the market." Going forward, Montgomery notes that Morningstar has reported that growth stocks have finally outperformed their core and value brethren the past fiscal year 2010 for the first time in ten years. In his latest outlook, Montgomery concludes that due to this shift, "we believe that large-cap growth stocks represent a relatively attractive segment of the market for investments inside a well-diversified portfolio."

Solution Funds

With the launch of the Alternative Energy Fund in June 2007, Calvert expanded its offerings and focus from the traditional Signature SRI approach to include more targeted and innovative products through its Solution Funds. According to the Calvert Web site, Solution Funds "are portfolios that selectively invest in companies that produce products and services geared toward solving some of today's most pressing environmental and sustainability challenges." Solution Funds strive to attract a new investor who has become more aware of the impact of human activity on Earth and wants to help provide capital to those companies searching for innovative solutions to the planet's biggest problems, such as access to cheap, renewable energy and clean, abundant water. Furthermore, in a break from Signature Funds practice, Solution Funds are benchmarked to specific indexes created to track companies in nontraditional fields. For example, the Alternative Energy Fund is benchmarked to the Ardour Global Alternative Energy Index, and the Global Water Fund (launched in October 2008) is benchmarked to the S-Network Global Water Price Index. Like many of the funds at Calvert, the two Solution Funds are not managed in house. As and when the company increases its number of portfolio managers and analysts, more funds will be run by Calvert directly.

To be included in a Solution Fund, a company must pass both screening criteria and exclusions in a similar manner to the Signature Funds. For the Alternative Energy Fund, for example, companies are screened for their commitment to the environment, their commitment to improve social standards through their investments, and internal corporate governance issues. Companies then are excluded if they are currently invested or have future plans to invest in new nuclear power facilities. For the Global Water Fund, analysts are looking for "disclosure and transparency, equitable and affordable access to water, measures taken to mitigate the effect of climate change, and willingness to participate in stakeholder engagement." Companies then can be excluded for investing in tobacco products, offensive weapons manufacturing, or repressive regimes (such as a company that does business in a country with a brutal dictatorship such as Burma).

The Alternative Energy Fund has experienced a –17.14% return since its inception on May 31, 2007. The fund is also down both year to date and quarter to date, tracking its benchmark in lockstep since late 2009 the fund is matching the performance of its benchmark (comparative) index while being down overall during the periods mentioned. While performance has been negative for the life of the fund, companies within the fund have been hit unusually hard by the global recession that started in late 2007. The fund invests in primarily small-cap companies because most alternative energy companies are trying to break into a market dominated by large, traditional players. As the financial crisis intensified, investors pulled their money out of these supposedly riskier ventures, causing large sell-offs. Additionally, the financial crisis caused oil prices to tumble from $147 a barrel to approximately $33 a barrel. As oil becomes cheaper, the incentive to invest in alternative energy goes down; therefore, the amount of capital available to these companies dries up, although the situation is changing rapidly as oil prices are up once more. However, Calvert is a long-term investor and is not making a play in alternative energy for a quick profit. As the market begins to recover and investors return, Calvert believes there will be additional capital and interest available for the alternative energy sector, especially if the price of traditional energy, such as oil, stays high. Portfolio manager Jens

Peers also sees a boost from overseas as "news regarding energy regulation announcements in China is likely to act as a tailwind for the Alternative Energy sector." On the individual security level, one of the current holdings of the Alternative Energy Fund is Iberdrola Renovables, the "largest global wind-farm operator and a market leader within this mature and scalable renewable energy sector."[5] The company not only has emerged as an industry leader in installing, designing, and managing wind farms but also has projects in the pipeline that will increase its megawatt capacity over fivefold.

In contrast to the Alternative Energy Fund, the Global Water Fund has experienced positive growth of 4.97% since its inception on September 30, 2008. It is also currently returning positive both over the most recent year and quarter, as of this writing. According to Freeman, the Global Water Fund is the "only water fund in America with an advocacy commitment." It has been a complicated challenge for Calvert but also a profitable one due to the "big and growing market for water." Unlike the Alternative Energy Fund, the Global Water Fund had the good fortune of launching close to when equity markets were at their lowest points in recent years and has been able to ride the momentum on the way up due to "an appetite for risk return at the start of the third quarter [2010] as better-than-expected corporate earnings and improving economic news from Europe boosted investor sentiment," according to Peers. Going forward, Peers looks to continue to be "biased toward quality companies that have strong balance sheets, a sustainable competitive advantage, and attractive valuations." At the individual security level, one of the Global Water Fund's top ten holdings is Flowserve Corporation, which operates in the water treatment, chemical, oil and gas, and power generation industries. The company is a leader in the design of pumps and valves that help to transport water from its source to where it is needed. The near future for Solution Funds appears to be to try to strengthen current offerings. Freeman says that currently "no new Solution Fund is being actively developed." He also notes that "timing means a lot in launching new funds" and Calvert wants to make sure that there is a market for these funds.

SAGE Funds

Calvert launched the SAGE Funds in December 2008 as a strategic shift from more traditional SRI funds. According to Stu Dalheim, Calvert's director of shareholder advocacy, the SAGE approach came about from a recognition that the screening process applied to the traditional SRI vehicles was a very "black-and-white approach," whereas in reality the progress companies were making was happening along a spectrum. In recognition of that spectrum of progress, the first SAGE Fund, called the Calvert Large Cap Value Fund, was created "to challenge the sustainability commitment and performance of companies [Calvert had] never held before, and to broaden the impact of SRI at the same time."[6] Companies held in the fund, which have included General Electric (GE), British Petroleum (BP), Dow Chemical, and Wal-Mart, are the targets of "enhanced engagement," which involves developing a "high-quality relationship" with management and working with them to achieve specific ESG goals.[7] According to Freeman, "SAGE brings to bear the full range of engagement tools—from proxy voting and filing shareholder resolutions to holding dialogues with senior management and participating in multi-stakeholder initiatives to raise standards for entire industries."[8] If those tools do not result in the company meeting or significantly approaching those goals, Calvert will publicly divest its shares. For example, after two years of engagement, Calvert sold its shares of BP in June 2010 in the wake of the oil spill in the Gulf of Mexico. Calvert had been working with the oil giant to "improve its safety practices, be more transparent in its Canadian tar sands exploration, and reverse its decline in alternative energy investment"[9] but was unsatisfied with the company's progress on those goals as well as with BP's financial performance since the spill.

GE has formed part of the Calvert Large Cap Value SAGE Fund since its inception, and Calvert has been working with the company on several objectives, most notably "ensuring the quality and accountability of stakeholder engagement with local communities affected by the company's enormous clean-up of polychlorinated biphenyls (PCBs) in the Hudson River in upstate New York." However, as Calvert senior sustainability analyst Jules Frieder notes on the Web site, Calvert's interest in the quality of the cleanup and GE's commitment to the communities affected does not arise from purely altruistic motives: "as a GE shareholder, Calvert also cares about the cost of the cleanup" and the extra costs associated with doing it incorrectly (further lawsuits, government fines, and more). The company hopes that GE will learn from this experience "by completing the Hudson cleanup the right way, [and move forward to focus on the] innovative 'Ecomagination' investments in renewable energy and other environmental technologies that can potentially reap rewards for the company's reputation and share price alike."

Calvert's efforts with companies often seen as the "bad guys" have met with some success. According to Dalheim, the biggest victory to date has been the inclusion of a revenue transparency provision in the financial reform legislation passed in July 2010 that requires gas, oil and mining companies to reveal payments to foreign governments. The company "wrote an investment case for revenue transparency [which was] quoted on the Senate floor and submitted to the" Securities and Exchange Commission as investor support for the "Publish What You Pay" provision. Support for that legislative effort had been a key objective for seven of the companies held in the SAGE Fund. Upon passage of the bill, Calvert had achieved public support from

Newmont Mining and avoided outright opposition from Royal Dutch Shell and BP. While the SAGE investment strategy has ruffled a few feathers among Calvert's more traditional investors, it appears to be a permanent fixture in the SRI portfolio. As Freeman notes, "SAGE embodies [Calvert's] conviction that the time has come to offer a fund that puts investors in the trenches—as owners—trying to influence some of the largest companies in the toughest industries on the most important sustainability issues in the world."[10] As the corporate social responsibility movement continues to expand across industries and job functions, and investors remain interested in the ramifications of their investments, engagement with companies that have farther to travel along the socially responsible spectrum will remain a valued tool for the company.

CALVERT'S PERFORMANCE

With its expansion into Solution and SAGE funds, Calvert now has an impressive portfolio of innovative SRI products that it can market to both niche and mainstream investors. However, if the firm is truly going to win institutional and high-net-worth money, it is going to have to prove that the returns of its funds are competitive with industry leaders. After all, Calvert is an asset manager, and people use a particular asset manager because they believe that their money is put to better use through that asset manager's funds. Therefore, the question that Calvert asks is this: How do its funds compare to more traditional competitors?

Comparing Calvert to Its Competitors

In order to make a solid comparison between Calvert and its mainstream competitors, we looked at three different fund styles, all within the Signature category: large-cap growth, mid-cap growth, and small-cap growth. For comparison, we took a sampling of Calvert's more traditional peers in the asset management industry, including Fidelity, American Funds, Janus, Dodge and Cox, Columbia, Franklin Templeton, T. Rowe Price, Legg Mason, and Blackrock. Due to the different products offered by each firm, we were not able to include every firm listed in each of the three styles we researched. Also, not every firm offered a product that was an exact match to the style that Calvert offers. Therefore, we looked at the stated benchmark for each fund and chose funds that were competing against the same standards. For large-cap funds, we used the S&P 500 and the Russell 1000. For mid-cap funds, we used the Russell Mid Cap Growth Index; and for small-cap funds, we used the Russell 2000.

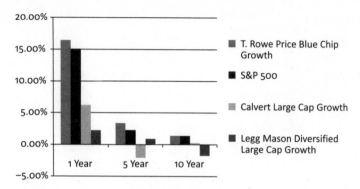

FIGURE 8.1   Large-Cap Growth Funds

In order to compare funds, we looked at total return minus sales charges over one-, five-, and ten-year periods. These three time periods help to eliminate those funds that happened to have strong short-term returns and demonstrated the abilities of managers and analysts over a difficult ten-year cycle that began with the bursting of the tech bubble and saw the explosive growth of the mid-2000s and then the crash and subsequent rocky recovery of the Great Recession. The data show that Calvert has placed in the middle of the pack over the past one, five, and ten years. Never once was Calvert the top performer, nor did it ever beat its benchmark in any of the three time periods, but its funds did beat out those of many well-known companies, such as Legg Mason and BlackRock. Furthermore, Calvert's funds were not alone in their underperformance of benchmarks.[11]

Figures 8.1, 8.2, and 8.3 highlight each fund's performance over those three time periods. Each figure includes four returns for each one-, five-, and ten-year period: one for a leading performer, one for the relevant benchmark,

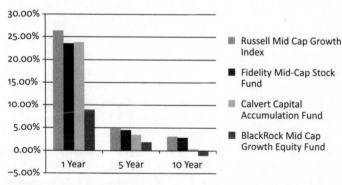

FIGURE 8.2   Mid-Cap Growth Funds

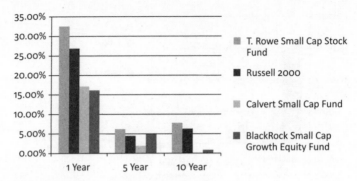

FIGURE 8.3   Small-Cap Growth Funds

one for Calvert, and one for a lagging performer. It is important to note that
even the best-performing funds barely beat their benchmarks over a five-
and ten-year period due to the difficult market conditions and the unique
economic environment we have been experiencing in recent years. In the
large-cap growth universe, the fund that performed best was the T. Rowe
Price Blue Chip Growth fund, which returned 16.42% over the past year,
3.38% over the past five years, and 1.41% over the past ten years. The
benchmark S&P 500 returned 15.06% over the past year, 2.29% over the
past five years, and 1.41% over the past ten years. Calvert's Large Cap
Growth fund returned 6.22% over the past year, –2.04% over the past five
years, and 0.26% over the past ten years. Finally, the Legg Mason Diversified
Large Cap Growth fund returned 2.27% over the past year, 0.93% over the
past five years, and –1.73% over the past ten years.

In the mid-cap growth universe, the best-performing fund was the Fidelity Mid-Cap Stock fund, which returned 23.57% over the past year,
4.52% over the past five years, and 2.88% over the past ten years. The
benchmark Russell Mid Cap Growth Index returned 26.38% over the past
year, 4.88% over the past five years, and 3.12% over the past ten years.
Calvert's Capital Accumulation fund returned 23.83% over the past year,
3.44% over the past five years, and 0.36% over the past ten years. Finally,
the BlackRock Mid Cap Growth Equity fund returned 8.99% over the past
year, 1.91% over the past five years, and –1.07% over the past ten years.

In the small-cap growth universe, the best-performing fund was the T.
Rowe Small Cap Stock fund, which returned 32.53% over the past year,
6.27% over the past five years, and 7.79% over the past ten years. The
benchmark Russell 2000 returned 26.85% over the past year, 4.47% over
the past five years, and 6.33% over the past ten years. Calvert's Small Cap
fund (in existence since October 1, 2004) returned 17.09% over the past
year and 1.89% over the past five years. Finally, the BlackRock Small Cap

Growth Equity fund returned 16.14% over the past year, 4.96% over the past five years, and 0.83% over the past ten years.

Three conclusions can be drawn from these data:

1. Due to fund constraints, market timing, economic cycles, and randomness, it is difficult to beat stated benchmarks. For example, in the mid-cap universe, not one of the funds analyzed beat the Russell Mid Cap Growth Index over either a one-, five-, or ten-year period.
2. Calvert's funds have performed solidly but not spectacularly. Investors who chose Calvert funds would be satisfied with their performance relative to some of the mainstream competitors but would have seen better returns by investing in an index fund.
3. Calvert Signature Funds are more constrained than these competitors due to the screening restrictions and industry exclusions. Calvert believes that over a long-term investment horizon, this extra layer of due diligence will help its managers create portfolios that will return on par or better than both their nonscreened competitors and their chosen benchmarks.

However, based on the available performance data, that belief cannot be proven. That said, given Calvert's commitment to social responsibility, it can be argued that Calvert's funds have a social return component that can be added on to a traditional portfolio return. Investors in Calvert's funds may be willing to give up a few points of total return in exchange for knowing that they are not investing in companies that degrade the environment or fund governments with a history of human rights violations. Overall, Calvert's advocacy work and sustainability research is unparalleled in the asset management industry, and it has made great inroads in expanding SRI into the mainstream. Calvert still has more work to do to in order to prove that SRI techniques result in superior financial returns, but it certainly has proven that it is possible to compete in the financial world as a responsible, socially committed company.

SUMMARY

Going forward, Calvert is focused on integrating sustainability and financial analysis to be able to manage more funds in house. The company has hired a new chief investment officer of equities, Natalie Trunow, and is working to train its sustainability analysts in financial metrics. The company has a strong base on which to build and feels positive that its focus on sustainability has provided it with a superior risk management strategy. CEO Krumsiek considers the "sustainability metrics to be a lens through which to evaluate risks with more granularity and precision,"[12] and that lens allowed the company to avoid any investments in subprime mortgage-backed securities or credit default swaps during the run-up to the recent financial crisis. While proud of that track record, Krumsiek isn't satisfied. She never wants to reach a moment where the focus becomes conserving what the company already has rather than seeking to grow and adapt in a changing marketplace. As the future unfolds, Calvert will "embrace change, creativity and innovation" in order to bring more of the world's assets into socially responsible funds and work with the world's most influential companies to bring about positive change.

NOTES

1. www.socialinvest.org/directory/detail.cfm?key=4295
2. www.socialfunds.com/news/article.cgi/1957.html
3. www.calvertfoundation.org/about/mission/mission-history
4. http://finance.yahoo.com/q/pr?s=SVT.L+Profile
5. www.calvertgroup.com/ae/examples.html
6. www.greenmoneyjournal.com/article.mpl?newsletterid=53&articleid=768
7. Interview with Bennett Freeman. Calvert offices, April 2011
8. www.greenmoneyjournal.com/article.mpl?newsletterid=53&articleid=768
9. www.triplepundit.com/2010/07/calvert-investments-drops-bp-from-sage-ethical-fund/
10. www.greenmoneyjournal.com/article.mpl?newsletterid=53&articleid=768
11. We decided not to use a risk-adjusted return measure, such as the Sharpe or Treynor ratio, because such ratios require a risk-free rate to be subtracted from the total return in the numerator. This raises the question of what determines an appropriate risk-free rate for these funds (i.e., three-month Treasury bill or ten-year Treasury bond). Furthermore, if we are trying to calculate a risk-adjusted return for a historical five-year total return, do we use the historical five-year risk-free rate over that period or do we use a current five-year risk-free rate? In addition, both ratios require the total return minus the risk-free rate to be divided by a measure of volatility (standard deviation in the Sharpe ratio and beta in the Treynor ratio). This leads to further ambiguity due to the fluid nature of measures of volatility, such as standard deviation and beta. Since these measures are constantly changing with the market, what is the appropriate time period to use to get an accurate measure of volatility? Furthermore, should we use historical volatility measures, or should we use forward-looking measures (which bring up questions about forecasting)? Therefore, we decided to keep the analysis to comparable data reported by each fund company, total return minus sales charges, over a one-, five-, and ten-year period.
12. Interview with Barbara Krumsiek, April 2011

CHAPTER 9

Winslow

Amrita Vijay Kumar

Jack Robinson founded Winslow Management Company in 1983, one of the first investment firms focused solely on environmental opportunities in the United States. Winslow is accustomed to being a pioneer, although the world finally may have caught up with it. A closer look at the firm shows how it is evolving—trying, as it always has, to stay ahead of the curve.

Winslow Management Company has been recognized over the last decade or so as having been something of a trailblazer, investing exclusively in companies offering so-called green solutions, well ahead of almost anyone else. This definition of "green" has evolved over time, although Winslow's stated investment philosophy has not: Winslow believes that a concentrated portfolio of financially and environmentally sustainable businesses will deliver attractive returns over time. The company continues to position itself for what it refers to as the ongoing "green shift" in our economy—a combination of regulatory, environmental, and technological changes that will enable new investment opportunities across many sectors.

BLAZING A TRAIL

Winslow utilizes a comprehensive approach to green investing, because it believes that many companies—from the newest solar or biodiesel company, to the traditional manufacturer using recycled materials or low-emission production technology—can achieve high levels of financial performance

107

through dedication to high levels of environmental performance. Winslow's strategy is to find hidden opportunities among these companies—companies that appear poised for growth but whose stocks are undervalued or unrecognized by the broader market.

This approach differentiates Winslow from many of its competitors, which focus exclusively on renewable energy opportunities or other specific green niches. It also differentiates the firm from the more values-based forms of socially responsible investment (SRI) that continue to dominate the field in the United States. Most SRI fund managers limit the universe of companies that they pick from using negative screens to weed out companies that do not match their ethical values and invest in most everything else. This is fundamentally different from Winslow's strategy of opportunity-driven idea generation.

Winslow's original investment offering, the Winslow Green Growth Fund, was established in 1994. The Green Growth Fund targets a variety of green solutions investment themes, offering exposure to clean energy, green transportation, and other companies that are directly solving environmental challenges. The fund's investment process is built around a core concept of bottom up fundamental research and long-term investment, designed to ride out the inevitable short-term volatility experienced by small companies often involved in emerging green markets.

Winslow's newer strategy is its Green Large Cap strategy, which was launched in partnership with Winslow's parent company, Brown Advisory, in 2009. Unlike the thematically oriented Green Growth Fund, this large-cap offering provides a fully diversified portfolio of companies across all industry sectors; portfolio managers select companies that they believe are strongly positioned for growth within their core markets and that also stand to benefit from their various environmental strategies.

INVESTMENT PROCESS

Ideas are generated across both of these strategies using a similar process: Winslow's ideas come from a combination of thematic research by analysts and a very strong information flow from a prescreened network of proven technology, policy, and industry contacts who have been carefully cultivated over many years. Key to both strategies is identifying companies whose fundamental or environmental value is not yet recognized broadly by the market.

A prime example of this sort of company is Horsehead Holdings. Horsehead is a zinc alloy producer, but it sources zinc by recycling electric arc furnace (EAF) dust, a waste product from steel grinding mill operations.

The company has figured out an economical way to extract value from a waste product and make money at both ends of its value chain. Horsehead's suppliers, the steel mills, pay them to take this EAF dust offsite, and customers pay Horsehead for converting the dust into a useful by-product. This is a fairly good example of a green story that wouldn't be obvious to the average analyst or investor, and Horsehead went on to be one of five companies that Winslow Green Growth cited as being among the biggest positive contributors to its returns in 2010, along with Schnitzer Steel (resource efficiency), BioExx Specialty Proteins (sustainable living), Nalco Holdings (water management), and Acuity Brands (green building).[1] Winslow analysts are trained to look for cases where the market has not yet recognized the underlying opportunity, where the related potential value has, in theory, not been priced in.

The portfolio construction process, however, is quite different across the two strategies.

Winslow Green Growth

The Green Growth Fund's portfolio is typically invested in small-cap and mid-cap companies, and Jack Robinson's portfolio philosophy has always been to focus the portfolio on a limited number of companies with strong upside potential. Of course, this sort of strategy is accompanied by risk—there will inevitably be winners and losers. The theory is that if Winslow stays focused and picks enough winners, it has every chance to outperform over the long term, although this sort of focus also has the potential to provide somewhat volatile returns, as the fund has experienced at times. Noted private equity investor Vinod Khosla takes a similar approach, anticipating an even higher failure rate. So long as he picks enough winners, he figures they will more than offset the inevitable downside of some of his choices.[2]

One of Winslow's successful long-term bets has been First Solar, which has consistently been the global low-cost leader—by a significant margin—in the manufacture of solar panels. Over time, the company has leveraged its material and process cost advantages into a rapidly growing business with an emphasis on utility-scale solar farms. The firm's business in its early years focused in countries such as Germany, which provided generous solar subsidies; the company is now expanding its presence in the United States. First Solar also benefited from a decision to get into the business of project development itself. Its success in this area is exemplified by its recent sale of its Agua Caliente project in Arizona to NRG Energy; the project eventually will generate over 290 megawatts of power, making it the largest facility of its kind in the world.

An example of a less successful bet is found in a recent Winslow foray into the LED illumination space, Rubicon Technologies. The investment was made based on the long-term potential for the LED general illumination, which many analysts believe is the future of illumination in this country. However, Winslow's analysis could not predict the volatility inherent in the demand for LED televisions and the display market. The slowing growth in the economy meant a large standing inventory of televisions, which impacted the sales of all component manufacturers. Timing is everything. While Winslow analysts still believe in the long-term potential of Rubicon, Winslow's investment here was too early to fully capitalize on the expected LED wave.

Green Large Cap

Quite different from the Green Growth Fund, Winslow's newer Green Large Cap strategy looks primarily at larger and theoretically more stable companies that are well positioned to succeed using a sustainability focus. This may mean that the company provides a product or service that solves an environmental problem directly or indirectly, or it could mean that the firm simply has superior environmental attributes compared to industry benchmarks. This fund's portfolio is also built using a bottom-up philosophy but primarily is motivated by generating risk-adjusted performance relative to its benchmark. As such, the strategy is less focused on finding home-run investments than the Green Growth Fund and more focused on building a portfolio of solid, dependable base-hit growth investments.

An example of a company that attracted the Green Large Cap strategy's managers is Denbury Resources. Denbury is in the tertiary oil recovery sector, an unusual company for a green portfolio. However, the company has access to technology that allows it to extract oil from already degraded sites. This improves the efficiency of oil extraction economics for the primary producers while allowing a more efficient and complete extraction that otherwise would have gone wasted. What interested Winslow's analysts was the company's expertise working with carbon dioxide, the gas Denbury uses to pressurize old oil wells. Because of this expertise, Denbury is at the forefront of the fledgling carbon capture and storage (CCS) sector, and it is the recipient of U.S. Department of Energy funds targeted at piloting and researching CCS projects. Winslow is particularly attracted to these sorts of situations, what it calls "environmental call options," where a company stands to benefit from a future event but is not dependent on it. In this case, the event is potential regulation to price carbon emissions; if such regulation becomes a reality, Denbury stands to be a major beneficiary. If it does not, the company is still profitable in its own right.

Another example of a Green Large Cap holding is IBM. The firm has targeted four major growth initiatives, and one of them is its "Smarter Planet" business, which it plans to grow to over $10 billion over the next five years. Leveraging its huge and highly skilled workforce (including the world's largest aggregation of mathematicians) and the highest amount of research and development spending ($6 billion a year) of any of its peers, IBM is directing massive consulting and service projects for universities, cities, and countries that are driving energy efficiency, reducing pollution, and increasing water efficiency worldwide. Winslow believes that IBM is one of only a very few companies in the world, perhaps the only company, that can pull off many of these projects. As a result of this effort, its Smarter Planet initiative is expected to contribute 20% of IBM's revenue growth through 2015.

Winslow's investment committee meets twice per week; through these meetings, the team decides which new ideas will be subjected to a full round of deep due diligence, which includes financial, strategic, and environmental evaluation. Winslow's research process focuses on understanding the real environmental investment story (i.e., what environmental drivers position the company for growth into the future); evaluating the strategic and financial strength, as well as the strength of the management team, of each potential investment; and performing valuation analysis, which includes scenario and sensitivity analysis to future potential stock movements.

The analysts are integrated in their approach. They are not siloed into niche specialty categories, and this in theory allows them to be impartial and integrative in their analysis. The main thing that differentiates them from typical analysts is that they look at more factors before making a decision. Winslow tries to uncover environmental risks and opportunities by looking at third-party sources and by identifying investment risks that other analysts may not uncover.

The criteria for selection include financial, strategic, and environmental factors:

Financial/Strategic

- Revenue/earnings patterns
- Capital allocation decisions
- Cost and competitive advantages
- Balance sheet strength/debt levels

Environmental

- Attractiveness of green market opportunity
- Company position within its green market
- Environmental impact of product or service

Winslow's long-term ownership philosophy guides its sell discipline. Significant up-front research goes into identifying portfolio positions that can be maintained for the long term, and positions are adjusted or sold over time when the environmental or fundamental thesis breaks down, the stock approaches or exceeds upside or downside price targets, or a superior new idea displaces a current position.

PERFORMANCE CONSIDERATIONS

The Green Large Cap strategy was started on January 1, 2010; it grew out of the recognition that there was a need among clients for a more diversified product that offered stable returns—such stability is inherently not characteristic of high-growth green stocks with smaller market caps. The Green Large Cap strategy had a solid first year, demonstrating that the strategy can work. The risk and volatility was at or below the benchmark, and attribution analysis showed that outperformance was driven primarily by stock selection as opposed to sector allocation. It is still early days, but Winslow seems confident in this strategy.

The Green Growth Fund is a different story, and performance versus benchmark has been a challenge. While it has performed well since its inception, more recently it has failed to provide adequate returns to investors, having plunged more deeply during the 2008 financial crisis than most funds on the market after outperforming its peers for most of the previous decade.

Ethan Berkwits, Winslow's marketing director, suggested that the Winslow Green Growth Fund's strategy is in fact very difficult to benchmark against traditional stock indexes; thus, the fund is a square peg that many investors often struggle to fit into traditional allocation strategies. The fund is not a pure clean-tech play per se, and it does not seek a particular sector focus that would allow it to ride a particular growth spurt as demand picks up; yet it is clearly not a diversified strategy that is likely to correlate highly with small-cap stocks in general. Communicating this concept to mainstream investors has been a challenge for Winslow, and to date the company has had the most success with investors who are environmentally passionate or long-term believers in the green economy.

SUMMARY

Winslow seeks to distinguish itself from other investment management firms by staying on the cutting edge of green markets and by being ahead of the curve and spotting green opportunities that other analysts are not identifying. However, as sustainability trends and drivers become better understood and more mainstream, it is becoming harder for companies like Winslow to stay on top of new technologies and the competition. Winslow has had a fascinating run and, in many ways, continues to blaze a unique trail, with an approach that few undertake. The challenge for Winslow will be staying on top of the rapid evolution of its market, in terms of both new environmental innovations and increased competition in its investment niche. Given its approach, it may be well positioned in some ways to find these opportunities first, but it will have to stay sharp.

NOTES

1. Winslow Green Growth Annual Report, December 2010. www.winslowgreen .com/forms/default.aspx
2. www.economist.com/node/18304172

CHAPTER 10

Portfolio 21

Ashley Hamilton

Portfolio 21 is a Portland, Oregon–based mutual fund manager that strives to use a sustainable investing framework. Portfolio 21, the Winslow Green Growth Fund, and Pax World Global Green Fund, subadvised by Impax Asset Management of the United Kingdom, set the highest bar available for sustainable investing in the United States so far as publicly available mutual funds are concerned. Let's read about how they do it.

Portfolio 21 Investments has grown from a little-known investment firm managing $2 million in mutual funds to a notable player in the sustainable investment space. As of the end of 2010, it managed approximately $403 million in retail and institutional money according to a unique investment philosophy informed by The Natural Step and the Global Footprint Network. What sets the fund apart is its mandate to not invest in companies involved in the extraction of oil, gas, and minerals. It was one of the few sustainable and responsible investment funds in the United States that was not invested in BP at the time of the Gulf incident. Thus, its brand as a sustainable investing leader remained unscathed following the Gulf of Mexico oil spill in 2010. And despite the restrictions within its investment mandate, Portfolio 21 has enjoyed decent financial performance, returning 4.61% since inception.[1]

PORTFOLIO 21: A HISTORY

The company was founded in 1982 as Progressive Investment Management, based in Eugene, Oregon. Progressive's founder, Carsten Henningsen, opened shop when he was just 22, believing that investors could make the world a better place by using capital to influence corporate behavior. His firm joined a small but growing group of socially responsible investment funds in the United States that viewed themselves as activists first and money managers second. The company has since grown to become a well-respected money manager and shareholder activist.

In 1999, Progressive Investment Management started a year-long process to develop comprehensive environmental selection criteria. That same year, it launched Portfolio 21, a global equity mutual fund aimed at the retail market and named for the firm's twenty-first-century outlook. It was the first sustainability-themed mutual fund to launch in the nation. And while it started small, assets have steadily risen over the years. The success of the fund led the company to start offering an institutional share class in July 2007. In November 2007, Progressive Investment Management changed its name to Portfolio 21 Investments after its flagship fund.

As of December 31, 2010, the fund managed approximately $403 million, invested across 99 securities. Approximately 60% of the fund's assets come from the retail mutual fund business and 40% from institutional investors. Top holdings include Novo Nordisk, Google, Roche, Novartis, and Telefonica.

In addition to its global equity mutual fund, Portfolio 21 also offers separate account portfolio management for high-net-worth individuals and institutions. Separate account clients are offered the option of investing in the global equity mutual fund as well as Portfolio 21's fixed income products, which favor taxable corporate bonds with a maturity of seven to ten years. The firm also offers clients the opportunity to invest in a Local Economies Income Fund, which provides capital to local community projects through regional bonds, deposits, and real estate–backed private loans.

Portfolio 21 is a very small niche player in the responsible and sustainable investing space. With only $403 million, it is small potatoes compared to some of the larger socially responsible mutual fund companies in the country that manage billions in retail assets. However, it has positioned itself as the largest screened mutual fund in the international/global category, and its flat-out refusal to invest in oil and gas and other high-impact sectors sets it apart from many of its competitors.

THEORY OF SUSTAINABILITY AND CHANGE

Understanding the company's core philosophy gives us some insight into how Portfolio 21 picks stocks and why it avoided investing in BP. Portfolio 21 bases its investment decisions on the belief that the greatest risk facing companies today is ongoing ecological degradation caused by human consumption and destruction of the natural environment. It works from a definition of sustainability that was first developed by Mathis Wackernagel, the codeveloper with William Rees of the Ecological Footprint analysis. According to Wackernagel's definition, sustainability means "securing people's quality of life within the means of nature." With this lens as its starting point, Portfolio 21 has developed an investment strategy based on the theories and scientific calculations of the Ecological Footprint as well as the sustainability framework of The Natural Step.

The Ecological Footprint is a resource accounting or budgeting tool that uses ecological data, such as yields from croplands, forests, fisheries, and grazing land, to determine the carrying capacity of our global and local ecological systems. Based on current technology and environmental management systems, the measurement calculates how much land is required to support the population while maintaining Earth's ecological integrity. The process then calculates how much of that system each individual or organization "uses" every day. The resulting "footprint" represents the amount of land and water required to support our consumption habits. For example, one often-quoted calculation concludes: "If everyone lived the lifestyle of the average American we would need five planets." The process can be applied to individuals, cities, businesses, or even countries.

The Ecological Footprint is used as a tool to assess a company's current consumption patterns and trends in relation to the natural environment's ability to support that consumption on an ongoing basis. Companies that consume resources at a faster rate than is ecologically sound are determined to be overshooting their allotted ecological "budget."

The Natural Step (TNS) is a model for sustainability planning based on complex systems theory. The premise is that small changes in one part of the system will affect other parts and therefore the system as a whole. Developed by a Swedish oncologist, Dr. Karl-Henrik Robèrt, TNS subscribes to the process of "backcasting," whereby sustainability planning starts with a vision of the desired outcome.[2] These guidelines ensure that decisions are not made in isolation and that all new products and services are innovative, flexible, and adaptable to changing environmental and social conditions.

According to TNS, four conditions have to be met in order to create a truly sustainable society.

1. We must eliminate all industrial activities that contribute to the buildup of heavy metals and fossil fuels extracted from Earth's crust.
2. Society must stop the spread of persistent and toxic chemicals that accumulate in our air and water.
3. All activities that result in the destruction of natural ecosystems should be stopped.
4. Society should bring an end to all economic activities that undermine people's ability to meet their basic needs.[3]

Put into practice, TNS approach is a game-changer for investors. Oil and gas companies are significant players in the U.S. national economy. One report estimates that in 2007, the industry's total value-added contribution to the U.S. economy was approximately 7.5% of gross domestic product.[4] In addition, the estimated value of production from U.S. metal mines was $29.1 billion in 2010, and industrial minerals contributed an additional $34.9 billion to the U.S. economy.[5] Calling for an end to this activity may seem radical to some, yet Portfolio 21 seems to make it work while continuing to post good returns.

If not oil, then what?

When news of BP's Gulf oil spill hit the headlines in 2010, Portfolio 21 was unabashed. Unlike many of its competitors, it did not own shares in the oil giant. In keeping with its commitment to the TNS system, Portfolio 21 does not invest in oil companies. Not one. Nor does it invest in mining companies. The reason for this decision is grounded in the sustainability principles espoused by TNS. It also makes good business sense, given Portfolio 21's evaluation of the long-term risk of oil and gas extraction: "The sector is generally in the position of chasing increasingly scarcer resources at higher costs and greater risk."[6] With the looming threat of climate change and the dwindling reserves of easy-access oil, there is no guarantee that companies in the oil and gas sector will maintain wide profit margins over the long term. Not to mention the fact that the ecological footprints of the mining, oil, and gas industries are significant, given both their physical disruption and carbon intensity.

Instead, Portfolio 21 chooses to invest in companies developing new technologies and services to help society use energy more efficiently and ultimately transition us to renewable sources. The firm prefers companies developing smart-grid systems and alternative energy technologies that do not depend on the extraction and accumulation of fuels and heavy metals. As Carsten Henningsen explains, "Portfolio 21 invests only in companies that are integrating intelligent and forward-thinking environmental strategies into their overall business planning."[7]

This is a unique approach. In comparison, many of Portfolio 21's competitors subscribe to the "best of sector" or "best in class" approach to investing where companies rated as more sustainable or responsible than their competitors within the same sector are eligible for investment. This includes mining, oil and gas, coal, and other companies with high environmental impacts.

As Henningsen explains, "Portfolio 21 does not subscribe to the best in class approach because we feel that there are certain sectors in which the ecological risks are so high that the companies operating within them will not remain financially competitive over the long term." Portfolio 21 does apply traditional negative screens, including on tobacco, nuclear energy, gambling, and weapons. It is also quite cautious about investing in automobile companies because of the impact of car transportation on global climate change. To date, Henningsen says, it has invested in only one vehicle-manufacturing firm, Volvo, citing its use of biogas and other alternative technologies to reduce greenhouse gas emissions.

IN SEARCH OF FORWARD-LOOKING COMPANIES

When evaluating potential investments, Portfolio 21 starts from the assumption that there is no such thing as a truly sustainable company and that no one company excels in all areas of sustainability management. The challenge is to find companies with forward-looking approaches to business that address the ecological constraints they face and take steps to reduce their impacts. Portfolio 21 also looks for firms that are spending money to research and develop ecologically superior products or create technologies aimed at solving some of our most pressing problems. Finally, analysts seek companies that can demonstrate their understanding of the complexities and future challenges in an increasingly resource-constrained world.

What are the signposts Portfolio 21 uses to identify these forward-looking companies? Well, other than refusing to invest in oil, gas, and mining stocks, the criteria don't differ much from what other sustainable and responsible investing firms look for in a company. Evidence of sound environmental management and accounting systems, transparency, resource efficiency, and low exposure to environmental risks and liabilities (such as fines and penalties) are some of the indicators used. Support for progressive environmental legislation is another key factor analyzed. Finally, Portfolio 21 evaluates labor and human rights standards.

While the process of evaluating companies according to these key sustainability principles seems straightforward, things can get complicated when examining certain sectors. For example, many clean-tech companies are developing products that are good for the planet but rely heavily on products obtained from mining; for example, they use precious and rare earth metals. So will Portfolio 21 invest? The firm takes a prudent approach, investing in clean tech companies that comply with the Restriction on Hazardous Substances directive of the European Union, which sets targets to reduce the accumulation of toxic products and e-waste in the electronics industry, have implemented life-cycle assessments and electronics take-back programs, or that subscribe to environmental design practices that minimize the use of raw materials.

Ultimately, companies that excel in multiple areas of sustainability performance and that have a good financial outlook are good candidates for Portfolio 21. The evaluation is robust. In 2003, Carsten Henningsen described the process: "When we began applying our criteria to the selection process, we looked at over 2000 companies, out of which we've been able to qualify 52 so far. This gives you an idea of how stringent the screening is and how few companies really do 'get it.'"[8] In 2010, approximately 200 companies were qualified and eligible for investment by Portfolio 21.[9]

To date, the fund has identified the majority of these companies outside the United States. In fact, less than one-third of the companies that Portfolio 21 has invested in are American. According to chief investment officer Leslie Christian, "Much more is happening on the sustainability front outside the U.S."[10] Favorites of the fund for 2011 include companies like Cisco, which is improving online collaborative technology that can reduce business travel, and Schneider Electric, a manufacturer of energy-saving devices and power supply equipment for solar and wind power projects. Its long-term investing philosophy is reflected in its stock turnover rate, which is low, at only 10% per year.

RESULTS

Portfolio 21's approach to company evaluation has led it to reject some big-name companies over the years because they did not live up to its high environmental and social standards. Companies recently rejected include Deere and Company for not incorporating life-cycle analysis into its product design and Canadian firm Shoppers Drug Mart for not disclosing enough information on food sales and the use of genetically modified organisms.

Portfolio 21 has enjoyed relatively positive results. Five- and ten-year returns show a healthy profit of 4.88% and 4.70%, respectively. Even during the 2008 recession, it managed to beat the MSCI World Equity Index and the Standard & Poor's 500, losing only 2.59% over a three-year period.

More recently, the firm's one-year return numbers are good at 9.30%, but well below those posted by its stated benchmarks over the same period, and the fourth-quarter results for 2010 are also lower than expected. The more recent lackluster financial results are due to its higher allocation to large-cap European stocks, which experienced a significant downturn in 2010. The firm also attributes its lower performance compared with its benchmark to the fact that it does not invest in the commodities and raw materials industries, which experienced a boom in 2010.[11]

In addition to its stringent company evaluation and divestment strategy, Portfolio 21 is a shareholder activist, partnering with well-respected advocacy group As You Sow to press companies on improving their social and environmental practices. It has a long history of shareholder advocacy, filing its first shareholder proposal in 1992. Portfolio 21 has filed a number of high-profile shareholder proposals over the years, including one at Whole Foods in 2008, asking the company to separate the positions of chair and chief executive. The proposal won 27% shareholder support. The fund participates in various collaborative investor letters calling for greater environmental responsibility from companies and regulators.

In keeping with best practice, Portfolio 21 also votes its proxies and discloses how it votes on its Web site. It was a founder of CERES, a coalition of environmentalists and investors working to improve corporate disclosure of environmental risks. Portfolio 21 has also taken great strides to practice what it preaches to companies and has sought to embody the principles of sustainability taught by TNS and the Ecological Footprint. Its offices are located in a LEED-certified green building in Portland, and the company has been carbon neutral since 2001. It strives to reduce office waste, encourage sustainable employee commuting, and offset its greenhouse gas emissions. Portfolio 21 also goes a step further, tracking employee emissions from business travel and deducting the final cost of carbon from each employee's annual bonus. In addition, the company cofounded Upstream 21, a small regional holding company that acquires privately owned firms and operates them according to strict sustainability guidelines. Upstream 21 is currently invested in three private companies located in the Pacific Northwest and is poised to expand its portfolio over the next few years.

SUMMARY

Portfolio 21's approach is unique, perhaps even radical by some investment management standards. By not investing in oil, gas, and mining companies, the firm chooses instead to deploy its capital to support progressive companies striving to meet society's demands for more sustainable and responsible products and services. And it has been successful, beating its benchmark by nearly two percentage points since inception. Challenges still remain. Portfolio 21 struggles to identify energy and food companies that meet its stringent assessment criteria, so it often misses out on the short-term windfalls from growing global demand for commodities. However, as its past performance shows, taking the longer-term approach can pay excellent dividends, in terms of both financial return and social and environmental impact.

NOTES

1. Performance as of December 31, 2010 (inception date September 30, 1999). Portfolio 21, 2011, "Performance." Available at www.portfolio21. com/in_depth_perf.php. See www.footprintnetwork.org/en/index.php for specific details about Portfolio 21 and the Global Footprint Network.
2. The Natural Step, "Our Approach," 2011. Available at www.naturalstep. org/our-approach#quick-overview
3. Businesses that rely on the abuse of power, poverty wages, poor working conditions, and insecurity are considered unsustainable, according to TNS, because they encourage exploitation and overconsumption by the "haves" at the expense of the "have nots." Bob Willard, "Four Reasons Why Our Current Business Model Is Unsustainable," The Natural Step, 2010. Available at www.naturalstep.org/fr/comment/reply/1736
4. PricewaterhouseCoopers, "The Economic Impacts of the Oil and Natural Gas Industry on the US Economy: Employment, Labor Income and Value Added," Report prepared for the American Petroleum Institute, 2009. Available at www.api.org/Newsroom/industry-supports.cfm
5. U.S. Geological Survey, "Mineral Commodity Summaries 2011." Available at http://minerals.usgs.gov/minerals/pubs/mcs/
6. Leslie Christian and Carsten Henningsen, Portfolio 21 Investments Annual Report, Letter to Shareholders, June 30, 2010. Available at www.portfolio21.com/pdfs/report_6-10.pdf
7. Author personal communication with Carsten Henningsen, March 15, 2011.
8. As quoted in Bill Baue, "When Lightning Strikes: Portfolio 21 Applies The Natural Step's Sustainability Theories," Social Funds, 2003. Available at www.socialfunds.com/news/save.cgi?sfArticleId=1081
9. Author personal communication with Amanda Plyley, March 22, 2011.
10. As quoted in Ilana Polyak, "Greener Approach," *On Wall Street*, August 1, 2010. Available at www.onwallstreet.com/fp_issues/2010_8/greener-approach-2667986-1.html
11. Author personal communication with Henningsen.

Northwest and Ethical Investments

Dana Krechowicz

Canada is its own interesting case in point: rich in natural resources and at the same time aware of the environmental and social impacts of resource development. It's interesting to observe the approach of Canada's largest socially responsible investment fund manager and how it manages to balance achieving strong financial performance while remaining true to its values.

With its roots in the Canadian credit union movement, Northwest and Ethical Investments LP (NEI)[1] considers itself to have strong values of respecting the environment and human rights, which it aims to adhere to while maintaining a steadfast focus on returns. NEI is a Canadian leader in engagement, unafraid to tackle controversial issues, such as the oil sands of Alberta and elsewhere.

With a dedicated sustainability team and after a merger of Ethical Funds with a conventional fund manager (Northwest Funds) in 2007, NEI now has almost CA $5 billion in assets under management and is Canada's largest socially responsible investment (SRI) fund manager. While NEI's base and home market remains in Canada, it has begun to see interest from European clients. European asset owners are quite active on the issues NEI has expertise in, particularly environmental and social issues regarding the resource sector (including unconventional fuel sources, such as shale gas and oil sands). Since the merger, the ongoing challenge for NEI is how to build on its history while continuing to evolve with the shifting marketplace.

HUMBLE BEGINNINGS

Vancouver is often considered the greenest city in Canada, with ambitions to be the greenest in the world by 2020. Its citizens have a long history of environmental activism and concern, so it's no surprise that this city would produce home-grown companies with strong community values, such as the Vancouver City Savings Credit Union, founded in 1946, known as VanCity. By the 1980s, VanCity's members were looking for financial products that would enable them to invest according to their values. To fill this need, the Ethical Growth Fund was launched in 1986.

In the early years, the investment approach was based on excluding companies that the fund's advisory council believed were incompatible with the fund's values. Research was outsourced, and while the fund's assets grew steadily, not much changed in the methodology. The brand now known as Ethical Funds was founded in 1992 when the Provincial Credit Union Centrals bought the Ethical Growth Fund as well as four other small mutual funds from other credit unions in the system.

As with many companies, such as Shell with Brent Spar, Ethical Funds encountered a seminal event that dramatically altered the status quo. In 1997, the long-running investigative consumer program, *Marketplace*, of Canada's public broadcaster, the Canadian Broadcast Corporation (CBC) did a story on Ethical Funds. *Marketplace* reported that at least one of the companies in Ethical Funds' portfolio should have been excluded according to the firm's stated values and investment strategy.

NEW DIRECTION

Due to the attention from the CBC story, Ethical Funds took a close look at its socially responsible investing policies and procedures. At the time, it had 12 funds and owned hundreds of companies but was still outsourcing its research and had only one staff member whose role was responding to customer inquiries and communications and liaising with the advisory council. In the wake of the *Marketplace* story, the fund company decided it was time to build in-house research capacity. This led to Ethical's hiring of Robert (Bob) Walker in 1999 to head up its sustainable investing program. Given that Walker is now NEI's most senior and long-running environmental, social, and governance (ESG) services employee, his worldview and background has helped shape the company's approach to responsible investment.

Walker came to Ethical Funds with experience in corporate engagement gained from leading the Social Investment Organization (SIO) as executive director. Between 1996 and 1999, the SIO helped some West Coast pension funds initiate shareholder campaigns on the issue of sweatshops in retail company supply chains. Socially responsible shareholder action at this time in Canada historically had been the provenance of faith-based investors. For pension funds and mutual funds, this was virgin territory. Hence, Walker's experience was invaluable to Ethical Funds as it aimed to develop its own engagement program, formally introduced in 2000.

Walker had an unconventional path to entering the world of responsible investment, though perhaps that is typical of those who entered the field in the 1990s, while it was still in its infancy. Following high school and a series of jobs in construction, Walker attended a vocational school and trained to become a commercial diver. Upon graduating, he worked winters on the west coast of Vancouver Island harvesting geoducks and summers on natural gas drilling rigs of Lake Erie, near Leamington, Ontario, site of some of North America's earliest offshore drilling. This experience gave him an appreciation for the environment—Lake Erie has one of the world's largest and most intensively managed inland commercial fishing industries—and for health and safety issues associated with the drilling process and for the people working in the sector; later this appreciation would prove useful while working on energy and mining issues at Ethical Funds. After a few years of diving, Walker went back to school and eventually earned a master's degree in international political economy at Dalhousie University in Halifax, Nova Scotia. Inspired by the professors he worked with (not to mention their lifestyle), Walker decided he wanted to become an academic and pursue a PhD in political science, focused on decision theory and policymaking. While the PhD didn't work out, he did complete another master's degree, this one in planning. He also leveraged his interest in the wine sector into a major report for this degree, which involved interviewing many of the local wine entrepreneurs in Ontario's Niagara region. These entrepreneurs' perseverance had ensured the industry's survival, despite all predictions to the contrary, which Walker greatly admired. This experience piqued his interest not only in wine but in business, entrepreneurship, and the role of public policy in fostering the responsible development of an industry, themes that would continue to weave their way through his career.

Just as Walker was defending his final paper, a colleague offered him a research position at the new Canadian SIO. Walker's extensive academic background prepared him well for the job, which also gave him a front-row seat in witnessing the development of the SRI industry in Canada. Since the organization was small, he was able to gain experience in many different areas, including micro-loan fund development, SRI evaluation methodology, and shareholder action.

When Walker joined Ethical Funds in 1999, his initial focus was creating a more systematic internal approach to company ESG evaluations and corporate engagement. He first moved to initiate an internal review of corpo-rate social and environmental profiles provided by external service providers. In 2000, he drafted and published on the Canadian mutual fund industry's first publicly disclosed proxy voting guidelines. Also in 2001, Ethical Funds filed a shareholder proposal with Citigroup asking the financial giant to ensure an end to predatory lending practices associated with its subprime lending business. This was the first proposal on a social issue ever filed by a Canadian mutual fund company.

After the dot-com boom went bust in the early 2000s, Walker found that there was a huge surge in interest from mainstream investors in responsible investment. As demand grew, Ethical Funds began to build out its internal team of ESG professionals, taking in-house all its evaluations in 2004 and increasing the scope of its corporate engagement program to target 20% of assets each year. A key hire came in 2001 when Jennifer Coulson joined as an analyst. Coulson's eye for detail, balanced perspective, and negotiating skills soon became apparent as she became the driving force behind corporate engagement at Ethical Funds.

EVOLVING INVESTMENT APPROACH

NEI's approach to evaluating the companies it invests in is constantly evolv-ing, reflecting the dynamic external environment. One major evolution oc-curred in 2004, when, to reflect its growing in-house expertise, Ethical Funds dismantled its advisory council and added more new faces to the sustain-ability team. At the same time, it created a socially responsible investment committee of the board to provide oversight of its expanded SRI activities. It also launched its Corporate Sustainability Scorecard (CSS), its methodology for evaluating a company's ESG performance.

Since 2009, and under the direction of Christie Stephenson, manager of ESG Evaluations, NEI has been working on developing a new evaluation process. NEI observed that many companies had become adept at maximiz-ing their rating under ESG scoring systems and that ESG evaluations based on aggregating large numbers of indicators to produce a score can mask underlying firm-specific risk. As a result, NEI has retained CSS's sectoral approach while continuing to evolve its ESG research process. NEI's ESG evaluation methodology includes: a material risk analysis of the primary ESG challenges facing companies; the establishment of baseline expecta-tions to determine eligibility for investment; and conducting headline risk and management breach investigations to monitor performance. Though its program has evolved considerably in terms of sophistication, NEI still em-ploys automatic exclusions related to tobacco, weapons, and nuclear power.

It also has "core violations" that would prohibit investment in a company, such as the absence of environmental management systems for extractives companies.

The oil sands sector is one that NEI has been extensively engaged in for many years; NEI's ESG evaluation process will be explained using an example from this sector, Suncor, which merged with Petro-Canada in 2009. The ESG Services Department starts by identifying sector-specific material ESG risks and baseline expectations for each sector. Baseline expectations include both management systems and performance benchmarks and represent the minimum requirements that a company must meet to be considered for inclusion in NEI's portfolio. Companies are monitored on an ongoing basis to ensure that they continually meet NEI's baseline expectations ("headline risk"). If NEI's ESG analysts find an incident that suggests a violation of baseline expectations, they may conduct a management breach investigation, where they examine the fundamentals of an incident. Companies found to be in violation may be targeted for corporate engagement or, in extreme cases, divested altogether.

Some of the most significant ESG risks facing Suncor are associated with future carbon regulation and liabilities and those associated with unconventional extraction in the oil sands, such as water availability and potential contamination of air, water, and snowpack. The baseline expectations for oil and gas companies include evidence of the existence and implementation of polices regarding health and safety and human rights. Suncor has a sophisticated health and safety policy and accompanying management system, including a board committee responsible for oversight of the safety program. The company has also made a public commitment to protect human rights within its sphere of influence and has a very strong Aboriginal engagement policy. As a result of the company's evidence of high-level commitment and implementation of ESG risk management, Suncor exceeds NEI's baseline expectations for the oil and gas sector. However, it still brings risks to NEI's portfolio, which must be monitored on an ongoing basis using targeted analytics. NEI's ESG Services Department identifies targeted analytics for the most material ESG risks in certain sectors; these are policy and performance indicators that provide a comprehensive picture of ESG areas for improvement.

For the oil and gas sector, the ESG Services team monitors tailings management, water use, and greenhouse gas (GHG) emissions, among other indicators. Suncor is actively reducing its tailing, as well as the water and GHG emissions intensity of its operations. All of the data collected and analysis conducted on companies provides the basis for corporate engagement. For Suncor, in 2009, NEI raised the issue of lack of disclosure of future carbon costs, though the company's public disclosure is generally good.

Subsequent to a dialogue with Ethical Funds and a shareholder proposal, the company agreed to provide details for potential carbon costs for all new projects as well as a detailed five-year GHG emissions forecast, so analysts can determine exposure to current and future carbon regulations.

Beyond purely company-specific risk analysis, the NEI team also examines cross-cutting, emerging ESG risks in more detail. This research, managed by Michelle de Cordova, manager of Public Policy and Research, is also used to inform internal policy and shareholder action. In 2005, Ethical Funds began publishing white papers on issues considered most material to the companies in its portfolio, including international humanitarian law and Canadian mining companies; corporate obligations when operating in countries with high prevalence of HIV and AIDS; and the concept of free, prior, and informed consent for indigenous peoples. One recent research focus has been the oil sands, where NEI seeks to develop a deeper understanding of the risks unique to this sector. It has published a series of research reports examining the sector in detail, including benchmarking the ESG performance of the major companies active in the oil sands. In cases where the ESG Services Department determines that minimizing the risks associated with an issue necessitates a regulatory response, NEI will engage policy makers to encourage the adoption of appropriate legislation and regulation.

CORPORATE ENGAGEMENT PROGRAM

NEI's corporate engagement program is extensive. In 2010 alone, NEI engaged with more than 60 companies over seven thematic areas, including oil sands, disclosure, and green buildings. Every year, 20% of portfolio assets are targeted for corporate engagement. NEI's experience has shown that it is possible to engage with companies on difficult and controversial issues while still maintaining good relations.

NEI does not consider itself a shareholder activist; rather, it is a well-informed shareholder seeking to assist companies improve their performance in key areas, so that they can continue to be successful (and NEI can continue to invest in them confidently). NEI's experience has been that many companies acknowledge the value of these interactions.

The focus list of companies to engage with is determined by the NEI ESG Services Department. Companies are identified both from a bottom-up and top-down approach. From the bottom up, by researching companies during the ESG evaluation process, analysts get to know which companies are potential candidates for engagement and which issues are hot topics. From the top, Walker and other senior members of the team stay connected to trends through their involvement in various external initiatives. In addition, investors are also surveyed on a regular basis about which issues they feel are important. The team then comes together to decide which themes and companies should be targeted for the year's focus list.

Once companies and sectors are identified, sector analysts gather all the relevant information on a company—its score relative to its peers, the key risks it faces and how it is currently managing them, as well as other relevant information that will be used to craft any initial letter to the company.

If the company responds to the letter, then a meeting is arranged, in person if possible. NEI is usually represented by Coulson, Walker, and the analyst covering the company. At the meeting, they go over the letter and present NEI's issues to the company. NEI also lets the company know where it stands relative to its sectoral peers, information that companies tend to find useful. NEI generally has one to two interactions with a company before it outlines the actions it would like the company to take to address its concerns. NEI generally has a "three strikes and you're out" approach. It gives a company three chances to demonstrate that it has addressed NEI's concerns; if the company is unwilling or unable to do so, NEI may choose to disinvest. Sometimes the person NEI met with within a company who was in charge of an aspect of ESG management tells NEI that he or she was unable to gain traction on NEI's concerns with management. Many companies state that they wish other investors would raise these issues. In some cases, company managers have urged NEI to file a shareholder proposal, although NEI prefers to build trust and credibility with companies by engaging in a constructive dialogue. NEI's view is that shareholder proposals do not always necessarily deliver the best results due to time pressure and the negative effect filing proposals can have on the dialogue with a company over the longer term. In addition to direct engagement with companies, NEI also regularly votes on proxies and is extremely transparent about its voting record. NEI takes its proxy voting responsibilities very seriously. Its analysts vote every proxy wherever legally permitted to do so. That adds up: In 2010, NEI voted 6,960 items at 619 meetings.

In general, NEI finds that it is alone in engaging with some companies on certain issues. NEI is not afraid to take on high-profile, controversial issues, such as oil sands and human rights issues in the gold mining sector. In several cases, engagement with a company has led to a disinvestment.

The Forzani Group Ltd. is Canada's largest national retailer of sporting goods. Ethical Funds considers it to be a well-run company but had concerns that despite the fact that it sources a lot of materials from developing countries, it does not have a supplier code of conduct in place. Ethical Funds requested that Forzani put such a code in place, which it did. However, the company was unwilling or unable to share details about how the code has been implemented. As a result, in late 2006, Ethical Funds disinvested in Forzani.

NEI's portfolio has benefited from its decision not to invest in high-ESG-risk companies. For example, NEI's ESG analysts' concerns about the risks associated with Taseko Mines' proposal for the Prosperity open pit mine in British Columbia, including significant First Nations opposition, meant that the company was excluded from its portfolio. In November 2010, the Canadian federal government stated that it would disapprove the mine proposal, which resulted in a sharp decline in Taseko's share price.

In 2010, NEI had a number of significant corporate engagements. It persuaded Le Chateau to adopt and disclose a supply chain code of conduct that requires suppliers to adhere to international labor standards. NEI also tracked Le Chateau's progress in implementing the code, including supplier audits, and being more transparent on an ongoing basis. NEI was also active in encouraging companies in the food sector, such as Kellogg's and General Mills, to develop water footprints and conservation policies. NEI is extremely active in tracking risks for companies operating in Canada's oil sands. In 2009, it released a report that benchmarked the performance of 13 major energy companies on air, land, water, First Nations, and overall strategy. The report was used to inform its corporate engagement program, which achieved several successes in 2010. For example, Husky Energy published its first sustainable development report in 2009. NEI is also active on the issue of unconventional (e.g., shale gas) fuel extraction and its impact on water quality, namely through engagement with Encana and Talisman.

KEY PRODUCTS AND PERFORMANCE OVER TIME

NEI's main product is responsible mutual funds, though it is currently expanding its product line by beginning to offer in-house expertise, especially in corporate engagement, to clients. NEI has 26 funds and since 2004 has administered the broad-based Ethical® Canadian Index. NEI's largest fund, the Ethical Balanced Fund, A Series, dating from June 1989, has about CA $360 million worth of assets.

In 2009, NEI launched its Ethical Select Portfolios, Canada's only responsible fund of fund target risk portfolios featuring NEI, Acuity Funds, and Phillips, Hager & North Funds.

Since 2005, NEI has also made its funds available to institutional clients through its partnership with Guardian Capital (known as Guardian Ethical Management, GEM).

NEI's track record is proof that investors can adhere to strong values and still generate returns. Its largest fund, the Ethical Balanced Fund,

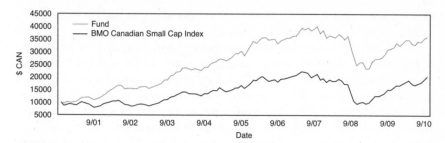

FIGURE 11.1 Ethical Special Equity Returns from 2000 to 2010
Source: NEI Investments, "Ethical Special Equity." Available at: www
.neiinvestments.com/NEIFiles/PDFs/FundFeatureSheets/en-CA/ET67.pdf. For more
information about the long-run return for all of NEI's Ethical products, see
www.neiinvestments.com/Pages/Products.a spx#4.

A Series, has a ten-year average return of 2.74 %. Some funds have outperformed conventional competitors by a wide margin. Its Ethical Special
Equity, a Canadian small/mid-cap equity fund, has consistently achieved
higher returns than a competitor fund, as shown in Figure 11.1.

LOOKING FORWARD: NEI'S MERGER WITH NORTHWEST FUNDS

In 2007, Ethical Funds joined forces with Northwest Funds to create Northwest and Ethical Investments LP, now known as NEI Investments. Northwest has been known for its traditional risk focus, while Ethical is known for
its ESG focus, as described. The merger was designed to increase Ethical's
market reach, especially through the distribution channels of the two shareholders of the merged entity, Desjardins Group and the Provincial Credit
Unions Centrals, with Desjardins now utilizing NEI's ESG evaluations and
engagement services for its Desjardins Environment Fund

While each family of funds has retained its original branding, the company has been integrating its processes and technology behind the scenes.
In 2009, NEI began using one operational platform, which allows advisors
and investors to seamlessly purchase and switch among Northwest Funds,
NEI Investments, and Credential Funds.

Bob Walker and his team are focused on expanding its line of services
to include advisory services, mainly on corporate engagement strategies for
pension funds. NEI recently won an extensive request-for-proposal process,
to become the preferred supplier of the Swedish national pension funds. Its
main product offering will be engagement with any company on the Toronto

Stock Exchange Composite but with a natural focus on ESG challenges related to the energy and mining sectors.

NEI will also continue its public policy work, focused on promoting transparency and environmental and human protection in the development of natural resources. In 2011, NEI will continue to encourage global stock exchanges to improve the transparency and corporate governance practices of listed companies, partially through the Sustainable Stock Exchanges initiative. Continuing its focus on the oil sands of northern Alberta, NEI will keep up the pressure on both companies and the Alberta government to minimize the environmental and human impacts of the oil sands.

NOTE

1. In December 2007, a strategic partnership between Northwest Funds and the Ethical Funds Company created Northwest and Ethical Investments LP. NEI Investments is owned 50% by the Provincial Credit Union Centrals and 50% by Desjardins Group. In this chapter, the company is referred to as "Ethical Funds" prior to 2007 and as "NEI Investments" after 2007.

CHAPTER 12

Looking for a Green Century

Passive-Indexed versus Active Portfolio Management

Fernando Viana

The elimination of entire sectors—those considered to be too oner-ous from a sustainability standpoint—is an extreme case, perhaps. Arguably, any portfolio or positions heavily invested in industries that are unsustainable in the long run are timing the market, knowing they may well have to get out sometime in the future. More investors mov-ing their equity away from such sectors could encourage companies to consider changing their business models in a race for efficiency and innovation-seeking capital. This chapter focuses on how Green Cen-tury Capital Management applies these basic tenets.

Green Century Capital Management (Green Century) is the sponsor and investment advisor to the Green Century Equity Fund and the Green Cen-tury Balanced Fund. These two funds combined manage approximately $115 million and aim to offer "mutual funds whose portfolios have been screened to include companies with strong environmental performance records as well as those companies that are in the business of solving environmental problems."[1]

BACKGROUND

Green Century was founded in 1991 by a consortium of nine nonprofit environmental advocacy organizations: California Public Interest Research Group (CALPIRG), Citizen Lobby of New Jersey, Colorado Public Interest Research Group (COPIRG), ConnPIRG Citizen Lobby, Fund for the Public Interest, Massachusetts Public Interest Research Group (MASSPIRG), MOPIRG Citizen Organization, PIRGIM Public Interest Lobby, and Washington State Public Interest Research Group (WASHPIRG).These nonprofit public interest groups, part of the Public Interest Network (PIN) that includes traditional public interest research groups (PIRGs) as well as affiliated civic organizations, seek to preserve and protect the environment by, among other things: campaigning for the conservation of clean air, clean water, and open space; filing lawsuits against companies that pollute illegally; and advocating for lower use of toxic chemicals and the reduction of greenhouse gases causing global warming. In the early 1990s, when there were few socially responsible investing (SRI) options, PIRGs had a large membership interested in environmental and social issues and were motivated to provide members with the ability to invest in line with their values.

Green Century has incorporated environmental criteria into its investment strategies since its inception. Now more than ever, Green Century believes its mission is to consider and measure the environmental impact of the companies in which its mutual funds invest, both to promote greater corporate environmental responsibility and to temper the risks of investing in high-carbon companies in the transition to an overall greener and less carbon-intensive economy.

Green Century also distinguishes itself in its active shareholder advocacy role. In addition to being an active shareholder, it devotes 100% of its management fee profits to its founding advocacy organizations to fund environmental and public interest advocacy work.

GREEN CENTURY FUNDS

The Green Century Equity Fund seeks to achieve long-term total returns to match the performance of the MSCI KLD 400 Social Index (formerly the Domini 400 Social Index), which is comprised of 400 stocks selected using environmental and social criteria. The index is screened to include those companies with the best sustainability records.[2]

The Green Century Balanced Fund similarly seeks to promote environmentally responsible corporate behavior, a cleaner environment, and a sustainable economy. In contrast with the Equity Fund, however, the Balanced Fund also holds fixed-income securities to "balance" equity risks with credit risks, such as interest rate, credit, and inflation risk. Accordingly, the Balanced Fund seeks *both* capital growth and income from a diversified portfolio of stocks and bonds that meet Green Century's standards for corporate environmental performance.

Green Century's two diversified fund products, a *passively* managed equity-indexed fund and an *actively* managed fund with both stocks and bonds, offer a choice of investment styles and preferences to match investor goals as well as meet changing macroeconomic conditions. When an SRI-indexed fund underperforms the market during some cycles—for example, when oil company stocks are very high—many socially and environmentally focused investors will be comfortable riding out those cycles with a solid core of long-term sustainable holdings. Indexed funds may offer competitive or better return performance than "mainstream" active investment managers over the long term, from lower transaction costs and potential tax advantages through lower capital gains taxation. More actively managed funds, while potentially more expensive from a fee standpoint, offer more discretionary opportunities to revise holdings according to macro conditions or investor goals.

GREEN CENTURY EQUITY FUND

As mentioned, the Equity Fund seeks to achieve a long-term total return that matches the performance of the KLD400 Index, a market-cap-weighted index of 400 stocks selected using environmental, social, and corporate governance criteria. This is the oldest and best known of the SRI indexes; indeed, it is the flagship index most often used as a benchmark by other SRI funds. The stock components of this index were compiled originally from a larger universe of securities screened by MSCI to include only those companies with the best sustainability records. The five categories of "negative" screens applied are tobacco, alcohol, gambling, nuclear power, and firearms and/or military weapons.

Northern Trust[3] serves as a subadvisor to the Equity Fund, which had approximately $55 million under management as of June 30, 2011. Northern Trust's role is essentially to re-create the composite 400 securities in the KLD400 Index and trade securities for the Equity Fund. This is a straightforward role of passive indexed portfolio management, not an active investment role involving the bottom-up selection of securities.

The fund's sector allocation and stock selection follow closely the KLD400 Index's criteria for excluding companies with the "worst environmental and social records" on issues such as waste disposal, toxic emissions, environmental fines/penalties, emissions reductions, product and service performance, corporate citizenship, employee relations, and the like. Nevertheless, even relatively environmentally unfriendly sectors (even after applying screens) remain included in the final allocation, such as capital goods (6.09% as of March 31, 2011), energy (6.02%), materials (2.81%), and utilities (1.52%).

This postscreening "best in class/breed" approach to the remaining sectors of the economy (after screens have been applied) results in a portfolio containing many well-known large-capitalization companies commonly found in a more mainstream non-SRI portfolio. Not surprisingly, the Equity Fund's major holdings as of June 30, 2011, were IBM, Microsoft, Johnson & Johnson, Procter & Gamble, Google, Intel, PepsiCo, Merck, Qualcomm and McDonalds. Seven of these ten top holdings are Dow Jones Dividend companies and among the most widely held stocks in the United States.

Given the broad environmental, social, and governance (ESG) criteria of the Equity Fund, it is appropriate to compare the fund's returns with overall market returns, as represented by the Standard & Poor's (S&P) 500 Index. The fund's return over the last three, five and ten years to June 30, 2011, were 4.06%, 2.52%, and 1.55% versus 3.34%, 2.94% and 2.72% for the S&P 500 Index. The Equity Fund's performance surpassed the benchmark return for the three years (average annualized) to June 30, 2011, which is remarkable since the fund's results are after management fee expenses. (The total annual fund operating expense ratio was 0.95% as of the prospectus dated November 29, 2010.)[4]

Aside from looking at the Equity Fund returns versus the benchmark, investors may also consider that their "returns" also include a healthy dose of shareholder advocacy to improve the ESG performance of selected fund holdings, while mainstream firms are typically hands-off investors.

TRILLIUM ASSET MANAGEMENT AND THE BALANCED FUND

Green Century's Balanced Fund offers an excellent case study on how investors seeking to follow a narrower, more focused, and more aggressive environmental agenda can diversify their holdings around the large-cap companies commonly found in many SRI funds, including the Equity Fund. With approximately $60 million at June 30, 2011, the Balanced Fund differs significantly from the Equity Fund in that it seeks *both* capital appreciation and income from a diversified portfolio of stocks and bonds, and it specifically *excludes* certain environmentally unfriendly sector allocations and does not hold fossil fuel stocks directly. Specifically, it excludes investments in traditional fossil fuel–based energy and utilities, and it rebalances these exclusions by proactively overweighting new or emerging sectors, such Healthy Living (2.01% at March 31, 2011), Renewable and Efficiency [Energy] (9.20%), Telecom Services (5.72%), and Software & Services (7.31%).

The fund typically holds 60 to 80 equity securities and 20 to 30 fixed-income securities. As of January 2011, it held about 70 equity securities. Its asset allocation was approximately 65% common stocks, 30% bonds, and 5% cash. The common stock portion of the Balanced Fund, which is never to exceed 75% of net assets, is multicap, broken down in this way (all as of November 30, 2010):

34.6% mega cap (>$50 billion in total capitalization)

31.3% large cap ($10–$50 billion)

20.6% mid cap ($2.5–$10 billion)

13.5% small cap (<$2.5 billion)

Thus, while it invests in both large and small companies, it may be relatively biased toward small and midsize companies with the advantages of greater growth prospects as well as the challenges of greater risk and price volatility. Bond holdings are typically at least 25% of all net assets, of investment-grade quality, and may be of any maturity.

The Balanced Fund also allocates small amounts to community investing, as in Self Help Credit Union and Shorebank Pacific's EcoDeposits. Finally, it has invested in innovative Green Bonds recently developed by the World Bank.[5]

TRILLIUM ASSET MANAGEMENT CORPORATION

The Balanced Fund is actively managed by Trillium Asset Management Corporation[6] in Boston, a subadvisor to the fund. According to Erin Gray, responsible for Marketing and Strategic Analysis at Green Century, Trillium "conducts day-to-day investment management function of the fund consistent with the mission and guidelines set by Green Century." The Balanced Fund is currently the only mutual fund Trillium manages.

According to Lisa MacKinnon, Marketing Manager of Trillium, which was founded in 1982, the company has had a consistent mission and values-driven approach to investing in its almost 30-year existence and manages close to $1 billion today.[7] "It is the oldest and largest independent investment management firm in the United States solely devoted to sustainable and responsible investing."

It invests in "companies with strong ESG profiles [that] are better managed for the long term, have lower risk profiles, and are positioned to outperform their peers." Trillium's name is derived from and represented by the tripetal trillium flower, which equates with the three prongs of sustainability: environment, equity, and economy.

Like Green Century, Trillium also engages directly in "shareholder engagement and advocacy, and indirectly, through allocating capital to companies and sectors with positive economic, ecological, and social impact."

Trillium offers investors with varying profiles—individuals with significant wealth, families, foundations, endowments, religious institutions, corporations, and other nonprofits—equity, balanced, and fixed-income portfolios driven by a "Growth at a Reasonable Price (GARP)" or "Core" investing style, a hybrid growth and value approach to investing. This investing style aims to hold securities of companies that, compared to their industry or sector peers, offer the best possible balance of above-average historical and prospective growth, below-average debt, above-average return on equity, and below-peer-group valuations.

As ready-made investment options, Trillium offers four distinct portfolios suited to various investor goals: Large Cap Core, Small/Mid Cap Core, All Cap Core, and Sustainable Opportunities. To meet more specific investor objectives, Trillium creates customized portfolios, as with the Balanced Fund, including holdings that are animal testing free, fossil fuel free, and weapons free, as well as portfolios that reflect Catholic values.

As a result of its long ESG track record and commitment to advocacy work, Trillium is a logical choice to implement the investment objective of the Balanced Fund. At a more micro level, Trillium uses various industry-specific methods to further screen prospective holdings. Tiffany, the jewelry and luxury specialty retailer, is an interesting case in point. Tiffany may not be viewed by many as a "sustainable" or even appropriate holding for a green or SRI fund, but it is exposed to the risks associated with diamond and gold mining and is in a position to manage its global supply chain expertly.

Diamond and gold mining are high-risk industries notorious for many negative environmental and human rights issues. However, Tiffany has long demonstrated strong leadership in sourcing diamonds from suppliers that address and minimize such concerns. Tiffany has worked for over ten years with interest groups and suppliers to apply ethical standards in diamond sourcing as well as transparency and credible codes of conduct. Among other examples, Tiffany stopped selling "coral jewelry in 1998 because it could not be sustainably harvested, has not sourced rubies from Burma since 2006, and opposed gold mining from environmentally damaging mines (name) in compliance with the 'No Dirty Gold' initiative in 2007."[8] The company's senior management has also taken an active public advocacy role in support of voluntary standards for mining, including the No Dirty Gold Campaign's Golden Rules and the Framework for Responsible Mining.[9]

The end product of Trillium's methodology for selecting securities is then a customized list of approximately 200 securities ranked by approximately half a dozen metrics, or "alpha" scores, including a technical score, a quantitative score, and an ESG alpha score, among others. This selective list of prospective holdings is then fed into a portfolio optimization model for sensitivity and other analyses. Moreover, since the Balanced Fund also holds fixed-income securities, a similar process is conducted for bond selection process. Ongoing monitoring and tracking of the selected portfolio occurs through a monthly review of financial as well as "sustainable" performance, mainly through a review of the alpha scores, applied not just to individual stocks but also to the overall fund against typical benchmarks.

A "macro layer" is also used to review fund positions and performance, given overall economic conditions. For example, in 2008, the fund took a somewhat more defensive posture as the economy deteriorated and early signs of the financial crisis emerged; in 2009, following the decline in most asset values early that year, the fund adopted a more aggressive stance. In 2010, following a large run-up in values, the fund had an approximately 50% rotation of its equity positions, higher than the approximately 30% turnover more typical in less volatile time periods.

According to Gray, the Balanced Fund's returns over the last three, five, and ten years (to June 30, 2011) were 4.25%, 3.10%, and 1.14% versus 4.41%, 4.40%, and 4.36%, respectively, for the Lipper Balanced Index.

For the last year to June 30, 2011, the Balanced Fund's return came close to matching the Lipper Balanced Index at 19.27% versus 20.32% for the benchmark. In fact, it surpassed the benchmark for the six-month period to June 30, 2011, at 5.28% versus 4.67% for the benchmark. (Unlike the benchmark, the fund's returns are after operating expenses, which were 1.38% of assets as of the prospectus dated November 29, 2010.) As investor sentiment turned more positive over the sustainability of the economic recovery in late 2010 and early 2011, gains in equity values were particularly strong in cyclical sectors such as energy, industrials, and materials. Since the Balanced Fund does not have any traditional fossil fuel energy holdings, it did not participate in the strong returns in this sector. However, alternative fund investments in the clean energy and clean technology sectors have performed well in recent quarters.

CARBON FOOTPRINT OF THE BALANCED FUND

In 2009, Trucost, a leading environmental data and analysis firm, conducted a carbon footprint study of the Balanced Fund, a first for the U.S. mutual fund industry. It concluded that the carbon intensity of the portfolio was 66% lower than the carbon intensity of the S&P 500 Index benchmark, as measured by tons of carbon emissions of the companies held by the Balanced Fund compared to those of companies included in the S&P 500.

The majority of the fund's low-carbon intensity is attributable to the underweighting or avoidance of heavy carbon dioxide emission sectors, namely Oil and Gas (0% in the Balanced Fund versus 11.9% of the benchmark at April 30, 2009), Utilities (0.8% versus 3.9%), Basic Resources (0% versus 1.2%), and Chemicals (0.8% versus 1.9%).[10] The carbon footprint of the Balanced Fund, at 126 tons of carbon per $1 million of revenue of each of the fund's portfolio holdings, is almost half the average footprint of 16 other sustainability and socially responsible investing funds (226 tons of carbon per $1 million of revenue of each of those funds' portfolio holdings) analyzed by Trucost.

According to the Trucost study, for example, the top ten carbon contributors to the fund were:

1. Air Products and Chemicals (Sector: Chemicals)
2. General Mills (Food and Beverage)
3. 3M (Industrial Goods and Services)
4. Jarden (Personal and Household Goods)
5. J. M. Smucker Co. (Food and Beverage)
6. Canadian Pacific Railway (Industrial Goods and Services)
7. Goldman Sachs (Financial Services)
8. Expeditor International (Industrial Goods and Services)
9. Interface (Personal and Household Goods)
10. Pentair (Industrial Goods and Services)

The top three holdings alone, while accounting for only 5% of fund value, represented approximately 28% of the portfolio's carbon footprint.

SEEKING SAFER PACKAGING: THE BISPHENOL-A REPORT

Another unique feature of Green Century's shareholder advocacy profile involves publishing reports on specific environmental concerns or issues.

For example, in partnership with As You Sow, a nonprofit proponent of enhanced corporate environmental and social responsibility, Green Century published *Seeking Safer Packaging*, a study that ranked and outlined the actions of 20 publicly traded food and beverage companies regarding bisphenol-A (BPA). BPA is a controversial chemical traditionally used for lining food and beverage cans and other items, such as hard clear plastic bottles and containers, including baby bottles. Studies have long established linkages between BPA and child developmental problems, heart disease, and diabetes.

Seeking Safer Packaging was originally published in early 2009 and updated in 2010. The report not only alerted investors to the health and environmental concerns from the use of BPA but also argued that companies could face financial risks and liabilities harmful to corporate reputations and shareholder value.

The study's findings were summarized in a scorecard of corporate efforts to explore substitute packaging. The 2010 report update ranked 20 companies according to these efforts: companies that ranked highly (A or B rankings) include Hain Celestial, ConAgra, H.J. Heinz, General Mills, and Nestlé for using BPA-free can linings and committing to eliminating overall use over time, active testing of alternative linings, and transparency. Lower-scoring companies in the study (F ranking) include Coca-Cola, Del Monte, Kraft, Unilever, Kroger, Safeway, Supervalu, and Wal-Mart: These companies were not transparent on their use of BPA and did not commit to alternative linings in their products (at the time of the study). Green Century and others became effective and powerful watchdogs on the food and beverage industry to limit the use of BPA.

SHAREHOLDER ADVOCACY

Green Century's primary mission is to achieve a portfolio composition in its funds that is fundamentally driven by the firm's values and environmental focus. Another priority function of the firm is to push an environmental agenda through very active shareholder advocacy efforts, including even the purchase of poorly managed environmental securities, as discussed below. Green Century views active ownership as a critical component of sustainable investing. Its advocacy efforts encompass many activities, "from strategic dialogue with management and top executives, to raising issues with the public and other shareholders through the filing of shareholder resolutions, to responsible proxy voting at the companies in which the Green Century Funds hold shares. Green Century employs numerous strategies to encourage improvements in corporate behavior," as noted on its Web site.

Green Century has organized its shareholder advocacy efforts since 2007 by focusing on six key "priority issues." (Environmental issues generally have of course been the macro focus of the firm since its inception.) These six priority areas are:

1. Climate and Energy
2. Wilderness and Biodiversity
3. Toxics and Environmental Health
4. Corporate Accountability and Responsibility
5. Water
6. Food and Agriculture

Green Century has tackled significant problems in each of these areas, including protection of the Arctic National Wildlife Refuge from oil drilling, termination of corporate sponsorship of the U.S. Chamber of Commerce over opposition to climate legislation, corporate transparency over "sustainability efforts," protection of ocean ecosystems, and many others.

Recently, hydraulic fracturing (fracking) has been a priority issue for Green Century. Fracking is a well-established but controversial natural gas extraction method that entails, as described on the company's Web site, the injection of high volumes of water, chemicals, and particles underground to create fractures through which gas can flow for collection. According to the industry, fracturing has been used in roughly 90 percent of wells in operation today and 60 to 80 percent of new wells will require fracturing to remain viable. Hydraulic fracturing operations have been linked to environmental risks that could have significant financial implications for the companies involved and are leading to increased regulatory scrutiny.

Following the 2010 BP oil spill in the Gulf of Mexico, investors and environmental activists alike have sought to improve corporate disclosure of the environmental risks and other liabilities associated with fracking as well as policy responses companies could adopt to reduce or eliminate adverse impact from those activities.

Regarding the company's achievements, Larisa Ruoff, the Director of Shareholder Advocacy for Green Century Capital Management, has said on the Web site:

> *This recent [BP] blowout demonstrates that drilling in unconventional natural gas reserves using hydraulic fracturing brings with it serious risks that could have financial implications for the companies involved. We believe the strong vote at EOG Resources, Inc. [. . .] demonstrates there is investor demand for improved transparency around environmental and business risks associated with this process and that more clarity is needed on company practices to minimize them.*

And on this issue, "at all companies where the shareholder resolutions went to a vote, the proposals received 7 to 14 times the percentage of votes required by the Securities and Exchange Commission to refile the proposals next year. The highest vote was at Williams Companies Inc. where 42% of the shares voted supported the proposal."

A second example of shareholder advocacy activism by Green Century and others involves "tar sands" oil exploration. For several years, Green Century has pressured major oil and gas companies to increase their disclosure on the environmental damage resulting from the expansion of their operations in the Alberta tar sands. At Chevron's 2008 annual meeting, 28.6% of shareholders representing 31.4 billion of shares voted in support of a resolution filed by Green Century requesting increased disclosure on the environmental impacts of company operations in the Alberta tar sands. In 2009, the resolution was filed again. Although the resolution was not included on the company's proxy statement, Chevron announced in June 2009 that it was putting its only majority-owned project in the oil sands on hold. In 2011, Green Century achieved similar resolution results on this issue at Exxon Mobil and ConocoPhillips at the companies' annual meetings.

In a third important example of priority issue advocacy, Green Century has sought increased transparency and disclosure of corporate political contributions. As trade associations and lobbyists play an increasingly key role in shaping policy, many argue that companies must be transparent and accountable for their political contributions. Interested shareholders need to know that corporate funds are not used in a way that may harm the environment or the long-term interests of the company.

Green Century has filed nearly 20 resolutions encouraging companies to adopt comprehensive policies to ensure transparency and accountability in their political spending. Perhaps the firm's most significant accomplishment on this issue was to achieve more extensive political contribution transparency from Amgen, a publicly-traded biotechnology company that pioneered the development of therapies and products based on advances in recombinant DNA and molecular biology, when the company not only agreed with Green Century's proposal but also asked its shareholders to vote in support of the resolution. An overwhelming 75% of shareholders supported the resolution, the largest positive vote Green Century has ever generated and one of the largest ever achieved for a shareholder resolution.

Finally, Green Century is innovative in its shareholder advocacy with "companies that have the most egregious impact on the environment [but] do not pass the Green Century Funds' environmental screens and thus are not included in either of the Funds' holdings." Green Century Capital Management—the parent company, not the funds—maintains a small investment portfolio for the sole purpose of conducting advocacy with those companies. (A $2,000 investment is required to be held for one year before proposing a shareholder resolution.) Thus, investors can be confident that while they are directly investing in clean, green companies, they are also supporting an organization that can actively engage with *all* companies on environmental issues as needed.

SUMMARY

Green Century's investment practices show that passive-indexed investing, even with an SRI or sustainable orientation, may result in a mostly large-cap equity portfolio that does not meet more aggressive environmental or sustainable goals, such as achieving a less carbon-intensive or truly innovative clean-tech portfolio. By performing active shareholder advocacy on these companies, however, Green Century aims to achieve positive ESG improvements even in the most mainstream companies. Investors seeking truly differentiated environmentally-sustainable returns may choose to identify funds willing to modify their sector allocation or use other criteria to more directly achieve those returns while maintaining strong traditional criteria for financial soundness, quality of management, and social and corporate governance.

NOTES

1. Unless otherwise noted, information in this chapter has been taken from www.greencentury.com. Interview with Erin Gray, head of Marketing and Strategic Analysis. on February 28, 2011.
2. http://us.ishares.com/product_info/fund/overview/DSI.htm
3. www.northerntrust.com
4. Interview with Gray.
5. http://treasury.worldbank.org/cmd/htm/WorldBankGreenBonds.html.
6. http://trilliuminvest.com/
7. (Telephone) Interview with Lisa MacKinnon, Marketing Manager, on December 28, 2010.
8. www.diamondfacts.com/conflict/eliminating_conflict_diamonds.html
9. Interview with Stephanie Leighton, Chief Investment Officer and Portfolio Manager for The Green Century Balanced Fund, and Lisa MacKinnon on December 28, 2010.
10. www.greencentury.com/funds/Green-Century-Balanced-Fund

CHAPTER 13

Pictet Water

Jenna Manheimer and Nancy Degnan

Water continues to be a key topic of concern. Agriculture relies on fresh water, which is increasingly scarce in many parts of the world, especially China. A growing number of large global corporations face strategic decisions regarding future licenses to operate for water-intensive facilities. Climate change is expected to affect fresh water supplies, especially where increasing temperatures put glaciers at risk. Entire populations face shortages, if not the need to seek new sources. There is a need to be more efficient with water use while replenishing these vital resources. Desalination and other new techniques have emerged, each with its strengths and weaknesses, as have efficiency and water management solutions, among other emerging opportunities. A growing number of fund managers offer dedicated portfolios and strategies focused on niche themes within alternative energy, as discussed elsewhere in this book. Water emerges as one more key theme in this regard.

Ethical questions abound: Can or should fund managers attempt to profit from a resource as vital as water, especially in the developing world, or is their participation essential from an infrastructure requirement standpoint? How are individual consumers, especially in poor areas, affected by shortages? Should water be a public or a private endeavor? This chapter looks in detail at one leading European fund and its approach to the subject of water.

Unless otherwise indicated, details about Pictet are available at the company site, http://pictet.com

As the global population continues to increase exponentially, innovative companies with long-term agendas for efficient resource use will drive the sustainability of this planet, and our future. Fresh water is arguably the most crucial resource, and the amount available on the surface of Earth is dauntingly scarce. According to the United Nations, by 2025, almost 2 billion people will be living in countries or regions with severe water scarcity.[1] Recognizing the value of clean water in a growing market, private investors have increasingly recently paid more attention to this resource, as it poses an opportunity for profit through conservation, increasing efficient use, and advanced treatment. The Bloomberg World Water Index, which tracks 11 utilities, returned 35% to investors annually since 2003, more than the 29% for oil and gas.[2] Understanding the value of this vital resource, as well as the ecological strains of increasing demand for a scarce commodity, the Pictet Water Fund has become one of the largest shareholders of the water market in the world.

Established in Geneva in 1805, Pictet is today one of Switzerland's largest banks, privately owned by just six partners. The company limits its services to managing the investments of individuals and institutions, as opposed to conducting investment banking or issuing commercial, mortgage, or unsecured loans. In the past decade, rather than follow the growing wave of environmental investing, Pictet has taken the initiative to be a trendsetter, venturing into multiple sectors of sustainable development. Recognizing the potential for increased efficiency across expanding fields of resource management that are essential to ecological survival as well as providing key opportunities for business, this seemingly traditional bank is moving forward faster than many of its long-standing peers. The various environmental funds Pictet manages allow for diverse investment needs and interests among sectors such as water, timber, clean energy, and agriculture. Each invested project focuses on new and developing science and technology at every level of operations, utilizing financial capital provided by investors to improve, develop, and implement the most modern and efficient tools. With a fundamental conservation philosophy of reusing and recycling, backed by advanced science, Pictet is transforming agricultural waste into fuel and feed and a universal need for fresh water into a profitable venture.

A crucial element of survival for all living creatures, water is not just essential to life but is becoming a strategic economic commodity, requiring forward-thinking to ensure usability, delivery, treatment, and reusability. Fresh water helps determine worldwide economic conditions for individuals and nations, measuring success and prosperity. And while the human population soars, total water usage worldwide is estimated to have increased by a factor of six since 1900.[3] Yet infrastructure often remains rudimentary, and water shortages in countries at every economic level of development are increasingly common.

Pictet is cashing in on this increasing need for fresh water, which is projected to rise sharply due to agricultural, industrial, and individual demands along with growing populations. By attracting patient investors willing to accept steady albeit long-term gains, the fund provides the capital many local utilities and suppliers lack to improve systemic infrastructure and increase distribution efficiency. In this way, private investment serves the dual purpose of granting access to clean water for people all over the world, even where piping systems are outdated and in need of replacement, while also creating a promising source of financial return for investors who commit monetary resources to the long-term goal of aqua sustainability.

EVOLUTION OF INVESTMENT STRATEGY OVER TIME: ORIGINAL VERSUS CURRENT MISSION

Today, Pictet manages a water fund that has expanded steadily since its inception in 2000. The debut of several environmental funds now managed by the company, including investment in a resource easily taken for granted such as water, was a novel concept in the market at the time. Currently managing assets of $3.2 billion, the venture initially met with poor returns and skepticism by analysts who dismissed the idea of profiting from an essential natural resource widely available. But although water has traditionally been viewed as a public good, supplied and regulated by government, increasing demand in both quantity and quality necessitates investment beyond what public utilities can provide. "The worldwide water infrastructure is completely outdated," explains Hans Peter Portner, one of the fund managers for Pictet Water. "Required investments to cover basic services worldwide are between 60 billion and 80 billion euros a year, but only 40% is effectively invested now."[4] That's when the deeper resources of the private sector come in to help bridge the gap in resource distribution. And Pictet estimates the total global value of this private investment at $260 billion per year.[5]

Human populations across the planet enjoy bountiful access to fresh water unequally, and the suffering of many does not occur without ramifications for the rest of global society. As goes the hierarchy of needs, unless the most basic of human requirements are met—adequate food and water supply—no further function is carried out, and no other desires are sought after. Without accessible, usable water, people do not contribute to the workforce or pursue education, and society's potential is not realized. Large suffering populations will inevitably have serious global ramifications, only some of which can be imagined in advance. In addition, in an era of growing local public awareness and concern over contaminants found both naturally and artificially in drinking water sources, stricter regulations mandate more complex monitoring and filtration systems than were traditionally in place.

During the early stages of Pictet's venture into the water market, it dealt mostly with companies that managed, purified, bottled, distributed, or treated water, and 24% of its assets were invested in French companies.[6] According to Phillipe Rohner, senior investment manager at Pictet, this was due to France's initiative to privatize water management, a concept that had its roots in Napoleonic times, and facilitated the fund's entry into the market. Pictet also favored those companies employing advanced technologies, for example the purification of water with ultraviolet. Over the last decade, however, Pictet has spread its aqua investments over a much broader market, with core holdings currently in the United States and the United Kingdom. In a public communication, Senior Product Manager Denis Schmidli stated: "The European Union intends to invest a total of nearly €350 billion in new [water] infrastructure between 2006 and 2025, and the United States is expected to invest some $900 billion in this same segment by 2019."[7]

FOUNDERS AND KEY DECISION MAKERS

Hans Peter Portner joined Pictet Asset Management in 1997 and has been managing the Water Fund since 2005 as head of the Sector and Theme Funds team. Currently the senior investment manager, he received his master's in economics from the University of Bern and is a chartered financial analyst with 18 years of experience in the industry. In addition to the Water Fund, Portner manages a global high-dividend infrastructure portfolio for Japanese investors.

Another key player managing Pictet's Water Fund is Philippe Rohner, also with the bank since the late 1990s, originally as a financial analyst for the Swiss chemicals sector. He comanages the fund along with Portner, as senior investment manager on the Specialist Equities team. Rohner joined Pictet with 14 years experience in various positions, having worked in the petroleum and chemicals industries with Texaco and Ciba-Geigy in Switzerland, the United States, and the United Kingdom. His academic studies include several technical and financial degrees, with bachelor's and master's degrees in industrial and chemical engineering from the University of South Carolina and Lamar University, respectively, and a doctorate in the same area of study from the Swiss Federal Institute of Technology. He also holds an MBA in finance from the University of Strathclyde in the United Kingdom.

The third manager of Pictet Water is Arnaud Bisschop, the newest member of the company, joining the Sector and Theme Funds division in 2007. He holds a bachelor's degree in engineering from the Ecole Polytechnique in Paris and a master's in science from the Ecole Nationale du Genie Rural, des Eaux et des Forêts (Paris). Bisschop brought five years of experience with him onto the team, having worked as a project leader in the sales department at Suez, one of the companies in which Pictet has significant holdings. In addition to experience in the financial sector, Bisschop was previously a senior consultant on the Sustainability Services Team at Ernst and Young in Paris.

Besides the chief managers of the Water Fund, Pictet relies on an advisory board of five individuals, all chief executive officers (CEOs), chairs, or directors of their respective companies and offering experience from an array of backgrounds. Members include Henri Proglio of Veolia Environment, a waste disposal and recycling company; David Owen of Envisager Ltd., who contributes a monthly column to *Global Water Intelligence* (GWI) and Michael Deane of the National Association of Water Companies.

METHODOLOGY

By assigning prices to the water market and projecting future values, Pictet attracts investors with the potential for perpetual growth. Denis Schmidli estimates that the total size of the world water market is $500 billion and expanding by 6% annually.[8] Managing this resource in an economically sound manner benefits everyone by providing society with public access to free or low-cost sanitary fresh water while generating revenue for private stakeholders.

The Water Fund operates by investing at least two-thirds of its total assets in companies conducting business in the water or air sector, focusing especially on those involved in water supply and treatment, which represented 43.1% of total investments as of December 2010. The next biggest sector is water technology, representing 40.7%, followed by environmental services, representing 12.3%. The goal of each investment is to make water utilizable through efficient operations, logistics, and technology, affecting multiple points in the pathway from source to consumer.

The geographical region representing the largest proportion of the fund is the United States, comprising almost half of the fund's resources at 41.7%. Since regulation is performed at the state level in this country, there is greater room for flexibility, with numerous potential regionalized smaller markets. According to *Forbes*, the 55,000 municipal water systems in the United States are operating on an extremely localized level, limiting the ability of each to make improvements in technology or undertake the large-scale projects necessary to sustain the increasing growth in demand while keeping up with advancing technologies becoming available.[9] Other countries where Pictet has significant holdings include Great Britain, Brazil, France, Japan, Hong Kong, and Switzerland itself, where the fund is headquartered.

Water assets in western Europe and the United States are becoming increasingly privatized, which is a heated political issue, with many pros and cons on both sides. But in an interview with *The Street*, Rohner stated that Pictet prefers that municipal governments own the utilities in question while the private sector should be contracted to provide resource management services only. In this approach, there is no capital investment, less taxes are spent on operations, and guaranteed revenue for services are provided by an investor-backed company. [10] However, privatization does signify an opportunity for external investment, and the trend toward this issue of contention is certainly of interest to financial institutions such as Pictet. Although perhaps overly optimistic in 2002 in predicting 65% privatization in the United States by 2015, water privatization is gradually becoming more common, especially in Europe and the United States.[11]

Pictet collects its own revenue by charging a management fee of 1.6%, a custody fee of 0.02%, and an administration fee of 0.31%, which can add up to a substantial return for the manager when attracting large-scale investments. Shares purchased are liquid, with quarterly redemptions, and the fund's board reserves the right to limit net withdrawal and subscriptions to 10% of overall net asset value.[12]

METRICS: WHAT IS IMPORTANT AND WHY

Water is a renewable resource; however, a mere 2.9% of Earth's total water content is fresh water, and about 20% of this is tied up in glaciers.[13] The amount of utilizable fresh water is measurable, and the reality of its scarcity necessitates the most efficient use of this resource. Proper treatment of wastewater is a vital step in the effort to conserve and maximize utility; as a result, it has become a growing focus of considerable investment by Pictet. Across all sectors and companies, the Water Fund has about 40% of its current holdings in wastewater management at various levels, as this sector is expected to grow fastest in coming years from increasing private investment, especially in southeast Asia.[14] Insufficient treatment of wastewater has multiple levels of environmental consequences, as hormones in human waste end up in rivers and lakes and diminish fish populations while precious fresh water often drains into oceans and becomes unusable.

Rohner views the water market as four distinct blocs: operators, systems integrators, equipment suppliers, and consumable suppliers.[15] Pictet employs a "defensive holdings" strategy by focusing on water systems operators instead of water technology, since utilities have more modest but sustainable profit margins. GWI, a company that tracks the total price of stock investments in water worldwide, announced a 9% increase in the Global Water Index in June of 2010, the largest jump since April 2009, which was driven primarily by the United States.[16]

One way to determine which companies are appropriate for investment, according to Portner, is based on the enterprise multiple: the sum of a business's market capitalization and total debt minus cash and marketable securities over its earnings before interest, taxes, and amortization.[17] In other words, the ratio of a company's enterprise value over its gross earnings is examined and considered the "minimum price an acquirer must pay for a dollar of gross earnings." Other key qualities sought in a company are liquidity of its assets and overall size, as a tiny firm will not hold enough value.

PICTET'S INVESTMENTS

Limiting its investments to publicly traded companies while looking for potential long-term growth, Pictet's investments currently are diffused across several key companies. The single largest is American Water Works, with 4.5% of total fund investment. Providing services such as drinking water and wastewater disposal to approximately 16 million people in North America, this is the largest investor-owned water utility company in the United States, in terms of people served and revenue generated,[18] with 5% of U.S. residents utilizing some form of its water-related services. In line with Pictet's growing interest in wastewater, American Water Works has increasingly focused on this sector for residential, commercial, and industrial consumers, building and operating treatment systems and repair services as well as improving infrastructure in the utilities sector. Subsidiaries providing any water-related services are subject to regulation by the states in which they operate.

As its largest single investment, American Water Works is attractive to Pictet, and perhaps rightly so. Founded in 1886, the sheer size of this long-established company is impressive. In the 12 months preceding September 2010, it saw revenue of $2.64 billion and a gross profit of $1.12 billion, with an enterprise value of $9.91 billion as of November 2010.[19] American Water Works focuses efforts on improving technology, providing granular activated carbon for water purification, and managing the disposal of biosolids.[20] With clients ranging from local utility companies to real estate developers, as well as across big industries and developing communities, its services are well diversified. This enterprise also enters into public-private partnerships throughout various sectors, a relationship preferred by Pictet due to lower operating costs, and perhaps preferred for political motives as well, due to the resistance toward total privatization in recent years.[21]

Pictet's second largest investment is in Suez Environment, a French company that specializes in the treatment and management of wastewater as well as the production and distribution of drinking water. This large organization has enjoyed stable returns in its domestic market and is anticipating growth in emerging markets. Much like American Water Works, Suez operates through numerous smaller subsidiaries across 35 countries.[22] These diversified holdings, along with stability and growth potential, are the main reasons for Pictet's interest; in addition, Suez's focus on sustainable wastewater treatment is consistent with Pictet's view that this methodology is a crucial solution to future limited fresh water availability.

Suez Environment has committed itself to the preservation of natural resources and maintenance of biodiversity through sustainable development. Wastewater or contaminated groundwater is collected and managed with the most efficient technologies available. Waste from the sanitization and purification processes is recycled as compost, a sector that saw a 2% increase in recovery rates from 2006 to 2009.[23] This water giant also succeeded in decreasing greenhouse emissions between 2006 and 2009 and increasing production of renewable energy. As of the last fiscal year, Suez attained revenues of over $16 million, with $86 million invested in research and development.

Veolia Environment, with operations in 77 countries, is the world's leading water services and supply company, and currently represents 3% of the Pictet Water Fund's holdings. As a company providing comprehensive water services, Veolia withdraws fresh water from the environment, delivers clean drinking water, and handles wastewater treatment and disposal while assuring that water is either recycled properly or safely released back into the environment. Committed to environmental sustainability and conservation, Veolia maintains efficient management of its water delivery systems and works to conduct operations that limit greenhouse gas emissions and capture renewable energy.

According to Portner, Veolia offers good growth prospects, an attractive share valuation, and exposure to the fast-growing Chinese market, all reasons for being among the largest holdings of the fund. Interests are also diversified over several sectors besides water systems, such as hazardous and solid waste removal and disposal, and industrial maintenance and cleaning services. Veolia chair and CEO Henry Proglio serves on Pictet's Water Fund Advisory Board.

Despite the challenges of breaking into the market in the developing world, one company that has sparked major interest in Pictet is Sabesp, currently a major holding of the fund as well. A private Brazilian water supplier, Sabesp serves São Paulo, the largest city in the Americas and in the southern hemisphere, with a population of over 11 million just in the city proper.[24] With 26.7 million people serviced by either water delivery or sewage systems, Sabesp is one of the largest private water companies in the world.[25] The only business from a developing country in which Pictet has made substantial investments, Sabesp represented 3.6% of the total fund in late 2010.

Like other companies that have grabbed Pictet's attention, Sabesp attempts to prevent water waste while keeping up with the continuous expansion of the population it serves; impressively, it has accomplished this goal since its inception in 1994. Armed with a strong financial portfolio, Sabesp also seeks economic sustainability and social responsibility. The recipient of various governmental and organizational awards for providing clean drinking water across economic strata, among other accomplishments, Sabesp conducts community outreach programs aimed at educating youths on both water and environmental conservation.

Some examples of newly made investments or reinvestments by Pictet include Idex Technologies, which has demonstrated strong secular growth in diagnostics for metering the flow of liquid pumps involved in water treatment systems; Aalberts Industries, with specialized industrial products for flow control, which show potential for increasing margins; and Valmont Technologies, with promising sales in center pivot irrigation for agriculture.

COMPANIES PICTET HAS *NOT* INVESTED IN, AND WHY

In a change from its initial approach, Pictet has sold most of its holdings in bottled-water producers such as Nestlé and Danone, predicting a decrease in global sales as concern over the environmental impacts of plastic waste takes hold in developed countries while developing countries seek regionalized production in order to lower associated packaging and delivery costs.[26] The United Kingdom's market has also posed challenges for private investors, as the regulatory environment has become "less comfortable," according to Rohner, since the country maintains "a high level of control over pricing and tariffs."[27] Holdings in the British market have therefore been reduced.

In the water technology sector, Pictet recently lowered investments in water solutions provider Pentair "due to a decrease in US consumer spending, in ITT (water & industrial services) due to a fall in their backlog, and in Flowserve on relative valuation." "If you look at Pictet, we just do asset management and are not entangled with any major problems that may be facing the industry. We are a private partnership with no debt," says Laurent Ramsey, CEO of Pictet Funds, who is charged with developing and selling products for the private bank's distribution arm.[28]

PERFORMANCE REVIEW

With over two centuries of expertise in banking, Pictet is a well-established financial institution, having drawn solid investors seeking stability for years. Recently, the company has recognized both environmental potential and financial opportunity and has become a pioneer with substantial resources in the field of sustainable investment. In October 2010, GWI praised Pictet Water Fund as a sound investment, reporting a 9% growth spurt in the water market and encouraging "anyone looking to mount a bid" to "get into bed with the two largest shareholders—Invesco and Pictet—who between them hold nearly 20%."[29] A considerable change from early skepticism at the start of the millennium, GWI's acclaim reflects a global market trend that will continue long into the future as demand continues to rise while technology and efficiencies follow suit.

Compared to the rest of the world, Europe leads the way toward sustainable investing, and Pictet was even slightly ahead of its continent's trend. From 2005 to 2007, total equities in environmental and ecological funds in Europe jumped from 0.6% to 15%.[30] Pictet initiated multiple equity theme funds devoted solely to this purpose (some before 2005), many of which have received awards for outstanding performance. Such recognition has been provided by diverse groups such as Asiainvestor, Lipper, and Morningstar.

Fund managers and other businesses everywhere globally are starting to catch on to this trend, many maintaining a certain percentage of sustainable investment. Pictet is a giant step ahead of the herd. An option for any Pictet investor to allocate a sustainable portion to their overall holdings increases overall attractiveness, whether the motives to invest arise from environmentalist ideals or from the perception that anything "sustainable" offers steady returns with lower risk.

At the end of 2007, Pictet Asset Management as a whole managed approximately $126 billion, a figure that has remained relatively constant through late 2010, despite high market volatility in recent years.[31] From inception, Pictet Water Fund has seen cumulative positive performance of 51.7%, while the MSCI World has lost over 15% of its value over the same period. According to Rohner, Pictet has strongly outperformed this MSCI index; investors would have lost 3.5% a year while Pictet gained on average 4% annually.[32] The company's total expense ratio is 2%. And according to GWI, Pictet Water Fund it is "not particularly high risk or volatile," with "both income and growth characteristics, and a reliable dividend stream."

SUMMARY

In an interview in 2002, Rohner discussed global prospects for the privatization of water in developing countries; he claimed that the United States and Europe were rapidly heading toward something like more than 50% privatization. This trend would help make Pictet's stated goal of sustainability through improved technology easier to implement in these markets. Invested companies would then have the necessary flexibility and opportunities to have a chance to become fully established. Although this prediction has failed to materialize rapidly, a slow trend toward privatization suits Pictet well, especially given the ongoing political, financial, and infrastructure issues that surround assuming absolute control of water systems. In coming years, public-private partnerships might gain trust and acceptance by both government and the public, recognized as a beneficial means to help improve water technology for growing populations in the face of shrinking resources. As far as prospects for investors, Portner predicts returns on water of 8% annually through 2020.

Future prospects in the developing world also remain a lingering question. Geographic areas most in need of large-scale infrastructure investments can be assisted by investment funds otherwise not available through local government funding or otherwise. By encouraging conservative management of a precious resource and diffusing access across populations, institutions such as Pictet have the power and position to change the status quo in the parts of the globe most in need while providing key ongoing opportunities for investors.

NOTES

1. Food and Agriculture Organization, UN Water Statistics, "Water Resources," 2010. www.unwater.org/statistics_use.html
2. Kishan Saijel and Madelene Pearson, "Water Outperforms Oil, Luring Picket, GE's Immelt" (Update 1), Bloomberg News, June 26, 2006. www.bloomberg.com/apps/news?pid=newsarchiveandsid=a823kgVOs5Zoandrefer=canada

3. Food and Agriculture Organization, "Water News: Climate Change and Water," Graph: "Estimated World Water Use." www.fao.org/nr/water/news/climchange.html

4. Marie Maitre, "Pictet Sees Gold in Water-Related Stocks." Reuters UK, 2007. http://uk.reuters.com/article/idUKNOA32934020070323

5. Denis Schmidli, "Pictet—Communication: Water Is One of the Strategic Resources of the 21st Century," 2010. www.pictet.com/en/home/communications/pictet_press/water_source.html

6. Beverly Goodman, "10 Questions with Pictet Global Water Fund's Philip Rohmer," *The Street*, 2002. www.thestreet.com/story/10043555/10-questions-with-pictet-global-water-funds-philip-rohmer.html

7. Schmidli, "Pictet—Communication: Water Is One of the Strategic Resources of the 21st Century."

8. Ibid.

9. Andrew T. Gillies, "The Water Business Boils Down," *Forbes*, February 20, 2002. www.forbes.com/2002/02/20/0220sf.html

10. Goodman, "10 Questions with Pictet Global Water Fund's Philip Rohmer."

11. National Association of Water Companies, Submission of the United States to the Round Table on Competition and Regulation of Water Supply, DAFFE/COMP/ WP2/WD 11.4, February 2004. www.ftc.gov/. . ./international/. . ./2004–Roundtable%20on%20Competition%20and%20Regulation.pdf

12. "Pictet Launches Water Fund," FINalternatives, April 23, 2008. www.finalternatives.com/node/4169

13. Steve Graham, Claire Parkinson, and Mous Chahine, "The Water Cycle," NASA Earth Observatory, October 1, 2010. http://earthobservatory.nasa.gov/Features/Water/

14. Kishan Saijel and Madelene Pearson, "Water Outperforms Oil, Luring Pickens, GE's Immelt," Bloomberg News, 2006. www.bloomberg.com/apps/news?pid=newsarchiveandsid=a823kgVOs5Zoandrefer=canada

15. Patrick Collinson, "Pictet Taps into Rising Water Levels," Fund Strategy: Features, June 21, 2010. www.fundstrategy.co.uk/opinion/patrick-collinson/pictet-taps-into-rising-water-levels/1013650.article

16. Ibid.

17. Andrew T. Gillies, "The Water Business Boils Down," *Forbes*, February 20, 2002. www.forbes.com/2002/02/20/0220sf.html

18. American Water Works company site, FAQs. www.amwater.com/About-Us/faqs.html

19. Capital IQ, AWK Key Statistics, American Water Works Company, Inc., Stock—Yahoo! Finance. http://finance.yahoo.com/q/ks?s=AWK+Key+Statistics

20. AWK Profile, American Water Works Company, Inc., Stock—Yahoo! Finance. http://finance.yahoo.com/q/pr?s=AWK+Profile

21. Many see the privatization of water systems as a beneficial way to improve public access to clean water, generate revenue, and reduce overconsumption; others argue that forcing people to pay for this essential resource, especially

in poor countries, is not ethical. Also, the infamous Cochabamba Water Wars of 2000 in Bolivia drew massive international attention, signaling the repercussions of a costly development project that increased access but raised each household's monthly water bill to an amount few could afford. As the middle ground, public-private partnerships are becoming more commonplace, often incorporating benefits from both systems.

22. Suez company site, Suez 2009 Reference Document. www.gdfsuez.com/document/?f=files/en/gdf-suez-ddr09-vus-interactif.pdf

23. Suez company site, "Suez Environment: 2009 Sustainable Development Brochure." www.suez-environnement.com/en/profile/corporate-publications/corporate-publications/

24. Instituto Brasileiro de Geografia e Estatistica, Census 2010. www.ibge.gov.br

25. Sabesp company site. http://site.sabesp.com.br/site/interna/Default.aspx?secaoId=3

26. Elena Logutenkova, "Pictet Prefers Wastewater That 'Stinks' to Perrier, Evian," *Bloomberg News*, March 14, 2010. www.bloomberg.com/apps/news?pid=newsarchive&sid=ajlNVk6fUsQM

27. Collinson, "Pictet Taps into Rising Water Levels."

28. Yuri Bender, "Pictet Targets Cash Conversions for Funds," Private Wealth Management, September 2, 2010. www.pwmnet.com/news/fullstory.php/aid/2983/Pictet_targets_cash_conversions_for_funds.html?current_page=1

29. "Water Index Posts 9% Monthly Gain," *Global Water Intelligence* 11, No. 10 (October 2010). www.globalwaterintel.com/archive/11/10/gwi-water-index/water-index-posts-9-monthly-gain.html

30. S. Johnson, "Fears over Rush into Green Funds," *Financial Times* (London), September 24, 2007. Adapted from C. Krosinsky, p 10.

31. "Pictet Launches Water Fund."

32. Collinson, "Pictet Taps into Rising Water Levels."

CHAPTER 14

Inflection Point Capital Management and Strategically Aware Investing

Matthew J. Kiernan

Building on his experience running sustainability research provider Innovest, Matthew Kiernan now puts his money where his mouth is, managing Inflection Point Capital Management. Here's a rundown on the company's approach, preceded by his plea for common sense, via investing that is simply strategically aware.

Inflection Point Capital Management portfolios are constructed in stages, progressively adding streams of analytical inputs. The company utilizes seven different alpha source inputs and signals, and the process is outlined toward the end of this chapter.

Here's a radical and counterintuitive proposition for you: What the sustainable finance and investment field desperately needs at this critical juncture is—wait for it—*another* acronym!

A casual observer might well have thought that with socially responsible investing (SRI); corporate social responsibility (CSR); environmental, social, and governance (ESG); responsible investing (RI); and sustainable investing (SI) already in hand, we were already amply provisioned in this regard. Well, we're *not*. In fact, I think that we desperately need one more, and adopting the right one just might alleviate some of both the intellectual and commercial anarchy of the current situation, where everyone clamors for more "mainstreaming" while the mainstream itself seems sublimely content with leisurely (glacial?) movement at best.

I truly believe that one of the primary causes of this excruciatingly slow rate of uptake of sustainability factors by mainstream investors (but by no means the only one) is the enormous confusion and conflation between and among the alphabet soup of acronyms in common use today. The sad result has been the stigmatization of most if not all of the acronyms by mainstream asset owners and their traditional advisors and asset managers. A number of perfectly robust sustainability strategies have in effect been babies thrown out with metaphorical bathwater.

This situation would not be so alarming were it not for the bizarre and pernicious real-world consequences that it has spawned. Ponder for a moment just a few of the most outrageous results of the almost Pavlovian rejection of all of the cited acronyms, tarring them all with the same brush:

Some of the world's largest and most prestigious foundations give away literally hundreds of millions of dollars worth of grant money to advance environmental and social causes each year while having fully 95% of their assets invested without even the faintest regard for their environmental or social impacts, which could easily be—and often is—undoing all of their good work on the program side.

The same is true for the staff pension funds of both the United Nations (UN) and the World Bank, despite the enormous efforts that both organizations devote to ameliorating environmental and social conditions worldwide. In the case of the former, the UN came within a hair's breadth in 2006 of not signing its own UN Principles for Responsible Investment (PRI). (I am not making this up.)

By some estimates, less than 2% of the assets pledged to support—and implement—the UN PRI are currently subject to a consistent, systematic assessment of their environmental and social impacts or risk. Sadly, some of the most derelict signatories still can be found adorning the podiums of SI/RI conferences, professing their undying devotion to the principles. This, folks, is not good.

So what is the new, silver-bullet acronym? Well, I propose SAI, which stands for "strategically aware investing." Words matter, and if sustainability concerns could be shorn of their historical, ideological, and emotional baggage—on all sides—we'd all be a good deal further ahead, and so would global environmental and social conditions, not to mention investor returns.

STRATEGICALLY AWARE INVESTING

Just think about the various global megatrends currently reshaping the competitive landscape for both companies and their investors:

- The dramatically increased complexity, transparency, and velocity of change in companies' competitive environments, which places an unprecedented premium on strategic management and innovation skills as well as corporate adaptability and responsiveness
- Substantially increased demand for energy as well as water and other critical natural resources, driven by a combination of explosive population growth, urbanization, industrialization, demographic shifts, and growing consumer affluence and consumption, particularly in emerging markets
- A general decline in both the credibility and the financial capacity of governments worldwide, with a corresponding increase in the necessity for corporations to shoulder more of the responsibility for tackling environmental and social challenges
- Substantially increased stakeholder expectations for improved sustainability performance from both companies and investors, accompanied by much greater information transparency with which to assess that performance and more effective communications tools with which to disseminate criticism
- An inexorable shift in the world's center of economic gravity toward emerging markets, where sustainability-driven risks and opportunities are greatest
- Growing threats to social and political stability, driven by income inequality and public health issues such as HIV/AIDS and malaria
- The incipient trend among state and sovereign wealth funds, especially in Asia, to diversify and internationalize their investment strategies in search of the higher returns necessary to provide adequate retirement and health benefits for rapidly aging populations
- The emergence of a new fiduciary paradigm for investors, requiring much greater transparency and attention to sustainability issues

Now, few if any thoughtful investors would dispute the existence or direction of these megatrends. Some will undoubtedly even claim that they are already taking them on board. But we're talking here about taking them on board in a meaningful, *systematic* way. This means, inescapably, two things: new analytical models and tools, and company-specific research—across a substantial potential investment universe.

None of these megatrends (or companies' responses to them) can be captured adequately in traditional analysis of price/earnings ratios, balance sheets, or consensus forward earnings estimates. In that very narrow sense, they are "extrafinancial" factors. But labeling or dismissing them as such in no way mitigates their capacity to propel companies to the top of their industry league tables or to eviscerate them entirely. For a recent example, think BP.

So: Is paying careful—and systematic—attention to these secular global megatrends a particularly controversial or ideological act? No, it's simply strategically aware investing—SAI. Perhaps if it could be rebranded and conceived as such rather than stigmatized or ghettoized as ESG/RI/SI investing, more institutions and asset managers might actually try it. Even more important, so might the legion of asset consultants and advisors who currently wield grossly disproportionate power and generally abuse it by reflexively discouraging their clients from using *any* of the acronym investment styles. Who knows, if they did, both the planet and their risk-adjusted returns would likely be the better for it!

BEYOND ENVIRONMENTAL, SOCIAL, AND GOVERNANCE TOWARD A NEW MODEL OF CORPORATE SUSTAINABILITY

The dominant current convention in this area is to equate corporate sustainability with ESG factors. While each of these three dimensions is unquestionably an important component of the sustainability dynamic, even taken together, they are not, in my view, sufficient. I believe that a single-minded and exclusive focus on ESG has had at least two pernicious effects:

1. It has blinded advocates and critics alike to several other corporate sustainability drivers that are of at least equal importance.
2. In so doing, it has lost an important opportunity to bridge the two solitudes of sustainability and mainstream finance and to accelerate their necessary—and inevitable—convergence.

What are these missing pieces of the corporate sustainability puzzle? In my view, the two most important are companies' innovation capacity and their adaptability and responsiveness.

In today's complex, high-speed, multistakeholder, competitive environment, companies lacking those two critical capabilities are courting the very real risk of impairment or even extinction, no matter how strong they might be on ESG factors. (Of course, all five attributes can often be found—or

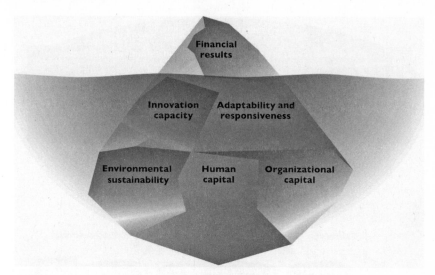

FIGURE 14.1   Five-Factor Model of Inflection Point Capital Management
Source: Inflection Point Capital Management.

absent—together.) I would, therefore, propose strengthening the conventional three-factor ESG definition of corporate sustainability with a new, five-factor model:

Corporate sustainability is about more than just ESG. (See Figure 14.1.),

While it would be overreaching to claim that these five factors explain the *entirety* of the 75% to 80% of companies' true risk profile and value potential that financial statements cannot capture, I believe that they come a good deal closer than ESG factors alone. And the two "new" factors: innovation capacity and adaptability—have two additional virtues: They actually can be linked directly and empirically with alpha generation,[1] and they are intuitively plausible (unlike ESG factors) to *mainstream* analysts and investors.

PORTFOLIO CONSTRUCTION

Just to be abundantly clear, however, while sustainability factors are an essential and necessary input to any sensible, twenty-first-century investment strategy, they are not, however, sufficient by themselves. Two further preconditions must be met:

1. Sustainability analysis must be complemented by, and integrated with, traditional financial analysis. The most "sustainable" company in the

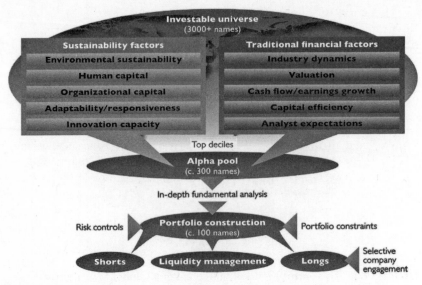

FIGURE 14.2 Investment Process of Inflection Point Capital Management
Source: Inflection Point Capital Management.

world will not generate attractive returns for investors if, for example, it is grossly overpriced or has a profoundly suboptimal level of capital efficiency.

2. That integration must occur from the outset. Unfortunately, it remains far more common today for one of the two key analytical pillars (usually it is the sustainability side) to be simply bolted on after the "real" work of the "proper" financial analysis has been done. Even if the sustainability research is of high quality and generated internally (both are heroic assumptions), merely tacking it on ex post facto trivializes the sustainability factors and is virtually guaranteed to produce suboptimal results.

A schematic representation of a more robust approach is offered in Figure 14.2.

INVESTMENT PROCESS

Portfolios of Inflection Point Capital Management (IPCM) are constructed in stages, progressively adding "streams" of analytical inputs. We utilize eight different alpha source inputs and signals:

1. Quantitative sustainability
2. Quantitative fundamental

3. Qualitative sustainability
4. Qualitative fundamental
5. Quantitative sustainability delta technical analysis
6. Industry sector views
7. Traditional price action technical analysis
8. Currency adjustments

Our portfolio construction process proceeds in sequential steps.

1. Our overall investment universe is a group of approximately 2,500 publicly traded large and mid-cap securities, diversified by both industry sector and geographic region, and selected to maximize liquidity. Those securities are drawn from our benchmark, the MSCI All Country World Index (ACWI).
2. We rate these securities based on the relative quantitative sustainability metrics in our proprietary factor model. To maximize the robustness of these ratings, we utilize at least three leading third-party specialist research providers. In reaching a single, composite score for each security, we apply a proprietary weighting algorithm that reflects our house view of the relative strengths, weaknesses, and merits of each provider, based on our 15-plus years of experience in this research field. The nature of the sustainability analysis is long term (three to five years).
3. We then apply a second layer of ratings based on approximately 20 traditional quantitative fundamental metrics (with a significant tilt toward value rather than toward growth). The nature of the fundamental analysis is medium term (one to two years).
4. The sustainability and fundamental ratings from steps 2 and 3 are then blended into a combined rating, and all 2,500 securities are then ranked from top to bottom.
5. For our long-only portfolios, we extract a subset of the highest-scoring companies from step 4.

    The size of this subset is typically 200 securities. This becomes the long-only portion of our Alpha Pool, which will be narrowed further at a later stage, using more detailed, qualitative analysis of both fundamental and sustainability factors.
6. For our long-short portfolios, we extract a subset of both the highest- and lowest- scoring companies from step 4. The size of the overall Alpha Pool is typically 200 names on the long side, and an additional 100 on the short side

Now, working solely within the Alpha Pool:

7. We perform detailed qualitative analysis of both sustainability and financial factors. At this stage, the sustainability analysis utilizes IPCM's

proprietary five-factor model. A separate score is created for each of the two dimensions for each company.

8. We next apply sustainability rating delta analysis (sustainability technical analysis), which consists of measuring trend/reversion signals of our historical quantitative sustainability rating changes since 2005. (This step adds a dynamic, multiyear trend perspective to the static current ratings developed in step 2). We then convert these results into an additional set of scores. The nature of this analysis is medium term (one to two years)

9. This is the stage at which we incorporate our views on the medium-term financial performance prospects of the various industry sectors. If we have strong positive or negative views on particular sectors, we adjust the portfolio positions accordingly.

10. We then apply traditional price action technical analysis of trend, volatility, and overbought/oversold conditions. We convert these into scores. The nature of this analysis is short term (1 to 12 months)

11. We then apply currency adjustments for the purpose of (a) reducing beta via limiting the impact of adverse exchange-rate movements on foreign equity holdings and (b) generating alpha from tactical foreign exchange views via adjusting country weightings. The nature of this analysis is short term (1 to 12 months).

12. At this stage, each security in the Alpha Pool has eight parallel scores, assessing these factors:
    a. Quantitative sustainability
    b. Quantitative fundamental
    c. Qualitative (five-factor) sustainability
    d. Qualitative fundamental
    e. Sustainability delta
    f. Industry sector views
    g. Technical price action
    h. Currency adjustments

13. Proprietary weights are then applied to each of the eight ratings, to create the final combined ranking of each security.

14. These combined final security scores are ranked from top to bottom.

15. For the long-only portfolios, the highest-ranked securities are selected to establish positions.

16. For the long-short portfolios, the highest-ranked securities and lowest-ranked securities are selected to establish positions.

17. For the long-short portfolios, the threshold between long and short positions is demarked, depending on the net directional bias sought, and a final long-short portfolio of approximately 80 to 100 securities is created, for review by the investment committee.

18. The investment committee must ratify all positions before the trades are executed.
19. The resulting final, netted positions are then executed in the market-place.
20. The portfolios are monitored carefully in real time, to ensure that the desired exposures and risk parameters are being maintained. To minimize trading costs and adverse tax implications for clients in the absence of major adjustments that may be required in exceptional circumstances, the portfolios generally are rebalanced quarterly at most. Our targeted portfolio turnover is typically in the 30-40% range, which is substantially lower than the norm.
21. Once the investments have been made, we also "engage" selectively with companies in our long portfolios. We do so in cases where we believe that we can make an effective contribution to companies' sustainability performance where such interventions can realistically create additional shareholder value, within the investment horizon of our funds (3–5 years).

SUMMARY

It is my devout hope that this style of a sustainability model, built into a truly integrated methodology and framework for portfolio construction, will make this approach considerably more user-friendly and attractive to mainstream investors. If it does, and if it thereby helps accelerate the necessary rapprochement between the two currently warring camps of mainstream and social investors, a great leap forward will have occurred (with apologies to Chairman Mao). Until and unless this rapprochement does occur, however, sustainability investment may be doomed to remain a peripheral, marginal phenomenon in the global capital markets, and its extraordinary transformational—and profitability—potential will remain unfulfilled.

NOTE

1. While a discussion and demonstration of this alpha generation is well beyond the scope of this short chapter, the author would welcome reader inquiries and further discussion. Please write to mjk@inflectionpointcm.com

CHAPTER 15

Environmental Metrics

James Salo

It's a real pleasure whenever I get to let my colleague Jamie do the talking. When it comes to sustainability and ESG, the state of the data industry is in a state of flux. Standards are lacking and the data industry is rapidly consolidating, ironically perhaps at the exact time when this sort of information has never been more important.

Environmental performance metrics are a unique and potentially valuable if not essential resource to investors. They provide a direct measure of the efficiency of companies to deliver goods and services to the market by highlighting resources required and waste generated. They provide an indication of compliance costs as well as ongoing risks from current and future regulation, litigation, and reputational challenges. Perhaps most important, they can offer insight into strategic positioning and organizational capacity to adapt and innovate during changing times.

Recent research warns that costs associated with climate change could increase investment portfolio risk by 10% over the next 20 years as a result of new regulations, extreme weather events, and other associated impacts.[1]

Investors, going forward, will need to be equipped with data and tools which can help them traverse the changing landscape and take advantage of market opportunities.

THEORETICAL AND PRACTICAL NEEDS FOR SUSTAINABLE INVESTMENT

Sustainable investment is an approach to investment that systematically integrates environmental, social, and economic factors into the long-term valuation of assets.[2] Therefore, the practice of sustainable investment requires the blending of financially material environmental performance measures into the applied investment management strategy in order to maximize long-term returns.[3]

In order to apply this approach, the sustainable investor must:

1. Identify the most important areas of environmental performance for each asset held or considered.
2. Develop an understanding of the drivers of value and risk for the important areas of environmental performance identified to allow for data collection and measurement.
3. Standardize and prioritize the environmental performance data to allow for the inclusion of the valuation and/or asset comparison, ultimately allowing investment integration with social and economic factors.

Identifying the Most Important Areas of Environmental Performance for Each Asset

Thousands of different environmental metrics could be utilized for investment decision making. However, the sustainable investor needs to be able to focus on the areas of environmental performance that will most significantly affect the long-term value of each asset. The overall significance and areas of environmental performance for a particular asset will depend significantly on the asset type (equity, bond, commodity, real estate, insurance, and cash/currency), the sector(s) of operations, and the specific economic-generating activities conducted. In addition, each organization has its own particular products and services, legal and regulatory exposure, data collection and management systems, and/or environmental impacts.

Understanding the Underpinning Drivers of Value in Each Area of Material Environmental Performance

While the specific environmental performance metrics that are most important to the value/risk of investable assets can differ significantly, the areas of derived value can be classified into several broad performance areas.

Operational Efficiency   Enhanced environmental efficiencies in organizational operations and supply chains can reduce costs and increase profitability. This is true both for input requirements (price of energy or required natural resources) and outputs generated (waste disposal, pollution, and any associated regulatory compliance/violation costs). Organizational capability to measure and manage resource needs, waste, and emissions generated is very important.

Organizational Adaptability and Innovation Capability   Organizational research and development capabilities, strategic positioning, and organizational ability to adapt can position companies to take advantage of potential environmental innovation opportunities. This is true both for direct operations and within supply chains. The ability to adapt to the changing pressures caused by the effects of climate change, pollution, resource scarcity, and changes in consumer demand, in addition to minimizing future environmental risk exposure (regulation, litigation, financing/underwriting costs, etc.), will increase the long-term value of the organization and its investors' holdings. Organizational measurement and analysis is important to this as it will allow for better management decision making.

Branding/Reputation   Benefits associated with greater awareness and public perception of environmental performance credentials can include:

- Sparking interest among retail and institutional consumers by associating with a set of desirable values to differentiate the product from the competition
- Improved stakeholder relations
- Greater employee recruitment and retention

However, environmental reputation is not controlled solely by the company. Other contributors to a company's image include stakeholders like the news media, journalists, labor unions, environmental organizations, and other nongovernmental organizations (NGOs), which can negatively brand the organization if it fails to meet stakeholders' environmental performance expectations.

Standardizing and Prioritizing Each Area of Environmental Performance to Allow Investment Integration

Sustainable investors need a way to compare environmental performance data that likely differ in importance across a universe of assets and to blend these data with other financially material investment criteria. Currently, the metrics used to blend environmental performance with social and other economic factors occurs through either monetization or ratings.

The monetization of environmental performance allows for the most straightforward integration with other financial measures and allows many different kinds of environmental performance metrics to be valued financially and be summed, compared, and prioritized by both managers and sustainable investors. However, this process of monetization requires very detailed performance information and the application of many underpinning assumptions for valuation calculation, making this process quite labor and resource intensive. Trucost, this author's employer, has worked with a panel of leading environmental economists to create a unique database that quantifies environmental impacts of investable assets and places a cost on them to allow for easy assessment and integration.[4] For investors, environmental costs can be apportioned by the total value held of each asset, allowing for portfolio-level assessments that can highlight the areas that are most and least exposed to environmental costs.

A number of international research efforts are also focused on monetizing environmental performance. These efforts include Lord Stern's *Review on the Economics of Climate Change*, the 2010 report of the United Nations (UN) *Universal Ownership: Why Environmental Externalities Matter to Institutional Investors*, and the work of TEEB (The Economics of Ecosystems and Biodiversity), which provides tools for citizens, businesses, and policy makers to improve the valuation of ecosystem services, biodiversity, and environmental impacts.[5]

An alternative to the monetization of environmental performance is benchmark ratings. These ratings often use a graded scale, similar to investment credit ratings, to rate assets with letter grades (A–F) or numerical scales (1–100). These graded performance ratings are produced by both private research companies and NGOs. Environmental performance ratings are examined further in the next section.

AVAILABLE DATA AND METRICS

As mentioned, there are thousands of different environmental performance metrics that investors can use to evaluate investible assets. Two major sources of data are available to investors: public disclosures and third-party research/databases. A third source of data used to evaluate corporations is membership information and especially adherence to voluntary guidelines and initiatives (e.g., the Ceres principles or the broader United Nations Global Compact).[6]

Public Disclosure

Public disclosure is the first major category of environmental performance information available to investors. Many companies voluntarily self-report environmental performance data in their annual reports. Over 7,500 companies have published reports that include information on environmental performance, corporate social responsibility, or sustainability, according to the corporateregister.com. Almost 3,750 reports were published in 2009 (700+ first-time reports), a considerable growth from roughly 500 total reports in 1998. Of course, in addition to company reports that may have environmental performance data included, many companies disclose data directly on their Web sites and provide data to third parties.

While the number of reports that include environmental performance data is considerable and is continuing to grow, it is still a very small number when compared to the total number of public companies. Even when companies do disclose, the contents of sustainability reports may have little value to the sustainable investor because the information in these reports is almost exclusively voluntary. Companies may choose not to disclose the environmental performance data that are most material to their business, and investors then end up with incomparable, nonstandardized, and financially insignificant information.

The Global Reporting Initiative (GRI) is a multistakeholder effort to provide some focus to company reports; currently it includes 30 suggested areas of environmental performance disclosure.[7] The idea for a global reporting standard is a good one. If all companies disclosed these metrics in a standardized and comprehensive way, the sustainable investor would have some good data on which to base investment decisions. However, there are limitations with regard to the number of companies reporting using the GRI (under 1,800 reports in 2010, only 180 in the United States) and the number of the GRI metrics each company chooses to voluntarily report on. The GRI has three declared reporting levels and all but the highest (A) level requires the disclosure of only one environment metric toward the total required, so a company can pick and choose to avoid environmental metrics.[8] Reporting at the A level requires an organization to report on 17 core environmental areas, which just over 500 companies did in 2010.

Since reporting is almost exclusively voluntary, even when companies do disclose on similar areas of environmental performance, there still is a considerable amount of variation in the sophistication of the data. For example, reported greenhouse gas emissions data may cover only individual emissions (carbon dioxide only, not methane, nitrous oxide, etc.), may include only emissions from a percent of the total operations of the company, or may include only emissions from direct operations, electricity, and purchased goods and services, or a combination of the three. Clarity and completeness of company-reported information is very important in order for environmental performance metrics to be useful to the sustainable investor.

Third-Party Research/Databases

The second major category of environmental performance information available to investors is third-party research/databases. Because of the increased amount of disclosure and the resources required to appraise it accurately, there is a growing need for a way for investors to access and evaluate such data. A number of third-party companies and NGOs produce environmental performance ratings to fill that need. Over 100 different ratings exist that examine different areas of corporate performance, and about 80% of these include environmental performance metrics.[9] These ratings are of varying sophistication, quality, comprehensiveness, and focus. However, they do provide the sustainable investor with a compiled set of data to work with, which would be difficult to achieve by using company disclosures alone.

Private environment, social, and governance (ESG) research organizations are one of the major aggregators and providers of environmental performance data. These include Sustainalytics, MSCI (including the legacy KLD and Innovest data sets), EIRIS, ASSET4 (Thomson Reuters), and Oekom Corporate Ratings. Increasingly, NGOs are also conducting environmental performance rating assessments; examples are Climate Counts' Company Score Cards and the Carbon Disclosure Project's Carbon Leadership Indexes. To create their ratings, these organizations rely on a combination of public disclosures, feedback from companies on questionnaires, and proprietary rating models to collect and analyze environmental performance data.

Trucost is a specialized environmental data company that aggregates and standardizes disclosed company environmental impact data, discarding any data that is misleading and filling in data gaps using a sophisticated multisector impact profiling model. Further, it prioritizes areas of environmental performance by monetizing the environmental impacts to allow investors to see the total environmental cost of each company. I want to emphasize this because this is one rare source of standardized, quantitative, and complete data that can be readily integrated into a financial assessment of the risks and opportunities of companies across a large research universe.

Recently, there has been a growing trend to create ratings based on a combination of third-party research providers. These include the *Newsweek* Green Rankings of companies, the Global 100 Most Sustainable Corporations in the World, CSRHUB's Company Ratings (based on 90+ data sources), and Goodguide's product ratings. These rankings are useful as they provide a high-level benchmark for overall performance, but they lack disclosure of their underlying sophistication, which is required for sustainable investors to be able integrate measures of environmental performance directly into their own investment research. Another notable benchmark is GreenBiz's annual State of Green Business Report, which reviews a number of important environmental performance measures, from energy efficiency to e-waste, and whether progress is being made.[10]

Of course, in each case, these third-party research/databases are limited by the information available to them. About one-third rely solely on publicly disclosed information, another third on surveys and directly provided information, and the final third on a combination of data sources.[11] It is worth emphasizing that company involvement is essential in the collection of environmental performance data; therefore, there is an increasing need for transparency and for third-party validation of environmental performance.

CHALLENGES AND OPPORTUNITIES MOVING FORWARD

We have already identified a number of challenges posed when trying to integrate environmental performance into a sustainable investment strategy: the lack of availability of comprehensive and consistent data, the need to identify and gather the material data from the low-quality/materiality noise, the need for standardization, and the need for valuing/integrating the data with other financially material information. Next we focus specifically on several key areas where improvement is needed to support the sustainable investor.

Role of Companies: Voluntary Reporting Is Not Nearly Enough

Companies need to play a key role in resolving the issues outlined thus far by collecting and distributing material environmental performance data. However, doing this may pose a significant challenge. Companies may resist disclosing the most material information because there is a cost associated with collecting such data. In addition, they may, perhaps understandably, consider this information to be sensitive, as a source of competitive advantage, or as a trade secret. Recent research has found that current company statements do not provide accurate assessments of environmental liabilities and that companies can understate or omit these disclosures altogether due to lackadaisical reporting standards (if an argument can be made that a reasonable estimate is not feasible).[12] Similarly, disclosure of environmental opportunities may be hindered if there is value creation associated with innovative environmental strategy. Disclosure or transparency could potentially lead to loss of that value by others imitating the strategy or product.

There is a clear tension between companies desiring to profit from innovation and a desire for more disclosure. There are significant challenges to relying solely on voluntary corporate disclosures, but the active involvement of companies is essential. Regulatory inclusion of key environmental performance data in annual reporting to investors is likely the only solution. There have been small steps made in this direction, such as the *Commission Guidance Regarding Disclosure Relating to Climate Change*[13] of the U.S. Security Exchange Commission released in 2010 that requires public companies to disclose to investors material information concerning climate-related risks and opportunities. Regulation requiring disclosure of environmental performance may not be a pipe dream. Governmental bodies, such as the European Commission, are considering mandating ESG disclosures, and investors from around the globe are lobbying for the same.[14]

Need for Sophisticated Accounting Standards

Even with mandated reporting requirements, companies still need a significant amount of guidance to properly account for and report on their key areas of environmental performance. The current development of integrated reporting guidelines and the reporting guidelines available from the GRI offer a starting point for companies.[15] Ultimately, investors should expect environmental data to have the same level of quality as reported financial data. However, this is not currently the case.

The Greenhouse Gas Protocol is a widely accepted method to account for greenhouse gas (GHG) emissions. However, company-reported GHG emissions are not universally standardized or reported in a comprehensive way. Only 400 of the 3,000 companies disclosing to the Carbon Disclosure Project (CDP) in 2010 report greenhouse gas emissions within a 5% certainty range and can support that claim with documentation.[16] The majority of reporting companies does not provide any information about the scope and uncertainty of reported data and may not evaluate it at all.[17] Similarly, the disclosures reported to the CDP vary widely in quality and sophistication. Research organizations like Trucost are needed to aggregate this publicly disclosed data and to work with companies to ensure that high-quality data are reported, specifically through adherence to the Greenhouse Gas Protocol.

Whereas the GHG Protocol provides an excellent accounting and reporting standard for GHG emissions, global standards do not exist for many important areas of environmental performance, including for corporate water use disclosure.[18] A growing number of company-level environmental performance standards are beginning to compete for membership. These include UL's ULE 880 Sustainability standard for Manufacturing Organizations, Green Seal's sustainability standards, and the more broadly used International Organization for Standardization (ISO) 14000 environmental management standard.[19] Overall, there is a great need for sophisticated accounting practices and comprehensive assessment to empower better disclosure of environmental impacts, opportunities for innovation, efficiencies, and savings in addition to risks and liabilities. The lack of standards will hinder the efforts of companies that are trying to disclose meaningful and comparable information.

Supply Chain: Indirect Risks/Opportunities

The evaluation of supply chain environmental performance can offer the sustainable investor further insights important for identifying long-term investment opportunities and risks. The long-term value of organizations is tied to cost they pay for required input commodities and also to the cost of disposal of undesired emissions and waste by-products. For many companies, up to 80% to 90% of total energy, GHG emissions, and water required by the goods and services they sell originate from the supply chain as opposed to from direct operations.[20]

On the input side, oil is a commodity that can significantly impact companies through sudden price hikes. This was felt in 2008 when the price of oil quickly soared above $100 a barrel over worries of peak oil and instability in the Middle East. The price fell in 2009 with the global financial downturn, but in early in 2011 it is again surpassing $100 after the price per barrel jumped almost 50% since 2010. The increasing political instability in the Middle East following the Egyptian revolution of 2011 appears to promise a continued uncertainty on the price of oil, but one that is liable to spike in response to supply threats. An increased price of oil affects almost every sector either directly or indirectly through increased costs from energy or oil-based products. For example, the cost of plastic bottles has increased with the price of oil. The prices of other commodities, including cotton, corn, wheat, sugar, and steel, are volatile and rising sharply.[21]

The increased price of input commodities demands both increased efficiency and reuse where possible. Lowering waste and increasing efficiency also provides output benefits by lowering the cost of waste disposal and decreasing emissions. This is particularly important in markets where emissions are regulated, as with GHG emissions under the European Union

Emissions Trading Scheme (average cost of €14 per metric ton of carbon in 2010).[22]

How can the sustainable investor incorporate a supply chain evaluation into an investment strategy? Currently, this is a challenge because there is a dearth of public information available on companies' supply chain exposure. However, there is considerable interest and momentum in assessing and accounting for supply chain environmental performance. Measurement and disclosure standards are being set through multistakeholder processes, notably the GHG Protocol's three-year process setting emissions accounting and reporting standards for supply chain (Scope 3) and products in use which are due to be finalized in the summer of 2011.[23] Companies and major purchasers are becoming the most significant drivers to collect this information as they push to understand the risks and opportunities in their supply chains. Ambitious efforts have been undertaken by the City of London to assess the carbon footprint associated with 120,000 suppliers and by Wal-Mart, whose supplier sustainability assessment sent to 100,000 firms since late 2009 has sent ripples of action through its supplier companies.[24] The number of company supply chain data collection initiatives is limited but growing, and without standardization, risks leading to supplier survey fatigue, which would harm the quality of the data collected. The U.S. federal government is also in the process of asking suppliers to disclose their GHG emissions, energy, water use, and waste, to enable federal agencies to set improvement targets toward sustainability goals beginning January 31, 2010, as part of a White House executive order.[25] This directive includes laying out how each federal agency will reduce its overall GHG emissions by 30% by 2020.[26] The information increasingly disclosed by suppliers and collected by purchasing organizations then will be shared, allowing sustainable investors to identify more adaptive companies with lower risk and better-managed supply chains.

SUMMARY

Key environmental performance metrics are an essential tool to ensure the effectiveness of sustainable investors. They have a strong potential to drive investment outperformance in the long term by directly identifying efficiency opportunities; reducing regulatory and reputation risk; and improving adaptability, capacity for innovation, strategic positioning, and branding, all of which currently are difficult to recognize or value in the market.

The environmental performance information currently available to investors is limited but growing thanks to many voluntary initiatives and research providers. There is an urgent need for continued focus on quality, completeness in scope, and materiality in disclosure. This may prove difficult without adoption of mandatory reporting requirements for companies. Even then, there will be a continued need for data standardization and validation.

For sustainable investors making investment decisions, environmental performance data provides insights into future winners and losers. Companies are increasingly investing in improving their environmental performance, but there is a disparity between the leaders and the laggards who have not focused on energy cost savings, material efficiency, and risk mitigation. For both companies and investors, it is important to measure financially the value of environmental performance even with its challenges, as there are going to be long-term value benefits to moving early, even with incomplete information.

Environmental performance metrics are providing information that is increasingly important to a firm's long-term ability to succeed. Sustainable investors need to be guided by comprehensive and standardized disclosures on the material risks of environmental impacts, the benefits of investment in research and development to pursue innovation, and the ability of organizations to adapt in a changing competitive and increasingly resource-constrained landscape. By integrating environmental performance data throughout their investments, investors will benefit from improved value into the future.

NOTES

1. www.ifc.org/ifcext/sustainability.nsf/AttachmentsByTitle/p_ClimateChange Survey_report/$FILE/ClimateChangeSurvey_Report.pdf
2. Cary Krosinsky and Nick Robins, eds., *Sustainable Investing: The Art of Long Term Performance* (London, Earthscan, 2008).
3. Unlike arguments for or against the profitability of corporate social responsibility activities or socially responsible investing, the theory for sustainable investment focuses primarily on investing with a lens regarding the most material long-term issues.
4. www.trucost.com/advisory-panel
5. www.hm-treasury.gov.uk/sternreview_index.htm; www.unpri.org/files/6728_ES_report_environmental_externalities.pdf; www.teebweb.org/
6. www.ceres.org/Page.aspx?pid=416. www.unglobalcompact.org/AboutTheGC/TheTenPrinciples/index.html
7. www.globalreporting.org/NR/rdonlyres/DDB9A2EA-7715-4E1A-9047-FD2FA8032762/0/G3_QuickReferenceSheet.pdf

8. The A Level Requires the Reporting of 17 Core Performance Indicators. www.globalreporting.org/ReportingFramework/ApplicationLevels/FAQsApplicationLevels2010.htm

9. www.sustainability.com/library/rate-the-raters-phase-two

10. According to GreenBiz, positive progress is being made in 7 of the 20 evaluated areas; there has been no change in 11 areas; and, in two areas, carbon intensity and e-waste, performance decreased in 2010.

11. www.sustainability.com/library/rate-the-raters-phase-two

12. Rob Bauer and Daniel Hann, "Corporate Environmental Management and Credit Risk," December 23, 2010. Available at Social Science Research Network: ssrn.com/abstract=1660470

13. www.sec.gov/rules/interp/2010/33-9106.pdf

14. www.responsible-investor.com/home/article/eu_close_to_making_corporate/ and www.globalreporting.org/NR/rdonlyres/BA446A5C-613C-4717-B79E-FB5067D87EC9/3924/2010GRIEUNote.pdf. www.socialfunds.com/news/article.cgi/2913.html

15. www.integratedreporting.org/ www.globalreporting.org/ReportingFramework/ReportingFrameworkOverview/

16. www.cdproject.net/en-US/Results/Pages/overview.aspx

17. www.pwc.com/en_US/us/corporate-sustainability-climate-change/assets/creating-value-from-corporate-responsibility.pdf

18. www.sam-group.com/htmle/yearbook/downloads/SAM_Yearbook_2011.pdf?CFID=2882945andCFTOKEN=a6de2cbed33fc567-6CB9E551-DE48-324C-0831C21B361239EC

19. www.ulenvironment.com/ulenvironment/eng/pages/offerings/standards/organizations/; www.greenseal.org/GreenBusiness/Standards.aspx; www.iso.org/iso/pressrelease.htm?refid=Ref1363; www.iso.org/iso/iso_14000_essentials

20. www.nsf.org/business/sustainability/SUS_NSF_Trucost_Report.pdf

21. Joe Glauber, "Prospects for the U.S. Farm Economy in 2011," February 24, 2011. www.usda.gov/documents/Glauber_Joe_Speech.pdf; Sarah Johnson, "Commodity Prices: High and Volatile," *CFO* Magazine, March 1, 2011. www.cfo.com/article.cfm/14558010/c_14559200

22. "Globally Carbon Markets Gain One Percent in Value from 2009 to 2010," Point Carbon, January 14, 2011. www.pointcarbon.com/aboutus/pressroom/pressreleases/1.1496966

23. www.ghgprotocol.org/standards/product-and-supply-chain-standard.

24. www.trucost.com/capital-ambitions-partnership-with-trucost; walmartstores.com/Sustainability/9292.aspx and www.greenbiz.com/blog/2009/09/24/walmart-sustainability-index-means-big-business

25. http://edocket.access.gpo.gov/2009/pdf/E9-24518.pdf; www.whitehouse.gov/the_press_office/President-Obama-signs-an-Executive-Order-Focused-on-Federal-Leadership-in-Environmental-Energy-and-Economic-Performance

26. www.gsa.gov/portal/content/183229

CHAPTER 16

Crawford Chemicals

Carbon Risk Management in an Uncertain Environment

Thomas J. Nist, Pavel Yakovlev, and Becky Weisberg

Environmental data is a burgeoning field with still-emerging standards. Government regulation is but one risk category, but the uncertainty that has emerged has not kept companies from acting. Global organizations from Wal-Mart to IBM, Unilever to Nike, Sprint to Dow Chemical, and many more, are taking an active role in innovating and managing their environmental impacts. The more environmentally intensive sectors have harder decisions to make, as their business models innately expose them to risk. This case study on Crawford Chemicals highlights the situations companies face and shows how using environmental metrics is critical for companies and their strategic thinking. It is also critical for investors to consider.

Adam Johnson, newly hired as the coordinator of sustainability for Crawford Chemicals, faced a daunting task. Until recently, Crawford Chemicals, a 40-year-old company with seven locations throughout the United States that specialized in manufacturing diversified chemicals, and its

---

For teaching notes on this case, please visit this book's Web site, www .investchangingworld.com. Information contained in the case in this chapter is based on actual firm and industry participants, modified to support the learning objectives of the case. The situation presented is purely fictional.

executives never believed that the company's environmental impact played a significant role in the success of its business.

The environment had recently become a topic of discussion among its executives due to a problem faced by one of Crawford's competitors. In the past month, the competitor had become a popular subject with the media and had been described as "a dirty company that's also in the chemical business." Nongovernmental organizations and environmental activist groups had helped bring attention to this competitor, reporting that the company inflicted more damage on the environment than the public considered acceptable. To mitigate Crawford's risk of being viewed by the public in the same negative manner, Ronald Smith, the chief executive officer (CEO) of Crawford, decided to take a proactive stance.

CRAWFORD'S ENVIRONMENTAL DILEMMA

Smith approached the board of directors with an idea to hire a coordinator of sustainability. Eight of the ten board members dismissed Smith's concern about environmental risk but supported the broader definition of sustainability as a corporate priority. Smith recruited Johnson immediately. Johnson's job description included determining the environmental risks that Crawford faced, evaluating the steps that Crawford could take to lower those risks, and providing semiannual reports describing Crawford's sustainability efforts and recommendations for improvements.

Johnson had graduated three years earlier with his master of science degree in environmental sustainability. Since graduating, he had worked for a consulting company focused on providing businesses with clean energy solutions. Smith knew about Johnson's background in alternative energy and thought that he was an obvious choice for the position. When Johnson was interviewed, the CEO revealed that the board did not fully support the creation of his position on the basis of environmental risk. Nevertheless, Johnson accepted the position because of his strong belief in the importance of reducing negative impacts on the environment. He was aware, though, that it would be a challenge to convince Crawford's board of directors of the importance of lowering the company's impact on the environment. To do so, Johnson knew that he would have to present a solution that proved both the environmental and the monetary benefits of altering operations. Smith requested that within three months of joining Crawford, Johnson be prepared to present to the board preliminary research explaining Crawford's primary environmental risks and his solutions on how to mitigate those risks.

Johnson began his research by reviewing Crawford's utility bills. Crawford's water usage was not significant relative to other companies with which

Johnson had consulted; Johnson was also pleased to learn that Crawford's production processes did not produce a large amount of pollution or hazardous materials. Unfortunately, Johnson quickly learned that Crawford's rate of fossil fuel combustion was exceptionally high. In order to produce carbon black, one of the company's main sources of revenue, Crawford was using a process developed over 50 years ago that was very carbon intensive. Johnson quickly determined that he needed to convey the significance of this problem to the board of directors.

Carbon Dioxide's Role in Atmospheric Problems

Carbon dioxide (CO_2) emissions are a growing concern in the scientific and political communities around the world. Before 1850, Earth's atmosphere contained only 280 parts per million (ppm) of CO_2. Currently, the atmosphere contains 380 ppm of CO_2, an increase of 35.7%. By 2050, the Intergovernmental Panel on Climate Change estimates that the atmosphere could contain up to 550 ppm of CO_2.[1] CO_2 is one of six elements that are classified as greenhouse gases (GHGs). Increasing attention has been paid to GHGs because of the effect that they have on global average temperature. GHGs trap heat, which causes global average temperatures to rise. Among these six gases, CO_2 is the most prevalent and thus has become the focus of many actions taken to stop the progression of global warming.

CO_2 is released, in large part, through burning fossil fuels. Technological advances and the growth of the world population have led to an increase in fossil fuel combustion. In the United States, this trend has increased GHG emission levels by 17% since 1990 as measured by CO_2 equivalency levels.[2] Climate change has become a highly debated topic because of the impact that it will have on the world population. Former chief economist of the World Bank, Nicholas Stern, predicted that climate change may cost the global economy \$9.6 trillion, reduce global economic output by 3%, and displace 200 million people within the next 100 years.[3] A report released by Trucost stated that in the long term, a failure to cut GHG emissions could lead to a climate change that will cause a 5% to 20% reduction in gross domestic product.[4]

Need for Government Intervention

For many years, Johnson had been aware of the negative effects that an increasing amount of CO_2 has on the environment. After consulting with many companies that wanted to change their practices but were hesitant to do so, he understood why CO_2 reduction processes face such internal resistance. In many countries, carbon emissions are "externalities" that take

TABLE 16.1 39 Countries Named in the Kyoto Protocol

Country	Quantified Emission Reduction Commitment (percentage of base year or period)
Australia	108
Austria	92
Belgium	92
Bulgaria*	92
Canada	94
Croatia*	95
Czech Republic*	92
Denmark	92
Estonia*	92
European Community	92
Finland	92
France	92
Germany	92
Greece	92
Hungary*	94
Iceland	110
Ireland	92
Italy	92
Japan	94
Latvia*	92
Liechtenstein	92
Lithuania*	92
Luxembourg	92
Monaco	92
Netherlands	92
New Zealand	100
Norway	101
Poland*	94
Portugal	92
Romania*	92
Russian Federation*	100
Slovakia*	92
Slovenia*	92
Spain	92
Sweden	92
Switzerland	92
Ukraine*	100
United Kingdom of Great Britain and N. Ireland	92
United States of America	93

* Countries that are undergoing the process of transition to a market economy.
Source: http://unfccc.int/resource/docs/convkp/kpeng.html

lower priority in company planning. A negative externality is an effect that one party has on others, with the first party incurring no cost in producing the externality. Although many businesses are aware of the negative externalities that their production processes cause, they do not have an incentive to change their operations. Companies must stay competitive in order to remain in business, and it would be a challenge for one company within an industry to incur a cost that no other companies in that industry incurred and still maintain its competitive position. Deciding to invest in lower-emissions operations could put a company at a disadvantage. Without a uniform regulation forcing all businesses to alter their operations in the same manner, it will be hard to convince some firms that changing operations in the name of carbon reduction is a justifiable decision. These concerns have led to a widespread belief in the need for government intervention in the marketplace in the presence of significant carbon externalities.

Regulatory compliance is viewed by a large majority of business executives as the means by which the largest change will be enacted.[5] Many businesses will not voluntarily change their practices to exert less of an impact on the environment; government regulation will be necessary to force businesses to change. PricewaterhouseCoopers interviewed executives of 700 companies in 15 countries, focusing on top companies as measured by turnover rate (total sales).[6] The interview determined that the two highest motivators to induce businesses to change their approach toward the environment are governmental regulation and tax incentives, with 95% of those interviewed agreeing that regulation and incentives would help the world reach a consensus on solving the climate problem.

In 1997, 183 governments endorsed the Kyoto Protocol. The Kyoto Protocol is the first international treaty directly addressing the emissions of CO_2. The treaty requires that 39 industrialized nations reduce greenhouse gas emissions by approximately 5% below 1990 levels by 2012. (See Table 16.1.) The protocol's passage helped lead to an increased interest in curbing CO_2 emissions.[7] One of the three solutions set forth in the protocol to solve the problem of increasing carbon emissions involves implementing a market for trading carbon permits.

MARKETS FOR CARBON PERMITS AND CAP AND TRADE

Pollution permits are a commodity traded on a market similar to the Chicago Board Options Exchange. Permits can be bought and sold through brokers or independent parties. The market for CO_2 permits is supported by a cap-and-trade system. Cap-and-trade systems are comprised of two components that work together to lower global carbon emissions. The "cap" is a limit that the government places on each industry in relation to what is considered an appropriate level of CO_2 to be emitted. Companies are either allocated or forced to purchase credits that allow them to emit a certain accepted level of CO_2. The "trade" component of this system allows companies and individuals to put any unused credits on the market. Companies that have lower-than-permitted emission levels can benefit from selling carbon credits to companies that cannot reduce their emission levels at a cost lower than that of purchasing carbon credits. The market creates tangible economic incentives for businesses to lower carbon emissions while providing an alternative to firms that cannot respond quickly. Excess allowances can be sold at a price determined by the market. One allowance provides the right to emit one ton of CO_2.[8] Since CO_2 is a gas, its weight is measured by how much an equivalent amount of solid carbon would weigh. Under a cap-and-trade system, companies are given three options for means by which they are permitted to reduce their carbon emissions. They are permitted to (1) reduce emissions through altering operations, (2) purchase carbon credits from other companies, or (3) use a combination of the first two methods. When a limit or cap is established on the amount of CO_2 that is acceptable, trading emerges as the primary solution behind reducing global emission levels.

Although cap-and-trade markets have only recently been utilized to help restrict carbon emissions, such operations are not a recent development. The United States has had a market for sulfur dioxide (SO_2), another GHG, for over 12 years. SO_2 is emitted from power plants and is one of the primary causes of acid rain. Since the trading market was implemented, SO_2 levels have dropped 41% below 1980 levels.[9]

Arguments in support of cap-and-trade systems look at the benefits of pricing each ton of emitted carbon. When the government puts a cost on emissions, it forces businesses to focus on low-carbon improvements. This focus will help move businesses toward alternative, cleaner, renewable sources of energy. Successful cap-and-trade systems have devoted significant investments to supporting business' efforts to achieve low-carbon emissions and innovative, clean technologies.[10] By allowing those businesses with low carbon emissions and aggressive reduction initiatives to sell credits and earn higher profits, the world is supporting the use of cleaner energy systems.

Alternatives to Cap and Trade

Johnson had written his master's thesis on the benefits of cap-and-trade markets. He was aware, however, that many believed that alternatives to emissions markets were a more viable solution. One popular alternative to cap and trade is a corrective tax, also known as a Pigouvian tax. In this scenario, a tax is aimed at the negative externality, forcing parties to pay for the environmental cost of pollution. A tax on carbon might lower the emission level of carbon via reduced fossil fuel combustion, more efficient forms of energy usage, and new technologies, among others. Some people who support taxes believe that they, rather than a cap-and-trade system, will make it restrictive for companies to continue to pollute, forcing them to lower their carbon emissions.[11] Others who support a tax do so because they believe it will be an inexpensive way to reduce pollution. Business executives in Europe believe that a carbon tax would be easy to administer and would provide a stable source of environmental regulation.[12] However, previous proposals for a tax on carbon emissions have been difficult to implement, and some taxes have been set too low to have a significant impact.[13] Consequently, some experts view existing environmental taxes as not very effective.

There are those who oppose cap-and-trade systems simply because they do not believe that these systems deliver the intended results. The World Wildlife Fund, for example, claims that the existing European market for carbon permits results in companies within the market importing too many inexpensive carbon credits from developing countries without reducing carbon emissions in Europe.[14] Companies in developed countries may not lower their own carbon emissions because they have been given an inexpensive alternative (carbon credits) to doing so. In the European system, the cost of reducing pollution is dependent on each country's rate of economic growth. Russia, for instance, has had slow economic and emissions growth since 1990; thus, it is relatively inexpensive for Russia to reduce its pollution levels to a rate below that of 1990.[15] Consequently, Russia can inexpensively produce a large number of carbon permits that other countries can buy. If all countries agree to reduce their emissions level to a certain percentage below the level that existed in 1990, some will have to reduce their emissions by a higher amount than other countries will.

Some business executives wonder if trading markets simply allow for monetary transfers between borders but do not force lowered overall emissions. Catrinus Jepma, professor of energy and sustainability at the University of Groningen in the Netherlands, says that although the motivation behind the Kyoto Protocol was to deter companies from polluting by forcing them to pay a high price to pollute, in fact, the cap-and-trade system has put a low price on polluting, allowing companies to continue to pollute with few repercussions.[16] In summary, the many criticisms focus on implementation of a cap-and-trade system rather than on cap-and-trade systems themselves.

EUROPEAN UNION EMISSIONS TRADING SCHEME

The European Union (EU) includes 27 member states. On January 1, 2005, the EU created a single market for CO_2 emissions. The market for carbon permits, titled the Emissions Trading Scheme (ETS), is the world's first international company-level cap-and-trade system that controls carbon emissions and other GHGs through the use of an allowance system.[17] The implemented ETS is part of the EU's three-phase plan. The first phase of the plan started on January 1, 2005, and involved a three-year pilot phase to establish best practices for carbon trading and determine appropriate market prices. Phase 2 started three years later, on January 1, 2008. This phase includes complying with emissions targets set forth in the Kyoto Protocol. For the EU, this requires reducing emissions to 6.5% less than CO_2 levels of 2005. The third phase will begin on January 1, 2013, and will last seven years. During this phase, the EU is hoping to strengthen and grow the ETS and continue to support long-term investments in initiatives taken to reduce carbon emissions. The EU intends to reduce its overall emissions by at least 20% relative to levels in 1990 and also obtain 20% of its energy from renewable sources by the year 2020.

The ETS's success is based on four basic characteristics:

1. It is a cap-and-trade system.
2. Participation is mandatory for businesses in the covered sectors: energy activities, ferrous metals production, cement and lime, ceramics/bricks, glass, pulp and paper, and renewable energy.[18]
3. Compliance with the ETS is strong.
4. Emission reductions schemes are shared with the rest of the world.

By enforcing mandatory participation, the EU requires that compliance be strong; companies are obligated either to lower their emissions or to purchase carbon credits. Additionally, sharing carbon emissions credits with other countries has allowed companies that must purchase credits to do so from a wide variety of sources, some of which may offer lower-priced credits. The ETS is currently the largest operating market for carbon permits, and it has capped emissions at more than 10,000 companies.[19]

How the EU ETS Operates

The EU grants factories, power plants, and other firms the right to emit a specific level of CO_2 known as carbon allowances. Any allowances that are

FIGURE 16.1 EU ETS Carbon Pricing
Source: Bloomberg, L.P.

not used by one company can be sold to other companies within the same year. However, during phase 3 of the EU's three-phase plan, ETS intends to treat all allowances as "auctioned off" rather than granted at no cost. In this manner, all companies will be required to pay to pollute. A provision may be granted to energy-intensive industries that would no longer be able to compete internationally if complete auctions were implemented.

Companies are permitted to trade carbon allowances directly with other companies or through carbon intermediaries. The carbon trade system is overseen by a general moderator. The price of carbon is determined by supply and demand and, since the inception of the ETS, has risen and fallen both with the price of other fossil fuels, such as oil and natural gas, and also with the general level of economic stability.[20] In 2007, too many allowances were given out and the CO_2 market was flooded with credits. (See Figure 16.1.) Since the market is based on supply and demand, when the supply drastically increased, the price dramatically decreased. The price of carbon fell to record lows, and the EU was forced to lower the level of the emissions cap and the number of allowances issued.[21]

PROS AND CONS OF THE MARKET FOR CARBON PERMITS

One of the benefits of a market for carbon permits is the revenue that it generates for firms that take an aggressive approach to carbon reduction. As the volume of carbon permits traded between the years 2005 and 2007 grew, the value of the global market rose from $8 billion to $63 billion.[22] Proponents of a market for carbon permits point to the increase in global economic output as one reason that this type of market is beneficial both to the environment and to society. Risks also are incurred in the implementation of this market. Across business sectors, carbon risk varies greatly. The four least-carbon-intensive industries—personal and household goods, retail, travel and leisure, and food and beverage—account for a total of only 4.18% of all GHG emissions.[23] Conversely, the two most-carbon-intensive industries, utilities and oil and gas, account for 78.66% of all emissions. The utility industry, the highest-emitting sector, would be affected the most by a carbon emission price. At a price of $28.24 per ton emitted, utility companies could recognize a reduction in combined earnings of up to 50%.[24] In the five highest-emitting sectors, earnings before interest, taxes, depreciation, and amortization (EBITDA) could fall between 1% and 117% due to carbon regulations, which suggests that some firms will sacrifice their entire profit picture if they do not take corrective action.[25] The risk that carbon legislation places on companies involves an increase in operating costs. Companies likely will attempt to pass carbon costs onto customers, driving up the price of goods and giving consumers an incentive to reduce consumption or switch to less carbon-intensive alternatives. This is beneficial to those companies that are not carbon intensive but can be detrimental, if not fatal, to those that are.

Currently, no national laws in the United States regulate carbon emissions. Fortunately, Johnson has kept abreast of the progress of the carbon regulation debate in the nation. President George W. Bush did not endorse the Kyoto Protocol, citing restrictions that would be placed on businesses as too large of an expense to reasonably incur.[26] In the 2008 presidential election, both candidates Barack Obama (Democrat) and John McCain (Republican) spoke about the importance of regulating U.S. carbon emissions through a cap-and-trade program. After Obama was elected president, he continued to discuss the ways of increasing environmental protection at the minimal cost to the economy. He claimed that utilizing clean-energy alternatives would create jobs in those sectors. He even insisted that he would enact legislation to reduce heat-trapping gases by 17% below 2005 levels by 2020.[27]

Although it has often been the intent of politicians to enact a cap-and-trade policy in the United States, no such legislation has been passed. Recently, the federal government has discussed intentions to introduce a cap-and-trade system in the year 2012. This system would introduce requirements for all six greenhouse gases and would auction off 100% of allowances.[28] Other plans include reducing greenhouse gas emissions by 6% below 2005 levels by 2012, 14% below 2005 levels by 2020, and 80% below 2005 levels by 2050.[29] An estimated price of $20 to $30 per ton of carbon emitted is proposed under these plans.[30] Currently there are state-level and regional programs in the United States dedicated to reducing carbon emissions. These programs vary depending on their geographical location, and they have not come together to form one unified regulation. The lack of unified regulation causes problems for the local programs. For example, the lack of support in the Senate for climate legislation caused the Chicago Climate Exchange, a voluntary cap-and-trade scheme, to shut down at the end of 2010.[31] The closing of this exchange effectively eliminated the trading of any emissions permits across a North American market.

The 2008 economic recession and high unemployment rate have taken precedence over enacting any cap-and-trade policies. The country is divided over the importance of passing these policies due to the costs that the regulations will place on businesses and the potential job losses that might occur. Although some believe that supporting alternative energy sources will stimulate the economy, many more feel that alternative energy will come at a cost to businesses and that there is no logical way to stimulate the economy when businesses are incurring additional expenses. Some believe that the proposed cap-and-trade bills are too harsh for businesses, will not lead to a significant change in carbon emissions, and will merely increase energy costs.[32] American citizens are increasingly concerned with the high unemployment rate, and they are interested in an energy bill that is viewed as creating jobs rather than one that could potentially eliminate jobs.

Measuring Carbon Risk

Johnson is not sure whether carbon legislation will ever pass in the United States. Although legislation has not been successful yet, he thinks that due to the progress made in the EU and the tide of global public opinion, if companies within the United States want to remain competitive, they must address their carbon output. "Carbon risk" is the potential risk that U.S. companies with currently high levels of CO_2 emissions will face in terms of increasing costs and decreasing profits if regulatory restriction is implemented.

As carbon emissions and global warming become areas of increasing importance, financial analysts will begin to consider a company's carbon risk when evaluating its investment potential. Environmental risk cannot be quantified in any exact terms because legislation has not passed in the United States. Establishing the risk profile involves considering if and when a regulation will be implemented and how it will impact companies with large carbon footprints. There are those who believe that legislation will be passed in the near future; others believe that it will never be passed. Determining carbon risk involves evaluating the impact of what other countries have done and making predictions about what action steps the United States might take, and when.

Fortunately for Johnson, he recently uncovered an important source of information to support his analysis from a company called Trucost. Trucost focuses on providing environmental data and has been developing its expertise since 2000.[33] Trucost manages a database containing information about the environmental profile of over 4,500 companies, making it the world's largest database on greenhouse gas emissions. The company produces "carbon footprints," quantitative measures of carbon risk that are based on converting greenhouse gas emissions to CO_2 equivalent emissions. The carbon footprint is measured in terms of metric tons emitted per million dollars of revenue. By measuring carbon emissions relative to revenue, the carbon footprint indicates how dependent a company is on fossil fuels and other processes that emit CO_2 to generate revenue. In order to determine carbon footprints, Trucost reviews information that companies publish, such as annual reports, environmental/sustainability reports, public disclosures, and company Web sites. When there is no available public information regarding carbon emissions, Trucost uses its proprietary environmental profiling system to analyze over 720 different types of environmental impacts. All of the information regarding carbon risk is measured and presented against data from same-sector peers. It is important to consider carbon risk as relative to a firm's peer group because if legislation is passed, it most likely will impact companies on an industry-specific basis. Comparing a high-carbon-intensive company to a low-carbon-intensive company that operates in an entirely different industry will not accurately depict firm-level carbon risk. It is more useful to compare the highly carbon-intensive companies to those that are less carbon intensive within the same industry and to measure the variability of intensity within an industry or sector. Caps for carbon emissions in the EU have been implemented based on sector-specific targets; it is reasonable to assume that similar emission limits passed in the United States will focus on emissions within specific sectors.

Emissions that are regulated by the government tend to fall into three distinct categories. Scope 1 emissions are direct emissions released by a company's fuel combustion or industrial processes. Scope 2 emissions are indirect emissions created through purchased electricity. Scope 3 emissions are also indirect emissions that are released from sources not owned or controlled specifically by the company under consideration, such as suppliers' emissions.[34]

PREDICAMENT OF SUSTAINABILITY IN THE CHEMICAL INDUSTRY

Although Johnson had three years of experience working with companies that were intent on becoming less dependent on fossil fuels, he did not have any significant experience with chemical companies. Smith agreed to meet with Johnson before his presentation to the board of directors to make sure that he fully understood Crawford and the diversified chemical industry. Since Johnson did not have a particularly strong financial background, Smith explained the meaning of some of the industry averages to him, including the fact that carbon black is the chemical from which Crawford derives 80% of its revenue. Crawford is one of a few companies in the United States that produce carbon black, with additional competition coming from companies based in China and India. Within the competition for carbon black, Crawford accounts for slightly less than 30% of the market. Most of its sales are to foreign countries, with the United States accounting for approximately 16% of sales; Japan and China are the two countries that comprise the largest amount of sales. Crawford differs from some of its competing North American diversified chemical companies because no other company has one revenue source accounting for more than 60% of its revenue.

Smith thought that it was important for Johnson to understand the supply and demand for chemicals. In Crawford's industry, demand is significantly more inelastic than the supply, meaning that producers are relatively more sensitive to price changes than consumers are, forcing consumers to bear most of the costs associated with potential carbon reductions. The chemical industry is comprised of a few firms that produce relatively homogenous products. As Johnson recalled, this type of market structure is called an oligopoly. He also remembered that collusion or cartel agreements among the firms in an oligopoly are prohibited by the United States anti-trust Sherman (1890) and Clayton (1914) acts.

Furthermore, Johnson recalled a conclusion from game theory that collusion, even if not detected by the U.S. Justice Department, is likely to fail in practice because of a strong incentive on behalf of each firm to break the agreement and price its products lower than those of its competitors. Based on this information, Johnson concluded that Crawford operates in a rather

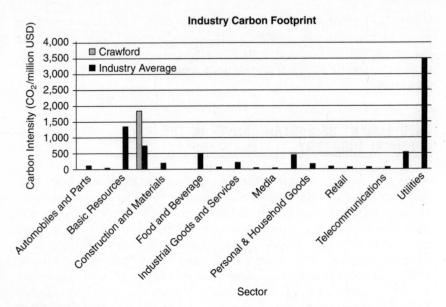

FIGURE 16.2 Trucost Analysis of Crawford's Carbon Risks Relative to Same-Sector Peers

competitive market and that it cannot singlehandedly influence the market price. Crawford, therefore, is a price taker. This means that it can pass the cost of carbon reduction per unit of output onto consumers in proportion to how much the market price increases in response to potential cap-and-trade regulation. The amount of carbon emission cost per unit of output that Crawford can shift onto consumers cannot exceed those of its competitors, which means that Crawford must absorb the remainder of the cost.

With less than a week until his meeting with the board, Johnson knew that he had to develop a position on Crawford's carbon risk and make a recommendation. He had gathered data that he thought would be helpful, beginning with a Trucost analysis of Crawford's carbon risk (see Figure 16.2 and Table 16.2). Then he collected financial information regarding Crawford's position relative to the top 12 other diversified chemicals industries in North America (see Table 16.3). Armed with the notes he had taken from his meeting with Smith, the chief financial officer, and the other data he had gathered, Johnson hoped to put together a presentation that would convince the board that reducing Crawford's carbon emissions was both environmentally and monetarily prudent.

As he began to prepare his recommendations, Johnson jotted down a few notes that would serve as key assumptions in establishing his

TABLE 16.2 Trucost Carbon Intensity by Sector

Industry Classification Benchmark Supersector	Carbon Intensity (t CO_2e/million USD)	
	Crawford Chemical	Industry Averages
Automobiles and Parts		109
Banks		20
Basic Resources		1,371
Chemicals	1,834	756
Construction and Materials		210
Financial Services		50
Food and Beverage		475
Healthcare		60
Industrial Goods and Services		212
Insurance		10
Media		29
Oil and Gas		453
Personal and Household Goods		179
Real Estate		84
Retail		67
Technology		58
Telecommunications		63
Travel and Leisure		539
Utilities		3,585

Source: Trucost, October 4, 2010.
Interpretation: The chemicals industry emits 756 tons of carbon per $1 million in revenue while Crawford emits 1,834 tons per $1 million.

recommendations. This list includes notes from his meeting with Ronald Smith of things to consider:

- Elasticity of demand and supply in the chemical industry (see Figure 16.3).
- Crawford is mostly a price taker.
- Its products are mostly commodities.
- Crawford's efforts concentrate on low-cost production and regulatory compliance.
- Crawford monitors the Herfindahl-Hirschman Index to measure fluctuation in market concentration (see Table 16.4—this index tracks concentration of market share, market power, and pricing power—in the

TABLE 16.3 Fictionalized Bloomberg Data Based on the Top Chemical Companies in North America, September 2010

Name	Revenue	Total Assets	Market Cap	CAPEX	PM*	P/E	P/S	P/B	Debt/ Common Equity	Dividend Yield %	P/EBITDA
Average	7,214,633,598	11,812,413,550	8,324,017,063	−316,418,002	1.33	19.27	0.89	2.50	93.37	1.72	6.52
ARMSTRONG	3,029,473	4,299,259	4,866,542	−64,021	15.93	20.00	1.60	1.20	0	0.00	9.90
TIOGA	262,029,000	258,244,992	53,521,008	−5,379,000	−25.35		0.20	0.62	71.83	0.00	4.04
DAUPHIN	541,880,000	338,632,992	400,568,992	−28,891,000	4.06	26.38	0.75	2.61	64.03	0.00	9.83
VENANGO	1,515,600,000	1,932,000,000	1,607,681,024	−137,900,000	8.86	45.11	1.05	1.95	45.12	3.95	7.60
CRAWFORD	2,754,000,000	2,676,000,000	2,132,580,992	−106,000,000	−3.43	12.18	0.76	1.73	50.15	2.21	5.48
LUZERNE	2,968,699,904	3,136,199,936	4,916,431,872	−161,200,000	8.09	15.17	1.65	4.26	51.31	0.74	7.71
JUNIATA	1,902,000,000	3,265,999,872	1,996,841,984	−44,000,000	−6.78	11.45	1.02	3.99	236.04	0.00	5.16
SCHUYLKILL	5,952,999,936	5,514,999,808	5,387,103,232	−310,000,000	2.69	12.51	0.91	3.21	88.73	2.36	5.10
FAYETTE	8,641,000,064	8,625,999,872	2,790,991,872	−189,000,000	1.47	27.79	0.32	1.68	237.34	3.43	3.70
CAMBRIA	8,742,999,808	9,447,000,064	3,857,005,056	−174,000,000	0.88	9.92	0.43	1.05	32.19	0.92	4.00
SOMERSET	14,924,999,936	14,240,000,000	12,070,800,384	−239,000,000	2.75	17.49	0.94	3.50	80.92	2.97	7.42
MCKEAN	20,079,998,976	38,185,000,960	40,657,059,840	−1,308,000,000	6.72	13.59	1.38	4.73	138.24	3.66	9.05
BEDFORD	25,500,999,680	65,936,998,400	32,336,769,024	−1,410,000,000	1.44	19.63	0.60	1.96	118.01	2.15	5.76

*In this data set, "profit margin" refers to accounting profit. Accounting profit does not account for the opportunity cost (implicit cost) of doing business in this industry. Crawford's opportunity cost can be approximated by the average profit that it could have earned producing another product or operating in a different industry altogether. If the opportunity cost for Crawford to continue producing its products is taken into consideration, its economic, or true, profit will be less than its accounting profit. CAPEX = Capital Expenditures, P/E = Price to Earnings Ratio, P/S = Price to Sales, P/B = Price to Book Value

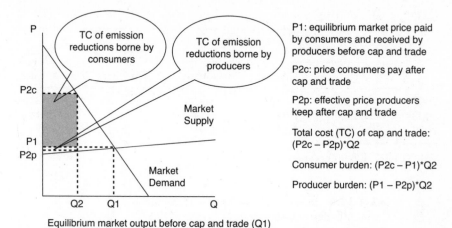

FIGURE 16.3 Supply and Demand for the Chemical Industry

context of this case, it suggests that firms will not be able to unilaterally pass along future carbon costs).

■ Crawford has little control over market price behavior in any product line.
■ Capital expenditures (CAPEX): historically conservative approach to investment spending, looking to milk the assets for all they can.
■ Price to Cash Flow (P/CF) versus price/earnings: P/CF does not account for depreciation.
■ Opportunities have been presented to upgrade plant and equipment with environmentally friendly technologies that could bring Crawford in line with industry emission levels within five years at a cost of $150 million.

In addition, Smith, the chief financial officer, provides these data:

Margin Analysis, 2009

	Crawford		Industry	
	% Sales	Margin	% Sales	Margin
Carbon black	1.6%	80%	1.1%	15%
All other products	(23.55)%	20%	1.37%	85%
Total	(3.43)%	100%	1.33%	100%

CAPEX Analysis

	Crawford		Industry		
	CAPEX	**% Sales**	**CF/Share**[*]	**Div/Share**[*]	**% Sales**
2007	$75.8 mil	2.70%	5.75	2.17	4.42%
2008	$84.3 mil	2.94%	6.14	2.28	4.51%
2009	$8.5.0 mil	2.91%	6.08	2.40	4.39%

[*]ABC has 27,500,000 shares outstanding.

TABLE 16.4 Industry Market Shares: Data Analysis of
Chemical Industry Concentration

Name	Percent of Market Based on Revenue
ARMSTRONG	0.001
TIOGA	0.003
DAUPHIN	0.006
VENANGO	0.02
CRAWFORD	0.03
LUZERNE	0.03
JUNIATA	0.02
SCHUYLKILL	0.06
FAYETTE	0.09
CAMBRIA	0.09
SOMERSET	0.16
MCKEAN	0.22
BEDFORD	0.27
Sum	**1.00**

Source: Bloomberg, September 29, 2010.

This market share data can be used to compute the Herfindahl-
Hirschman Index (HHI). The HHI is a measure of market concentration and, by extension, competition. The HHI can be com-
puted by squaring each company's market share and adding them
together. An HHI value less than 0.1 indicates a rather competitive market; an HHI value between 0.1 and 0.18 indicates a
moderately competitive market; and an index greater than 0.18 is
considered a highly concentrated or rather uncompetitive market.
An index greater than 0.4 could motivate the U.S. Department of
Justice to bring an antitrust lawsuit against the industry.

Therefore, a few of Johnson's assumptions based on the data included:

1. We do not want to create reputation risk of negative public relations for Crawford. We must address our position as an above-average carbon emitter, at least by preparing a plan.
2. There is a 50/50 chance of carbon regulation passing in the United States by 2013, with 2015 imposition of tax or cap-and-trade scheme.
3. Guidelines in 2015 will set industry average emissions in 2010 as the baseline for all participants with a 3% reduction per year through 2025.
4. Carbon prices will average $28.24 throughout the analysis horizon.
5. Short term: Crawford will not enjoy price flexibility above industry levels due to carbon regulation legislation. Some pass-through of carbon costs in price is possible in the short run.
6. Long term: The risk of product substitution requires that the industry find reduction or offset schemes that maintain historical price levels.

SUMMARY

Making decisions under uncertain conditions is something which all companies face, in different ways, depending on their sector involvements. In an uncertain age of global regulation, companies face strategic decisions that will affect their shareholders now and in the future. Analysts and investors therefore need to start factoring such considerations into their buy/sell decisions and valuation models, as well as asking these companies the right questions. Asset owners also need to make sure their external fund managers have the expertise needed to deal with the uncertain environment ahead.

NOTES

1. Stephanie Baker-Said, "Cashing in on Pollution," *Bloomberg Markets* (December 2007). www.bloomberg.com/apps/news?pid=nw&pname= mm_1207_story1.html
2. Trucost Plc, *Carbon Counts USA: The Carbon Footprints of Mutual Funds in the US Annual Report 2009*. Boston: Author, 2009, 4. www.pewclimate.org/ docUploads/CarbonCounts-USA_5_V-ONLINE.pdf

3. Robert O. Mendelsohn, "A Critique of the Stern Report," *Regulation* (Winter 2006–2007). http://environment.yale.edu/files/biblio/YaleFES-00000260 .pdf. Baker-Said, "Cashing in on Pollution."

4. Trucost Plc, *Carbon Counts USA*, 5. www.trucost.com

5. PricewaterhouseCoopers, *Appetite for Change: Global Business Perspectives on Tax and Regulation for a Low Carbon Economy*. Author, 2010, 10.

6. Ibid., 9.

7. A. Perold, F. Reinhardt, and M. Hyman, *The Market for Carbon Permits* (Boston: Harvard Business School, 2009), 3.

8. European Union, *The EU Emissions Trading Scheme. EU Action Against Climate Change* (Belgium: European Communities, 2008), 9.

9. Baker-Said. "Cashing in on Pollution."

10. European Union, *The EU Emissions Trading Scheme*, 5.

11. Baker-Said. "Cashing in on Pollution."

12. PricewaterhouseCoopers. *Appetite for Change*, 29.

13. Perold, Reinhardt, and Hyman, *The Market for Carbon Permits*, 1. PricewaterhouseCoopers, *Appetite for Change*, 16.

14. Baker-Said, "Cashing in on Pollution."

15. Jonathan Gruber, *Public Finance and Public Policy* (New York: Worth Publishers, 2005), 153.

16. Baker-Said, "Cashing in on Pollution."

17. European Union, *The EU Emissions Trading Scheme*. Unless indicated, details about the EU ETS are from this source.

18. Vertis, "Sectors Covered by the EU ETS." www.vertisfinance.com/ index.php?page=278&l=1.

19. Perold, Reinhardt, and Hyman, *The Market for Carbon Permits*, 3.

20. Ibid., 5

21. Baker-Said, "Cashing in on Pollution."

22. Perold, Reinhardt, and Hyman, *The Market for Carbon Permits*, 5.

23. Investor Responsibility Research Center, Institute for Corporate Responsibility, *Carbon Risk and Opportunities in the S&P 500*. Boston: Trucost, 2009, 12.

24. Trucost Plc, *Carbon Counts USA*, 4. Investor Responsibility Research Center, Institute for Corporate Responsibility, *Carbon Risk and Opportunities in the S&P 500*, 3.

25. Ibid.

26. Baker-Said, "Cashing in on Pollution."

27. John M. Broder and Krauss Clifford, "Advocates of Climate Bill Scale Down Their Goals," *New York Times*, January 26, 2010. www.nytimes.com/ 2010/01/27/science/earth/27climate.html

28. Trucost Plc, *Carbon Counts USA*, 4.

29. Investor Responsibility Research Center, Institute for Corporate Responsibility, *Carbon Risk and Opportunities in the S&P 500*, 3; Trucost Plc, *Carbon Counts USA*, 7.

30. Trucost Plc, *Carbon Counts USA*.

31. Aaron Smith, "Chicago Climate Exchange to Shut Down Emissions Trading," CNNMoney, November 17, 2010, http://money.cnn.com/2010/11/17/news/economy/climate_exchange/index.htm

32. John M. Broder and Krauss Clifford, "Advocates of Climate Bill Scale Down Their Goals," *New York Times*, January 26, 2010. www.nytimes.com/2010/01/27/science/earth/27climate.html

33. All details about Trucost are from Trucost Plc, *Carbon Counts USA.*

34. Investor Responsibility Research Center, Institute for Corporate Responsibility, *Carbon Risk and Opportunities in the S&P 500*, 6.

CHAPTER 17

Using Statistical Tools

Sam Brownell

Mainstream financial analysts often do not factor in sustainability; likewise, academic research all too often relies on correlations, calculations, and statistics whose names are foreign and unfamiliar. There are ways of bridging these gaps—of providing context and building a robust risk management framework that is more applicable to environmental and other sustainability-related inevitabilities. This chapter represents a first outreach across these realms—a call for a unification of terminology and content, towards recognizing what's truly important.

The most recognizable of all statistical distributions is the bell-shaped, Gaussian, or normal distribution. It is also the most recognized and widely used distribution throughout the financial world. It is used to model volatility of a security, to place a value on the potential losses from a portfolio of investments, and to discover a trend between variables to help forecast future values. The normal distribution has become embedded in the way we view financial markets, from the simplest expected return calculations to the most complex volatility models such as generalized auto-regressive conditional heteroskedasticity (GARCH). The benefit of the normal distribution is that it is easy to work with. All one needs to know is the expected value or average and the variance of a data set; then the normal distribution can describe the entire set of values.

While the explanatory ease works well to describe the height of a population, it has trouble capturing the true randomness of the financial markets. For example, financial analysts, portfolio managers, and traders like to calculate the correlation of one security to another so that they can understand whether their portfolio is diversified. Correlations run from positive 1, where every increase of security A means security B will also increase, to negative 1, where every time security A rises, security B falls. Investors like to have assets that are not highly correlated so that they can hedge their investments if a particular sector or company takes an adverse move.

Correlation is easy to use in practice but is unreliable when modeling real-world market moves. For example, correlations change over time as the markets move. Furthermore, correlation tends to be higher when measured over short periods of time and lower when measured over long periods of time, but the opposite can also be true. Finally, since correlations are built off an underlying distribution that is smooth, it cannot possibly hope to model the complexity of security markets, which are full of discontinuities and irregularities that are difficult to predict.

In fact, correlation is just one tenet of modern portfolio theory (MPT), the most predominant idea in investing today. MPT states that security markets are efficient and that the price of individual securities reflects all relevant information available to market participants. Within this construct, there are three levels of "efficiency": the strong form, the semistrong form, and the weak form. The strong form states that all public and private information is automatically integrated into the pricing of a financial asset. To believers in a strong form of efficient-market hypothesis (EMH), regardless of whether an investor is an insider, such as an executive, or an outsider, such as a mutual fund manager, there is no way that individual can outperform the market because there is no advantage to having additional knowledge since that knowledge is already reflected in the security's price. The semistrong form states that all publicly available information is automatically priced into an asset. Practitioners who believe in the semistrong form believe that company insiders have an advantage in material information likely to affect the price of the company's outstanding securities. Therefore, these practitioners may use strategies that follow the buying and selling of company management to gain an edge in return over their competitors. Finally, believers in the weak form of the EMH feel that security prices fully reflect all *past* publicly available information. Investors who believe in the weak form are those who most likely believe that outperformance is possible (albeit difficult) if their analysis can uncover possible future surprises, such as gross margin expansion, which would lead to a jump in security prices as investors bid up share values to their new fundamental level.

However, as anyone who has lived through the latest financial crisis can attest, markets are anything but efficient. Markets consistently display the types of discontinuities and discrete price movements that MPT advocates dismiss through their use of advanced mathematics that assume that markets are smooth and continuous and the distribution of security prices follows the central limit theorem (a basic statistical theorem that states that distributions should approach normality as the sample size increases or as the analyst combines multiple samples). In practice, security prices do not trend toward a finite variance, one of the necessary inputs for a normal distribution. Furthermore, information is not neatly assimilated into the price of a financial asset. Adherents to MPT who use the normal distribution because it is the "best" approximation for security prices also believe that security prices can be modeled as a continuous process. These practitioners model security prices with variants of Brownian motion (originally used to model the movements of particles in fluids), which makes the path of security prices move between price levels in a smooth increase or decrease. Once again, anyone who has looked at a stock chart would question whether prices actually assimilate information in such a neat and tidy manner. For example, when a company announces a buyout offer, the price of the target company makes a large discrete jump toward the announced buyout price.

UNDERSTANDING THE TREND

So why do we stake our money on such an ill-fitting distribution? Basic human psychology drives us to attempt to control the random environment and to fit events into a smooth and predictable pattern. As philosopher Karl Popper discusses in his seminal text *The Poverty of Historicism*, human nature programs us to use historical patterns (such as the explosive rise of communism or the benign advance of housing prices) in order to formulate our predictions of the future. Therefore, we have developed mathematical tools such as the normal distribution in order to fit a complex world into an understandable trend. However, as becomes painfully obvious in hindsight, we are no better at modeling our world or predicting the future than our ancestors. The only difference is that they were willing to give up a large degree of control to deities while we are too stubborn to realize our own limitations.

The question we need to ask is whether there is a better way to describe the financial markets. The answer is a resounding yes. While most veterans of finance admit that the normal distribution does not build in enough variation to explain extreme events such as the crash of October 19, 1987, they keep trying to rebuild their models with "fixes" to account for the last large market movement. The trouble is that these fixes still rely on an underlying distribution that is normal while assuming that the next market crash will look like past market crashes. These black swan, or highly improbable, events, however, never happen in the same way and therefore cannot be built into any standard financial model.

The path forward has been postulated by Benoit Mandelbrot, who took his study of fractals in nature and used them to describe financial markets. A fractal is a new way to look at geometry by embracing the roughness and irregularities that are hallmarks of our world. Fractals do not attempt to fit a set of data into a predetermined distribution. Fractals allow us to create lifelike charts of security prices and their corresponding variations that rely on the Lévy distribution, which by definition has an infinite variance and undefined excess kurtosis and therefore can account for extreme market movements.

By acknowledging the limitations of our ability to understand and to control the world and by using new mathematical tools such as fractals to describe the world as it actually is, with all its roughness and randomness, we can be better prepared to deal with a complex environment we will never fully grasp. For example, by constructing a base portfolio with 10% to 15% allocated to far out-of-the-money puts and the balance invested in the corporate debt of firms that produce sustainable, staple products (e.g., providing water or basic healthcare), we receive protection against unforeseen and highly impactful events that catch the market by surprise.

Consider that the since 1897, the Dow Jones has experienced 79 days with a decrease of more the 5% versus 63 days with an increase of over 5%. Furthermore, the magnitude of the largest down day is 27.96%, almost twice the magnitude of the largest up day, and multiple downward moves have eclipsed the largest one-day increase. Finally, there is evidence that upward trends tend to display long-term dependence whereas downward discontinuities tend to be independent and therefore unpredictable events. This evidence lends further support to the strategy of being prepared to take advantage of unknown market movements.

SUMMARY

In January 2011, a commission of six Democrats and four Republicans known as the Financial Crisis Inquiry Commission told us what "caused" the financial crisis of 2008. The majority finding was that Federal Reserve chairman Alan Greenspan allowed too much deregulation and that his replacement, Ben Bernanke, did not predict the financial crisis. These panel members have fallen victim to two well-known psychological traps: the hindsight bias and the narrative fallacy. Events are always easier to see with the benefit of all relevant data and the true outcome. After the fact, it is easy to build a convincing story about how certain causes (i.e., the Federal Reserve chairmen) led to the ultimate effect (the financial markets and economies around the world collapsed). As psychologist Baruch Fischhoff notes, "Even where records are available and unavoidable, we seem to have a remarkable ability to explain or provide a causal interpretation for whatever we see."[1]

Our penchant for trying to fit our irregular world into a neat, smooth thought process is difficult to correct. But it is important that our risk management and trading strategies reflect this inclination for self-delusion. Following the market crash of October 19, 1987, traders realized that the Black-Scholes model neglected to account for the fact that far out-of-the-money options were actually more valuable than most people thought. This realization spawned the rediscovery of the "volatility smile," where traders use increased measures of volatility to price options that are far out of the money, and also created new graphs of implied volatility that now had lower levels of fluctuation for at-the-money options, and increasing levels of volatility as one moved farther from current at-the-money options. The Black-Scholes model would have placed essentially a zero valuation on these out-of-the-money options due to a constant volatility factor. Because financial markets display volatility that can range from mildly random to wildly random,[2] using the Black-Scholes model vastly undervalues these options.

The October 1987 experience demonstrated that buying far out-of-the-money puts is a beneficial long-term investment and risk management strategy. These puts are usually undervalued due to the minuscule chance that they actually will finish in the money. Furthermore, the farther out of the money these puts are, the higher the implied volatility along the entire range of expiration dates (which is a primary driver of option prices). Fear associated with a market crash causes volatility to spike at an exponential rate, and this volatility provides immense value, especially to the short-term, far out-of-the-money puts.

One can combine these trading strategies to construct an overall portfolio that is designed to take advantage of large negative and positive market moves. At least 90% of options expire out of the money and therefore require investors who are patient and do not panic when the premiums are lost on these options. In fact, this is the most important piece of the strategy: The aim is not to beat the market every year but to put oneself in a position to reap the huge benefits when the unexpected event occurs. Of course, buying out-of-the-money puts to let them expire would be counterintuitive and would lead to depreciation of principal. Therefore, the portfolio would be constructed with about 10% to 15% allocated to a ladder portfolio of two to five month, far out-of-the-money put options. The balance would be invested in corporate bonds of companies that are in the business of manufacturing essential consumer goods, such as water and clothing, and are making an effort to look beyond traditional investment and project analysis to consider intangible factors, such as management quality, environmental issues, and solid human resources practices. By taking a different view of the same issues, these companies and investors have the opportunity to notice opportunities that most investors may have missed. Furthermore, traditional investment analysis approach has a woeful track record of actually predicting winners and losers. Consider that a 2008 *Wall Street Journal* study of the 12-month performance of sell-side analyst recommendations showed that the best performer correctly predicted equity movements only 27.8% of the time.[3] We owe it to ourselves to approach investment analysis from a different angle in order to uncover what true intangibles drive a company.

An example of such a company is Coca-Cola, which has begun to realize the importance of water as a resource, especially in emerging markets. Coca-Cola now has an executive-level sustainability position, vice president of environment and water, which encapsulates the importance of water as a resource to the Coca-Cola brand and to its product development going forward.[4] The importance of basic, staple resources is summed up by Matthew J. Kiernan, who notes that the price of rice, which is a staple for around 50% of the world's population, increased by more than 400% in 2008. Affordable and easy access to these goods will be necessary to the continued development of less developed countries. Companies such as Coca-Cola have positioned themselves to respond to the demands of the 4.5 billion people in these less developed markets.[5] However, the equity prices of Coca-Cola will continue to be at the mercy of the overall market and will continue to be influenced by extreme market movement. This is the reason to buy intermediate debt of companies that provide staple goods. Debt of these companies is not only more stable than their equity but also offers the opportunity to be repaid first if one of the holdings succumbs to unpredictable variance. Furthermore, the payments received on the debt will help cover the small losses when puts expire out of the money. Last, this strategy and the allocations cannot be static. If a particular sector or economy is growing at a nonsustainable pace, it is important for opportunistic investors to increase exposure to far out-of-the-money puts, thus creating the opportunity for greater payoffs when the market experiences a large discontinuity. Similarly, a large negative move would lead to a switch to a strategy that favors cheap, out-of-the-money call options to take advantage of a potential large positive discontinuity.

By understanding that the natural world eventually corrects self-fulfilling cycles (i.e., U.S. debt levels and the current gold craze), we are better prepared to take advantage of these corrections (even if we cannot predict how they will happen or, more important, their magnitude). No longer is it an acceptable excuse to state that "No one saw it coming" in response to an extreme and random event. We have the tools to model the world as it truly is, and we need to use these tools to benefit risk management and wealth accumulation.

NOTES

1. Daniel Kahneman, Paul Slovic, and Amos Tversky, eds., *Judgment under Uncertainty: Heuristics and Biases* (Cambridge, UK: Cambridge University Press, 1982), p. 345.
2. Benoit Mandelbrot, *Fractals and Scaling in Finance: Discontinuity, Concentration, Risk* (New Haven, CT: Yale University Press, 2010)
3. Matthew J. Kiernan, *Investing in a Sustainable World* (New York: AMACOM, 2008) page 36.
4. Ibid., p. 110.
5. Ibid., p. 104.

CHAPTER 18

Barriers to Sustainable Investing

Stephen Viederman

We have seen how markets fail to adequately price in environmental and other so-called externalities. Mispricing of risk has its perils—for just one example, consider what occurred in this regard with collateralized mortgage obligations during the recent financial crisis. This chapter poses another view that can help investors make better sense of overarching financial theory to take into account more tangible risks. Experts suggest, perhaps understandably, that efficient markets theories are possibly defunct. At minimum, they could use a tweak or two.

Nothing in life is to be feared. It is only to be understood.
—Nobel laureate Marie Curie

The world of finance exempts itself from nature and society. As Warren Buffett, well regarded longstanding value investor, observes, "In nature, every action has consequences, a phenomenon called the butterfly effect." But his investing does not appear to consider the risks and opportunities of societal and environmental issues. They are presumably externalities and intangibles, which he may address through his philanthropic endeavors.

This chapter is based on material available at www.unpri.org/files/Robins_ Krosinsky_Viederman_PRI2009.pdf.

MISSING PLANET PROBLEM

Warren Buffett's separation of vocation and avocation appears to be more the norm than the exception in the boardrooms and finance committees of many institutional investors and the investment managers who serve them. In the 1990s, a *New York Times* reporter asked a managing director at Lehman Brothers about his stance on a recent tax change. Noting that it benefited him and his clients, he went on to say "After six, when I get home from work, I worry about it as a citizen."[1] Too often it appears that "citizenship" is exercised before and after work and on weekends, much like going to the gym.

The lack of understanding of sustainable investing seems to arise from bounded awareness, which encompasses "a variety of psychological processes, all of which lead to the same error: a failure to see, seek, use, or share important and relevant information that is easily seen, sought, used or shared."

The culture of finance of institutional investors replicates what they know rather than what is needed for change. The internal incentive systems are not calibrated for environmental, societal, and governance (ESG) issues. They are not looking at fast-moving and complex trends, such as water availability and utilization, human rights, labor, climate, and resource scarcity, that will affect individual companies and economic sectors in their portfolios.

Board dynamics are crucial, but boards often have set patterns, providing too little time for real discussion of new issues and new ideas, for which there is no strong perception of need.

Consultants are more often than not gatekeepers for conventional investing. The culture reflects a closed mind to ideas that are outside the orthodoxy of traditional finance. Collateralized debt obligations rooted somewhere in what they have learned are acceptable even though some pundits in the field, such as Robert Rubin, have remarked that they do not understand them. Sustainable investing is definitely perceived as outside orthodoxy.

There is a Bermuda triangle within institutional investing in which new approaches to investing as if the future mattered, appear to get lost. At the corners of the triangle are the investment committees and boards, the investment staff members, and their consultants. They all come from the same business programs with the same outdated view of what constitutes their fiduciary duty and what investment is all about.

There is much talk of black swans, where the probably of a particular event occurring is low and not expected. Identifying these as low probability and unexpected absolves the culture from responsibility for many events and trends that, in fact, are "predictable surprises." These events, such as climate change and the onset of the housing bubble, could have been foreseen (and in these cases were) well before their onset was felt. Predictable surprises are different from black swans. And predictable surprises are often preventable surprises, a term that needs no definition.

OVERCOMING THE BARRIERS

Preconceptions about ethical and sustainable investing have converged in a prevalent myth of underperformance. Furthermore, the alleged absence of multiyear data sets on the use of sustainability factors has become another excuse for inaction. There is a sad irony in this as the market was brought down in 2008 by, among other things, financial instruments that seem to have been developed by the minute, with no track record and with no shortage of buyers and traders.

Language plays a powerful role in inhibiting discussion in institutional settings. The mainstream views such terms as "social," "ethical," "responsible," "impact," and in some places even "sustainable" as suspect, conjuring up images of Birkenstocks and peace symbols. Methodological differences among these approaches often are not considered.

Looking to past ESG performance is essential but not sufficient for sustainable investing. Retrospective analysis is not always a prelude to the future. Prospective methodologies that provide analysis of predictable surprises within a sector and at the company level are more likely to also identify preventable surprises and possible competitive advantage. Positive screening of "good companies" or negative screening of "bad companies," done every day on Wall Street as part of fundamental financial analysis, somehow becomes suspicious when financially tangible social and environmental factors are suggested. Beliefs play a part in *all* financial decision making, but apparently some beliefs are more important than others.[2]

Outdated interpretations of fiduciary duty are limiting factors in mainstream approaches to sustainable investing. An undue burden of proof is placed on investments that exhibit social and environmental parameters on sustainable investing. Maximizing return gives precedence to short-term thinking rather than long-term investing.

The latest insights that challenge this "conventional wisdom" of fiduciary duty have yet to impact the bedrock of investment opinion. Institutional investors ask their lawyers, "Can we do sustainable investing?" and all too often the answer is "No!" The question to ask should be "How can we do sustainable investing?"

The United Nations Environment Programme report, Freshfields II, recommends that investors ask their managers to include ESG issues in financial decision making. However, there is no discussion of how to move the institution to make that request. Given the institutional investors' typical culture there is a continuing dilemma. In addition, many investment managers are not capable of responding effectively.

Very few institutional consultants are well versed in sustainable investing. If asked, many consultants claim competencies that they do not actually possess; others with a reasonable degree of competency do not offer it unless asked.

Relationships are where the value driver is perceived to be, rightly or wrongly, and fear of jeopardizing these relationships is all too often the overriding motivation. Changing nothing becomes the default position and is perceived as the best way of preserving relationships.

There is now an urgent need to develop strategies of research and market reform that can make sustainable investing the norm. And that new norm must be accompanied by strategies to overcome the barriers to that exist within the institutional investor community to overcome willful blindness.

STRATEGY AND TACTICS

Much of the effort to introduce sustainable investing has been tactical. Many guides, for example, suggest that the first step is to write an investment policy that reflects ESG issues. They do not, however, offer strategies to address ways to encourage decision makers to demand a new investment policy.

A strategy is needed to influence the behavior of the key decision makers. A power analysis is needed to identify how to reach them. This process will require an understanding of the cultural and psychological barriers faced by the players, as well as analysis of the power dynamics and governance of the institution. A systemic approach is essential. Research to date on these issues has been limited.

Key to any strategy is developing a clearer conceptualization of what any of the adjectives of investing—social, ethical, responsible, impact, sustainable—really mean. Each has its own methodologies and views that often are strongly defended. But outsiders lump them together to the disadvantage of all. Words create worlds and can confuse as much as they can clarify.

We need a better understanding of the social, psychological, and cultural worlds of the key players in their roles as institutional investors. Anecdotes abound of the eleemosynary activities of members of boards, investment committees, and offices, who personally contribute to human rights and environmental groups while denying that these issues intersect with their day jobs. "Denial has always been a problem," writes Harvard Business

School historian Richard Tedlow. "What is different today is that the cost of denial has become so high. We are living in a less forgiving world than we once did."[3]

Decisions are made within organizations. The structure of decision making and the incentive systems facilitate or hinder discussion of sustainable investing. We need case studies on how a wide range of institutional investors have or have not engaged in aspects of sustainable investing.

Pension funds are like lemmings where innovation is concerned, in effect following each other with a herd mentality. The same is true of foundations and college and university endowments. Many smaller foundations, for example, have been involved in what is called mission-related investing for almost 20 years, but no large foundations are similarly engaged with a significant part of their endowments. The opportunity remains for champions of sufficient scale in the institutional investment world to effect change.

Academic researchers, to the degree that they have addressed sustainable investing at all, have approached it from the perspective of financial performance. However, the future will be different, and old, tired methodologies do not and will not capture the changes afoot or the affects of imbalance and injustice.

The challenge to business schools and others is to address the real world of institutional investing. We need a better understanding the circumstances that will encourage the broad range of institutional investors to consider and adopt sustainable investing.

Knowledge of the governance of institutional investors and institutional decision making are needed. Greater insight is needed to overcome "bounded awareness" and "denial" so that boards and finance committees will take the time to understand the emerging risks that societal and environmental issues raise for their financial performance and to act on this new awareness.

NOTES

1. Diana B. Henriques with Floyd Norris, "Rushing Away from Taxes," *New York Times*, December 1, 1996.
2. www.towerswatson.com/research/3795
3. http://drfd.hbs.edu/fit/public/facultyInfo.do?facEmId=rtedlow%40hbs.eduandfac Info=customandlinkId=1230

CHAPTER 19

The Silent "S" in ESG

Dan Viederman

> We turn now from the perspective of the barriers that prevent further uptake and application of sustainability into investment, and a view on the all-too-often missing consideration of risk to companies from social factors within investment portfolios. In an age of uprisings in the Arab world started by food shortages, these risks will become increasingly paramount.

For many environmental, social, governance (ESG) investors the "S" is silent. Social issues have proven complex to connect to financial performance, even more so than environmental and governance issues. Many investors compound this difficulty by asking companies the wrong things about social performance.

At Verité, we have seen this as we have worked to build labor rights in company supply chains since 1995. We have extensive expertise in apparel, footwear, electronics, agriculture, toy, and heavy industry supply chains, working both with brands—the mostly consumer-facing companies that sell a finished good—and their suppliers, which are mostly (but not exclusively) farms and factories in developing countries. Since 2001, we have provided information on labor rights risk and corporate performance to some of the largest pension funds in the world and helped asset managers and research firms better understand the levers of change available to them.

ASSESSING SOCIAL METRICS TO INCREASE BUSINESS PERFORMANCE

The common characteristic of the sectors in which Verité works—that they are heavily reliant on multitiered, contracted supply chains—is one of the main complicating factors in establishing a financial link between supply chain labor performance and the financial performance of a company. The way workers are treated in a contracted factory that spends part of its time making part of a brand's products has at best an indirect connection to the brand's stock price or short-term financial success. For this and other reasons, investors who seek a financial silver bullet may search in vain.

Yet there are ways to connect the management of labor rights on factories and farms with business drivers that brands, companies, and investors care about. From my interaction with chief executives, general counsels, and senior management, the strongest reasons why a company should pay attention to labor rights in its supply chain include:

- *Maintaining a reputation as a good employer.* Companies pay a premium to attract desired staff to a controversial workplace.
- *Avoiding surprises.* Companies do not like to find out that they are sourcing in an unauthorized location or wasting time and resources sourcing through several layers of agents where they could be sourcing directly.
- *Operating legally and ethically in risky business locations.* Companies ideally want to avoid operating in an illegal or unethical way, even when the operator is a contracted supplier.
- *Maintaining a positive reputation in the public eye.* The negative financial impact of a bad reputation is overemphasized—that is, companies generally do not suffer substantial declines in financial performance or stock prices when associated with sweatshops—but maintaining a positive reputation is, of course, of interest to companies.
- *Where the company is a supplier to other companies.* The closest connection between social performance and financial performance exists among the subset of suppliers that are of substantial scale or publicly listed. They must meet the social requirements of their clients and can suffer loss of contracts if they fail to do so.

RISK MANAGEMENT

In general, companies address supply chain labor rights issues as part of their risk management efforts. Unfortunately, much of what investors ask brands about this risk management gets to the heart of neither the risk nor management. The information that most investors seek tends to be related peripherally to the actual risk profile of companies.

Supply chain risk is determined by three factors: where companies source, what raw materials they use, and how they choose suppliers. The response to these risks cannot be one-size-fits-all, yet often that is what investors (as well as other stakeholders) expect of companies.

Geographic Risk

As Verité's Emerging Markets Research Program has shown over the past ten years, countries are not risky to the same degree or in the same ways. In China, almost every manufacturing company has difficulty controlling work hours to comply with the 60-hour-per-week limit embedded in most codes of conduct.

In India, the risk profile is different: Child labor, illegal subcontracting, and discrimination against women are common problems. In Mexico, one of the main issues is the often violent suppression of freedom of association. Effective management of supply chain risk requires that companies apply relevant tools to address the specific risks they face in different geographies.

Raw Materials

Companies that source commodities must address the difficult and often-uncontrolled circumstances in which they are exploited. Verité has documented the tight link between commodity sourcing and the egregious problem of modern-day slavery at www.verite.org/commodities.

But addressing labor conditions in commodity sourcing is particularly complicated. The main problem for brands coming to grips with commodity sourcing is that they must deal with many actors—traders, agents, government-run exchanges—that do not face the same consumer pressure the company does to improve labor conditions. Strengthening labor conditions in commodity supply chains requires these consumer-facing companies to collaborate with their competitors and shared suppliers, yet members of the collaboration face different incentives and pressures.

Choosing Suppliers

The most powerful risk management intervention a company can make is avoiding risk in the first place. Yet companies rarely choose suppliers based on the suppliers' ability to manage labor conditions effectively. To the contrary: The vast majority of companies do not factor supplier labor performance into their selection criteria when choosing a factory or farm.

SUMMARY

The risks outlined here highlight two overarching ways in which brands can manage labor rights risk: by making up-front decisions that minimize the risk that emerges from the three factors and by putting in place controls that address risk after the fact. Almost all investors focus on the latter effort. But the work that companies do to avoid risk rather than manage it has far greater impact and says a great deal about a company's approach to management.

Investors should look favorably on companies that address social responsibility up front in supplier selection. Investors should use shareholder engagement as an opportunity to give support to the idea that social performance should be equal in weight to a supplier's ability to deliver a quality good, on time, at an appropriate price. In doing so, investors will help drive brands and their suppliers to more impactful efforts to protect the rights of vulnerable people who work in supply chains while protecting the security and maximizing the potential of their portfolios.

CHAPTER 20

Sustainable Investing

A Ten-Year Perspective

Nancy Degnan

Data abounds on ESG factors, but the most important information is all too often not available, including, for example—what the tipping points are, what the distance to target is—that we need to achieve as a global society to avoid these potential tipping points. Standards are still emerging. In this chapter, Nancy Degnan from Columbia University discusses her perspective on what steps are now most critically important.

The beginning of the second decade of the twenty-first century offers us an interesting opportunity to imagine where we will be in 2021. If we could look ahead ten years, would we see how sustainable investing fostered social, economic, and environmental achievement? Would it have impacted climate change for the better? Would sustainable investing have supported the experience of humanity toward less poverty, greater prosperity, and deeper knowledge about our interconnectedness with each other, nature's resources, and the marketplace? Would sustainable investing mainstream the importance of investment decisions based on ecosystems and their value to business and industry? Would a general and widespread stewardship of biodiversity, water, and energy have found its central place in decisions about risk and resiliency? And would these have occurred while remaining steadfast to the core function of investing, which is to *pass money from the present into the future as savings and wealth*?[1]

THE NEW NORMAL

Imagining such a place for investment is intriguing. Many would speculate and dismiss such a role, especially given the economic and financial crises and suffering of the past several years. But from within precisely this context, the marketplace has revealed its state of resiliency—what investors call the *new normal*: "slower economic growth, fewer returns on investments, and higher unemployment." The phenomenon appears to be global.[2] Coupled with the "new normal," however, is a growing realization about a connection between investment and innovation—or, as a recent article suggested (not about sustainability but investment in general), maybe one positive, longer-term development to come out of the recession is more focus on our need to be innovative.[3]

The premise for the 2021 "looking back" is that the investment innovation that offset the "new normal" of 2011 was, in fact, *a sustainability innovation*. The deliberate and widespread coalescence of social, environmental, and economic well-being now afforded through the lens of sustainability could provoke innovation on a much broader basis, albeit localized and regionalized, than had occurred by the end of the century's first decade. The essential elements of sustainability innovation rest in climate change adaptation as a source of innovation, which could foster the:

- Design of predictive research and data from a local and regional scale
- Centrality of ecosystem goods and services, the biodiversity upon which ecosystems rest, and the interconnection with water and energy as integral to sustainability investment
- The shaping of data parameters and analysis within spatial and temporal levels to support medium- and longer-term investment in sustainability innovation

The remainder of this chapter further describes these three elements as foundational to sustainability investment.

CLIMATE CHANGE MITIGATION, ADAPTATION, AND SUSTAINABILITY RESEARCH

In considering a role of climate change adaptation as a driver of sustainability research and its application at local and regional levels, it is useful to look at climate change mitigation as a starting point. For nearly 20 years, climate change mitigation and carbon emissions and the efforts to lower, exchange, sequester, or substitute for them altogether has arguably opened the doorway for sustainability research specifically regarding greenhouse gas (GHG) emissions and more generally around the idea of sustainable development.

What has been revealed through the lens of climate change mitigation and sustainability research and application is the need to shift away from wholesale exploitation of nature's goods and services toward their stewardship. Seen from a perspective of stewardship, the role of nature is recognized as central to well-being. Natural capital contributes to the provision of water, natural water filtration, energy production, flood control, recreation, natural storm water management, and biodiversity.[4] It is estimated that worldwide dollar value of the goods and services nature provides, or, in other words, ecosystem services[5]—is $33 trillion per year. The value of all human-produced goods and services per year is about $18 trillion.[6]

On one hand, an elevated awareness has promulgated more public discourse on the role of the goods and services nature provides for human production and consumption. On the other hand, people, whether as professionals or as citizens, can be befuddled by deluges of data and the uncertainty of projections and trends, the preponderance "science speak,"[7] as well as accompanying norms of value neutrality emblematic of solid scientific research but problematic for decision making.[8] More, that climate change mitigation has become highly politicized is another complicating factor and is central to confidence in data and research. Lamentably, while research around mitigation and sustainability may be robust, deep understanding among the nonscience community and a trust in the data, particularly with regard to application of that research to climate solutions, may yet be elusive.[9]

The investment community may be experiencing the very same conditions. There is the growing realization that nature's goods and services, including energy, food, and water, are linked together, and that these connections matter in real and significant ways for investments. However, translating this realization into actual investment practice may be challenging. For instance, renewable energy investment has revealed unintended consequences of greater intensity and global impact, sometimes ending in market misalignment.

A good example of this phenomenon is the one of biofuels production as a substitute for fossil fuels and the policy that subsidizes U.S. farmers to grow and use corn for ethanol production. Besides being both an energy- and water-intensive process,[10] ethanol production directly competes with the world's grain markets, impacting poorer nations and the people within them in fundamental, life-and-death ways. The move by the U.S. government, farmers, and investors to substitute ethanol for fossil fuels has created great insecurity and risk on a global scale.[11] Touted as a measure of sustainability and a step forward in renewable energy production, the ethanol example epitomizes the consequences of "siloed" decision making based solely on a climate change mitigation perspective derived from a singular focus on carbon.

Climate change mitigation has been caught up in its own spatial and temporal character in at least three ways:

1. At the heart of mitigation is mandating carbon emission cuts and caps globally, neither of which has been wholly agreed to by the nations of the earth. There is little to suggest that this situation will reverse itself soon, even as international conferences continue to be held and the topic debated.[12]
2. The high degree of uncertainty in climate policy serves as a disincentive to investment in innovation in the renewable energy sector.[13]
3. While estimates of the global economic impact for warming up to 3 degrees Celsius exist, climate ensemble models project a mean warming by 2100 of 1 to 6 degrees Celsius, so impacts may be worse than expected.[14] There exists little consensus on how to handle such variation in data and modeling.

In the face of ongoing challenges for climate change mitigation, and the certainty of continued global warming from past and current emissions, how can the world move forward in its efforts to both cut GHG emissions and simultaneously steward nature's goods and services that stand to be adversely affected by warming?

ADAPTATION AS KEY TO INVESTMENT AND PRACTICE

Answers may be found in a strategic and holistic embracing of climate change adaptation as a key driver of research and its application to investment and practice. Such a statement does not suggest an abandonment of climate change mitigation efforts. That we must continue to work toward climate change mitigation remains unequivocal. However, in a complementary approach to mitigation, climate change adaptation may well offer platforms for innovation that both lower GHG emissions and honor the environmental interdependency sometimes missed by the mitigation's main attention to carbon. Together, mitigation and adaptation may provide a way forward in sustainability where the combination affords an effectiveness that is not achievable through either alone.

The local and regional contribution of climate change adaptation to sustainability is threefold.

1. Risk may be more manageable, because it can be assessed and monitored with greater frequency, although the caliber of data and research here is key.[15]
2. Empirical research has demonstrated that innovation processes have a pronounced regional dimension with the analog to location being the availability of knowledge.[16]
3. Because the scale of adaptation is different from mitigation, at least five benefits[17] are realized:
   a. The "free-rider" or collective action problem is significantly reduced.
   b. Contentious asymmetry between emissions producers and victims becomes less relevant.
   c. Private benefits of adaptation are more likely to exceed private costs.
   d. Short-term benefits are less uncertain and easier to finance.
   e. The existing weather and commodity risk management infrastructure can be adapted to reduce vulnerabilities (across sectors).

Taken as a full complement, climate change adaptation may be described as more immediately well informed, from a sustainability perspective. Across each of the five benefits is the opportunity to engage in climate change adaptation and the type of research design, data gathering, and analysis intended to inform adaptation solutions.

The International Research Institute for Climate and Society of Columbia University (the author also works at Columbia University) currently has over 866 publications on various aspects of climate change, risk, risk management, and application to a variety of sectors. It engages in 126 projects around in three regions of the world: Latin America and the Caribbean, Africa, and Asia and the Pacific.[18]

These research projects are driven by their regional focus as well as climate change. Research has applications that are tangible; reflect the importance of energy, biodiversity, and water—sometimes singularly and sometimes synergistically—and are contextualized within sectors such as agriculture, transportation, and energy production. One example is current research going on in the Southern Cone of South America, which holds the largest reserve of cultivable soil, "to identify main vulnerabilities (current and expected with a changing climate) of the main production systems ... to explore possible technological alternatives and policy interventions to improve their adaptability and sustainability ... and thus, build resilience to climate-related risk in the agricultural sector."[19] Among the stated objectives of the research is analysis of "possible climate scenarios for the next 10–30 years that include the measures of uncertainty ... as well as integrated seasonal climate forecasts to soil water balances for establishing early warning systems of droughts and floods."[20] The research is based in a partnership of 11 organizations including those in Uruguay, Chile, Paraguay, and Argentina as well as the Inter-American Development Bank and the Inter-American Institute for Cooperation—all of which have a profound regional knowledge of and connection to both the agricultural sector and the geographic location within South America.

It is arguable that each of the five aspects of the scale of adaptation is present and function productively, given the research design and inclusion of stakeholders. It is likewise arguable that the findings of such research would inform medium- and longer-term investment in sustainability innovation in agriculture, for instance, because it has been deliberate about addressing risks and vulnerabilities within the sector in those time frames. Such research promulgation may be critical to effective climate change adaptation.

ECOSYSTEM SERVICES

Engaging with climate change from an adaptation perspective also brings us closer to the realization of the interconnectedness of natural infrastructure with that of the human-built environment. Climate change adaptation offers a platform to consider the other services of environmental sustainability, that is, water and biodiversity with energy as nature's services—ecosystem services—for production and consumption. The deeper understanding of the type and function of ecosystem services emerges. Changes in one impact the other due, in part, to the identifiable boundaries of ecosystems themselves.

It is also here that sustainable economic development can be distinguished from traditional economic development, in that the essential role of the ecosystems is considered in investment decision making. Implications here are twofold:

1. Ecosystem goods and services, valued through a scientific framework, must likewise be valued through an economic and financial one.
2. These scientific, economic, and financial values need to be operationalized into the life cycle (LC) of loan approvals.

In 2007, the environment ministers of the Group of Eight + 5 countries commissioned a report to address what it would take to assign economic and financial value to ecosystem goods and services. "The Economics of Ecosystems and Biodiversity," or the TEEB Report, was published in 2010. Its goal was to "initiate the process of analyzing the global economic benefit of biodiversity . . . because the invisibility of biodiversity values has often encouraged the inefficient use or even destruction of natural capital . . . which is foundational to our economies."[21] Investment based on economic and financial valuation of ecosystems services would benefit sustainability efforts. In the report, the economic valuation of ecosystems services is demonstrated through case studies, rendering the analysis of valuation on an example-by-example basis. The authors note that economic valuation is a "challenging task which needs careful selection and application of methodologies ... requiring high levels of precision and reliability ... that is often time and resource intensive." The authors also indicate that access to best practices is key, yet difficulties remain when even making judgments about what is actually "best." Nonetheless, a core consideration for sustainable innovation is the fact that ecosystems are local and regional and as such interface with climate change adaptation research.

MAKING USE OF DATA AND FINDINGS

For sustainability investment decision making to occur, the next logical step is to make effective use of data and findings on climate change adaptation and ecosystems as applied to core business function of investing. One important way to do so is through the LC of loan approval, which has at least seven steps.[22] It begins with the articulation of what will be reviewed and all points of assessment and ends with ongoing monitoring and evaluation for the life of the investment:

1. Framing the guidelines for the loan
2. Reviewing applications to ensure that they are within those guidelines and can advance to evaluation
3. Evaluating
4. Engaging in due diligence
5. Selecting projects for investment through committee approval
6. Disbursing funds
7. Conducting ongoing monitoring and evaluation

One major step forward for investment in sustainability and innovation is to deeply embed the science and research of climate change adaptation, integrated with the science of ecosystems, ecosystem valuation, risk and uncertainty, within the LC. Moreover, the process requires emergent knowledge transmission, in an iterative way, to ensure the inclusion of new science and insights as these arise.

In order to do so effectively, sustainability investment and innovation must rely on a common base of knowledge, or body of knowledge, and the acquisition of such knowledge must matter to scientists, researchers, practitioners, and investors alike. Authors Michael Fritsch and Viktor Slavtchev state: "There is general agreement among economists and economic geographers that innovation activity is shaped by space and concentrated in certain areas"—or innovation clusters. General understanding, moreover, suggests that high levels of innovative activity found in these clusters are due to knowledge born of research and development (R&D) through both universities and private enterprise.[23] The authors also state that there is broad consensus that scientific knowledge plays an essential role in economic development and social well-being and that the basic knowledge from university R&D is an important input for private sector innovation activity.

These characterizations are central to the notion that climate change adaptation can support sustainability innovation. For such innovation to occur rapidly and robustly over the next decade, deeper and more detailed and dynamic engagements between universities and the investment sector—both private and public—need to take place. Innovation's success will be dependent on core groups of experts doing the hard work of understanding each other's role in sustainability and then making the deliberate effort to identify synergies and act on them for the benefit of adaptation.

The type of expert group probably includes at least these specialists:

- Ecologists
- Botanists
- Conservation scientists and agronomists
- Investment bankers from public, quasi-governmental, and private organizations
- Geographers
- Economists
- Economic geographers, finance
- Risk managers
- Operations research scientists and practitioners

For productive exchange to occur, the group will need to develop models of intentional learning to emphasize learning needs as an intended goal rather than just as a by-product of their engagement.[24]

Interestingly, sustainability innovation clusters can and ought to take some cues from 20th century sector clusters. One example is Ile de France's "special innovation clusters" that include optics and electronic software, automotive and public transportation, healthcare and biotech, cosmetics and perfumes, agriculture and finance innovation. These clusters required inter-sectoral cooperation, higher education research and concentration of financing and investment. For the 21st century, sustainability innovation would be focused on water, biodiversity, energy across existing sectors. Intact biodiversity is vital to healthcare and biotech, cosmetics and perfumes, agriculture. While energy is often cited in technology and optics, enormous amounts of water are necessary for these industries and present a looming challenge given the continued reliance of agriculture on water and the growing scarcity of water itself. Finally, it is arguable that financial innovation will likely be impacted by a consideration of nature's services as a part of risk analysis and risk management. For instance, healthy ecosystems can reduce the amplitude of disasters and, increase the levels of human and natural resiliency, that factor into overall financial recovery.

In terms of regional innovation, we might imagine regional innovation clusters to address industry issues of water and wastewater management to help drive more efficient and effective conservation and use of this critical resource.[25] With the recent focus on unconventional (shale) gas drilling, regional clusters could attract R&D investment to address the myriad of challenges currently facing the industry. For instance, finding ways to fix the design flaws in gas wells leaking fugitive gases is critical to gains in efficiency and safety as well as in reduction of the large amount of emissions of hydrocarbons and methane. Of course, other serious ongoing issues of unconventional gas drilling include the use of millions of gallons of water as part of hydraulic fracking fluid; and, the storing and cleaning the highly toxic flowback water which results from the drilling process. Investment in R&D specifically addressing these issues can support innovation in the energy sector with additional benefit accruing to the water sector.

The effort of sustainability innovation investment will be both complex and complicated. It will likely need to be embedded in a commonly held worldview of the essential, critical role of sustainability for all future well-being. It may require a change of culture supported by new sets of normative practice, habits, and assumptions to be shared among all experts within the investment industry and those who engage with the industry. Systematic scholarship, informed by both academia and industry, including the kinds of institutional arrangements and actual knowledge systems needed, has to be central to collective work if investment is to be broadly sustainable.[26] Moreover, making this knowledge productive in both medium and longer term requires the ongoing and dynamic flow of information that is both explicit to adaptation and ecosystems science and to risk and uncertainty.[27] Unlike the examples mentioned earlier, where incentives to consider risk were removed, sustainability investment can ill afford to take shortcuts with climate change or fail to consider the inherent interconnectedness of natural systems, lest wholesale, negative unintended consequences arise. Investment made in expanding the type of research that offers data, models, and analysis on time scales of 10 to 30 years will help investors more deeply understand the complexity of sustainability; and, thus likely make more sound decisions about the innovation to help achieve it.

SUMMARY

Climate change adaptation, seen as a complement to climate change mitigation, offers an important and critical opportunity to invest sustainably in innovation locally and regionally. A local and regional scale helps reveal our interdependency with nature's goods and services—ecosystem goods and services—and brings into focus risk and uncertainty from both a scalar and temporal level that is not readily available through mitigation research and modeling.

Nonetheless, for true sustainability innovation to occur, stakeholders across academia, investment, and development institutions need to develop and advance a body of knowledge that incorporates complex information about equally complex human and natural systems, all toward investment decision making. While the work is undoubtedly challenging, without it, investing in innovation for sustainability will fall short of the goal of balancing economic, social, and environmental considerations for the current and future well-being of Earth. Sustainable investment, arguably, has an enormous role to play and responsibility to fulfill. It will be very powerful to look back ten years hence and see that the investment community has done its part successfully.

NOTES

1. William N. Goetzmann, "An Introduction to Investment." Yale University, School of Management, 1998. http://viking.som.yale.edu/will/finman540/classnotes/class1.html
2. Tom Granahan, "The Economy Normalized," *IDD*, September 24, 2009. www.iddmagazine.com/blog/tom_granahan/the-economy-normalized-197961-1.html?zkPrintable=true
3. Ibid. The remainder of the quote is "Just don't tell Wall Street."
4. Biodiversity is often defined at three levels: (1) the variety of species on Earth from microscopic bacteria to "whales the size of city blocks"; (2) the variety of ecosystems across the face of Earth—tropical, savannah, grasslands, marshes, oceans, forests, and deserts; and (3) the variety and diversity of genetics or the diversity of genes within a species. www.biodiversity911.org/biodiversity_basics/why_important/BottomLine.html

   The Convention on Biological Diversity defines biodiversity as the "variability among living organisms from all sources including terrestrial, marine and other aquatic ecosystems and the ecological complexes of which they are a part; this includes diversity within species, between species and ecosystems." Text of Convention: 1992. www.cbd.int/convention/articles.shtml?a=cbd-02

5. Ecosystems are defined as "all the interacting living and non-living elements of an area of land or water. Ecosystem functions refer to the processes of transformation of matter and energy in ecosystems. Ecosystem goods and services are the benefits that humans (and all living creatures) directly or indirectly derive from naturally functioning ecological systems." Daly and Farley, 2004; Costanza et al. 1997; Daily, 1997; DeGroot et al., 2002; Wilson, Troy and Costanza, 2004 as cited in David Batker et al., *Gaining Ground: Wetlands, Hurricanes, and the Economy: The Value of Restoring the Mississippi River Delta* (Tacoma, WA: Earth Economics, 2010). www.eartheconomics. org

6. www.biodiversity911.org/biodiversity_basics/why_important/BottomLine.html

7. What I mean by "science speak" is that set of language, vocabulary, and normative practice of the science community. To be sure, investment banking, and every other profession can be said to have its very own version of communication designed to facilitate transactions and understanding within the community. However, language and norms also serve as a barrier to immediate understanding for those outside the community.

8. Sharachchandra Lele and Richard B. Norgaard, "Sustainability and the Scientist's Burden," *Conservation Biology* 10, No. 2 (April 1996): 354–365. www.jstor.org/stable/2386852. The article offers interesting insights into the dilemma that sustainability presents for scientists. The authors write about the challenges of "operationalizing" the concepts of sustainability from a natural science perspective and suggest that scientists should redefine terms of reference, methods of research, and problem definitions for scientific research as one way to address "value-loaded and social charged discourse" surrounding sustainability.

9. http://curry.eas.gatech.edu/climate/towards_rebuilding_trust.html

10. Experts differ on whether ethanol has net energy production versus net energy consumption. This difference seems to be based in the calculus of what is actually measured. See Phil McKenna, "Measuring Corn Ethanol's Thirst for Water." www.technologyreview.com/energy/22428/

11. Lester Brown, "Why Ethanol Production Will Drive World Food Prices Even Higher in 2008." www.openmarket.org/2007/01/08/ethanol-demand-will-drive-grain-prices-to-record-levels-lester-brown-warns/. The author wrote: "We are witnessing the beginning of one of the great tragedies of history. The United States, in a misguided effort to reduce its oil insecurity by converting grain into fuel for cars, is generating global food insecurity on a scale never seen before."

12. "Global Deal on Climate Change in 2010 Almost Impossible," February 2010. www.guardian.co.uk/environment/2010/feb/01/climate-change-deal-impossible-2010. Alex Kelly, "Is Cancun Climate Deal a Pig's Ear?" December 2010. http://ourworld.unu.edu/en/is-cancun-climate-deal-a-pigs-ear/

13. Pano Kroko, "Green Capital Index, Climate Change Companies: Sour Grapes and Good Wine." September 2010. panokroko.wordpress.com/2010/09/17/green-capital-index-climate-change-companies-sour-grapes-and-good-wine/. The author writes: "Renewable energy alone is the investment field, badly underperforming all other Climate Change global equities. Especially in the US where the lack of any Climate Change legislation, new energy policy and carbon price direction stumps the best business models."

14. Satyajit Bose, "Climate-Economy Models, Financial and Commodity Markets," presentation to the InterAmerican Development Bank, Washington, DC, September 30–October 1, 2010.

15. Manuel Guariguata et al., "Mitigation Needs Adaptation: Tropical Forestry and Climate Change," 2008. www.cifor.cgiar.org/nc/online-library/browse/view-publication/publication/2405.html. See also Shardul Agarwala and Martin Berg, "Development and Climate Change Project: Concept Paper on Scope and Criteria for Case Study Selection," Organisation for Economic Co-operation and Development, 2002. www.oecd.org/dataoecd/9/21/1950084.pdf

16. Michael Fritsch and Viktor Slavtchev, "The Role of Regional Knowledge for Innovation," 2005. www.feweb.vu.nl/ersa2005/final_papers/623.pdf

17. Bose, "Climate-Economy Models, Financial and Commodity Markets."

18. Available at http://portal.iri.columbia.edu/portal/server.pt?open=512andobjID=967andmode=2).

19. Walter Baethgen, "Climate Change and Variability in the Expansion of Agricultural Frontier in the Southern Cone: Technological and Policy Strategies to Reduce Vulnerabilities—ID:136," International Research Institute for Climate and Society , Columbia University. http://portal.iri.columbia.edu/portal/server.pt?open=512andobjID=967andmode=2

20. Ibid.

21. Pavan Sukhdev et al., "The Economics of Ecosystem and Biodiversity: Mainstreaming the Economics of Nature, a Synthesis Approach," Conclusions and Recommendations of TEEB, 2010. www.teebweb.org/Portals/25/TEEB%20Synthesis/TEEB_SynthReport_09_2010_online.pdf

22. Satyajit Bose, "Conservation," October 2010, Columbia University, Earth Institute. See also World Bank, "How the Project Cycle Works."http://web.worldbank.org/WBSITE/EXTERNAL/PROJECTS/0,,contentMDK:20120731~menuPK: 41390~pagePK:41367~ piPK:51533~theSitePK:40941,00.html

23. Michael Fritsch and Viktor Slavtchev, "The Role of Regional Knowledge for Innovation," 2–3.

24. Jan Van Aalst, "Distinguishing Knowledge-Sharing, Knowledge-Construction, and Knowledge-Creation Discourses," 2009. www.springerlink.com/content/y5l3752806321501/fulltext.pdf. Peter Senge and John Sterman, "Systems Thinking and Organizational Learning: Acting Locally and Thinking Globally in the Organization of the Future," 1990. www.systemdynamics.org/ conferences/1990/proceed/pdfs/senge1007.pdf

25. See: Water Technology Innovation Cluster, WTIC FAQs. www.epa.gov/wtic/faqs.html

26. David Cash et al., "Knowledge Systems for Sustainable Development," 2003. www.ncbi.nlm.nih.gov/pmc/articles/PMC166186/

27. David Gurteen, "Knowledge, Creativity and Innovation," 1998. www.emeraldinsight.com/journals.htm?articleid=883647. Serge M. Garcia et al., "Towards Integrated Assessment and Advice in Small-scale Fisheries: Principles and Processes," 2008. FAO Fisheries and Aquaculture Technical Paper No. 515. Rome, Italy: Fisheries and Aquaculture Department, United Nations. www.fao.org/docrep/011/i0326e/i0326e00.htm

CHAPTER 21

Bloomberg

Curtis Ravenel

> One large information provider, more than any other to date, has seen the opportunity and embarked on a path to provide environmental, social, and governance information. Here's Curtis Ravenel, who heads up Bloomberg's efforts in this regard.

When Michael Bloomberg started his firm, he had an idea that was unique at the time and filled a gap: the need for common information. And so the Bloomberg terminal was born, giving its users unprecedented access to information and increased ability to act on it. This access has transformed the securities industry globally by leveling the playing field between buyers and sellers.

This leveling of the playing field has reduced costs, increased participation, democratized access through transparency, and greatly improved liquidity—making markets more efficient. But financial markets display a strange dichotomy; with improved transparency and access to information comes increasing complexity and challenges to finding value and managing risk. And for all of the efficiency they bring to capital allocation, markets still do not address some fundamental externalities—most notably, climate change. "The problem of climate change involves a fundamental failure of markets: those who damage others by emitting greenhouse gases generally do not pay," said Sir Nicholas Stern in his seminal 2006 report on the economics of climate change.[1]

Given the complexities of climate change issues facing the globe, it is critical that government and business leaders focus on finding commonality and opportunity to move collectively toward a global deal or other means of mitigating impacts. Regardless, climate change will continue, with far-reaching implications requiring adaptation, and the world will respond in multiple ways—economically, politically, and socially—with or without a deal. These responses will create significant risks and opportunities across all economic sectors and geographic regions. How companies address these risks and opportunities is critical, requiring a more holistic view of "sustainability." One that focuses beyond traditional financial analysis to also include social impact and environmental management—not just to address these risks, but to also understand how to use these issues as a source of innovation and opportunity—all of which, for many mainstream investors, is a new concept

PROVIDING INVESTOR INSIGHT AND INCREASING TRANSPARENCY

The financial markets look to Bloomberg for their critical market information, and in our search for value in this area, we look for ways to provide more insight to our customers on emerging issues. Sustainability information is one such area. Recent studies from McKinsey and Accenture highlight that over three-quarters of executives believe sustainability contributes positively to shareholder value in the long term.[2] Additional research shows that most of a company's share value is attributable to cash flow expectations beyond three years out.[3] And there are important intangible or extrafinancial issues—such as human capital, risk, brand management, carbon exposure, and capacity for innovation—that cannot be accounted for with traditional financial analysis.

We began collecting environmental, social, and governance (ESG) data to try to capture some of the drivers of that value. Having developed our own internal sustainability program, we know firsthand that significant value can be derived from these efforts. Coupled with the proliferation of available company data, the regulatory circling of multiple, significant national and multinational agencies, and a significant increase in interest from institutional investors, we were led to believe that ESG data *are* fundamental to equity analysis.

But, like any new set of information, there are significant problems with its depth, breadth, and quality. Inconsistent disclosure, varying standards, questions of materiality, and data accuracy (verification) remain significant barriers to greater market integration. For those who lament the current state of affairs, please remember that it took hundreds of years to screw up traditional financial accounting. Given the relative youth of this field, we should not let the perfect be the enemy of the good. The multitude of organizations involved today reflect the enormous challenges (and opportunities) ahead. While nongovernmental organizations, specialty research shops, and socially responsible asset managers created the demand for transparency and pioneered sustainable investment strategies, the road ahead requires significant commitments from mainstream institutional investors and, by extension, their information providers.

For Bloomberg, this means leveraging our role in the market to encourage companies to disclose, to work with our partners to address the questions of materiality and set new standards. While there has been a lot of very good work by statisticians, academics, researchers, and even large institutional asset managers to demonstrate materiality and a correlation with risk and return, the challenge remains for sustainability data to be defined to a degree that will enable mass use. Nor is there enough historical data to draw real conclusions.

State Street did a fascinating study showing the volatility of various ratings applied to companies from independent ESG raters. Our own review of key performance indicators used across the world confirmed what many have known for some time: A social agenda still drives much of the industry. This, of course, means that "materiality" is not defined in financial terms, a fact that has stigmatized ESG data among mainstream investors as soft or subjective and qualitative, and has significantly hampered its integration into traditional financial analysis.

This is changing. A recent research note from Elaine Prior's team at Citigroup Global Markets highlights this fact:

> *"Non-Financial" or "Extra-Financial" Data: These terms are sometimes used for ESG data. We do not differentiate data this way. We believe that the raft of data and information that may influence assessment of a company's outlook can all be considered "financial." ESG data is simply one tool in conducting research, and must be combined with additional information to make useful "ESG-related" interpretations and judgments.*[4]

This sentiment is being pushed aggressively by the Integrated International Reporting Committee, whose mission is to create a globally accepted framework bringing together financial and ESG criteria, moving traditional CSR/sustainability reporting out of what has been a separate function, and insisting that both the overall and sustainability strategy of the organization is deeply embedded into their normal annual reports.

These efforts, along others such as the international expansion of the Global Reporting Initiative, the United Nations Principles for Responsible Investing, the UN Global Compact, the Carbon Disclosure Project, and

Ceres' Investor Network on Climate Risk all seek to mainstream ESG analysis.

And, as Farnum Brown commented in a recent blog, the team at Trillium Asset Management "will identify, test, refine and systematize an evolving set of demonstrable ESG 'alpha factors'—that is, quantifiable environmental, social, and governance factors that measurably improve corporate financial performance and investor returns."[5] This, he says, is SRI 3.0, which moves ESG from ethical alignment and shareholder activism to hard, statistical analysis. Trillium and many others have been doing this for years, but only recently have the data been available to do any significant regression analysis. In fact, it will be another five-plus years before we can truly appease hardcore quants.

But what others have done behind closed doors (as asset managers, their methodologies are their intellectual property and competitive advantage), UniCredit's Patrick Berger and the Responsible Investment Academy's Louise O'Halloran are working with Bloomberg to bring into the open and move the integration from the philosophical to the tactical.[6]

As fundamental tools for the financial community—one that works hard to understand participants' work flow—Bloomberg terminals are well positioned to integrate useful sustainability data and analysis into the valuation and decision-making process of the capital markets. By offering information transparency, we create visibility in new and often complex instruments and issues. This builds confidence in the public market and, in turn, drives liquidity and broader participation. Ultimately, our goal is to provide reliable information that drives responsible investment decisions—across the value chain.

SUMMARY

In the coming years, Bloomberg will collaborate with partners from industry, finance, nonprofits, and governments to identify best practices for ESG integration and develop new ones where necessary. While many firms have deep ESG data, they do not have Bloomberg's depth of critical industry and financial data, news assets, or the clean energy data of Bloomberg New Energy Finance. And most important, they don't have Bloomberg's user base: the most influential investors in the world. By combining these information sets with our powerful suite of analytical tools, we will create new opportunities for us, our customers, the environment, and society.

NOTES

1. http://news.bbc.co.uk/2/shared/bsp/hi/pdfs/30_10_06_exec_sum.pdf
2. How companies manage sustainability. McKinsey Global Survey results 2010. A New Era of Sustainability. UN Global Compact-Accenture CEO study 2010. http://download.mckinseyquarterly.com/sustainability.pdf; www.unglobal compact.org/docs/news_events/8.1/UNGC_Accenture_CEO_Study_2010.pdf
3. Ken Standfield: *Intangible Finance Standards: 21st Century Breakthroughs in Fundamental Analysis & Technical Analysis* (Burlington, MA: Elsevier Academic Press, 2005.)
4. Citigroup Global Markets, "ESG: The Quest for Standardized, Auditable, Comparable Data," February 2011.
5. http://trilliuminvest.com/news-articles-category/featured-articles/the-evolution-of-sri-introducing-version-3-0/
6. UniCredit's new ESG research methodology, The Halo's Creed, is publicly available and seeks to quantify ESG issues and incorporate them into stock evaluations. The Responsible Investment Academy launched a specialized course for financial advisors to integrate ESG issues. www.unicreditgroup.eu/ucg-static/downloads/UniCredit_ESG_report_The_Halos_Creed_Nov_2010.pdf

CHAPTER 22

Aviva

Malte Griess-Nega and Nick Robins

Institutional investors own or control the bulk of global equity, and by incorporating sustainability into the ways in which they allocate capital, they hold a key to unlocking corporate efficiencies and innovation.

Research is a commodity, analysis is not.
Steve Waygood, head of Sustainability
Research and Engagement

As institutional investors learn how to deploy sustainable investing approaches, one of the key themes to emerge is the dynamic between specialist strategies and broad-based mainstreaming. In some instances, fund managers with pre-existing ethical or socially responsible funds have found it harder to integrate sustainability factors into wider investment practice as ESG issues can be misperceived as the sole preserve of niche funds. In others, starting from a clean slate has enabled many large institutional investors to comprehensively insert ESG factors into routine investment analysis and decision-making. The most powerful dynamic exists, however, where specialist sustainability teams demonstrate through their superior performance track record in terms of risk and return the core rationale for wider integration by regular portfolio managers.

To explore how this dynamic can work in practice, it is instructive to look at the United Kingdom's Aviva.

AVIVA'S HISTORY AND INVESTMENT PHILOSOPHY

Aviva is one of the world's largest insurance companies with £240 billion in assets under management in early 2011. It took a strategic decision to promote sustainable and responsible investments (SRI) in 2001 with the launch of six Sustainable Future funds: Corporate Bond, UK Growth, Absolute Growth, Global Growth, Managed Growth, and European Growth. The team that managed the funds had over a decade of experience in sustainable investing and implemented a three-tier approach to company screening using thematic research to identify key sustainability trends, classic company analysis, and progressive engagement to effect change in corporate behavior.

Aviva's Sustainable Future funds aim to outperform mainstream investment benchmarks over a three- to five-year time frame by integrating material of environment, social, and governance investing (ESG) factors. The funds are based on the premise that capital markets are fundamentally mispricing the challenge of sustainability, in terms of both downside and upside risks. A range of market inefficiencies is at work. Although information is now becoming more available, mainstream investors generally underestimate the value of sustainable and responsible businesses. The main reasons is lack of expertise, too short a time horizon, and behavioral factors (herding). Aviva's SRI strategy aims to exploit this market inefficiency and capitalize on the long-term cash flow potential of those securities that are better place to benefit from the sustainability shift. But there are also market failures with social and environmental costs still not factored into asset prices. These more deep-seated problems require investors to work with policy makers to reform capital markets so that long-term value creation can continue.

As of July 2010, Aviva's SRI team now manages £3.8 billion in assets as of July 2010, and comprises16 dedicated investment professionals. It also offers a sustainability approach to sovereign bonds and emerging markets for institutional clients and manages the Aviva ethical fund. Its remit has also expanded beyond the management of specialist funds: Aviva's Corporate Governance and Corporate Responsibility policy applies to all assets under management. Aviva also periodically screens its conventional portfolios for breaches of core principles on human rights, labor standards, and sustainable development more broadly. The thematic analysis of the SRI team is available to other mainstream desks, and there is frequent interaction with the other mainstream teams.

AVIVA'S SRI INVESTMENT PROCESS

The investment process of Aviva's SRI team is designed to identify companies with a positive ESG outlook that are currently undervalued. Figure 22.1

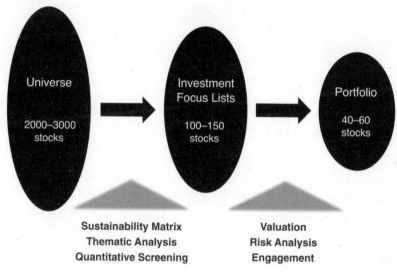

FIGURE 22.1   Investment Process Overview

shows Aviva's structured investment process. Using a sustainability matrix, valuation metrics, and thematic analysis, an investment focus list of 100 to 150 stocks is selected. Further sustainability screens, risk analysis, and direct company engagement are subsequently undertaken. Each element of the investment process will be discussed.

Sustainability Matrix

Aviva's sustainability matrix first assesses the sustainability impacts of different sectors based on their product mix, rating companies from A to E with A being the most sustainable. The management quality of individual firms is then rated from best (1) to worst (5) by assessing whether a company has the structures, policies, and practices in place to manage ESG risks. In Figure 22.2, companies above the line are candidates for Aviva's SRI portfolios. Aviva's engagement work is aimed to improve those companies rated outside the line on both management and business.

Aviva's SRI team has automated and outsourced the provisional industry and management scores. A third-party data provider, EIRIS, delivers an initial industry rating (based on internally established sector guidelines) and the environmental and social management scores for individual companies; this is supplemented by GMI's and PIRC's ratings for governance factors as can be seen in Figure 22.3. Once the provisional sustainability matrix rating has been established, Aviva's SRI analysts evaluate and review the ratings. Then the final company profile is produced. Individual judgment is

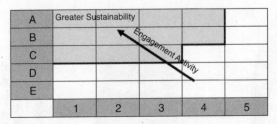

FIGURE 22.2   Sustainability Matrix

the final authority for the sustainability matrix. The profiles take a long-term view of industry sectors and company performance, and are reviewed every two years.

Thematic Analysis

A major source of Aviva's sustainable investment ideas is thematic research. The focus is on companies that are set to benefit from big structural shifts in the market, and Aviva's SRI team is currently following four main themes: climate change, quality of life, sustainable consumption, and governance

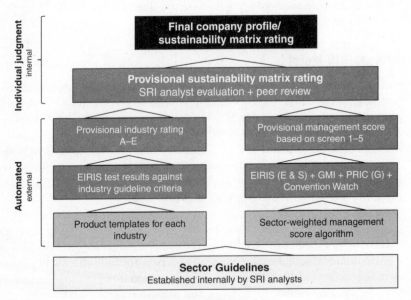

FIGURE 22.3   Sustainability Matrix Components

Sustainable and Responsible Investment Thematic Integration		
Sources of information	Identify the theme	Concentrate on a significant shift in the market where data are available and are likely to result in the investment recommendation that gets into the funds.
Internal colleagues Broker research Market data Academia NGOs GL channel check ESG news	Who are the winners and losers from this theme?	Companies are different. Some benefit from a given secular shift while others may lose out.
	Identify the theme	Use fundamental valuation tools such as comparative valuation analysis and/or discounted cash flow models to come up with a view on value. Then make an investment recommendation.

FIGURE 22.4   Three Levels of Thematic Analysis

and risk management. These themes are then divided into subthemes and microthemes.

The sources of information for the development of further themes and microthemes can be seen in Figure 22.4 and is not restricted to the more traditional information sources of investment managers. At Aviva, the analysts and the portfolio managers (PMs) can add to the core SRI ideas list. Analysts and PMs sit next to each other, and each contributes to the process; the traditional sequence of analyst recommendation followed by PM implementation no longer applies.

Aviva's thematic analysis can be used for short-term, reactive ESG and long-term emerging ESG themes. It is structured into three analysis levels. On level 1, the main question is how the theme can materially change cash flows and act as a financial catalyst over, for example, the next 18 months to three years. A presentation is prepared to discuss and decide the themes viability and potential. Level 2 looks at the winner and loser companies that are exposed to the theme. On the last level, the theme's impact on individual stocks and possible scenarios are reviewed, which ultimately results in the company's addition to, or rejection from, the investment focus list.

Valuation

Aviva's SRI team blends traditional analysis with sustainability research to revalue equity prospects. In the investment process, the emphasis is on assessing a company's future earnings using SRI tools, and then conducting valuation using standard mainstream techniques. The focus of the SRI team is on understanding changes in the business landscape, regulation, and societal expectations and how they might materially impact future earnings. External broker research, industry experts and NGO insights feed into this analysis alongside the opinion of Aviva's internal economists and strategists. These adjusted earnings are then scrutinized using the relevant metrics that are driving returns in a particular sector at the time. These will range across absolute and relative measures including forward price/earnings rations, EV/EBITDA, earnings growth, balance sheet strength, discounted cash flows and free cash flow (FCF) yield.

SRI PORTFOLIO CONSTRUCTION

Upon the successful completion of the thematic investment process and presentation to the SRI team, a stock will be added automatically to the Conviction lists. Stocks can be added at any time to the team's Buy list or Watch list. On the Watch list are stocks that are either strong on sustainability, but weak on valuation, or strong on valuation, but weak on sustainability. On the Buy list are sustainable companies that are attractively valued.

The optimal stock weight is based on fund manager judgment (either top down or bottom up). Top-down considerations include portfolio risk and overall factor exposures, including sector weightings, macro themes, market volatility, factors driving overall returns, tracking error, active weights, and beta appropriate for the fund. Bottom-up considerations are the risk and return characteristics of the stock (liquidity, beta, and risk profile), marginal risk impact, the conviction that emerges from meeting and assessing company management, and external analyst recommendations. Aviva's fundamental belief is that better long-term investment returns come from companies that are well governed and have responsible management practices. Prior to investing, Aviva endeavors to meet with senior management, and ongoing engagement with the companies it has invested in is central to the investment process.

CASE STUDY 1: GREEN TIRES

Identify the Theme

Within its Sustainable Consumption theme, Aviva's SRI team has been focusing for some time on the "Changing Autos" subtheme. The team looked at the entire value chain within the auto industry and identified the industries that will need to change as cars become lighter and more efficient largely as a consequence of ever-tightening regulations.

In 2009, Neil Brown, an analyst on the SRI team, looked at the core drivers of the auto parts sector. This generated a further subtheme within "Changing Autos" on Energy Efficient tires. At that time, new EU regulation was scheduled for implementation in 2013 that would benchmark various elements of tire quality which would be displayed in a consumer-facing badge very much like existing energy ratings for white goods. This would identify products with superior energy efficiency performance and, by setting a minimum threshold, potentially drive out poorly performing competitor products.

Pick the Likely Winner

Brown published an internal note in October 2009 outlining his view on Michelin. In it he wrote that "Michelin was taking sustainability seriously and had identified three key advantages to its future product portfolio: energy efficiency, longevity, and improved grip. They believed their R&D had developed a competitive edge and head start over their competitors." With significant spending already conducted on R&D, and a new regulatory driver set to show the benefits of this to the end consumer, Brown explicitly forecast both a lower R&D requirement as a percentage of sales over the coming three years as well as an uplift in sales relative to consensus by 2011.

Attractive Valuation

When Michelin's earnings were compared with its peers using these new assumptions, the stock looked attractively valued. Aviva's SRI team concluded that consensus numbers might be too focused on the short term, failing to appreciate the impact of energy efficiency regulation on sales. As a result, Michelin was being mispriced, providing an opportunity for sustainability investors.

How It Played Out

With further positive economic news, rebounding tire sales and competitors raising prices in December 2009, the stock performed well. Fears over protracted recession and rising input costs drove volatility in the sector through the beginning of 2010, but the stock had neared the target price set by the SRI team by June.

At that time, with earnings upgrades bringing consensus forecasts nearer those of the team, a review of the holding concluded that it should remain in the funds and on the Conviction list. Although a long-term conviction holding, the team reduced their exposure toward the end of

2010 as significant increases in the rubber price generated a headwind for the company. The stock was moved to the Watch list in January 2011 as team waited for rubber prices to ease. Rubber prices corrected sharply in March, and the stock was returned to the Conviction list and the funds.

CASE STUDY 2: THE RESPONSIBLE SUPPLY CHAIN

Identify the Theme

A number of retailers in the apparel sector have profited extensively from an outsourcing model relying on manufacturing capacity in developing countries, notably in Asia, to produce goods at very low cost. Over the past decade, the respect for human rights and labor standards have become central to the development of the "responsible supply chain." One key dimension which has often been overlooked in this trend is in the business value of retaining production close to the point of sale within developed markets. Proximity sourcing can help deliver both higher sustainability performance as well as business resilience.

Pick the Likely Winner

In early 2009, Brown conducted research on the sector which identified Inditex as a clear outperformer on responsible supply chain management—in ways that he believed could deliver material outperformance against peers. The investment thesis was based on the share price being driven by a combination of sales growth and operational efficiency. The company's focus on the quality of in-store staff and treatment of customers would, it was hoped, allow them to respond more rapidly to changing consumer demands and thereby maintain strong sales. In turn, Inditex's proximity sourcing model allowed it to deliver quicker response times along the chain, and therefore result in lower markdowns, better working capital, and lower U.S. dollar exposure. (Asian suppliers are paid in U.S. dollars.) Brown noted that "strong employee relations are the foundation of the proximity model. You can only order in small amounts and repeatedly revise designs is if you have a long-term relationship of trust you're your supplier. We believe Inditex has achieved this, and it delivers a number of advantages."

Attractive Valuation

Based on this belief that focusing on consumers and maintaining a responsible supply chain would deliver strong sales, Brown's report modeled a two-year earnings earnings before interest and taxes (EBIT) forecast 15% higher than consensus. This growth would give the company a similar performance to peers and yet Inditex was trading at around a 19% discount. This more responsible and operationally superior business model was not yet fully appreciated by market sentiment and the stock was added to the SRI team's Conviction list.

How It Played Out

With the financial crisis delivering an all-time market low in early March 2009, Inditex slightly missed both its top-line and its consensus EBIT numbers. Therefore, it started from a lower base with regard to the initial financial forecasts made by Aviva's SRI team. While sales were below expectations in the first forecast period at 7%, they subsequently picked up to forecasted growth rates in year two. More importantly, the company's supply chain enabled it to deliver above-expectation EBIT numbers in both forecasting years. The gross margin reached 59.3% in year two, 2.8% above forecast, confirming Aviva's above-consensus EBIT forecasts. For Aviva, this example highlights the importance of high labour standards in sustainaing business value.

ENGAGEMENT ACROSS ALL ASSET CLASSES

At Aviva, engagement is not just something for the SRI funds. With regard to voting, Aviva's responsible investment approach is applied across all investee companies, whether they are part of SRI or mainstream funds, as can be seen from the engagement management system in Figure 22.5.

Voting relates to one or all of three issues: the board, compensation, and disclosure. Aviva is looking for an effective board that is collectively responsible for the success of the company. The chairman and chief executive officer functions should be clearly separated, and the board balance should be evenly distributed and independent.

Second, remuneration should be clearly linked to corporate and individual performance. This process should be transparent, and no director should be involved in setting his or her own remuneration. Third, Aviva requires companies to disclose their exposure and management of key corporate responsibility risks. In the case of noncompliance, Aviva may well vote against the adoption of the report and accounts. In such cases, Aviva informs companies in advance of its voting intentions.

Aviva also engages with companies that rate poorly on its sustainability matrix. Vedanta, the Indian mining group, is such a case. In 2010, Aviva's SRI desk allocated Vedanta its lowest management score for sustainability.

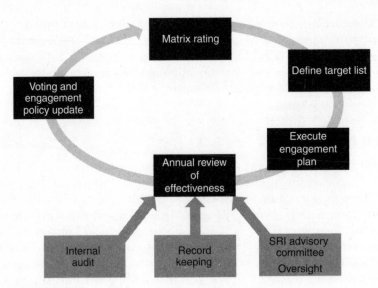

FIGURE 22.5   Engagement Management System

The team's mainstream investment colleagues shared the view on management; hence Aviva never actively owned the stock.

Vedanta had come under international scrutiny for its expansion plans on the Lanjigarh alumina refinery and its application for a bauxite mine in Niyamgiri, both in India.

Vedanta did not respond to requests from Aviva for a meeting to discuss the team's profound concerns over its poor corporate responsibility conduct. As a result, Aviva performed a major engagement exercise at Vedanta's annual general meeting in July 2010. Ahead of the Annual General Meeting (AGM), Aviva commissioned a report from EIRIS highlighting how Vedanta could improve its governance and responsible business practices. The recommendations included widening the remit of the board's health safety and environment committee to cover all ESG issues (especially human rights), linking management remuneration to ESG performance, and adopting international standards such as the United Nations' Global Compact and the Extractive Industries Transparency Initiative among others.

Following the AGM, the *Financial Times* published an article stating: "Vedanta hasn't suffered much to date. Its shares have outperformed those of most peers over the past five years. But more enlightened miners have seen the value of engaging with sensible campaigners. If Mr. Agarwal (CEO) wishes to continue reaping the benefits of London's abundant pool of capital, he must do a better job of justifying what Vedanta is doing and how it is doing it."[1]

The Indian government subsequently refused to approve Vedanta's expansion plans and turn down its application for the bauxite mine in Niyamgiri. The share price reaction at the time was considerable, and it suffered as the market was expecting approval. Vedanta is appealing the negative decision. Sustainability research was shown to be effective at anticipating market-moving events.

The company has now opened up dialogue with Aviva and has been seeking its opinion on corporate social responsibility and sustainability. It has taken some steps in the right direction, such as introducing a new position of chief sustainability officer. However, it is too early to judge whether underlying sustainability performance has improved. Progress will be measured against EIRIS's key recommendations.

CONCLUSION

The success of Aviva's sustainable investment strategy is not just measured in growing funds under management or relative outperformance of the funds against mainstream benchmarks. These are critical success factors in and of themselves. But they also lend critical credibility to the sustainable investment case, winning senior management support in the process. Aviva Investor's chief executive Paul Abberley, for example, argues: "We genuinely want to be responsible—as part of an insurance company we have a longer lens to look through," and adds that "we will do more publicly rather than less on the issue of sustainable markets."[2]

One expression of this is Aviva's Sustainable Stock Exchange initiative, now adopted by the United Nations Principles for Responsible Investment (UNPRI). The initiative aims to get the world's largest exchanges to make sustainability disclosure a mandatory part of listing rules—and as a major user of exchanges, Aviva's voice carries weight. Another project is to analyze what a sustainable economy could look like in 2040. This will be used to identify winners and losers – and to invest now in those companies that seek to exploit the move to a sustainable world in 2040. Now, that's really long term.[3]

NOTES

1. Andrew Hill, "Vedanta's Bad Press Risks Undermining Its Image," *Financial Times*, July 28, 2010.

2. Aviva had engaged with Michelin in the past to encourage it to improve its marketing to position the company as a fuel-efficient producer. Aviva had also engaged on the long-term issue of tire recycling.
3. Jo Confino, "Aviva Seeks to Change City's Unsustainable Habits," *Guardian*, February 4, 2011.

CHAPTER 23

Generation Investment Management

Malte Griess-Nega and Nick Robins

> Let us turn to another firm fully integrating sustainability into every-
> thing it does—the groundbreaking Generation Investment Manage-
> ment. Sustainable value creation has been part of the company's DNA
> since inception. Please seek out the excellent Harvard Business School
> case study on Generation for more detail on their methodology.

Sustainable investing has been criticized for introducing political factors
into what is perceived as the value-free practice of fund management. In
Generation's case one of its founders, Al Gore, was not just a politician, but a
former vice president of the United States. Yet, what Generation's experience
shows is how a deep understanding of long-term economic, environmental,
social, and yes, policy, factors have now become the "new normal" for
investment excellence.

Making the Long Term Pay

Generation Investment Management is an independent, employee-owned
partnership established in April 2004.[1] The brainchild of David Blood, previously the chief executive of Goldman Sachs Asset Management, and Al
Gore, former vice president of the United States, Generation is rooted in the
belief that a long-term perspective and the integration of sustainability factors will yield superior returns. To prove the case, it created an investment
boutique. "We believe sustainable solutions will be the primary driver of

industrial and economic development for the coming decades," Generation states in its investment philosophy.[2]

Seven years on, Generation has delivered the goods in its core Global Equity fund and has also diversified its investment strategies into new themes (climate solutions), regions (Asia), and assets (fixed income). As Colin Le Duc, Generation's head of research, puts it, "Our biggest contribution is generating alpha by taking sustainability seriously."[3]

A NEW MODEL FOR GLOBAL EQUITIES

By the end of 2010, Generation's long-only, global public equity fund had reached $6.6 billion in assets under management. Generation's clients for this fund include institutional investors, such as pension funds and insurance companies, as well as high-net-worth individuals. Although sustainability is central to its approach, Generation does not want to be seen as a traditional socially responsible investment (SRI) fund. According to Le Duc, "All the money in the fund is out of mainstream equity buckets: we're trying to show that sustainability pays." Alignment with client interests is a core principle at Generation. The fund charges a 1% management fee on average annual assets, with an additional 20% performance fee linked to its benchmark, the MSCI World index. Unlike many other boutiques and hedge fund managers, Generation's performance fee is calculated over a three-year period in order to align incentives and to reduce the temptation for short-termism.

Global Equity: Investment Philosophy

Generation takes traditional approaches to asset management and reshapes them in light of sustainability. Its strategy for selecting stocks is surprisingly conventional:

> We Buy High Quality Businesses: Dominant market positions, strong entry barriers, predictable future, pricing power, and secular growth trends
>
> With High Quality Management Teams: Culture of integrity, respect for shareholders, well managed for the long term
>
> At the Right Price: Key to our success is our price discipline and the ability to buy companies at sufficiently attractive prices to deliver performance[4]

What is strikingly different is *how* Generation delivers these objectives. This involves three fundamental pillars:

1. *The fund has a long-term focus*, not just because of the negative repercussions for the global economy of the myopic culture of modern capital markets but also because financial outperformance requires an extended outlook that addresses the underlying sources of enterprise value. In Generation's case, this long-term approach is encapsulated in its focus list of around 120 of the world's best businesses, which turns over very slowly; the actual portfolio is driven more directly by valuations with an annual turnover of around 50%, closer to market norms.
2. *The fund is based on high-conviction investing.* From the broader focus list, the actual fund comprises around 30 to 50 companies, which Generation believes allows "maximum leverage of an intense research effort." In essence, Generation has brought to the buy side the research intensity of the sell side with the ownership disciplines of private equity. Interestingly, with experience, Generation's strategy has become more concentrated over time. Today 10% of the stocks can make up to 25% of the fund as the level of confidence/conviction has increased.
3. *Returns are delivered through integrated sustainability research.* Generation's starting point is that "sustainability factors directly affect long-term business profitability" and that these factors are interrelated: Climate change is impossible to separate from poverty, demographics, water, and health, for example. Traditional SRI has tended to separate the qualitative analysis of companies from financial analysis. At Generation, the team of 15 analysts carries out both the fundamental equity research and the in-depth assessment of the economic, environmental, social, and governance issues that could determine a company's ability to deliver returns.

Global Equity: Investment Process

The structure of Generation's investment process follows a fairly standard three-step process of idea generation, investment decision making, and on to portfolio and risk management. The process flow can be seen in Figure 23.1. Again, what distinguishes the process is the manner in which it is driven by the philosophy of long-term sustainability convictions.

Idea Generation The core ideas that drive the fund flow from a combination of sectoral as well as thematic research. Generation has completed over 25 industry road maps that identify the critical success factors in each particular industry and how the industry will evolve over the long term:

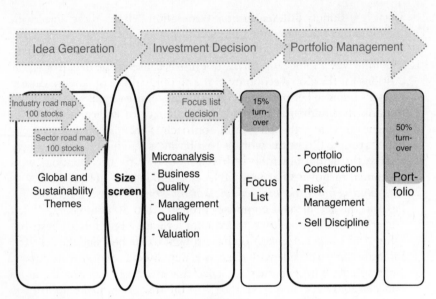

FIGURE 23.1 Generation's Investment Process
Data source: Generation Asset Management.

These roadmaps enable the analysts to identify those sectors and companies that are best positioned to benefit from these forces. The fund focuses on five sectors: Industrials, Financials, Consumer, Healthcare, as well as Telecoms, Technology, and Software. Its fundamental analysis means that it has limited or no appetite to hold stocks in a number of sectors, such as airlines and mining as well as oil and gas, because of the unattractive economic and sustainability characteristics.

On top of this, the research team also monitors a growing list of sustainability themes (see Figure 23.2). In the case of climate change, for example, the result of the research leads to a two-stage framework for evaluating companies. First, the carbon intensity of profits is evaluated to identify those companies at higher risk from regulatory and market shifts; this analysis incorporates both direct and indirect emissions along the value chain and gives the analysts a view on the quality of the business. Then management quality is assessed through the concept of carbon discipline, which involves assessing the extent to which a company's leadership both understands climate exposure and is actively managing these risks and opportunities. For a social imperative such as meeting real needs in the developing world—the "base of the pyramid"—Generation is looking not just for businesses that

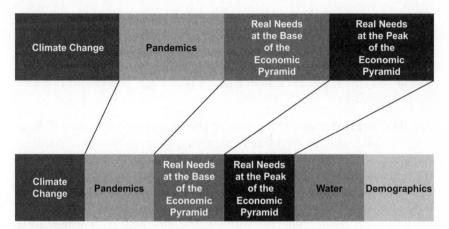

FIGURE 23.2 Generation's Evolving Set of Sustainability Themes
Data source: Generation Asset Management.

can identify new markets but also those that have the leadership capability to engage with the world's poorest.[5]

The team reviews industry sectors along these themes and creates maturity curves for each theme over time.

Investment Decision In the second step, Generation applies a two-step process to select companies for its focus list of about 120 companies. This involves grading a company's business quality (BQ) in relation to the themes that have been identified as future challenges and performing classic financial analysis. In general, Generation favors simplicity in business models, believing that it is often hard to add value in large, diversified conglomerates. The characteristics that Generation looks for are companies with positive cash flow and a hard-to-replicate business model (e.g., either number one or two in their market). It then assesses management quality (MQ) in terms of its long-term focus, integrity, track record, company culture, and respect for stakeholders.

To get a company onto the focus list, the analyst must present his or her findings to the rest of the investment team and win their support. Generation's conviction-based strategy rests on a collective approach to decision making. The team decides which rating each company should receive for its business and management quality. Ratings range from 1 to 5 with 1 being the best; a company with a BQ-MQ rating of 3-3 is unlikely to make it onto the focus list. Entry conditions are high, and the focus list has a very low turnover.

Accepting a company onto the focus list does not mean that the fund will immediately invest into stock. In fact, a few companies have stayed on the focus list for years. The investment decision will depend largely on the stock being attractively valued and offering on average a 20% upside to the current valuation. But once a company is on the list, analysts treat it as if the fund owns it.

Portfolio Construction   If the role of the analysts is to build the focus list, the fund managers specialize in the timing of investments and portfolio construction. The fund is highly concentrated with 10% of the companies constituting up to 25% of the fund. This targeted investment approach requires a high level of confidence and understanding of each position. The fund also has a relatively high exposure to emerging economies, such as Brazil, China, India, Indonesia, Mexico, and Thailand, with around 20% invested in these markets. Its largest sectoral allocation is in healthcare, notably medical technology. As for its investment horizon, the fund looks out three to five years but models companies on a 40-year research horizon.

The fund employs a strict selling discipline. Immediate sell orders are triggered when a stock leaves its valuation band. The fund also sells the stock should the company's business or management quality change adversely. However, the focus list approach enables Generation to move quickly when a company's valuation gets attractive, as happened when the financial crisis cut share prices. Generation's approach to responsible ownership covers stocks on its focus list as well as those in the fund. It organizes a chief executive conference every year to foster relationships with its focus list companies and hosts a client conference every two years to bring together its investors. The end result is a portfolio with a 50% turnover rate, about half as fast as that of mainstream fund managers. The fund has a tracking error of around 300 to 500 basis points compared to its benchmark.

Investment Results

As an institutional fund, Generation IM does not publish the performance of the Global Equity fund. However, its clients often do. For example, the UK Environment Agency stated in March 2011 that Generation had delivered a positive 17.38% outperformance over the benchmark since inception in the middle of 2008.[6]

SUMMARY

Generation's vision of investment extends beyond its funds to the economy as a whole, where it aims to promote "sustainable capitalism."[7] The firm donates 5% of profits to its foundation, which is dedicated to the promotion of capital markets aligned to sustainable development. One key theme is how to change the perverse incentive structures that work against long-term investing in current markets.

But what Generation can do best is show that sustainability not only makes sense from an investment perspective but is also a superior approach to conventional fund management. For this reason, it has launched a new fund focused on Asia as well as a fixed-income fund applying its method-ology to bonds. Looking ahead, "the financial crisis has only underscored our conviction that sustainability will be a critical driver of economic and industrial change over the next twenty-five years."[8]

NOTES

1. For a review of the first phase of Generation's evolution, see the Harvard Business School Case Study 9-609-057, September 2009.
2. www.generationim.com/strategy/philosophy.html
3. Interview with Colin Le Duc, January 2011.
4. Generation IM, "Global Equity: Our Investment Strategy."
5. See Generation IM, "Thematic Research Highlights," November 2010.
6. Howard Pearce, "The Environment Agency Pension Fund and Climate Change," March 2011, presentation to Mercers conference on climate change and asset allocation.
7. "We Need Sustainable Capitalism. Nature Does Not Do Bailouts," *Wall Street Journal*, November 5, 2008. www.generationim.com/sustainability/advocacy/sustainable-capitalism.html
8. James Cameron and David Blood, "Catalysing Capital towards the Low-Carbon Economy," Copenhagen Climate Council Thought Leadership Series 3, April 2009.

CHAPTER 24

Insight Investment

Reflections and Lessons Learned from Integrating Sustainability

Rory Sullivan

Fully integrating sustainability into all investment considerations by mainstream investors remains a major challenge and opportunity. One firm that was recognized for its approach in that area was Insight Investment in London. Rory Sullivan, the former Head of Responsible Investment at Insight, and one of the most authoritative writers and commentators on responsible investment and related issues, presents Insight's story here. He describes how Insight approached the challenge of investment integration and offers some practical reflections on the lessons learned in building an approach that added real value to investment decision-making.

The literature on how sustainability-minded investors integrate consideration of environmental, social, and governance (ESG) issues into their investment practices focuses almost exclusively on investment research, rather than investment decision making. There is a burgeoning body of academic and broker research on the financial implications of specific issues, such as climate change or environmental regulation, there are many studies identifying winners and losers from themes such as demographic change, and there is an increasing number of studies that demonstrate some sort of correlation between good ESG performance and financial or investment performance.

While the potential significance of ESG issues is increasingly recognized by investors (and not just by those involved in ethical or socially responsible investment), the reality is that making the case or evidencing that a particular issue is, or could be, financially material is just the starting point. The reality is that the effective integration of ESG issues into investment decision making has relatively little to do with the quality of the research that is conducted. Effective integration is much more dependent on factors such as the investment and other objectives of investment managers, on the interests of analysts and fund managers, and the nature of the relationship between the ESG analyst and the investment managers and analysts.

This chapter seeks to explain these points further and to offer some practical reflections on how ESG issues can be properly taken into account in investment processes and investment decisions.

ABOUT INSIGHT

Insight Investment was, until the end of 2008, the asset management arm of HBOS plc. Insight was, at that time, one of the United Kingdom's largest investment managers, with over £100 billion in assets under management. Following the takeover of HBOS by Lloyds Banking Group plc at the end of 2008, Insight continued to function as an autonomous subsidiary within the Lloyds Banking Group until its sale to Bank of New York Mellon in mid-2009.

Insight and its predecessor companies had a long record of activism on corporate governance issues extending back to the early 1970s. In 2002, Insight made a formal commitment to managing all of its assets according to a responsible investment policy. The policy committed Insight to:

- Integrating ESG issues into its investment process
- Engaging with the companies in which it was invested to encourage high standards of performance on ESG issues
- Working with other investors to promote responsible investment across the investment market more generally
- High levels of transparency in relation to its responsible investment activities[1]

The rationale was that the belief that these issues are important drivers of long-term investment value and that understanding them was critical to making good investment decisions and to delivering the returns that Insight's clients were seeking.

In 2002, Insight established a responsible investment team to implement its responsible investment policy. The team was initially headed by Craig Mackenzie and, from 2006, by Rory Sullivan. Over the period from 2002 to 2009, Insight established itself as a recognized market leader for its approach to responsible investment. Insight was consistently rated as one of the leading global asset managers for the manner in which it integrated ESG factors into its investment research and decision making across a range of asset classes, not just equities, and for the quality of its engagement with companies. Insight was a member of the expert group that developed the United Nations'-backed Principles for Responsible Investment (PRI), one of the founding signatories to the PRI, and the first asset manager in the world to publish a comprehensive annual report setting out how it complied with PRI.[2]

Adding value to Insight's investment process was an important part of the team's work since its inception, with the team having conducted research on a variety of ESG topics, such as the implications of the European Union's Emission Trading Scheme (EUETS) for the electricity sector and the EU's Registration, Evaluation and Authorization of Chemicals (REACH) Regulation for the chemicals sector.[3] However, investment integration (specifically, adding value to Insight's investment decisions across its equity and fixed-income platforms) became a much more important part of the team's work from early 2006. The next section describes Insight's research processes, focusing specifically on where and how ESG issues were integrated, and also presents a case study on climate change to illustrate the type of research that was conducted.

INVESTMENT RESEARCH ON ESG ISSUES

Insight integrated consideration of ESG issues into its investment processes for equities and fixed-income in three ways:

1. By conducting thematic research that identified sectors and companies that would benefit or lose as a result of structural changes in society and/or from long-term trends (e.g., growing public concerns about the environment)
2. By developing a series of risk indicators that could be applied across Insight's equity and fixed-income investment universes.
3. By analyzing specific ESG issues, whether in response to specific requests from analysts or fund managers or arising from Insight's engagement and discussions with companies on their approaches to corporate governance and corporate responsibility

Thematic Research

Insight's view was that significant investment value could be derived from understanding how structural changes or themes, such as climate change, access to water, and demographic change, could manifest themselves (e.g., through regulation, changes in supply or demand, the emergence of new markets or product opportunities or of new competitors or loss of existing competitors) and so affect companies. Insight had a rolling program of thematic research that sought to identify potential winners and losers associated with these themes. The starting point for this research was to assess whether the theme warranted in-depth analysis by asking questions such as:

- Would either supply or demand be restricted or enhanced?
- Would new markets be created or would incumbent technologies be disrupted?
- Could the consequences be predicted (rather than being random events)?
- Did the theme have global implications or, at least, affect several important regions?
- Did the theme cut across sectors rather than being sector-specific?
- Were there regulatory or other catalysts?

If the answers to some or all of these questions were positive, further research either on the overarching theme or on specific dimensions of the theme was triggered. For example, within the climate change theme, we researched areas as diverse as the implications of emissions trading for electricity utilities and the aviation sector, biofuels, solar technologies, and adaptation.

Where companies were identified as being beneficiaries of a theme, we first did some initial screening on the basis of basic financial indicators such as market capitalization and liquidity to assess whether they were suitable investments for our funds. If a company was considered an appropriate potential investment, it was subject to detailed analysis, so as to understand, for example, how the thematic driver might affect cash flows, returns, and other financial measures of success.

The key deliverables from thematic research were the generation of stock ideas for our portfolios and/or the identification of risks that were not highlighted by more traditional forms of investment analysis. The results of this research were generally presented in two ways. The first was through the production of written notes on the research that were posted to Insight's research database, which was available to all analysts and fund managers. The second, and more important, was through Insight's regular investment meetings, in particular the daily morning meetings and monthly theme meetings (where new ideas were raised and the outcomes of previous ideas or themes discussed).

Insight's Corporate Risk Initiative

Insight's corporate risk initiative sought to systematize information about material corporate governance and corporate responsibility factors across its equity and fixed-income investment universes. This was done through the development of a series of indicators for issues (corporate governance, pension liabilities, accounting, climate change, narrative reporting, and capital structure) that were of particular concern to the firm's equity and fixed-income investments; the indicators covered both exposure and quality of management.

Insight developed a standard spreadsheet that captured data relevant to these indicators and that was then used to generate performance scores. For each of the major indicators, Insight developed a flag system, from 1 (low risk) to 5 (high risk). Scores of 4 to 5 triggered further analysis of these aspects of performance. For example, one of the flags related to how Insight had previously voted its shares; companies where Insight had abstained or voted against management in any of the last three years were highlighted together with commentary on the reasons for Insight's decision and an analysis of how the market as a whole had voted on the resolution. This particular flag enabled analysts and fund managers to spot companies with less-than-ideal governance records, to understand the reasons for Insight's concerns, and then to consider this information when making their investment recommendation or decision.

Fundamental Analysis

Insight also examined ESG issues at the stock or company level, where the research assessed both the company's exposure to the issue in question and its quality of management of the issue. Examples of research that Insight conducted included:

- How food companies addressed consumer health, in light of concerns about rising obesity levels in many developed countries. What were the implications for their revenues, margins and profits?
- How European airlines were positioned to respond to the increasing regulatory and other pressures to reduce their greenhouse gas emissions. What were the implications for airfares within the European Community?

- The implications for BP's capital and operating expenditures of the accident at its Texas City refinery in 2005. Were there implications for other companies in the sector?
- How European electricity utilities were provisioning for the decommissioning of their nuclear reactors.
- The commercial opportunities for industrial gas companies of electricity utility interest in carbon capture and storage and integrated gasification combined cycle power plants.
- Investment opportunities of appropriate scale and maturity in the aquaculture sector. Would the scale of these opportunities increase in the future?
- The ability of mid- and small-cap building materials companies to profit from the green building trend in Europe.
- Investment opportunities presented by marine (wave and tidal) energy.

CASE STUDY: CLIMATE CHANGE

Climate change was an important focus for Insight's investment research for a number of years. Insight's research projects in this area included:[4]

- The exposure of European electricity utilities to climate change-related regulation (specifically the EU ETS).
- The implications of including aviation in the EU ETS, including an assessment of the strategic positioning of companies within the European airline industry to the increasing regulatory and other pressures to reduce their greenhouse gas emissions.
- The implications for motor vehicle manufacturers' research and development and capital costs of the EU's proposals for reducing greenhouse gas emissions from motor vehicles.
- The opportunities for alternative fuels in power generation and transport sectors in Europe and the United States.
- Adaptation and the physical impacts of climate change for the real estate, oil and gas, water, and electricity sectors, with the aim of identifying the major direct, physical climate change and weather-related risks (and associated opportunities) faced by companies in the sector; the potential implications for cash flows and balance sheets; and the disclosures required by investors to enable them to evaluate corporate exposures to climate change risks.[5]
- The business opportunities for industrial gases companies resulting from carbon capture and storage (CCS) and integrated gasification combined cycle (IGCC) power plants.

CASE STUDY: EUROPEAN ELECTRICITY UTILITIES

From mid-2005 to early 2006, we analyzed how 12 European electricity utilities where we had significant equity or bond holdings were positioning themselves to respond to the risks and opportunities they faced from the EU ETS directed at reducing greenhouse gas emissions between 2008 and 2012 (the Kyoto compliance period) and beyond. Our analysis considered company performance in the areas of:

- Climate change policies
- Governance and management
- Operations
- Emissions inventories (i.e., current and future greenhouse gas emissions and current and future regulatory exposures)
- Emissions management strategies (including investments—capital and operating—to respond to climate change and the outcomes expected from these investments)

For each company, we modeled, on a country-by-country basis, current greenhouse gas emissions, projected changes in emissions taking into account plans for new investments and the closure of existing plants, and likely changes in emissions allocations under the EU ETS. Doing this allowed us to quantify the expected emissions surplus/deficit for each company and, hence, the expected cost of purchasing additional emissions credits. We then looked at a company's market position, in particular its ability to pass the costs associated with emissions trading through to its final customers and the attitude of regulatory bodies to potential increases in electricity prices.

Assessing exposure was only part of the picture. We also analyzed each company's quality of management in relation to climate change risks and opportunities. In doing this, we considered the company's own analysis of climate change risks and opportunities, the company's objectives and targets, carbon dioxide abatement and offset strategies, and the manner in which the company was integrating climate change into its overall strategy.

This case study is adapted from R. Sullivan, and J. Kozak, "Investor Case-Studies: Climate Change—Just One More Investment Issue?," in W. Oulton (ed.), *Investment Opportunities for a Low Carbon World* (London: GMB Publishing, 2009), pp. 270–280.)

The analysis allowed us to draw some clear investment conclusions and led to a number of changes in the holdings in Insight's fixed-income portfolios.

1. While much of the literature on climate change and the electricity sector suggested that coal-fired power plants were likely to be affected most negatively, companies with a significant proportion of coal-fired generation in their portfolios were—due to the manner in which emission permits were allocated—major beneficiaries in Phases 1 and 2 of the EU ETS.
2. The financial impacts were—notwithstanding the overarching framework provided by the EU ETS—very country-specific. A proper assessment of exposure could be obtained only through analyzing national supply-demand balances and national positions relative to the Kyoto Protocol targets and the country's views on how much of this target would be delivered through national emissions reductions and how much through the use of the Kyoto Protocol flexibility mechanisms.
3. The financial impacts were dependent on the degree of market liberalization (i.e., the ability of generators to pass carbon costs through to their consumers).
4. The research provided important insights into management views and strategies. While some companies had a clear focus on renewable energy and were seeking to maximize the use of emissions offsets and trading to minimize their exposures, a number were quite unprepared. For example, one company stated that it did not believe that, when push came to shove, governments would take serious action to reduce emissions and that, as a consequence, the company did not feel that it needed to invest significant resources in this area.

CASE STUDY: BIOFUELS

Throughout 2005 and 2006, driven by high fuel prices, energy security fears, and concerns about climate change, governments around the world introduced targets or standards to make the use of biofuels mandatory and/or introduced tax breaks or subsidies to make biofuels more competitive. These regulations catalyzed significant growth and investment in the sector. By mid- to late 2006, however, there were signs of trouble: Biofuels ignited a fierce so-called food versus fuel debate; some biofuels were implicated in

This case study is adapted from Insight Investment, *Putting Principles into Practice: 2006* (London: Author, 2007) and Insight Investment, *Putting Principles into Practice: 2007* (London: Author, 2008)

causing significant environmental damage; and the carbon dioxide footprints of some biofuels were determined to be not as small as once purported. It soon became clear that first-generation biofuels were not a panacea for the world's energy security and environmental woes.

Throughout 2007, we closely tracked developments in the sector, including changes in regulation, feedstock prices, capacity and production volume changes, and end product prices. What we found was that high feedstock prices began to squeeze the profit margins of many biofuels producers, including D1 Oils (UK) and Verbio (Germany), while Biofuels Corp. (UK) was forced to delist from AIM (the London Stock Exchange's market for smaller and growing companies) after having to secure significant debt financing to keep itself afloat. Other companies experienced problems at the project level. For example, Neste Oil (Finland) and Total (France) canceled a joint pilot biodiesel project; Abengoa (Spain) suspended bioethanol production at its biggest plant for several months during the year; and BP, British Sugar, and DuPont, which canceled a biobutanol joint venture after determining that the technology was not yet ready for commercialization. For other companies, concerns about the sustainability of biofuels caused them to reevaluate their initiatives. For example, RWE npower canceled its project to convert its Littlebrook power station in the United Kingdom to run on palm oil because it could not secure enough feedstock from sustainable plantations, and National Express (UK) canceled biodiesel trials at its U.K. operations after consulting "green" groups regarding sustainability issues.

Our conclusion, at that time, was that the longer-term prospects for first-generation biofuels were uncertain. While, as at the end of 2007, the policy drivers were still strong, the sustainability challenges of these types of biofuel threatened to erode support, particularly in Europe. We therefore moved the focus of our research from first-generation producers to identify other potential opportunities in the value chain as well as those exposed to alternative and second-generation biofuels. For example, we added to our holdings in Novozymes, a producer of enzymes used in the conversion of grains such as corn, barley, wheat, and rye into bioethanol. The company was also at the forefront of research into enzymes suitable for the production of bioethanol from cellulosic feedstocks, a second-generation biofuel that may still be five to ten years from commercialization.

REFLECTIONS/TAKEAWAYS FROM THE CASE STUDIES

In many ways, the process and examples outlined in this chapter are typical of the manner in which investment research has developed over the past few years. Depending on how their research process is structured, most large fund managers are likely to analyze financially material ESG issues as a matter of course, are likely to recognize that company performance on ESG issues may provide useful insights into the quality of a company's management or strategy, and may see ESG performance as a partial proxy for overall quality of management. From the perspective of the ESG analyst, the critical question is not how to conduct research on ESG issues but how to ensure that this research is recognized and used by decision makers (i.e., analysts and fund managers). From our experience at Insight, there are four key lessons:

1. Effective integration begins with the investment process.
2. People are key.
3. ESG issues can be material . . . but not all the time.
4. ESG performance may not be a good proxy for corporate risk.

Lesson 1: Effective Integration Begins with the Investment Process

ESG integration must begin with understanding the investment process for the asset class or funds in question. That is, the central question is whether and how ESG factors can be built into the investment process (or how the investment process can be refined to accommodate these factors) rather than seeking to impose ESG factors on the investment process. Doing this requires paying attention to understanding:

- The investment process, in particular where and how ESG issues are relevant to the investment analysis and decision-making process. In some processes (e.g., where thematic research or fundamental analysis is central to the investment process), the potential contribution of ESG-related research may be clear. In others—for example, funds that are run on a strictly quantitative basis—the relevance of ESG issues may be limited.
- Which issues are already well understood by the market and which issues are not. While limited investment value may be derived by focusing research resources on topics such as tobacco litigation or the implications of the EU ETS for the electricity industry, themes such as innovation or human capital management may provide fertile areas for research and analysis.
- Investment time horizons. If fund performance is evaluated over relatively short time horizons, fund managers may be less interested in how longer-term issues such as climate change adaptation may affect the companies in which they are invested.

Lesson 2: People Are Key

Investment management and, by extension, ESG integration is about people as much as about process. One of the major conclusions to be drawn from Insight's experience is that establishing an expert responsible investment team is nowhere near enough. Maximizing the value of the research produced by this team required that Insight bring its research and investment teams and the research platform together in a manner that added real value to investment research. Insight's starting point was the acknowledgment that analysts following different asset classes (and specialists covering specific topics including ESG issues) may have quite different views on whether securities issued by the same company are good investments or not. Insight's objective was not necessarily to create a common view but to ensure that these different views were recognized and understood.

Insight, therefore, actively developed the links among its equity, credit, and responsible investment research teams and encouraged analysts and fund managers to interact with each other, including holding joint meetings with companies. Research meetings (e.g., daily internal team meetings, stock, sector and thematic research meetings) were open to all, and ESG issues or views on the ESG performance of specific stocks or credits were routinely discussed. In addition, Insight circulated weekly updates on forthcoming research and company meetings across the three research teams; and the heads of the equity research, credit research, and responsible investment teams met monthly to review research priorities and ensure the effective coordination of the research process.

Insight also had an open access research system where research from the different teams could be accessed and reviewed by all analysts and fund managers. The aim was to ensure that views on specific securities, shares, and bonds issued against different parts of a company's capital structure took account of the full range of analysis Insight had done on the company.

While formal processes such as those just outlined were important, of equal importance was understanding the attitudes, beliefs, and interests of the investment decision makers. We invested significant time in understanding the needs and interests of individual researchers and analysts (e.g., if there were specific types of ESG research that would be particularly relevant to their investment activities). We also understood that there were a range of views on the importance of ESG issues and, by extension, the value of ESG integration—from strongly supportive and engaged, through to cynical and skeptical. We understood that our role was not to be advocates but rather to support analysts and fund managers in their work; over time, we found that many became more supportive as we were able to provide practical examples of the utility of our work.

While analysts and investment managers inevitably have different interests and see different data points as being of more or less interest, our experience was that ESG research was most likely to be valued if we were able to:

- Offer a clear opinion on the implications (e.g., views on winners and losers, a robust assessment of the financial implications of the issue in question).
- Make clear links to recognized investment value drivers or, if not linked to such a value driver, a clear argument as to why the issue is relevant.
- Have a clear view on the time frame over which the issue manifested itself.
- Deliver research promptly so that it could actually be used by the analysts or fund managers.
- Locate our views in the context of what the market is thinking, particularly if our view is nonconsensual.

Lesson 3: ESG Issues Can Be Material . . . but Not All the Time

Clearly, ESG issues can be important drivers of investment value. Over the past few years, we have seen many cases where these have significantly affected company cash flows, balance sheets, and reputations. Examples include government legislation in areas such as waste and water management, economic incentives such as the EU ETS for greenhouse gas emissions, tobacco litigation, and consumer and media campaigns on topics such as the use of sweatshop labor in the apparel and footwear industries.

However, these examples should not be interpreted as an argument that all ESG issues are financially material in the short to medium term. First, while there is no universally agreed definition, financial analysts frequently use numerical thresholds—5% of a company's revenue or 5% moves in a company's share price are common rules of thumb—to assess the financial materiality of a particular issue. In this frame of reference, the majority of social or environmental factors—notwithstanding examples such as tobacco litigation and climate change—are not material. Second, time horizons are key. While issues such as climate change adaptation clearly present huge challenges for society with potentially major financial implications for companies and their investors, the timeframe over which these impacts manifest themselves may be well be beyond conventional investment time frames.

Our experience with ESG integration was that clarity around materiality was often our key contribution; being able to say that a specific ESG issue (e.g., a new regulation) is unlikely to have a material effect on costs or prices can be as valuable as analysis establishing that there is a material effect. For example, a common trajectory in relation to accidents is for the market to assume the worst and to exaggerate the damage or liability and then progressively wind back its estimates to closer to the true costs to the company. Such market overreactions to news flow (whether positively or negatively) can, in turn, create investment opportunities.

Lesson 4: ESG Performance May Not Be a Good Proxy for Corporate Risk

There has been significant discussion on whether ESG performance (as measured in terms such as total greenhouse gas emissions) is a good proxy for wider corporate risk. This argument has some plausibility. It is possible to derive useful insights into the quality of a company's management (e.g., its ability to identify and assess the significance of wider business risks, its ability to respond to and engage with stakeholders) based on its management of ESG issues. In addition, companies that manage these issues effectively are likely to be better investments over the longer term.

However, as illustrated well by the electricity utilities case study in this chapter, ESG performance is only part of the picture. First, ESG performance is just one of a whole series of factors—for example, the nature of the company's activities, the quality of the company's management, cash flows and balance sheet strength—that investors consider when making investment decisions. Second, where ESG issues are or may be material, investors do not consider the ESG performance measure in isolation but rather consider how the issue will affect a company's cash flows and balance sheets. For example, in relation to greenhouse gas emissions, whereas some commentators have argued that investors should preferentially invest in companies with lower greenhouse gas emissions (on the grounds that that these companies are less exposed to climate change regulations and so should be a better investment), prudent investors will consider not only total greenhouse gas emissions but also:

- The likelihood that the company will be required to reduce some or all of its greenhouse gas emissions
- The emissions reductions that are or will be required
- The time frame over which the emissions reductions are required
- The cost to the company of reducing or offsetting its emissions

- The ability of the company to pass some or all of these costs through to its customers

SUMMARY

The integration of ESG issues into investment decision making is a central part of responsible investment for three reasons.

1. It should enable investors to make better decisions and thereby generate better returns while also delivering on their wider social obligations.
2. It sends a clear signal to companies that ESG issues are an important factor in investment decisions, thereby providing an additional incentive for companies to manage these issues.
3. It is an important element in ensuring that investor engagement with companies is effective, providing a key lever in support of arguments that companies should take a more proactive approach to the management of their ESG issues. Investment integration needs to be seen as an integrated part of a holistic approach to responsible investment, encompassing active promotion of high standards of corporate governance and corporate responsibility, explaining to companies how ESG issues are built into investment processes and decisions, and playing a supportive role in public policy debates on corporate responsibility.

NOTES

1. For a more detailed description of Insight's approach to responsible investment, see: Insight Investment, *Putting Principles into Practice: 2006* (London: Author, 2007), Insight Investment, *Putting Principles into Practice: 2007* (London: Author, 2008) and Insight Investment, *Putting Principles into Practice: 2008* (London: Author, 2009).
2. Insight Investment, *Putting Principles into Practice: 2006* (London: Author, 2007).
3. S. Waygood, S. Erler, W. Wehrmeyer, and H. Jeswani, "Integrated Investment Analysis: Investment Implications of the REACH Regulation," in R. Sullivan and C. Mackenzie (eds.), *Responsible Investment* (Sheffield, UK: Greenleaf Publishing, 2006), pp. 62–80.
4. This research was a subset of a wider program of work on climate change that included major engagement programs to encourage companies to reduce their greenhouse gas emissions, to respond appropriately to the risks and opportunities presented by climate change, and to improve their disclosures on these issues. Insight also participated in a series of collaborative initiatives as a signatory to

the Carbon Disclosure Project, member of the steering committee of Institutional Investors Group on Climate Change (IIGCC), member of the Advisory Board of The Climate Group, and active engagement with public policy (in particular through the public policy activities of IIGCC).

5. For a further description of this project, see R. Sullivan, D. Russell, S. Beloe, F. Curtiss, and J. Firth, *Managing the Unavoidable: Investment Implications of a Changing Climate* (London: Acclimatise, Henderson Global Investors, Insight Investment, Railpen and USS, 2009).

CHAPTER 25

The Unexpected Role Model

Chinese Environmental and Energy Policy

J. Jason Mitchell

How does one short a company that is overvalued but a leader in its field as a sustainability play? While some might balk at the concept of a sustainability-focused hedge fund, the approach actually makes sense, especially when one considers the large pool of asset owners seeking maximum performance through hedge funds. That sentiment isn't going away any time soon, especially with shortfalls abounding and universities taking increasing annual expenses from endowment returns. So why not blend a sustainability-focused lens, using the full flexibility that a hedge fund structure offers? That's what GLG Partners, now part of Man Group, the world's largest listed hedge fund manager, is doing.

Jason Mitchell manages a sustainability fund at GLG, whose primary investment strategy focuses on secular themes and industries driven by environmental and demographic change. Rather than allocate on a country or sector-weighted basis, the fund emphasizes the entire food chain of key sustainability themes and is designed to capture shifts between regional or sector trends. The fund takes an integrated approach, matching the development of themes that include the effects of urbanization, resource scarcity, agricultural efficiencies, energy security, regulatory change, and increased investment healthcare provisioning, social housing, and education services vertically against industries and companies best positioned to benefit. Themes are remapped continually to examine the interrelationships among changes in regulatory regimes, resource scarcity, demographics, and supply and demand balances. Once investment themes are mapped, the fund then performs company-specific financial analysis and assesses of environmental, social and governance metrics. Additionally, the portfolio focuses on mid- to large capitalization, liquid stocks in order to facilitate active position size management.

GLG is one of the largest alternative investment managers in the world, managing approximately 50 funds and several private mandates following long-only and alternative hedge fund strategies. It is a wholly owned division of Man Group Plc and offers clients a diverse range of alternative investment products and account management services. As of December 31, 2010, Man Group Plc managed $68.6 billion.

This chapter offers Jason Mitchell's views on the opportunities and challenges emerging in China. The so-called emerging markets have now very clearly emerged. China is expected to become the world's largest economy within a decade, and other, smaller countries in the region appear well positioned to become a larger percentage of the world's economy. This dynamic alone suggests that an overweighting to Asia would make sense for any portfolio, simply to ride this wave of momentum. However, challenges loom on the road to this potential success. China relies on an energy mix that has made it the world's largest emitter of greenhouse gases, and it has serious water and pollution problems affecting the health of its growing population. Asia is so significant a topic that we provide the views of three leading thinkers in the space, starting with Jason Mitchell. As he bridges the world of hedge funds, sustainability, and the opportunities that emerge from the developing world, he is an ideal observer to start our tour of the world and the regional issues that emerge.

From the purist's perspective, the notion of sustainability makes for a near-impossible pairing with developing countries like China and India. The chief engine for economic growth—industrialization via conventional coal- and gas-fired power generation—runs counter to still-immature renewable energy and efficiency technologies. China, however, represents an important paradox: the country with the highest annual carbon dioxide emissions and, at the same time, the country most willing to mandate, fund, and enforce corrective change as national policy.[1] In directly confronting its coal and oil scarcity and managing its energy and emissions intensity levels through a national industrial policy, China could potentially present a carbon mitigation and efficiency model to countries where climate change debate has stalled action. Chinese efficiency-linked investment is already offering investment opportunities in companies driving lower-cost economics and innovation through efficiency themes like alternative forms of energy.

China's long-term national planning provides the chance to witness command-and-control environmentalism against the progress—or lack thereof—of environmental policy formulated and negotiated democratically. Developed countries would be wise to keep a watchful eye on China, as China's running budget marks the largest-funded national program of its kind aimed at cutting greenhouse gas (GHG) emissions and energy consumption per unit of gross domestic product (GDP). The center of the China paradox—its material outlays in technology and investment complemented by policy and norms-driven reframing—is perhaps best manifested through the draft 12th Five Year Plan (FYP) submitted to the National People's Congress in March 2011 for review and approval. The draft 12th FYP means that government agencies are actively reshaping the economic and social normative assumptions around the GDP-growth-at-all-costs psychology that characterized much of the industrialization since early 2000. This has already been reflected in new, penalty-loaded measures, elevating the efficiency gains in existing plants alongside new production. The significance of this national efficiency prescription cannot be underestimated. Chinese planning along efficiency themes represents, in some sense, a microcosm of what much of the rest of the world—particularly western countries, such as the United States, that have delayed national-level energy efficiency planning—also will have to undergo. Importantly, this national prescription around efficiency gains does not attempt to open or draw lines in the climate change debate. These policies address the more basic requirement for implementing functional efficiencies in order to accommodate future environmental and demographic growth.

By being the first to address and architect the need for environmental and efficiency-related investment on a national scale, China benefits not only from greater efficiencies, lower energy intensity ratios, and a much-needed reduction to its current carbon dioxide emissions trend line but on an industrial level as well. In the course of policy-driven investment, empirical necessity is nurturing the development of new Chinese industries in clean technologies, such as wind and solar, and in broader manufacturing and industrial efficiencies. China is undergoing its own "ideational turn," a shift running parallel to material growth where the government is actively reframing GDP-growth norms around environmental conservation and efficiency. These changes potentially could result in two significant by-products: China assuming a greater leadership role in policy-setting international, and the development of massive economies of scale in industrial technologies that currently are unable to reach grid parity. One likely outcome is that China could present an argument for why environmental and industrial efficiency agenda setting on a national, command-and-control basis proves compelling relative to the kind of unproductive, democratic environmentalism attempted through multilateral organizations and fora like the Kyoto Protocol and the United Nations Climate Change Summit.

CHINA'S RESOURCE SCARCITY AND ITS EMPIRICAL NEED FOR EFFICIENCY

That China's energy intensity represents the highest in the world should be no surprise. Industrial inefficiencies built at breakneck speeds over the last 20 to 30 years to facilitate 8% to 10% annual GDP growth have resulted in China having consistently added more than 50% of the world's incremental power capacity since 2000.[2] Western media often highlight only the fact of asymmetric energy consumption (Figure 25.1) in addition to

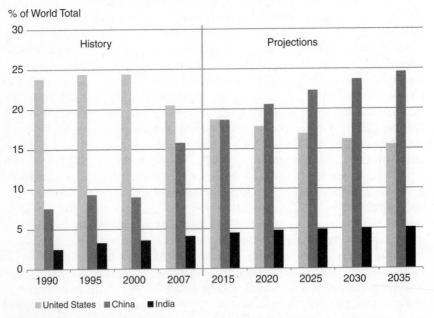

FIGURE 25.1 World Energy Consumption: United States, China and India, 1990–2035 Forecast
Source: U.S. Energy Information Administration, International Energy Statistics database (as of November 2009), www.eia.gov/emeu/international. Projections: EIA, World Energy Projection System Plus (2010).

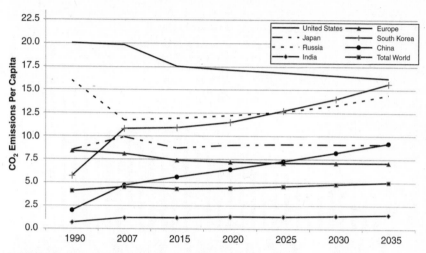

FIGURE 25.2 Energy-Related Carbon Dioxide Emissions
Source: Historical derived from U.S. Energy Information Administration,
International Energy Statistics database (as of November 2009) www.eia.gov/emeu/
international. Projections: EIA, World Energy Projection System Plus (2010).

profiling issues involving trade protectionism surrounding renewable technology or accusations of government subsidization that violate World Trade Organization free trade rules. However, to focus on this argument alone is to miss the larger structural issues that are unique to China, namely its dependence on domestic and imported coal as a primary fuel source.

The rhetoric of climate change politics also often overlooks the fact that Chinese net exports account for more than 20% of energy consumption,[3] implying that developed countries that outsource their manufacturing to China are in some sense exporting their emissions on a penalty-free basis. Put another way, developed countries can be seen to owe some part of their reduction in carbon dioxide emissions to the outsourcing and physical relocation of manufacturing plants, particularly in heavy industries, to China. This strategy ultimately translates into a lower degree of carbon-intensive, industrial capacity building in developed countries and displaces the environmental externalities to China. (See Figures 25.2 and 25.3.)

To tackle these issues, Chinese companies in the power generation, renewable energy, manufacturing, and capital equipment sectors are now navigating policy change as China transitions between five-year plans. The draft 12th FYP—the latest in a series of national, skeletal blueprints pushed downstream to the provincial level for interpretation and implementation every five years—has introduced wide-ranging reforms and measures for industrial growth, touching on sectors ranging from power grid and

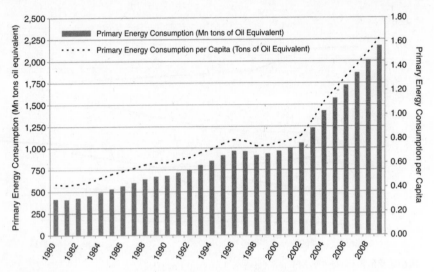

FIGURE 25.3 China's Energy Consumption, 1980–2009
Source: BP Statistical Review 2010, CEIC Data Company Ltda (CEIC), IMF and
Citi Investment Research & Analysis (CIRA) estimates.

transportation infrastructure to healthcare and social housing systems. Fittingly, the topic of energy efficiency—compared to previous policies that endorsed unregulated energy capacity expansion—plays a prominent role throughout the plan.

Under the draft 12th FYP, China has committed to a wide range of environmental targets. Over the 2011 to 2015 period, they include reducing energy consumption by 16% compared to 19.1% for the 11th FYP. (The lower targeted energy reduction is a result of recent plant closures and lower GDP growth of 7%.) The FYP looks to lower carbon intensity by 17% per unit of GDP and to cut the release of major pollutants by 8% to 10%. Having finished the 11th FYP at 9.6%, the new draft 12th FYP stipulates for 11.4% of primary energy consumption derived from non–fossil fuel sources, keeping China on track to meet its 15% objective by 2020 and reduce its coal and oil dependency. To accomplish this, Premier Wen Jiabao outlined plans for the construction of 235 gigawatt (GW) non–fossil fuel capacity within the 12th FYP, including 70 GW of wind, 120 GW of hydro, 40 GW of nuclear, and 5 GW of solar power.[4] Figure 25.4 illustrates the magnitude in new, nonfossil capacity growth between the 11th FYP and the draft 12th FYP. Generation from alternative energy sources effectively doubles between FYPs. This appears matched through efforts by the People's Republic of China Ministry of Land and Resources, which suspended the

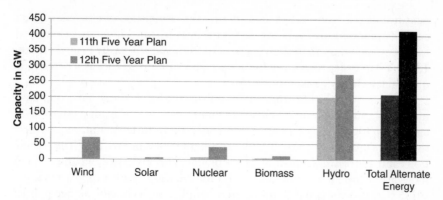

FIGURE 25.4 China's Draft Five-Year Plan, Alternative Energy Targets
Source: National Development and Reform Commission (NDRC), Credit Lyonnais Securities Asia (CLSA) Research.

issuance of new coal mining development licenses until the end of 2013 as a means to prevent overcapacity and to regulate investment relative to the ramp-up in nonfossil generation.[5]

The draft 12th FYP also articulates objectives across other environmental factors: Water consumption per unit of value-added industrial output will be reduced by 30%; stricter emission control standards imposing Euro V European exhaust standardization by 2012 in major cities, such as Beijing; and as-yet-undefined reductions for pollutants, such as sulfur dioxide and nitrogen oxides, as well as annual grain production, farmland reserve growth, and social housing construction quotas.[6] Several of these targets will come under scrutiny, specifically the hydro targets, as a majority of the new capacity is derived from damming up rivers in Tibet, which has implications for other countries, such as India, that depend on the rivers. As of the writing of this chapter (mid-March 2011) and in the context of the recent explosion and partial meltdown of the Fukushima Daiichi nuclear plant in Japan, China has announced it would *not* slow its 40 GW of nuclear capacity build.[7] China's State Council has, however, recently has placed a moratorium on the approval process for new nuclear power projects, noting that while its plants are deploying the latest Generation 3 AP1000 reactors,[8] the Fukushima incident warrants more safety and planning precaution. Such a downward revision of the 40 GW nuclear target seems unlikely from the most recent statements by the Ministry of Environmental Protection which has expressed support for nuclear. Depending on further Chinese assessments of the risk of nuclear generation, alternative forms, such as hydro and wind, may incrementally supplement power generation plan over the next five years. Nonetheless, considering the magnitude of efficiency-linked capacity planning and building across the breadth of technologies employed, energy efficiency as an underlying structural theme will easily extend into the 13th FYP in order to achieve the 15% target non–fossil fuel as a percentage of primary energy consumption by 2020.

It is not surprising, then, that the nature of Chinese environmental measures and long-term efficiency planning derives not from western-style, climate change–charged politics but from a more fundamental requirement to sustain high GDP growth while simultaneously improving living conditions and addressing industrial development. This makes China unique in its motivation for carbon mitigation and remediation. It also represents a position that is orthogonal to the western emphasis on climate change politics as the primary catalyst to induce policy and investment change. From the social constructivist perspective, the notions of sustainability and efficiency defined by China have less to do with the logic of appropriateness and the western mind-set of socially responsible investing than it has to do with the logic of consequences and the need facilitate growth while accommodating trends such as urbanization and an aging population.

For China, the issues of dwindling coal resources, industrialization, and a national move to elevate living standards are core, empirical causalities driving environmental policy enactment. Efficiency as a theme plays particularly into the confluence of scarce natural resource factor endowments and the diminishing rate of existing natural resources. Figure 25.5 illustrates the energy imperative that faces China's coal scarcity. Despite its 14% share of global coal reserves, Chinese coal consumption accounts for over 47% of global coal consumption.[9] In 2010, coal imports of 165 million tons

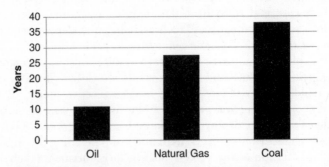

FIGURE 25.5   China's Energy Reserve Life, 2009
Source: Deutsche Bank, BP Statistical Review.
Note: Reserve life is calculated as proven reserves/actual production volume in the year.

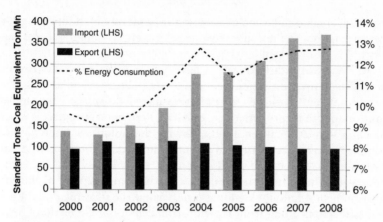

FIGURE 25.6 China's Energy Trade Balance, 2000–2008
Source: Deutsche Bank, CEIC.

accounted for more than 5% of total coal consumption, marking a 31% increase relative to 2009 and significantly outpacing national raw coal consumption growth of 5.3%.[10] Although no official Chinese estimation exists for 2011, Citibank estimates that coal imports could growth as much as 60%, to 233 million tons.[11] This step function increase in coal imports is a sign that China's energy trade balance has begun to skew toward factoring imports out of domestic supply constraints. Moreover, BP estimates that the country faces the potential for its own peak coal scenario within the next 40 years; in comparison, the U.S. domestic supply comprises roughly 30%—or 245 years' worth—of global reserves.[12] While this 40-year estimate reflects reserves relative to current extraction costs and omits undiscovered coal resources in the vast Inner Mongolian region, it is nonetheless a sobering profile of the disequilibrium between China's coal consumption and its diminishing reserves. (See Figure 25.6.)

Add to this the fact that 2009 represented the first year that Chinese domestic crude production saw a year-to-year decline (–0.1%), and China's shift to a large-scale net importer of oil should have profound ramifications across all parts of the global energy food chain.[13] Just 6% of domestic demand in 1993 when China first began to import crude, oil imports currently account for more than 50% of total domestic consumption and are estimated to reach as high as 64.5% by 2020.[14] In short, China faces a near-deterministic trajectory of energy consumption that its scarcity in resource factors such as coal cannot sustain. Confronted by the possibility of a future where the reliance on coal imports makes economic growth vulnerable to commodity pricing shocks and shortages, China's alternatives realistically include only the widespread adoption of efficiency measures and the commercial development of non–fossil fuel energy sources.

The effects of industrialization have accelerated the promotion of energy efficiency up the Chinese economic and political agendas considering the environmental damage and pollution-linked deaths of past industrial expansion, not to mention the drag on GDP. Premier Wen stated as much in a speech in May 2010, when, foreshadowing the ambitions of the 12th FYP, he elevated resource conservation and environmental protection to national priorities.[15]

Areas of China, to a certain degree, are now microcosms of the effects of environmental fallout extending well beyond the miasmic pollution that stretches to Hong Kong from the industrial centers of Guangdong. One of the simplest illustrations of this is CLSA's assertion that 39% of China's fresh water is polluted beyond potable standards. In a 2007 report, the World Bank estimated that pollution cost China 5.8% of annual GDP while acid rain cost $5.6 billion worth of crop and building damage;[16] it also estimated 750,000 pollution-related deaths per year. With environmental damage bearing negative externalities like these, China's political system has little time for U.S.-style partisan positioning or a Copenhagen-like impasse. The cleanup job alone will not be inexpensive. He Ping, chairman of the International Fund for China's Environment, estimates 2% of GDP or roughly $100 billion per year will be required to address existing environmental damage.[17]

The momentum starting to gather in China is a stark contrast to the lack of global, collective action as well as the oil and coal special interest groups in the United States that have managed to coalesce significant support against renewable energy policies. As a means of achieving its 11th FYP target of a 20% reduction in energy consumption per GDP by the end of 2010, China implemented penalty-loaded policy reforms to accelerate efforts and outline its seriousness. China's National Development and Reform Commission (NDRC) announced the closure of 11 GW of smaller, thermal power plants, exceeding Premier Wen's official target of 10 GW for 2010 and following the 26 GW worth of thermal plant closures in 2009.[18] Few countries, developed and developing alike, are politically capable of this much change through national policy coordination. To put this into context, 11 GW of power generation closures equates to nearly 20% of 2010 gross thermal coal capacity additions or more than 12% of total blended capacity additions for 2010.[19] This represents a staggering number of decommissioned plants that, unless precisely correlated against new capacity, could have easily cost the Chinese economy GDP growth. To accomplish closure targets, the Ministry of Industry and Information Technology published in August 2010 a list of 2,087 plants across 18 industries that it deemed to be outdated and inefficient, and were forced to close by September. By September 2010, provincial governments in Jiangsu, Zhejiang, and Anhui had already instituted power shutdowns, while local media reported corresponding power suspensions at cement and steel mills in the provinces of Fujian, Shanxi, and Hebei. The estimated compositional changes in energy consumption patterns in China through 2020 can be seen in Figure 25.7.

Clearly, these efficiency reforms carry an immediate cost to the Chinese economy. UBS forecasts that plant closures cost as much as 2% of GDP growth in the second half of 2010.[20] Chinese companies all offer their own anecdotes supporting claims of more stringent energy efficiency enforcement measures. Companies such as China Power Resources, an independent power producer, saw 4% to 5% fluctuations in coal spot prices in the second half of 2010 alone, as steel and cement mills closures shifted typical seasonal demand patterns.

SHAPING CHINESE ENERGY-EFFICIENCY NORMS

Efficiency as a theme is by no means a normative novelty to China, and an understanding of its ideational development is necessary in order to fully appreciate the extent of China's past commitment to energy efficiency and its future implications. Efficiency represents a continuation—interrupted only for the last ten years—of a policy agenda first implemented by former Chairman Deng Xiaoping in 1980. Prescriptive in nature, these early reforms were essentially an attempt to regulate what traditionally had been a singular focus on the growth of gross energy supply initiated during the Soviet-style policy planning of the late 1940s.

During the period of these first reforms from 1980 to 2002 under Deng, China demonstrated the efficacy of national energy planning by managing to reduce its annual average energy consumption per unit of GDP by 5%.[21] For these two decades, policy setting translated into heavy government regulatory oversight around energy capacity building balanced quantitatively by efficiency and energy intensity metrics. However, two pivotal events reversed these gains leading to the current situation of increasing capital formation as a percent of GDP: China's entrance into the World Trade Organization in 2003 driving exports followed by the rushed infrastructure build-out into the 2008 Beijing Olympic Games.

Fortunately, Chinese policy took effect as early as 2005 when the Politburo, expressed through the NDRC—one of the main government

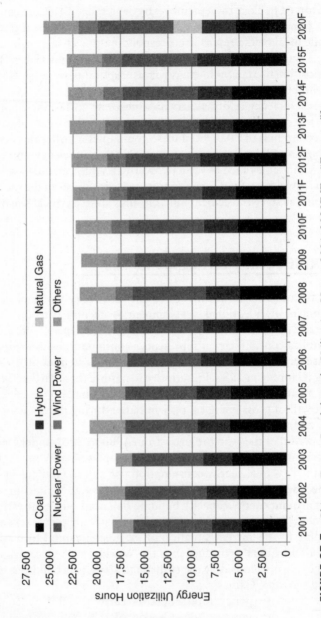

FIGURE 25.7 China's Energy Breakdown by Utilization Hours, 2001–2020F [F= "Forecast"]

Source: China Electricity Council, State Power Grid Company, National Development and Reform Commission, and Citigroup estimates.

agencies overseeing China's economic growth—enacted the "Ten Key Projects" initiative, which subsequently was integrated into the 11th FYP. This initiative, which included energy efficiency measures for buildings, coal-fired industrial boiler retrofits, district-level combined heat and power projects, and oil conservation, helped to reorient China back toward the trend begun by Deng in 1980, and its effects were perceptible almost immediately.[22] In 2006, energy intensity declined by 1.7%; in 2007, by 3.7%; and in 2008, by 4.6%, enabling China to reach its 20% reduction target at the end of 2010 and redoubling efforts to target a 17.3% reduction by 2015 in addition to a 40% to 45% reduction in carbon intensity by 2020.[23] The draft 12th FYP, presaged by the State Council's October announcement and Premier Wen's speech in May 2010, formally elevates the normative importance of energy savings and environmental protection to the first of seven efficiency themes to be promoted as industries. These moves were reinforced by the revision and establishment of new, more empowered regulatory bodies. In 2008, the State Environmental Protection Administration—China's version of the U.S. Environmental Protection Agency—was transformed into the more powerful Ministry of Environmental Protection supported by independent funding. It also meant the establishment of the National Bureau of Energy under the NDRC's oversight and the formation of the State Energy Commission that counts among its members the premier, a vice premier, and a number of ministers—accentuating the gravity of energy efficiency as a national directive.

A number of earlier policy realignment moves laid the foundations for the 2011 release of the draft 12th FYP. For example, in June 2010 the NDRC issued a directive outlining for the first time explicit penalties for officials at the provincial level and the management of state-owned enterprises (SOEs) responsible for achieving FYP emissions reduction targets and efficiency quotas. As a means of inculcating government agencies and SOEs, this process begins at the national, policy-setting level and then extends down to the provincial and local levels. It also introduces penalties for nonadherence that go beyond corporate-level enforcement and toward forms of individual liability. The NDRC directive further explains that performance assessments potentially could result in the lack of promotion or even job dismissal, depending on how far performance misses national targets. The Politburo has begun to require provincial and SOE officials to attend national training at the Central Party School in Beijing to create a uniform approach to shape the ideational as well as the material significance of this efficiency regulatory regime.[24] In short, the NDRC directive also serves to reinforce the fact that efficiency and emissions reduction targets are not merely window dressing to fulfill current FYP objectives.

The language in the NDRC notice suggests meaningful change to the shape and composition of Chinese industrial growth from an expansion-at-any-cost, shortsighted approach to one more concerned with long-term social and environmental welfare. In practical terms, beyond the statistical ranking of companies meeting or failing the emissions targets, there is an unequivocal emphasis on corrective action and career penalties for companies that jeopardized the 2010 20% emission per unit reduction target. Significantly, the NDRC has deemphasized its traditional system of GDP-driven growth targets for a broader, more holistic set of 47 indexes—half based on green-oriented criteria, such as water and clean coal consumption—that reward provincial officials on sustainability-loaded factors, such as energy conservation and the mitigation of greenhouse gas emissions. With policy architecture more entrenched on the national level, similar moves have begun to filter to the provinces. In November 2010, the NDRC issued a "demand-side management approach" measure designed to help provinces manage energy usage or demand pull as a means to optimize supply-side growth. In addition, these measures parse five-year energy-savings objectives down to annual targets in an attempt to smooth out the linearity of investment and implementation for provincial officials.

CHINESE POLICY SETTING

Thus far, international climate change negotiations have been driven largely according to the win sets of developed countries with superficial acknowledgment of the implementation issues and funding costs faced by developing countries, such as China. Issues posed by special interests in the United States, Japan, and Canada have prevented collective policy setting toward a revised Kyoto Protocol commitment, threatening to devolve international cooperation into regional or even bilateral environmental alliances.

At the UN Climate Change Summit in December 2009, criticism of China's resistance to working within a multilateral mechanism was widely reported. Yet the announcement of China's internal target to reduce carbon intensity by 40% to 45% by 2020 went largely underreported and was relegated to the Annex of the Copenhagen Accords. More important, the 2020 target still remains unmatched by notional climate change leaders, such as the United States. COP16—the most recent UN summit held in Cancun, Mexico—provided an opportunity for climate policy makers to readdress the negotiations and funding mechanisms necessary to replace and improve on the Kyoto Protocol as it nears expiration at the end of 2012. COP16 negotiations also displayed signs of China's increased willingness to assume a greater role in international environmental agenda setting, and

Chinese officials have already called for a binding, global climate treaty to be finalized and signed at COP17 in South Africa in December 2011. Emissions reductions targets laid out originally in the Kyoto Protocol clearly need to be readdressed and renewed in a form that carries more weight and collective ownership, particularly by the countries that did not ratify it. For this to happen, domestic-level politics must support policies around environmental change. In fact, because of inaction at the multilateral level, ultimately more countries may move toward the China model of stronger, more progressive unilateral policy setting buttressed by heavy investment and incentives.

One of the ways in which policy setting is supporting environmental and efficiency-related capital investment in China is the formation of national-level emissions targets in parallel with a renewable portfolio standard (RPS) mechanism. RPS mechanisms, which require utilities and independent power producers gradually to increase renewable energy sources as a percentage of their overall energy output, are seeing increasing implementation in developing countries. By comparison, the United States remains mired in legislative gridlock around a national energy policy, and partisan politics and lack of a consensus around tackling energy efficiency mean a watered-down proposal in 2011 at best. While the Obama administration maintains its own goal of 17% of U.S. energy consumption produced by renewable sources by 2020, this target lacks essential congressional ratification within a comprehensive energy bill. Thus, we can single out the United States as one of the few major developed countries without a national RPS mechanism. As it stands, only 24 states in the United States operate under a penalty-loaded RPS mechanism, and the piecemeal state schemes provide only an extrapolated path toward a 13% to 15% blended renewable goal by 2020. This fact reveals another paradox of the U.S.-China emissions standoff: The lack of a national RPS plan in the United States could mean that China's own RPS objectives by 2020 actually exceed U.S. nonfossil energy mix. This argument applies as well to other developing countries, such as India, that have implemented RPS plans. India case, like China, tracks renewable energy contribution as a percentage of overall power generation from 5% currently to 15% by 2020.

Realistically, these issues mean that the next two to three years have extraordinary weight in their ability to rebalance and shape some semblance of a collective, international energy agenda and emissions mitigation policy. Global energy and climate change policy has largely been hamstrung by the United States, due to its problems with domestic special interests groups in reaching a two-thirds legislative consensus to ratify any international accord. However, the diminished probability of a renewed Kyoto Protocol that represents signatories of all major countries or, as another alternative, does not mean the end of progress toward decarbonizing economies. Rather,

China and India, motivated by their own industrial ambitions and domestic energy security concerns, could increasingly represent new linchpins capable of coalescing developed and developing world agenda setting.

TRANSLATING CHINA'S ENVIRONMENTAL POLICIES INTO INDUSTRIAL OPPORTUNITIES

Although the reverberations of China's energy policy setting will be felt over the next ten years, the Chinese focus on efficiency already has materialized in the formation of new industries and national champions meant to consolidate manufacturing production at some point. China is successfully converting its base necessity for functional efficiencies into vast economies of scale where new capital investment, both government financed and direct foreign investment, is driving down cost per watt economics in solar, wind, and biomass.

The benefits of these cost curves reach far beyond China's borders, most notably to downstream integrators and renewable energy developers in areas as diverse as India, Europe, and South Africa, where developers continually work to solve for projects with bankable internal rates of return (IRRs) set against cascading feed-in-tariff regimes. Without the pressure on cost per watt economics from Chinese manufacturing, developer IRRs would become uninvestable, which would stall incremental renewable energy capacity building. By comparison, the willingness of many western countries to commit to long-term funding mechanisms needed to develop such areas as renewable energy remains a critical question; the fallout of economic austerity measures in the United States and Spain, for example, has exacerbated funding shortfalls and the development of new mechanisms. In China, the empirical need for energy reform is being pragmatically converted into functional efficiency and utility while policy shapes industrial innovation as much as industrial scale. In China's draft submission of the 12th FYP, seven key strategic industries (see Table 25.1) will see heavy investment. These seven emerging industries mark a distinct move away from previous sectors that were designated strategic, such as national defense, utilities, airlines, shipping, telecommunications, media, and basic resources. In addition, they carry enormous expectations with their aggregate value-added output reaching 8% of GDP by 2015 and 15% by 2020 from the current level of just 3%.[25] This path equates to roughly $171 billion of collective output derived from the development of these seven industries, depending on one's 2020 Chinese GDP assumptions, reaching as much as $3 trillion by 2020.[26]

In its simplest form, the draft 12th FYP translates into a multiyear runway of structural investment aimed at the improving China's biggest sectors

TABLE 25.1   12th Five-Year Plan: Seven New and Emerging Industries to Be Promoted

1.	Energy Savings and Environmental Protection	Energy-efficient products, including technologies in recycling, energy savings, environmental protection, emissions and pollution mitigation, control, clean coal; high-voltage inverters and energy management software.
2.	Advanced Information Technology	Information technology efficiencies and integration: cloud computing; high-end software and server; virtual digital technology; display technology; IPV4 core equipment.
3.	Biology, Biotechnology	Technologies in biomedicines, biochemicals, diagnostic reagents, disease prevention vaccines and control; advanced medical devices, equipment, and materials; biobreeding, green agriculture; bioproduction; marine biology.
4.	High-End Manufacturing Efficiencies and Advanced Capital Equipment	Aerospace, satellite engineering, and applied regional and general-purposed aircraft technologies. Track-based mass transit transportation equipment: passenger train and metros. Offshore equipment: digital, flexible, integrated intelligent equipment
5.	New Energy Efficiencies	Advanced power generation technologies including nuclear power plants; solar; wind power equipment, wind power plants, smart grid and related systems that can accommodate new energy sources; bio and waste to energy generation; smart grid; demand-side management software technology.
6.	New Materials	Advanced material technologies and extraction, including rare earth, high-performance synthetics, biomaterials and membranes, special-usage glass, functional porcelain/ceramic, LED; high-performance special steel, new alloy, and engineering plastics; advanced fibers and composites; nanotechnologies, superconducting, intelligent materials.
7.	New Energy Vehicles	Advanced battery and fuel cell chemistries, electric motor, power systems, electric control system; plug-in hybrid car. Natural gas automotive systems and downstream infrastructure.

Source: Morgan Stanley Research, "China Economics: Chinese Economy through 2020: Not Whether but How Growth Will Decelerate," September 10, 2010. Morgan Stanley assumes an average 3% appreciation of the renminbi against the U.S. dollar per annum, with 2010 GDP of $5.7 billion reaching $20 trillion by 2020.

in need of energy-efficiency measures, including power generation, manufacturing, industrial automation, and inefficient mills that specifically produce chemicals, metals, paper, and cement. These objectives are also meant to address persistent problems hindering Chinese economic growth, increasing the level of basic provisioning services such as healthcare, and building out a more robust infrastructure capable of supporting more advanced iterations of FYP agendas going forward.

To this end, China has stated a commitment to invest as much as $760 billion on new energy development planning over the next ten years. This is a systematic form of capacity planning that matches national targets with funding, going well beyond the short-term stimulus packages of developed countries. Under this program, many of China's energy-intensive industries will undergo accelerated cycles of plant decommissioning. The full extent of these upgrade cycles and efficiency improvements will impact import and export trade, as 2010 saw China's Customs and the Ministry of Commerce temporarily prohibit the export of 44 processing items, including materials that consume significant amounts of energy to produce, such as polysilicon. In January 2011, the Ministry of Industry and Technology announced additional guidelines for new polysilicon production, reinforcing its commitment to consolidating production and shrinking areas of energy inefficiency. These latest rules, for example, mandate production of at least 3,000 metric tons of polysilicon, the removal of equipment running at power consumption ratios in excess of 200 kilowatts per kilogram, and 95% water recycling rates; they also impose a more restrictive qualifying process for plants projects in areas with energy shortages or near farmland and nature reserves.[27] In short, China's endgame—ultimately, the consolidation and improvement of infrastructure around national leaders—should produce leaner, greater economies of scale more able to absorb domestic and export demand on competitive terms. This consolidation is already occurring in the renewable energy industry through companies such as GCL-Poly Energy, one of the largest Chinese polysilicon producers, and through solar module manufacturers, leading to powerful production cost advantages and closer parity to coal and oil economics. Similar ambitions exist for wind, with official domestic demand estimated at 100 GW by 2015 and 150 to 200 GW by 2020.[28] Chinese standing wind capacity at the end of 2010 of 41.8GW has already exceeded U.S. wind capacity of 40 GW.[29] The draft 12th FYP ensures that, like polysilicon production, wind turbine capacity is regulated to prevent overcapacity situations and avoid subscale production inefficiencies. This fact was reflected in the Ministry of Industrial and Information Technology's parallel announcement to the draft 12th FYP outlining industrial objectives. For wind, this means minimum quotas around annual production capacity (1 Gigawatt hour (GWh)), minimum turbine length (2.5 Megawatt hour (MWh)), and minimum equity investments (30%).

China's power grid stands as another major point of investment within the draft 12th FYP. Having historically lagged power generation investment, grid capital expenditure exceeds power capacity additions since 2009, driving upgrades for ultra-high-voltage (UHV) lines capable of transmitting renewable-generated power from Inner Mongolia and western China to the manufacturing and production hubs in the East, easing demand for coal. According to estimates, the combination of historical underinvestment and compounded capacity growth that will mean UHV capital investment accounts for 25% of total annual grid spend over the next several years (having comprised only 3% previously); by 2020, China expects to have built out about 11,000 miles of UHV lines compared with the current 1,250 miles of lines currently.[30] While Chinese companies already produce low- and medium-voltage lines, multinationals should benefit from the spending in UHC deployment. Within overall grid spending, smart grid technology will be a significant beneficiary of investment and a key contributor toward expected future energy savings. As a part of China's more than $60 billion annual investment in grid infrastructure, the $7 billion commitment by China's State Grid Corp means the basic construction of an integrated smart grid able to integrate energy sources on a feed-in basis including wind and solar by 2015. This, in addition to plans toward smart meter rollouts and advanced metering infrastructure upgrades over the next five years, could place China in a leadership role in the development and deployment of smart grid technology, despite this being a traditional strength of U.S. utilities.

China has started on an ambitious course by recognizing and acknowledging the ESG costs of the GDP-oriented policies of the last ten years. The follow-on effects are clearly evident: Chinese companies—and Indian companies in the renewable energy space as well—have proven agile at tapping public markets to finance their expansion plants, often at significant premiums to their European and American counterparts, which suffer from unclear regulatory environments. While 2010 saw a number of shelved initial public offerings with U.S. renewable energy exposure and significant discounts, the year also finished off with a number of Chinese renewable energy IPOs, including China Goldwind, Datang Renewables, China Suntien Green Energy, Shanghai Taisheng Wind Power, and Trony Solar, and many more were waiting fill the capital-raising pipeline for 2011 and 2012.

Another significant indicator that China's 12th FYP increasingly recognizes the need for greater policy coordination supporting technological innovation is the parallel establishment of a more robust institutional framework that both induces and protects patent development, a competence that historically has handicapped the country's rate of innovation. In November

2010, the State Intellectual Property Office of China published the *National Patent Development Strategy (2011–2020)* outlining objectives that run in parallel to overall five-year planning.[31]

This document reemphasizes patent development in key industries that reappear as upcoming FYP priorities: renewable energy, large-scale battery, manufacturing technologies, telecommunications, and information technology.[32] The deliberate emphasis of utility patents over intellectual patents is in itself revealing. It is policy anchored deep within national strategic demands meant to support the development of infant industries and industrial consolidation, reasserting the point that empirical and industrial necessity are propelling China toward applied technologies more than theoretical science. To meet targets such as 2 million annual patent applications by 2015, patent processes themselves are being streamlined. Examination review periods have been shortened to 22 months of inventions compared to 24 to 36 months in the United States, and a mere three for utility and design patents.

These dynamics are most notably playing out in renewable energy technologies, such as wind and solar. For solar, China's domestic demand in 2011 is estimated to account for little more than 500 megawatts, or roughly 3.5% of installed solar capacity in what is estimated to be a 14 GW global market for 2010;[33] yet Chinese solar module manufacturers controlled more than 26% market share in 2009. In spite of the criticism for all of China's coal-powered capacity needed to drive near-term GDP growth, the case can be made that the nation is establishing itself as a policy leader for renewable energy and, more broadly, functional efficiencies, in both the development its own domestic energy consumption as well as in technology exports.[34]

SUMMARY

The Chinese flavor of environmental policy under a command-and-control regime may be the kick start developed countries need to formulate and enact more ambitious objectives around emissions reductions and energy efficiency. This approach, bolstered by the evidence of measures already implemented in the 11th FYP, could see China increasingly considered as a leader on environmental change as climate negotiations in COP16. Just as the draft 12th FYP updated efficiency and emissions targets, the 13th FYP is expected to extend these targets, pointing to ongoing heavy spending and ideational reframing around efficiency themes for the next ten years. But for China, handicapped by resource scarcity, the upshot is more significant: The empirical necessity for coal substitutes, lower run rates of energy intensity, and national policy setting are a powerful blend of industrial drivers, the effects of which already are evident. China's ability to develop efficiency from abstract theme into specific industrial objectives will carry heavy implications for future, illustrating the differences between the West's norms-heavy, investment-light approach and China's norms-light, investment-heavy strategy.

NOTES

1. Carbon Dioxide Information Analysis Center, British Petroleum, Earth Policy Institute, 2010. www.earth-policy.org/index.php?/indicators/C52/
2. Credit Lyonnais Securities Asia, "China's Energy Binge," September 2010. www.clsa.com/member/index.asp but only subscribers can access research.
3. Bert Yahua Wang and Jiaochen Liang, "China Fights Climate Change through Energy Conservation Policy: An Empirical Analysis of Provincial Energy Intensity," Tsinghua University: Center for Industrial Development and Environmental Governance, School of Public Policy and Management, 2009.
4. China's National People's Congress, remarks by Premier Wen Jiabao on energy and environmental goals within the draft 12th Five Year Plan, March 6–7, 2010.
5. Bank of America Merrill Lynch, "Coal Output and Renewable Energy Development Update," March 8, 2011.
6. Xinhua press, quoting Zhang Lijun, vice minister of environmental protection, March 11, 2012.
7. Zhang Lijun, Chinese minister of environmental protection, indicating that China will not change its nuclear development schedule due to Chinese using AP1000 Generation 3 reactors as opposed to older technology deployed in less earthquake-sensitive areas, press conference comments, March 11, 2011.
8. State Council press release, March 16, 2011. www.gov.cn/ldhd/2011-03/16/content_1826025.htm
9. BP Global, "BP Statistical Review of World Energy," 2010. http://bp.com/statisticalreview.com
10. Xinhua News Agency, National Development and Reform Commission statistics, March 2, 2011. www.eiu.com/index.asp?layout=ib3PrintArticle andarticle_id=1987849183andprinter=printerandrf=0
11. Estimates from Pierre Lau, Citibank head of Asia Pacific Utilities Research, March 16, 2011.
12. BP Global, "BP Statistical Review of World Energy."
13. D. Winning, "China's Coal Crisis," *Wall Street Journal*, November 16, 2010. http://online.wsj.com/article/SB10001424052748704312504575617810380509880.html
14. BP Statistical Review of World Energy, June 2010, slide 14: www.bp.com/liveassets/bp_internet/globalbp/STAGING/global_assets/downloads/S/Stats_Review_2010_slide_pack.pdf
15. Chinese Academy of Social Sciences, *Blue Book of Energy* Report (July, 2009). http://rushanengine.com/en/newsshow.asp?id=660

16. Wen Jiabao's national teleconference speech to the State Council alluding to measures around emissions reductions, environmental conservation, and energy savings, May 5, 2010.

17. World Bank, Rural Development, Natural Resources and Environment Management Unit, East Asia and Pacific Region, "Cost of Pollution in China: Economic Estimates of Physical Damages," 2007, Washington D.C. www .worldbank.org/eapenvironment.

18. G. Sim and R. Feiwen, "China Is Set to Lose 2% of GDP Cleaning Up Decades of Pollution," Bloomberg News, September 17, 2010. www.bloomberg.com/news/2010-09-16/china-set-to-lose-2-of-gdp-fighting-pollution-as-doing-nothing-costs-more.html

19. NDRC-reported figure, February 11, 2011, http://news.sina.com.cn/c/2011-02-11/151021938747.shtml

20. Citibank Investment Research estimates, 2010. Estimates from Pierre Lau, Citibank head of Asia Pacific Utilities Research, March 16, 2011.

21. UBS Investment Research, "Trends and Changes: Chinese SRI," 2010.

22. Lawrence Berkeley National Laboratory and China Energy Group, "Assessment of China's Energy-Saving and Emission-Reduction Accomplishments and Opportunities During the 11th Five Year Plan," 2010.

23. M. Levine, N. Zhou, and L. Price, The Bridge, "The Greening of the Middle Kingdom: The Story of Energy Efficiency in China," 2009.

24. N. Zhou, M. Levine, and L. Price, Energy Policy, "Overview of Current Energy Efficiency Policies in China," 2009.

25. R. McGregor, *The Party* (London: Penguin, 2010).

26. Morgan Stanley Research, "China Economics: Chinese Economy through 2020: Not Whether but How Growth Will Decelerate," September 10, 2010. Morgan Stanley assumes an average 3% appreciation of the renminbi against the U.S. dollar per annum, with 2010 GDP of $5.7 billion reaching $20 trillion by 2020.

27. Ibid.

28. Statement issued by China's Ministry of Industry and Information on January 25, 2011; www.solarserver.com/solar-magazine/solar-news/current/2011/kw05/china-imposes-new-regulations-on-polysilicon-production.html

29. China Resources Utilization Association, Xinjiang Gold Wind, National Energy Administration, sourced from China Power Net and *China Securities Journal*, October 15, 2010.

30. U.S. figures from American Wind Energy Association; www.awea.org/learnabout/industry_stats/index.cfm; Chinese Renewable Energy Industries Association report from January 13, 2011. http://uk.ibtimes.com/articles/20110128/2011-hopefully-better-wind-power.htm.

31. http://graphics8.nytimes.com/packages/pdf/business/SIPONatPatentDevStrategy.pdf

32. Credit Lyonnais Securities Asia, "China's Energy Binge."

33. S. Lohr, "When Innovation, Too, Is Made in China," *New York Times*, January 1, 2010. www.nytimes.com/2011/01/02/business/02unboxed.html. A

translation of the National Patent Development Strategy document produced by the *New York Times* can be found at http://graphics8.nytimes.com/packages/pdf/business/SIPONatPatentDevStrategy.pdf.

34. Barclays Capital "Global Renewables Demand Forecast 2010–2014E," 2010. J. Weiss, "Export Growth and Industrial Policy: Lessons from the East Asian Miracle Experience," Asian Development Bank Institute Discussion Paper, No. 26, 2005.

CHAPTER 26

Ethical Asia

Simon Powell

Let's now turn to a different perspective on Asia, but one that's also practically focused—that of leading sustainability research house CLSA based in Hong Kong and its head of research, Simon Powell.

The concept of corporate social responsibility (CSR) is rooted in the western principles of liberal democracy, justice and social equity. We believe Asian firms, operating in fast-growing economies with different environmental and labor standards, face unique issues, where many of these western principles may not apply. Investors who have a focus on CSR need to assess regional CSR through a set of "Asian lenses." We analyze the CSR reports of 50 of Asia's largest companies. While the move to more reporting is positive, we are critical of the lack of disclosure and transparency in many companies.

The wealth gap in many Asian countries is significant. The region contains some of the world's fastest-growing economies alongside slowly developing legal and corporate-governance systems. A lot of regional corporations are run essentially as family businesses. An overarching sense of compliance-style management can hinder the practice and development of business ethics. The good news is that CSR reporting in Asia is rising fast. The region now accounts for more than 20% of global CSR reports versus 12% just five years ago, and China is delivering a big push toward more disclosure.

For the full report, contact Simon Powell at simon.powell@clsa.com

While CSR's deeper subtleties in the West are yet to emerge in Asia, we believe that here the emphasis is on environmental and labor standards. Related laws will only tighten over time, so firms that are doing the most in these areas should be able to maintain their returns on equity and outperform those that are lagging in CSR.

Investors should focus on supply chains and look at working conditions in Asian workplaces. Reputational risks exist in health and safety, pay and conditions, and environmental impacts. Increasingly, nongovernment organizations are taking a name-and-shame approach with some success in getting the worst offenders onto the front pages of the global press.

Across our coverage universe, we note that companies exercising higher CSR standards have marginally outperformed those that are lagging in the practice, especially when markets are in decline. Our analysis ties in closely with our corporate governance scores. Of the 50 companies we analyze for this chapter, Cathay Pacific Airways, Mitsubishi UFG, and Reliance Industries display the highest CSR standards. Meanwhile, China Merchants Bank, Dongfang Electric, SK Energy, Tata Motors, and Telkom Indonesia need to improve their disclosure significantly.

REPORTING IS ON THE RISE

Corporate social responsibility, if defined by the publication of CSR reports, appears to be on the rise in Asia. The region now accounts for more than 20% of global CSR reports versus 12% just five years ago. Based on the absolute number of companies, Europe still leads the way. We believe this reflects the pull effect of European funds and legislation in 2000 that required pension funds to reveal whether they take into account the ESG policies of the companies they invest in.

Banks and energy companies appear to have embraced the move to CSR reporting far more than other industries. Cynics could argue that those are the two industries that need to position themselves better in terms of public perception and relations, but our view is that different industries move at varied speeds.

Reporting Requirements: Forced or Voluntary?

Across the world, CSR reporting activity falls into two key camps, mandated or voluntary. For example, the UK Companies Act of 2006 explicitly mandates social and environmental reporting. Article 417 states that the director's report of a quoted company must "to the extent necessary for an understanding of the development, performance or position of the company's business, include... social and community issues, including information about any policies of the company in relation to these matters."

But even before the UK Companies Act mandated reporting, an amendment to the UK Pensions Act already required a higher level of disclosure in pension funds. It requires fund managers to tell members whether they consider the ESG impact of the companies they invest in. Managers have the option to state that they do not take these impacts into account, but the fact that they are required to disclose their policies puts greater pressure on them to justify their stances.

Other countries in Europe, including Austria, Belgium, France, Germany, Italy, and Sweden, have all enacted similar legislation. In Asia, CSR reporting remains mostly voluntary.

China The Chinese government has been promoting CSR by influencing the behavior of state-owned enterprises. For many years now, Article 5 of its Company Law requires corporations to "undertake social responsibility" in the course of business. In 2006, Beijing published *Guidelines for Publishing Corporate Responsibility Reporting in China*. It promotes CSR as a means to improve company brands, reputations, and competitiveness and encourages them to publish reports. The government has yet to implement sanctions or mechanisms to enforce such regulations. However, Beijing's stance on promotion and spreading awareness indicates that CSR is on its agenda. Shenzhen and Shanghai stock exchanges recently took action in promoting CSR disclosure. In August 2009, the Shanghai Stock Exchange also launched the Responsibility Index, selecting the top-100 socially responsible companies on the bourse.

Japan The Japanese government is as an advocate for CSR, in particular through it environment-related and climate-change-specific legislation. With the Environmental Reporting Guidelines and the Law Concerning Promotion of Environmental Consideration in Business Activities, enacted in 2004, it began promoting environmental reporting far earlier than other governments in the region. With the introduction of a mandatory greenhouse gas (GHG) accounting and reporting system, entities emitting large amounts of GHGs are now obliged to calculate and report these emissions.

Malaysia Bursa Malaysia has long promoted corporate responsibility and governance. In 2004, the Malaysian government came out in support of voluntary CSR reporting, but during the 2007–8 intersession, the prime minister announced support for mandatory disclosure of CSR activities in annual financial reports of publicly listed firms. The listing rules have since been amended to require CSR reporting or to state if there is none.

Philippines In August 2007, the Philippines Board of Investment started requiring CSR programs and reporting. Under the 2007 investment priorities plan, companies that were granted six-year income tax holidays need to issue annual reports on implementation of their CSR schemes during the last two years of the period.

Indonesia In July 2007, the government of Indonesia enacted a corporate law that required most companies outside of the financial sector to report their CSR activities. In addition, Article 74 requires all corporations that impact the environment to implement CSR programs.

Hong Kong In 2006, the Financial Services and Treasury Bureau launched a comprehensive rewrite of the local company ordinance with the aim of improving the city's attractiveness as a financial center. Expectations are that the new ordinance could be passed into law by the end of 2010. One proposed requirement is that companies will have to include in their annual reports "information relating to environmental and employee matters [that] is line with international trends to promote corporate social responsibility

Korea Businesses in Korea and Japan share many similarities when it comes to CSR reporting. Korean and Japanese companies show increased interest in global dialogue. There are ongoing improvements in governance, transparency, and stakeholder engagement. There also have been a number of initiatives to align Korean business practices with those of the United Nations' Global Compact.

Australia Since 1988, public companies in Australia have been under an obligation to report on environmental and social performance as stated in the Corporations Act section 299. Companies are required to provide details of their performance in relation to environmental regulation and any breaches of environmental laws and licenses, such as those relating to GHG management, in their annual reports. These obligations have been further enhanced by the Financial Services Reform act 2001, which requires disclosure as to the extent that labor standards or environmental, social, or ethical considerations are taken into account in investment decision making.

Singapore CSR reporting is entirely voluntary in Singapore. Section 201(c) of its companies' act requires directors to set out a profit-and-loss account and a balance sheet that complies with the requirements of the accounting standards and to give a true and fair view of the state of affairs of the company. Observers believe that Singapore remains a voluntary CSR market because the government takes a light regulation approach in order to appear more business friendly.

Thailand To stimulate CSR awareness among Thai companies, the local stock exchange has begun to award listed companies for outstanding CSR projects and established a CSR Promotion Fund at the end of 2008. In a related initiative, a CSR committee comprising both public and private sectors has proposed a CSR road map and developed a handbook for Thai-listed firms.

CSR WORKS WHEN COMPANIES AND SOCIETY ARE ALIGNED

When the interests of companies and society are aligned, companies pursuing profits will benefit society. Adam Smith spotted this when he famously identified the invisible hand and wrote *The Wealth of Nations*:

> [B]*y directing that industry in such a manner as its produce may be of the greatest value, he intends only his own gain, and he is in this, as in many other cases, led by an* invisible hand *to promote an end which was no part of his intention. Nor is it always the worse for the society that it was not part of it. By pursuing his own interest he frequently promotes that of the society more effectually than when he really intends to promote it. I have never known much good done by those who affected to trade for the public good.*

Where no alignment exists or even direct misalignment, business managers face a dilemma: Should they focus on their fiduciary duty to maximize shareholder returns and value? Or should they impose a tax on shareholders and work to benefit society?

It All Boils Down to Consumers

There appears to be a growing group of end-product consumers, who are increasingly asking about the source of the goods they buy. They are loosely tagged as conscious consumers.

- Is this product or service manufactured/provided in line with my values?
- Does this product harm or help the environment?
- Am I supporting my local economy?

- Are the people who produce this product/service treated and compensated fairly?

As a result of these questions, conscious consumers find themselves supporting organic agriculture, fair trade products, sweatshop-free products, and local and independent businesses.

One interesting side effect is an accelerated cycle: Conscious consumers appear to also be seeking what some describe as work-life balance, so they are likely to work fewer hours, which enables them to form closer bonds with their local community; hence the push toward locally produced goods for many. Given more free time, they can do more research on purchases. This research may make them more wedded to the idea of conscious consumerism.

FOCUSES IN ASIA: LABOR AND ENVIRONMENT

Looking at CSR in Asia requires a different set of lenses. The region is undergoing significant changes. The traditional concept of CSR is rooted in the western principles of liberal democratic rights, justice, and social structures. However, Asian companies could interpret these values and philosophies differently based on the cultures and traditions of their home countries. Given Asia's significant wealth gap and the fact that it contains some of the world's fastest-growing economies alongside slowly developing legal and corporate-governance systems, companies in the region face unique issues.

- Colonial and noncolonial experiences as well as ethnic and religious diversities shape their CSR perspectives of Asian economies.
- Predominantly homogeneous populations mean ethnic diversity at work isn't as relevant.
- Many Asian corporations are family/chairman-owned and run essentially as family businesses.
- Operations across multiple geographies and tax regimes in rapidly developing economies results in wide gaps in labor standards and legislation.
- Asia is undergoing much faster economic and demographic growth than the West, especially in terms of urbanization rates.
- An overarching sense of compliance-style management can hinder the practice and development of business ethics.
- Across Asia, the gap between rich and poor is significant.

While the deeper subtleties found in the West regarding CRS are yet to emerge in Asia, we believe that here the emphasis is on environmental and labor standards. Related laws will only tighten over time, so firms that are doing the most in these areas should be able to maintain their returns on equity and outperform those that are lagging in CSR.

Workshop for the Rest of the World

Asia has been a major manufacturer of global consumer products. In many industries, supply chains are disaggregated with multiple components going into a single product. Perhaps the most obvious example is electronics, with phones and computers made up of many parts from different factories spread across the region. News of low wages and long working hours increasingly prompt investors to query manufacturing companies' audit and management to ensure that illegal or unwanted work practices are identified and fixed. Pressures on the supply chain have become much more sophisticated than the earlier antisweatshop movement. Besides concentrating on labor and human rights abuses, attention is also paid on companies' impact on the environment and product traceability.

Many initiatives are taking place at an industry level with cooperation between large brands that deal with Asian manufacturers. One example is the Electronic Industry Citizenship Coalition (EICC), which promotes an industry code of conduct for global electronics supply chains to improve working and environmental conditions. Member companies of EICC include Dell, Microsoft, Hewlett Packard, and Samsung Electronics.

The suicides at Foxconn's factory in China came as no surprise to many observers. While the situation is complex, even Apple's published audits found wage issues and that employees at its supplier's factory were working longer than legally permitted. Almost all jurisdictions in Asia enforce minimum wages, maximum hours, and overtime remuneration laws. Health and safety standards exist in all countries, and most Asian countries are signatories to international conventions aimed at preventing child labor. However, we believe that there are many ongoing breaches of these standards and laws. One reason is that many employees are local people or overseas migrants, whose awareness of related laws is often low, or they are denied fair access to the rule of law.

Increasing Focus on Labor Practices

The risk for companies, and ultimately investors, lies in whether assemblers and their suppliers are complying with their contracts, codes of conduct, and relevant labor laws. It is virtually impossible to know what actually happens in factories.

We spoke to Impactt, which specializes in strategy consulting, research, training and social auditing to help businesses measure their supply chains. It shared with us data from all of its 2008 site visits, of which more than 68% were in Asia (49% in China and 19% in Southeast Asia). In total, it visited 98 factories: 51% in the apparel space, 19% in consumer goods, 15% in food, and the remainder in services.

The key takeaway is the significant number of factories that were not paying minimum wage and were breaching working hours and holiday requirements. This sample suggests that significant problems exist in the supply chains of many manufacturers. A high number of locations that Impactt audited for its clients (buyers of goods) were in breach of local regulations. Where employees are working longer hours, the number of sites in breach is always higher.

The fact that 24% of the 98 factories visited had some form of child labor will come as a shock to many investors. Impactt also states that social audit fraud is widespread in China and southeast Asia; more than 60% of the sites they visited reported significantly different numbers on minimum wage, and hours, and the like than were observed.

Move to Maximum Permitted Hours of Work

Numerous United Nations International Labour Organization conventions lay down work-hour standards for various occupations and workplaces. The general rule is that workers shall not be required to work more than 48 hours per week on a regular basis, that overtime hours shall be voluntary and restricted to 12 hours per week, and that workers are entitled to one day off in every seven-day period.

There is growing consensus on the need to include provisions in codes of conduct that provide for payment of a living wage. While a company should at the minimum ensure that, where applicable, legally mandated minimum wages are being paid and that the prevailing industry wage in the area is being met, it should also commit to ensuring that the wage paid is sufficient to meet workers' basic needs.

Industrial Action on the Rise

The right to join a trade union is mentioned in Article 23, Subsection 4 of the Universal Declaration of Human Rights, which also states in Article 20, Subsection 2 that "[n]o one may be compelled to belong to an association." Prohibiting a person from joining or forming a union, as well as forcing a person to do the same (e.g., closed shops or union shops), whether by a government or by a business, is generally considered a human rights abuse.

Environmental Laws Will Only Tighten

Rapid economic and population growth, as well as high rates of urbanization, characterize many parts of Asia. As a result, environmental degradation is significant. Until recently, companies that polluted were given relatively small fines with little or no impact to earnings. The situation is changing rapidly.

Corruption and Human Rights

While many companies are engaged in developing CSR reports, two big issues remain and are by their nature extremely difficult for investors to engage with companies on: corruption and human rights. We believe that, in Asia, these issues are linked in that acts of corruption tend to impact the rights of the poorest members of society.

China has launched a sustained anticorruption drive and intensified a crackdown on corruption in the public sector, investigating and prosecuting public officials and employees. Corrupt officials above provincial levels were disciplined.

Impacts on Shareholder Value

The big question: Do more responsible companies deliver better earnings and shareholder value than irresponsible ones? Backtesting suggests that companies with higher CSR scores outperform over the long term, but we believe that, ultimately, those demonstrating better corporate governance achieve more sustainable returns and that CSR is simply good corporate governance.

Our Corporate Governance Watch 2010 report, *Stray Not into Perdition*, highlights that companies with overall better corporate governance tend to outperform over the long term. Managers who act in an ethical and responsible fashion achieve greater returns for shareholders along a number of lines:

- Those companies avoid costly fines and impacts to brand and reputation.
- Companies increase their brand value through building social goods.

We believe that environmental and labor laws in Asia can only get tighter, and companies that are operating at or above current standards will maintain their higher returns on equity for longer.

SUMMARY

From our ongoing review of Asian companies CSR reports we see an emerging number of trends:

- CSR reporting seems like a box-ticking exercise for a lot of companies: Once the first company within an industry produces a report, others feel the need to follow to remain competitive.
- The first 25% of many CSR reports consists of preamble about values and principles that seem to be used as a filler to beef up these reports.
- A great deal of the initial focus of CSR reports is on financials, which are irrelevant but instead aimed at catching the eyes of prospective investors.
- We didn't see much emphasis on anticorruption measures and policies—for example, protecting employee whistleblowers. This is perhaps the most important measure, as it has important implications for investor relations and a company's trustworthiness.
- There is a lot of emphasis on certain policies if accidents occur. However, there is a lack of data when it comes to reporting work safety.
- Some companies that are not expected to report GHG emissions and fuel consumption do so, while some polluting companies do not report their emissions.
- Most of the CSR reports that are undeclared tend to be of lower quality, implying that a company will publish the report only if it believes it is publicly acceptable, which in turn suggests that reports are published only for public relations reasons.
- About 5% of the companies we looked at take CSR reporting extremely seriously. This can be observed when a company goes well beyond the expected G3 Guidelines provided by the Global Reporting Initiative.
- The quality of published CSR reports seems to be positively correlated with the size of the company as it will increasingly be in the public domain in terms of customers and media coverage. Newer and smaller companies usually have less detailed and comprehensive CSR reports.

CSR ties more easily into economic objectives and goals of certain companies or industries; for example, it is easier for a car company to claim it is green because it produces efficient cars but instead is responding to consumers' desire for lower fuel bills. And, finally, some top picks as of this writing include:

- Cathay Pacific—includes very comprehensive data in its report and was very transparent when certain goals were not met.
- Reliance Industries, an energy company in India, that provides very good data and goes well beyond required disclosure.
- Shenhua Energy is the only coal-mining company in China that is truthful about the number of deaths and injuries within the financial year reported. It produced a very thorough and honest report in FY2009.

CHAPTER 27

Mitigating ESG Risk in Asian Portfolios

Lucy Carmody and Laura Dodge

> We wrap up our triumvirate of views on Asia with a perspective from Responsible Research of Singapore, including thoughts on how ESG risks can be identified and possibly managed in the region. These are challenging issues, but at the same time they are critically important, not only for investor comfort and security but also for the ability of Asian corporates to succeed on a globally competitive basis.

In the past five years, over 800 global financial institutions collectively managing assets of about $25 trillion have signed the United Nations Principles for Responsible Investment (PRI). Yet investors and companies in Asia ex Japan comprise just a fraction of these signatories. Among major asset owners in the region, we still count just three: the National Pension Fund and the Teacher's Pension Fund of South Korea, and the Thai Government Pension Fund. The 20-plus Asia-based asset managers that are PRI signatories are mostly boutique firms specializing in alternative strategies. These early adopters, including Arisaig Partners, ADM Capital, Corston-Smith Asset Management and EISAL, use a variety of strategies to integrate environmental, social, and governance (ESG) standards into their operations.

The slow take-up of responsible investing (RI) across much of Asia is not surprising in light of the immaturity of many Asian capital markets and the composition of associated regulatory institutions, which have yet to fully recognize the advantages of stricter environmental and social standards. For example, in our 2010 report "Sustainable Stock Exchanges,"[1] we noted how rarely stock exchanges enact mandatory reporting requirements. Ownership structures and fiduciary duties of most stock exchange boards are designed to maximize returns to their own shareholders, and stock exchanges typically lack explicit mandates to improve sustainability in their country of operation. The short-term stances taken by many retail and institutional investors in these markets and the relative absence of robust civil societies to demand improved corporate accountability compound the disincentive to enact disclosure requirements.

Many exchanges in Asia, however, such as Bursa Malaysia, and the Taiwan, Shanghai, Shenzhen, Singapore and Thai stock exchanges, have already issued their own guidance on sustainability reporting. Hong Kong which is surprisingly late to this trend given the maturity of its market, is expected to follow suit in 2011. Officials, despite recognizing the long-term business and sustainable development benefits of improved ESG standards and disclosure, do not want to price themselves out of a very competitive initial public offering market by insisting on disclosure too onerous and expensive to provide.

Even in countries that have adopted relatively strict standards for ESG compliance, enforcement is lagging. Exchanges and enforcement authorities, particularly at the local government levels, often lack the resources to monitor companies adequately, especially on technical industrial environmental monitoring or human rights issues in remote locations. They may also lack incentives: Local governments and weak judiciaries are often reluctant to punish a business for ESG transgressions for fear of losing a key tax revenue source or one that provides them with illegitimate sources of funding.

THE CHALLENGE: LACK OF DISCLOSURE

ESG compliance of Asian companies tends to vary with market maturity as a result of systemic challenges. But in all markets, a lack of data hinders investors' ability to understand and monitor these risks. To address this lack of data, the Asian Sustainability Rating (ASR^{TM}) tool has been developed to benchmark the top Asian companies according to 100 ESG disclosure criteria.[2] The ASR awards some of the highest scores to South Korean and Taiwanese electronics companies and the lowest possible scores to about 50 Chinese companies (almost 9% of the 2010 total sample of 550 companies in Asia ex-Japan based on free float weighted market cap). Philippines-based companies were the second worst performers in the region, albeit with a much smaller sample size. India's less developed capital market structures and regulatory oversight did not prevent some of its largest companies, including the information technology services company Wipro, from ranking highest among Asian companies in terms of ESG disclosure.

Wipro's stellar performance in ESG disclosure rankings may be a harbinger of the future. Asia now accounts for over 20% of global corporate social responsibility reports[3] versus 12% just five years ago. And, according to our records based on reporting from 2009 and 2010, a third of the top Asian companies now produce comprehensive disclosure on ESG indicators in English. A further 15% report comprehensively, but only in their local language. Our universe of 750 listed Asian companies in our 2011 review is showing strong signs of improvements in reporting across the board.

ESG INTEGRATION IN ASIAN PORTFOLIOS

Fueling the trend toward better disclosure are the efforts of asset managers, regulatory bodies, research organizations, and social enterprises to help companies internalize the demonstrated material benefits of improved compliance, understanding, and reporting on ESG risk. Next we offer a look at some additional strategies.

Addressing the Low-Hanging Fruit: Governance Screening

Perhaps the most robust area of ESG monitoring in Asia is the "G"—corporate governance. Investors increasingly consider good governance critical to corporate performance, in particular disclosure and transparency, board skills, experience and diversity, remuneration practices, and relationships with regulators. Due to ever-tightening regulatory oversight on disclosure of board issues as well as nominations, audit, and remuneration committee structures, diligent institutional investors are able to discount valuations of companies with flagrant disregard for minority shareholder rights and basic governance standards.

Singapore and Hong Kong have strong government policies and reputations for bureaucratic efficiency, in part due to a lack of endemic corruption. Reflecting this, companies such as MTR and CLP Holdings in Hong Kong and SingTel and City Developments in Singapore therefore score very highly on our ASR. In spite of the recent political instability that rocked the market, the Bank of Thailand and the stock exchange have consistently stressed high standards of corporate governance. As a result, three Thai companies rank among the top in Asia in terms of governance disclosure: Siam City Bank, Bank of Ayudhya, and PTTEP.

Aberdeen Trust, a U.K.-listed international investment management group with a large Asian operation based in Singapore, has consistently been in the forefront of dialogue on governance issues in the region. Its emphasis on bottom-up stock picking and backing strong boards and management that protect minority interests has resulted in strong performance over the years. Peter Taylor, Aberdeen's governance specialist in Asia, was recognized by the Millstein Center for Corporate Governance at Yale as a "rising star" of corporate governance globally. It is particularly his work with Jamie Allen of the Asian Corporate Governance Association, which has driven widespread improvements in board governance in Asia over the past few years.

Collaborative Corporate Engagement

More and more investors throughout the region are engaging companies on issues key to the PRI, often with demonstrable effects. Responsible Research organizes regular investor roundtables in Hong Kong and Singapore that bring together investors, nongovernmental organizations, companies, and regulators to discuss sector-specific issues that could affect portfolio returns. In September 2010, we led a roundtable discussion hosted by Thomson Reuters on palm oil and forestry, one of the most challenging ESG issues in the region.[4] This event, supported by the Carbon Disclosure Project, First State Investments, ADM Capital Foundation, and Generation Investment Management was attended by about 100 Asian investors, corporates, and nonprofits. An investor grouping on palm oil has now formed under the auspices of the PRI. Similar events have been held on water in China, real estate in Hong Kong, and the beverages industry in Asia. An investor roundtable on "The Future of Fish in Asia" is to be held in Hong Kong in late 2011.

The Emerging Market Disclosure Project, an international coalition of asset managers and research companies led by Calvert and Boston Common Asset Management, is active in its aims of increasing corporate sustainability reporting in emerging markets. Separate work streams have been set up for South Korea, India, and Indonesia, and a report on disclosure in the top ten South Korean companies was released in 2010.[5]

In another example, in October 2009, PRI signatories, including Co-operative Asset Management in the United Kingdom, held a conference call with representatives from Total to discuss the human rights impacts of the company's pipeline operations in Myanmar to encourage its pipeline partner, Myanmar Oil and Gas, to communicate with junta officials and ask for a reduction in the level of forced labor.

Individual Corporate Engagement

Engagement with companies need not involve public displays of disaffection. Many of our clients say that faced with a lack of information, they simply pick up the phone and try to locate someone to speak to at the company. Others ask our local analysts to intermediate for them on certain issues. As a minimum, this highlights to the company that investors are interested in their ESG performance. The flip side is that many companies that are relatively good at reporting in Asia tell us that, despite allocating significant resources and funds to measuring, managing, mitigating, and reporting on their material ESG risks, few investors actually mention sustainability issues in investor meetings or raise identified risks at board meetings.

First State Investments is one of the few investors practicing responsible active ownership in Asia. The investor engaged with Tata Power after RepRisk®, a Responsible Research partner, highlighted concerns of the Indian State Forest Department over the proximity of the power company's proposed 1,000-megawatt-capacity thermal power project to the Chandaka-Domapara Wildlife Sanctuary and the Nandankanan Zoological Park.

First State's approach was to write a formal letter to the chief executive and chair of Tata Power, linking these concerns to long-term shareholder returns. At the time, First State owned, on behalf of itself and its clients, about 5% of the outstanding shares of the Tata Power. In entering into dialogue with the company, First State helped remind management that responsible investors expect it to do everything within its power to meet its environmental and social responsibilities, even if short-term profits may be compromised.

In 2005 Actis, a leading private equity investor in emerging markets, invested in Chinese solar voltaic panel manufacturer Suntech. Actis helped the company gain environmental certification (ISO 14001), bringing Suntech in line with international best practice. Suntech performed well during Actis's involvement: Between 2005 and 2007, revenues increased by almost 15 times and employment quadrupled. The company's visibility was enhanced by its involvement in public projects: In 2006, it won the contract to be the sole provider of solar power for the Bird's Nest Stadium, where the 2008 Olympic Games took place.

FUNDING ESG RESEARCH

Obtaining good-quality ESG research and information on Asian companies is challenging. Investors have begun to respond by allocating increasing commissions to investment banks that analyze ESG risk and independent research houses that specialize in sustainability analysis. They may also set aside additional funds for commissioning reports that identify risks and opportunities and for ESG initiatives pertaining to their investments.

Generation Investment Management, for example, allocates 5% of its profits to the Generation Foundation, which is dedicated to strengthening the field of sustainable development and sustainability research worldwide.

The partners of ADM Capital, a Hong Kong–based company that advises funds investing in distressed companies, have a different approach. They established a foundation in 2006 to support projects in several key areas of concern, such as marine ecology, forestry, and child labor. ADM jointly funded the Responsible Research report, "Water in China," which highlighted water pollution and scarcity problems in much of China.[6]

A final note should be made here of All Pension Group (APG), which administers over 30% of all collective pension schemes in the Netherlands and manages around €266 billion for about 4.5 million participants. APG has initiated and publicly backed many initiatives to raise awareness about ESG issues, with particular emphasis on palm oil, energy efficiency in the real estate sector, and labor issues in the information technology industry in Asia. Recently APG commissioned CLSA, an Asian brokerage firm, and Responsible Research to author a report called "Dying for Coal" that highlighted the poor health and safety standards in the Chinese coal mining industry.

BUILDING INSTITUTIONAL CAPACITY

Much of the credit for Asia's improving corporate governance record belongs to the Asian Corporate Governance Association (ACGA),[7] an independent, nonprofit membership organization. ACGA's work in research, advocacy, and education has been supported by several leading large pension and investment funds, such as MFC Global, IDFC Capital, Capital Research, Hermes EOS, and the Universities Superannuation Scheme. The organization has collaborated with governments, financial regulators, and stock exchanges on practical issues that affect the implementation of better corporate governance practices. It also produces reports, such as the recent policy document "ACGA White Paper on Corporate Governance in Taiwan." The association has also written letters to the Japanese Ministry of Justice on corporate law reform and to companies in Singapore on voting by poll.

Other collaborations between investors, companies, banks and researchers include the Association for Sustainable and Responsible Investment in Asia and the Asian Association of Independent Research Providers, which promotes independent investment research and advocates the un-bundling of research from execution services.[8] There is also a Korean Social Investment Forum, and a newly established Indian Responsible Investment Research Association intends to build a platform for a South Asia Social Investment Forum. The Sydney-based Responsible Investment Academy[9] should also help drive further ESG integration and capacity building in Asia.

A final mention should be made of CSR Asia,[10] a nonprofit social enterprise provider of information, training, and research and consultancy business practices in Asia, which has been helping companies to identify and report on material ESG issues for the past five years.

USE OF INDEXES, BENCHMARKING, AND SCREENING

The purpose of most investor-led ESG screening is to highlight areas of best and worst practices that can affect portfolio performance over time and that can then be researched more fully, if required. Most of our clients prefer not to use simple checklists for positive screening because ticking boxes often delivers skewed results that often lack insight. Investors may miss opportunities if they are not actively involved in judging each company on a case-by-case basis.

To this end, investors require comparable, consistent, complete, and comprehensive data sets on corporate disclosure and performance on a multitude of indicators. In addition to our Asian Sustainability Ratings, which covers 750 companies in 2011, a growing number of indexes cover Asian markets, including the Hang Seng Corporate Sustainability Indexes on Hong Kong and China A shares and the Kehati Biodiversity Index in Indonesia. There are also plans for ESG or sustainability indexes from Bursa Malaysia and by China Securities Index, a joint venture between the Shanghai and Shenzhen stock exchanges.

Negative screening for controversial issues such as child labor, gaming, gambling, weapons, and alcohol has been difficult for "ethical" investment practitioners to finesse in the region due to a lack of reliable data. However, the Norwegian Pension Fund screens this way using various tools, including RepRisk. The Ministry of Finance appoints a Council on Ethics, which produces a set of ethical guidelines and includes their criteria for screening and advice on exclusion from the funds. The council's screens include companies that sell weapons or military material to Myanmar and certain producers of hybrid cottonseed in India that use child labor and extensive pesticides. Their exclusions so far have included the mining company Vedanta Resources and subsidiaries, Sterlite Industries, and Madras Aluminium Co. Ltd, as well as weapons producers Hanwha Corp. and Singapore Technologies Engineering.

In another example where screening is used to enhance portfolio performance, Arisaig Partners, an independent investment management company focused on emerging market consumer sectors, has operationalized a strong corporate governance ethic by developing a financial controls and corporate governance checklist for all its holdings. This checklist is now overlain with the Asian Sustainability Rating to identify outliers in terms of sustainability.

SUMMARY

Investors are nothing if not pragmatic. As the Deepwater incident demonstrated, the incorporation of ESG analyses into investment decision making does not always protect investors from unexpected events. Exemplary reporting may disguise the fact that a company cuts corners on environmental and social risk issues. This fact, besides complicating how investors perform their fiduciary duties, has undoubtedly caused some investors to shy away from pursuing integration strategies. However, as more Asian portfolios demonstrate that long-term performance can be enhanced through an understanding of ESG risk and the business opportunities that arise from sustainability practices, more investors will join the trend.

Mention must be made that, due to lower consumer awareness and higher levels of state and single-family control in Asian companies, corporate disclosure is likely to be led by different drivers than in the developed world, where there is more minority shareholder and civil society activism. The trend is likely to be led by certain visionary owners, company management, and regulatory institutions to play a leading role in ESG integration in Asia. Aiding them will be the growing numbers of institutional investors, research organizations, and collaborative institutions dedicated to enhancing corporate performance in Asia.

NOTES

1. www.responsibleresearch.com/Responsible_Research___Sustainable_Stock_ Exchanges_2010.pdf
2. www.asiansr.com
3. www.acga-asia.org/public/files/CG_Watch_2010_Extract_Final.pdf
4. www.responsibleresearch.com/Palm-Oil-and-Forestry-Seminar.html
5. www.ussif.org/projects/iwg/EMDPReports.cfm

6. WATER_IN_CHINA-_Issues_for_Responsible_Investors_FEB2010.pdf
7. www.acga-asia.org
8. www.asria.org. www.asiairp.com
9. info@riacademy.org
10. www.csr-asia.com

CHAPTER 28

Sustainable Investing and Canada

Dana Krechowicz and Alex Wood

The Canadian perspective on sustainability is endlessly fascinating. Canada is a country rich in resources, including forests, potash and oil sands—especially in the province of Alberta, where extraction is particularly onerous on the local environment. Alberta as a province is so wealthy that some say that it is pondering creating a sovereign wealth fund. At the same time, Canada as a country is extremely aware of environmental issues. This natural tension is fascinating to watch. In many ways, Canada is ground zero for sustainability-related risks and opportunities.

Canada's investment and business landscape, like its geography, is one of variety and of extremes. It's a country that prides itself on the beauty and riches of its land, with a progressive, environmentally conscious population. And yet Canada has achieved no real progress toward reducing the carbon and resource intensity of its economy. Canadians seem to take their environmental riches for granted, and their sheer abundance may be a contributor to the country's lackluster productivity and innovation records.

At the same time, the Canadian economy is one of the most diversified and stable in the world. Its economic institutions and management are considered paragons of strength in the global economy.

THE BASICS

The Canadian investment scene is dominated by large national banks, credit unions, mutual funds, and private and public pension plans. Although Canada has 22 domestic banks, the banking sector is dominated by the big five national banks: Bank of Montreal, Canadian Imperial Bank of Commerce, Scotiabank, Royal Bank of Canada, and TD Bank. These five collectively account for almost 92% of Canada's banking sector assets.

The banking sector in Canada is highly regulated, which explains why Canadian banks fared better than their U.S. and other international counterparts during the global financial crisis. The big-five banks have integrated environmental, social, and governance (ESG) concerns into their core banking activities to varying degrees. Some have started to explore environmental products and services in their lending and commercial banking businesses, but there is very little integration of sustainability into investment banking or research.

Canada also has a thriving credit union sector; about a third of the country's population are members of one of the country's 945 credit unions, which have a collective asset base of US $229 billion.[1] Major credit unions include Vancity (British Columbia)[2] and Desjardins Group (Quebec), the latter being among Canada's largest financial institutions with CA $175 billion in total assets.[3] The core values of credit unions have a strong alignment with sustainable investing, and as such some of Canada's foremost sustainable mutual fund companies (such as NEI Investments, profiled in more detail in Chapter 11) arose out of the credit union sector.

On the product side, Canadian retail investors have a relatively large selection of sustainability-themed funds to choose from at various major financial institutions; in Quebec alone, there are over 70 such funds.[4]

Employer-sponsored pension plans, with assets of approximately CA $1.64 trillion, represent 58% of Canada's total pension assets.[5] Canada's public pension funds, mainly the Canada Pension Plan and Quebec Pension Plan, have a smaller pool of capital (7.1% of total pension assets) but affect the lives of more Canadians.[6] Most of Canada's largest public pension plans have sustainable investing policies and approaches in place, though they vary in terms of sophistication, depth, and implementation.

Venture capital investments in 2009 totaled just over CA $1 billion, with the majority concentrated in the information technology sector.[7] The "clean-tech" investment category is booming: It grew 47% during the recession of 2008–2009, which could increase to 117% between 2010 and 2012.[8]

GROWTH OF CANADA'S SUSTAINABLE INVESTMENT INDUSTRY

Sustainable investment has grown substantially in Canada in recent years. As of June 30, 2010, CA $530.9billion was invested according to socially responsible guidelines, representing almost 19.1% of total assets under management.[9] At the same time, Canada remains a small player internationally. As of late 2010, Canada had 34 (out of 833 global) signatories to the United Nations Principles for Responsible Investment, consisting of 10 asset owners, 16 investment managers, and 8 professional services partners. Of the 534 global signatories to the Carbon Disclosure Project (CDP), only 49 are Canadian.

Although Canadian investors may be slowly catching up with the global leaders in terms of integrating ESG criteria into their investment decision-making process, Canadian companies are generally lagging when it comes to corporate disclosure of ESG information. For example, less than half the Canadian companies surveyed responded to the 2010 CDP information request (92 out of 201).[10] Overall, the CDP ranked Canadian companies in the middle of the pack globally when it comes to disclosure of climate risks and found them to be particularly lagging in their adoption of emissions reduction plans and external verification of emissions.[11]

Canadians have played a role in the development of the sustainable investment research field. Two pioneering companies in the domain, Innovest (now part of MSCI) and Jantzi-Sustainalytics, have Canadian roots, although competitive necessity and consolidation in the industry has taken these companies international.

CONTEXT AND TRENDS

Two factors define the Canadian economic landscape. The first is the rich endowment of natural resources that have defined the country's economic development throughout its 400-year history.

Natural Resources

The huge quantity of Canada's natural resources also means that they are underpriced. The availability of cheap and plentiful energy, water, and natural resources has underwritten much of Canada's economic prosperity. Although Canada has evolved into a large and complex modern economy, the infamous label of Canadians as "hewers of wood and drawers of water" still has some salience. This has a direct impact on Canadian capital markets, whose default business is still the natural resource sector. In fact, the Toronto Stock Exchange is the third most carbon-intensive exchange in the world (the first two being from emerging economies), at least in part due to the oil and gas sector.[12]

Little wonder that the biggest Canadian business story of 2010 was the attempted takeover of Saskatchewan's Potash Inc. (a miner of the eponymous substance so critical to global fertilizer demand) by Australia's BHP Mining, which was vetoed by the federal government. The centrality of the natural resource sector to Canada's economic self-definition is further underlined by statements made by the Canadian prime minister during visits to Asia, declaring that Canada could be counted on to deliver the raw materials necessary to Asia's economic growth. Canada is also a net energy exporter, with huge reserves of natural gas and (mostly unconventional) oil. Whether these natural resources are developed in a responsible manner is a key concern for investors, as much of Canada's untapped resources are located in northern, underpopulated areas, giving rise to social concerns with regards to local Native populations and their rights.

Proximity and Access

The second important economic factor is proximity and access to the American marketplace. Hitching its economic wagon to the largest and most dynamic economy in the world—even if by the accident of geography—has been a winning proposition for Canada. The Free Trade Agreement negotiated with the United States in the early 1990s (and extended to include Mexico) concretized that dependency and has yielded some real benefits for Canada. According to the Organization for Economic Cooperation and Development, Canada has enjoyed the highest and most stable rate of growth of any of the Group of Eight (G8) economies over the past 20 years (recession included).

More generally, the dependency on the trade relationship with the United States reflects a larger truth: Canada's domestic market is small and fragmented. As a result, of all the G8 countries, Canada is the most dependent on foreign trade and foreign markets for its prosperity, now and in the future. As demand in those foreign markets starts to shift toward lower carbon- and resource-intensive products, Canadian companies will have to respond. That, more than domestic demand, may end up being the most important driver of change in the national market in the long term.

SUMMARY

For sustainable investors, the Canadian economy presents certain challenges and opportunities, mainly around the key themes of natural resources, energy, and emerging environmental risks.

Canada has warmed more than the global average so far (with the largest increases in the North). Given its varied geography and Arctic region, the country will face major, but uneven, climate change impacts—impacts the government currently is not prepared to manage. Given the country's economic dependence on natural resources, any increased unpredictability in their availability (e.g., changes to agricultural growing seasons) will greatly impact those sectors.

Moreover, Canada currently is not well positioned for a low-carbon future. Its economic dependence on carbon-intensive fossil fuels (i.e., the oil sands), lack of national policy framework or meaningful action to reduce emissions, and lack of innovation and research and development all provide large challenges for competing in the global low-carbon economy.

Canadians are awakening to the need to be better stewards of the country's illusory unending natural resources. Water is heavily embedded in the Canadian economy in sectors from forestry to energy, though water's historic abundance has given rise to waste and mismanagement. Some regions of Canada, such as the prairies, are subject to water scarcity, which has implications for the agricultural sector, and water quality is a concern in urban areas across the country.

On the opportunity side, several Canadian provinces have introduced policies encouraging the development of local renewable energy sectors. For example, the local content rules of Ontario's Feed-In-Tariff have already spurred millions in local investments, including the construction of the largest photovoltaic facility in the world.

The Canadian economy and lifestyle are very energy, carbon, and resource intensive. As many have noted, the Canadian economy will need to become much more resource efficient to remain competitive. That represents a daunting challenge for Canadian business but presents enormous opportunities for companies and their investors to play a role in transforming the economy.

NOTES

1. World Council of Credit Unions, "National Credit Union Data: Canada," 2009. www.woccu.org/memberserv/intlcusystem/icus_country?region=NAandc=CA

2. Credit Union Central of Canada, "Largest 100 Credit Unions (Outside of Quebec): Second Quarter 2010." www.cucentral.ca/Top100_2010Q2

3. "Desjardins: The Largest Cooperative Financial Group in Canada," September 30, 2010. www.desjardins.com/en/accueil/groupe-financier-cooperatif/

4. "Dossier: Les fonds éthiques," *Protégez-vous* (February 2011). www.protegez-vous.ca/affaires-et-societe/fonds-ethiques.html

5. Statistics Canada, "What Does the Pension Satellite Account Tell about Canada's Pension System?" 2008. www.statcan.gc.ca/pub/11-010-x/2009011/part-partie3-eng.htm

6. Ibid.

7. Canada's Venture Capital and Private Equity Association via Thomson Reuters, "Total VC Investment Activity by Sector," 2010. www.cvca.ca/files/Downloads/2009_VC_Investment_Activity_by_Sector.pdf

8. Russell Mitchell Group and Sustainable Development Technology Canada, "The 2010 SDTC Cleantech Growth and Go-to-Market Report," 2010. www.sdtc.ca/uploads/documents/en/CLEANTECH%20REPORT.pdf

9. Social Investment Organization, "Canadian Socially Responsible Investment Review 2010," 2011, p. 5. www.socialinvestment.ca/documents/Canadian SociallyResponsibleInvestmentReview2010_English_final.pdf

10. Carbon Disclosure Project, "Carbon Disclosure Project Report 2010: Canada 200," 2010, p. 10. www.cdproject.net/CDPResults/CDP-2010-Canada-Report-english.pdf

11. Ibid.

12. Trucost and Mercer, "Carbon Counts: Assessing the Carbon Exposure of Canadian Institution Investment Portfolios," September 2010. http://assets.wwf.ca/downloads/wwf_canada_report_final.pdf

CHAPTER 29

High-Risk Areas, Resources, and Sustainability

N.A.J. Taylor

Investing in conflict-affected and high-risk areas is a growing concern for responsible businesses and investors. Often companies based in developed countries operate in lesser developed foreign markets, where governance standards are lax, corruption is high, and business practices are poor.

This chapter focuses on one specific Anglo-Australian company that operates in West Papua, one of the poorest provinces of Indonesia. The risks for the company include the potential to contribute to environmental and social damage in a foreign market. The risks for investors include financing a company that does not get its risk management right. This is the story of how and why the Norwegian Pension Fund blacklisted Rio Tinto.

An ancient copper mine located near Huelva in southernmost Spain changed hands in 1873. A group of opportunistic Anglo-German investors, equipped with modern techniques that favored mining aboveground, acquired it from the Spanish government. The mine's copper had stained the surrounding water to such an extent that the indigenes named the river Rio Tinto—literally meaning red river.

The mine at Rio Tinto had supplied the Phoenicians, ancient Greeks, Carthaginians, and the Roman Empire. Its copper had paid for Carthage's numerous wars on Rome and had been held by both Scipio and Hannibal.

We can only assume that these investors, aware of such indelible marks on the environment and history, missed the irony, because they named their company, Rio Tinto.

However, the red river has since flowed a long way from home. The company has expanded its operations through Australia, North and South America, Asia, Europe, and southern Africa—across coal, aluminum, copper, diamonds, uranium, gold, industrial minerals, and iron ore. Rio Tinto is now so large that its dual listing on the Australian and London stock exchanges commands it a value of over US$100 billion.

What's left behind near the Spanish town of Huelva is a 58-mile-long river flowing through one of the world's largest deposits of pyrite, or fool's gold. Because of the mine, the river has a pH reading similar to that of automobile battery acid and contains virtually no oxygen in its lower depths. In the late 1980s, temporary flooding dissolved a power substation, a mandibular crusher, and several hundred yards of transport belts. More recently, NASA astrobiologists used the conditions of the river to replicate the conditions of Mars. "If you remove the green," one of them remarked, "it looks like Mars."[1] The thinking goes that if something could live in such an acidic river, then there is likely to be life on Mars too.

Every Australian—through public monies invested by elected governments, or their choice of superannuation fund, insurer, and bank—is funding this red river now too. Rio Tinto is so large and so profitable that, for the average Australian, investment in it is very near unavoidable.

BLACKLISTED

On September 9, 2008—amid the turmoil of the global financial crisis—the Norwegian government announced that it had liquidated its entire $1 billion investment in Rio Tinto for "grossly unethical conduct." Operating the second largest fund in the world, the Norwegians' decision focused solely on the Grasberg mine in West Papua on New Guinea, which it believed posed the "unacceptable risk" of contributing to "severe environmental damage" if it were to continue funding the Anglo-Australian mining giant.[2]

Rio Tinto had been blacklisted.

The following day, Rio Tinto's official statement relayed that the company was "surprised and disappointed," given both its recognized leadership in environmental sustainability and its noncontrolling interest in the Grasberg mine.[3] As with most claims of sustainability, the truth is otherwise.

Rio Tinto should not have been surprised by the Norwegian stance on Grasberg. Records show there had been months—in fact, years—of dialogue with the Norwegians about Grasberg's inadequate environmental and social performance.[4] Rio Tinto had faced a litany of signposts indicating that multinational and Indonesian involvement in West Papua was not meeting various standards, laws, and norms: Institutions such as the World Bank, Australian Council for Overseas Aid, International Finance Corporation, Overseas Private Investment Commission, United Nations Committee against Torture, U.S. State Department, and the Indonesian Environment Ministry, as well as many U.S. and European politicians, independent environmental assessments, international media, Papuan leaders, civil society groups, and shareholders had brought the problems to Rio Tinto's attention.

That an institutional investor should act on environmental, social, and corporate governance considerations is a newly evolving development within the global investment industry, and one in which many Australian institutional investors and service providers have been quick to claim leadership. However, the blacklisting of Rio Tinto by the Norwegian government was uniquely public, transparent, and forward-thinking. Yet this wholesale dumping of one of Australia's blue-chip stocks received only syndicated coverage in the local media.

Behind the headlines of the global financial crisis is a deeper, more systemic fault line that rewards rampant capitalism. Too many invest in and operate mines such as Grasberg without any consideration of the ethics of so doing.

BACKGROUND

New Guinea, geographically as well as historically, is Australia's closest relative. Separated from the mainland during the last glacial period, the waters filled in what now separates them: about 95 miles of the Torres Strait.

While Australia and New Guinea both have enviable mineral stores, economic and political exploitation has left the latter as home to many of the poorest people on Earth. New Guinea is also an island of two histories.

The eastern half forms the independent state of Papua New Guinea—a status it has enjoyed since breaking from Australia in 1975. With its natural resources of oil and industrial metals, Papua New Guinea has long been exploited for its minerals at places like Ok Tedi and Bougainville. Both projects ended in social and environmental disaster. The environmental impact of Ok Tedi was so great that in 1999, then BHP chief executive Paul Anderson conceded the mine was "not compatible with our environmental values."[5] But it did serve the company's pursuit of profit. It was not until the Ok Tedi environmental disaster three years later that the true impact of BHP's mining practices came to the attention of the global public. BHP subsequently sold its interest, established a fund to restore the sustainable development of the affected people, and received immunity from further prosecution.

The western half of New Guinea has had a lesser-known but equally tragic history centered around the Jayawijaya Mountain, home to the Amungme, and farther downstream, the Kamoro people. As with much of East Asia, the indigenes were under Dutch rule when a geological expedition in 1936 located a significant *ertsberg* (ore mountain) deep in the southwestern highlands. World War II intervened, and the Japanese claimed Indonesia and some of the western parts of New Guinea. Following defeat in the war, the Japanese were marshaled back to their home territory, and Dutch colonialism resumed. Importantly, when Indonesian independence was obtained from the Dutch in 1949, few knew of the *ertsberg* hidden deep in West Papua's wilderness. And so the Dutch began a ten-year Papuanization program in 1957 that would see West Papua handed back to the indigenes, creating the independent state of West Papua around 1972.

Despite multiple territorial claims, the ore mountain lay dormant for over 20 years.

West Papua

On March 6, 1959, the *New York Times* reported the presence of alluvial gold in the Arafura Sea just off the coast of West Papua.[6] Reminded of their earlier discovery, Dutch geologists were said to be returning to the ore mountain, now simply known as Ertsberg.

The indigenes, meanwhile, as part of their program toward independence, established a Papuan National Council and provisional government as well as their own military, police force, currency, national anthem, and flag. At the time, West Papua's independence was due before the United Nations Decolonization Commission, and representatives took part in various cultural and political activities throughout the region. By December 1, 1961, the West Papuan "Morning Star" flag had been raised alongside the Dutch for the first time. Many assumed that independence was imminent.

Unbeknownst to both the indigenes and the Dutch, U.S. mining company Freeport-McMoRan Copper and Gold was negotiating directly with Suharto—at the time an Indonesian army general—for a small group of its experts to prospect this ore mountain. The path into West Papua through Suharto promised to be fruitful for Freeport, since its board was stacked with the Rockefeller's Indonesian oil interests who already were versed in the general's way of doing business. An exploration agreement was reached, and soon after a geologist from Freeport was forging his way through the wilderness toward Ertsberg.

West Papua was about to change hands again.

Armed with Chinese and Soviet weapons, as well as an increasingly public friendship with the communists, Indonesia declared war on Holland. To protect western interests from the threat of communism, on August 15, 1962, the United Nations (UN) and the United States orchestrated a meeting between Dutch and Indonesian officials during which interim control of West Papua was signed over to Indonesia.

Six years of UN interregnum followed, after which a plebiscite would decide whether to form a separate nation or integrate into Indonesia. All 815,000 West Papuans were to vote in an Act of Free Choice.

To ensure a favorable outcome, the Indonesians worked to suppress Papuan identity. Raising the West Papuan flag and singing the national anthem were banned, and all political activities were deemed subversive. Indonesia ruled through force, for self-interest. Alarmed by ongoing media reports, on April 5, 1967, in the British House of Lords, Lord Ogmore called for a UN investigation.[7] By early 1968, with Suharto having assumed the presidency of Indonesia, a U.S. consular visit almost unanimously agreed that "Indonesia could not win an open election" in West Papua.[8]

West Papua still wanted its independence.

In a desperate attempt to secure West Papua's right to self-determination, two junior politicians crossed the border into Australian-administered Papua and New Guinea on May 29, 1969. They carried damning evidence of Indonesian repression; the hopes of a yet-unformed nation rested on the politicians reaching the UN. As Australia and its allies were amenable to Indonesian control of West Papua, the two were imprisoned upon crossing the border until after the referendum. Their brave plea was silenced.

Between July and August 1969, less than a quarter of 1% of the population—some 1,026 West Papuans—signed the country's freedom over to Indonesia. The election, held under the aegis of the UN, was far from an act of free choice. The following day West Papua was declared a military operation zone, the local people's movement was restricted, and expression of their national identity banned under Indonesian law.

Poor, neglected West Papua.

Ramifications

Control of West Papua proved a lucrative business deal for the Indonesians. Two years prior to the Act of Free Choice—coincidentally the same day the plight of Papua was raised in the House of Lords—Freeport signed a contract of work with the Suharto government entitling a jointly owned company, PT Freeport Indonesia (Freeport-Indonesia), full rights to the Ertsberg mine. In return, Indonesia would derive significant tax revenues and fees as well as a minority 9.36% shareholding. Without the authority to do so, Indonesia nevertheless cut itself into a deal that sold large tracts of West Papua to the U.S. company, intent on sifting it for copper and gold.

Although Ertsberg fulfilled its promise, as production slowed in the mid-1980s, Freeport-Indonesia began to explore surrounding mountains and ridges for other reserves. As is often the case, the best place to establish a new mine is next to another. Sure enough, significant copper and gold reserves were located at Grasberg only a couple of miles southwest of Ertsberg.

Grasberg has the largest recoverable reserves of copper and gold in the world. It's also Indonesia's economic beachhead.

Observing the Grasberg mine via Google Earth, one sees a scar like no other: Located about 13,000 feet (4,000 meters) above sea level, open-pit (above-ground) mining has bored a hole through the top of the mountain half a mile (1 km) wide. What they're digging for is more than $40 billion worth of copper and gold. Every day the operation discharges 230,000 tons of tailings (waste rock) into the Aghawagon River. This process is expected to continue for up to six more years, at which point exploration will go underground until there's no value left. Freeport estimates that it will be done by 2041.

The operation is so large that it has shifted the borders of the adjacent Lorenz National Park. Listed as a World Heritage site by the UN's Educational, Scientific, and Cultural Organization (UNESCO) in 1999, the park is "the only protected area in the world to incorporate a continuous, intact transect from snowcap to tropical marine environment, including extensive lowland wetlands."[9] For the Amungme and Kamoro indigenes, corporate imperialism had replaced European colonialism.

The ramifications are both environmental and social.

The social and economic condition of the indigenous Amungme and Kamoro poses fundamental human rights concerns. Although Freeport-Indonesia directly or indirectly employs a large number of West Papuans and is regularly Indonesia's biggest taxpayer, in 2005, the World Bank found that Papua remained the poorest province in Indonesia.[10] With a marked rise in military personnel and foreign staff has come a number of social issues, including alcohol abuse and prostitution such that Papua now has the highest rate of HIV/AIDS in Indonesia.

Indonesian control of West Papua has been characterized by the ongoing and disproportionate repression of largely peaceful opposition. Few sustained violent interactions have occurred; however, in one major conflict in 1977, more than 1,000 civilian men, women, and children were killed by the Indonesian military in Operasi Tumpas (operation annihilation) after a bomb slurry pipe was severed and partially closed the Ertsberg mine. More recently, in 1995, the Australian Council for Overseas Aid reported that the Indonesian army and security forces killed 37 people involved in protests over the mine in the preceding seven-month period. While the level of violence is difficult to establish, academics at the Centre for Peace and Conflict Studies at the University of Sydney maintain that up to 100,000 West Papuans may have been killed since Indonesian occupation. They call what's happening to West Papua "slow-motion genocide."[11]

There are also two primary environmental concerns over Grasberg.

1. As I have noted, the mine discharges 230,000 tons of tailings (waste rock) a day into surrounding waterways; given the escalating rate of processing, this rate is arguably against national law.
2. Acid rock drainage (outflow of acidic water) has resulted from the disposal of a further 360,000 to 510,000 tons a day of overburden and waste rock in two adjacent valleys covering 4 miles (8 km) up to 975 feet (300 meters) deep. The mine operators dispute both claims.

Riverine methods of waste disposal are banned in every developed country on Earth. The World Bank no longer funds projects that operate this way due to the irreversible ecological devastation, and the International Finance Corporation requires that rock be treated prior to disposal, which is not a practice carried out at Grasberg. Since the mid-1990s, a number of independent environmental assessments have found unacceptably high levels of toxicity and sediment as far as 140 miles away. Freeport and Rio Tinto maintain that riverine tailings disposal is the best solution, given the difficult terrain, the threat of earthquakes, and heavy rainfall.

Grasberg's reserves are so vast that extracting them is expected to create 6 billion tons of industrial waste.

President Suharto, who is now recognized as one of the most corrupt and tyrannical leaders in history, renewed Freeport-Indonesia's exclusive mining rights in 1991 for a further 30 years with an option of two 10-year extensions. The license included an option to prospect another 6.5 million acres (2.6 million hectares), as far as the Papua New Guinea border. "The potential is only limited by the imagination," Freeport's chairman, James

Moffett, remarked to shareholders in March 1995. "Every other mining company wants to get into Irian Jaya [West Papua]. Bougainville and Ok Tedi don't hold a candle to Grasberg."[12]

ENTER RIO TINTO

In February 1995, Rio Tinto announced three deals that secured access into Grasberg.

1. It agreed to invest $500 million of new capital in Freeport for a 12% stake in the U.S. miner's business.
2. Rio Tinto agreed to finance a $184 million expansion of the Grasberg mine. In return, it received 40% of post-1995 production revenue that exceeded certain output targets and, from 2021, a 40% stake in all production.
3. Rio Tinto would receive 40% of all production from new excavations elsewhere within West Papua.

Rio Tinto was effectively doing business with Suharto now too.

In response, Freeport told shareholders that Rio Tinto would "contribute substantial operating and management expertise" through proportional representation on the board as well as various Grasberg operating and technical committees, from which the "policies established by the [board] will be implemented and operation will be conducted." Speaking of the "exceptional potential" of the deal, Rio Tinto's then chief executive, Robert Wilson, agreed that "given [Rio Tinto's] experience in other major open-pit copper ore bodies such as Bingham Canyon, Palabora and Escondida, we anticipate considerable mutual benefit."[13]

Rio Tinto obviously liked how Freeport-Indonesia did business, especially at Grasberg.

By October 1995, an independent U.S. government agency had canceled Freeport's international political risk insurance. The insurer, the Overseas Private Investment Corporation (OPIC), specifically cited the Grasberg mine operation as contravening the Foreign Assistance Act of 1961, which required that "overseas investment projects do not pose unreasonable or major environmental hazards or cause the degradation of tropical forests." Freeport was the first policy holder to be terminated by the OPIC for ethical violations, despite President Suharto and Freeport director Henry Kissinger heavily lobbying the U.S. government to reinstate the policy. Following OPIC's decision, the company did not disclose the environmental performance of the mine again until 2003—it no longer had to.

For a brief time in 2000 and 2001, a particularly sympathetic Indonesian environment minister, Sonny Keraf, pursued numerous avenues to impose penalties and fines on Grasberg, including an unsuccessful attempt to invoke the criminal section of the 1997 Environmental Law to cease Freeport-Indonesia's riverine method of tailings disposal. Under pressure for his pursuit of the part-Indonesian-owned Freeport, Keraf was replaced following the 2001 election

As Suharto's reign came to an end, an increasing number of West Papuans also began to campaign against the environmental and social impact of Grasberg. Papuan leaders brought the matter before the U.S. Federal District Court in April 1996 and before the Subcommittee on International Operations and Human Rights of the U.S. House of Representatives in May 1999. Many more attempts, including one to address shareholders at Rio Tinto's 1998 annual general meeting in London, were foiled by Indonesian authorities.

Building on restrictions introduced in 1991, the U.S. government banned arms transfers to Indonesia for widespread human rights violations in East Timor in 1999. Consequently, Freeport's payments to the Indonesian military and security forces were more closely scrutinized. The *Wall Street Journal* found that between 1991 and 1997, Freeport guaranteed over $500 million in loans so that Suharto's family and allies could purchase a stake in the mine[14]—a great portion of which was written off by Freeport in 2003. An outspoken Australian academic, Lesley McCulloch, also found that the 1996 Timika riots adjacent to the Grasberg mine led to a spike in monetary demands by the Indonesian military, resulting in the funding of a $35 million army base.[15] Freeport and Rio Tinto refused to disclose details of the payments.

Then in August 2002, two American teachers and an Indonesian employed by Freeport-Indonesia were murdered at the Grasberg mine complex. Following one rebel's admission that he was a business partner of the Indonesian military, several New York City pension (superannuation) funds formally requested that Freeport disclose the nature of its Indonesian "security" payments. The shareholders were concerned that such payments violated the Foreign Corrupt Practices Act. Although Freeport was not required to put the proposal to shareholders, the company did begin to disclose its security-related payments. Filings with the U.S. Securities and Exchange Commission since 2001 have confirmed annual payments reaching an average $5 million per annum for government-provided security of the Grasberg complex and staff and fluctuating annual costs reaching $12 million for unarmed, in-house security costs. A spokesman for the company later told the *Jakarta Post* that these payments had been taking place since the 1970s.[16]

Sporadic accounts began to surface—in the *Sydney Morning Herald*, *Jakarta Post*, and *New York Times*—quoting internal sources that confirmed that the Indonesian had masterminded the killings to extort monies from the Grasberg operators. "Not surprisingly, the Indonesian military has exonerated itself," U.S. Congressmen Joel Hefley and Tom Tancredo said in June 2003. "American investigative teams, including the FBI, have not been able to complete their investigations mainly due to the Indonesian military's refusal to co-operate and tampering of evidence."[17]

Freeport remained steadfastly opposed to later demands by New York City pension fund investors to cease all payments to the Indonesians until they complied with official U.S. investigations into the August 2002 murders. At the 2004 annual general meeting, president and chief executive Richard Adkerson advised shareholders that "the management and Board believe that the stockholder proposal mischaracterizes the company's relationships with Indonesian security institutions and suggests actions that would undermine the company's relationship with the Indonesian government and the security of the company's operations."[18] Despite the ongoing human rights and corruption concerns in West Papua—including a report by the World Bank and a letter by U.S. senators to then–UN Secretary General Kofi Annan calling for the appointment of a special representative to Indonesia—after a vote by shareholders, the resolution was not passed.

On March 23, 2004, Rio Tinto announced it had sold its 11.9% shareholding in Freeport. Rio Tinto made a $518 million profit. Citing no environmental or social reasons, Rio Tinto's then–chief executive Leigh Clifford reassured shareholders that "the sale of [Freeport] does not affect the terms of the joint venture nor the management of the Grasberg mine" and that through "our significant direct interest in Grasberg, we will continue to benefit from our relationship with Freeport."[19]

Rio Tinto remained committed to the mining of Grasberg and would continue overseeing its management through various operating and technical committees.

Sensational claims that illegal payments to individual soldiers, units, and policemen had been routinely made to secure the Grasberg complex and its staff came to light in 2005. A report by Global Witness revealed that an additional $10 million had been paid directly to individual military and police commanders between 1998 and 2004. This included $247,000 between May 2001 and March 2003 to General Mahidin Simbolon, former head of the 1999 East Timor massacre, and monthly payments throughout 2003 to the police Mobile Brigade—a group cited by the U.S. State Department as having "continued to commit numerous serious human rights violations, including extrajudicial killings, torture, rape, and arbitrary detention."[20]

With the U.S. arms trade embargo still in place, Rio Tinto had reassured the market that payments to the Indonesian military were "legally required and legitimate" only months before the news broke. Now Rio Tinto and Freeport-Indonesia came under even greater public pressure. At Rio Tinto's next shareholder meeting, after several West Papuans refugees made statements to the board on Grasberg, shareholder activist Stephen Mayne suggested that "the most appropriate thing for Rio Tinto to do would be to exit."[21] After confirming that Rio Tinto's contractual obligations would permit such a move, then-chairman Sir Rod Eddington informed shareholders that they "make a considerable effort to ensure that the best that Rio Tinto can offer to Freeport in the management of that venture is available to them."[22]

An Indonesian ministerial decree in 2007 demanded that the security of "vital national objects" such as Grasberg be handed over to the police within six months. Evidence obtained by world news service AFP suggests this is not happening. In a filing to the U.S. Securities and Exchange Commission, Freeport disclosed additional direct payments of "less than" $1.6 million in 2008 to 1,850 soldiers, despite the fact that 447 policemen make up the official number of personnel responsible for security at the Grasberg complex.[23] The company's 2008 Sustainable Development report confirms that Freeport-Indonesia makes contributions to "security institutions (including both police and military)."[24] Alarmingly, according to Amnesty International, as recently as 2008, fundamental human rights violations such as the "torture, excessive use of force and unlawful killings by police and security forces"[25]—reports that have subsequently been confirmed by the UN Special Representative of the Secretary General on Human Rights Defenders, and United Nations Committee against Torture.

"There is no alternative to our reliance on the Indonesian military and police," Freeport chairman James Moffett said to the *New York Times* in 2005. "The need for this security, the support provided for such security, and the procedures governing such support, as well as decisions regarding our relationships with the Indonesian government and its security institutions, are ordinary business activities."[26]

ORDINARY BUSINESS ACTIVITIES

Ordinary business activities got both Rio Tinto and Freeport blacklisted.

First, Freeport. In October 2005, the Norwegian government began five months of deliberations over the company's "extensive, long-term and irreversible" environmental damage at the Grasberg complex. Entering into dialog with the company in December, the Norwegians found

Freeport's response gave little evidence otherwise, choosing to instead criticize the use of "outdated information or biased reports issued by non-governmental organizations that are anti-mining or have a political agenda." And so, in February 2006, Freeport became the first company the Norwegians blacklisted for environmental reasons. Although public disclosures of investment decisions are rarely made public, the Norwegians released a detailed 32-page recommendation report after the shares were sold in June 2006.[27]

Second, Rio Tinto. In December 2007, the Norwegians began eight months of deliberations over "severe environmental damage" resulting from the Freeport joint venture in West Papua. Entering into dialogue with the Norwegians in December 2007, Rio Tinto claimed that the tailings were "an engineered, managed system for deposition and control" and that the rock is natural rock with little environmental impact. And so, as with Freeport, the Norwegians made the decision to divest from Rio Tinto in February 2008 due to the "unacceptable risk that the Fund, through continued ownership in the company, would contribute to ongoing and future severe environmental damage." Referring to the earlier Freeport report, in September 2008, the Norwegians published an additional ten-page recommendation report on the Rio Tinto sale.[28]

For the Norwegians, it wasn't so much about what had been done in the past; it was what Rio Tinto and Freeport were going to do next.

The following day, Rio Tinto told the market that it was "surprised and disappointed" in the Norwegians' decision and that it had a "non-controlling" interest in the mine.[29] Following years of signals from the international community, knowledge of the Freeport divestment in 2006, and months of dialogue over the matter, this is not so. As 12% shareholders in Freeport between 1996 and 2004, Rio Tinto enjoyed proportional representation on the company's board as well as input through various operating and technical committees specific to Grasberg. For example, Rio Tinto's chief executive between 2000 until 2007 was also a director of Freeport from 2000 to 2004.

Curiously, a letter to the Norwegians from chief executive Tom Albanese claims that Rio Tinto had "not been asked by the Ministry to discuss its concerns prior to the sale." Citing the sustainable fashion in which Rio Tinto supplies diamonds and gold to Tiffany, Albanese reassured the Norwegians that the company makes a point of "carefully selecting our partners to be organizations with comparable standards to our own in environmental performance, as well as other areas such as community relations and human rights."[30] A company with good governance wouldn't have gone into business with Freeport, let alone a business deal in which Suharto had a stake.

There has been some criticism of the Norwegians' divestment within the investment community. Much of it centers on four issues.

1. Ethical divestments remove the opportunity for dialogue to influence the practices of companies, especially when the sale represented only 1% of Rio Tinto value.
2. The decision contravenes investment theory. By reducing the number of companies in which to invest, one interferes with the efficient market and thereby constrains the financial returns available to it.
3. Investors should focus on increasing shareholder value rather than adopting value-based positions—there are no sin stocks, only leaders and laggards.
4. The Norwegians are largely investing monies earned from the country's vast oil reserves, so how can they claim to be so ethical?

But in annual sustainable development reports, both Rio Tinto and Freeport position themselves as socially responsible businesses. We're told that Freeport was a pioneer in recognizing the land rights of the Amungme and Kamoro people, paving the way to compensation and dialog since 1974 and an updated Memorandum of Understanding in 2000. We find that 14 "invalid and unsubstantiated" land rights claims were made against the company globally in their 2008 report and that steps are being taken to process such claims better in future.[31] And we are told that Rio Tinto and Freeport set aside 1% of net revenues from the Grasberg complex, which has enabled the indigenous Amungme and Kamoro people "to become equity participants in the mine" since 1996. But we find the indigenous people are told, "the river upstream will largely recover naturally." The language of ethics has been hijacked such that what is claimed is not what is actually happening.

In June 2008, the Norwegians called for public input into the country's ethical guidelines. In his submission to the Norwegian Government, pioneering shareholder activist Robert A. G. Monks sets the tone with the line: "There's a fine saying that one should not blame Columbus because he was not Magellan."[32] Indeed, acting and striving to be ethical is a noble achievement in itself, especially when lured with the financial fruits of rampant capitalism.

The blacklisting of Rio Tinto is not an exemplar of capitalism. There are, to be sure, many equally compelling stories of what can go wrong when blinded by the relentless pursuit of wealth. But what the story of the Grasberg complex does teach us is that the global financial crisis was not caused by the limits of "extreme capitalism," as the Australian prime minister, Kevin Rudd, suggests his government can control,[33] but the rampant and uncontrollable nature of capitalism itself. Nearly all of Australia's financial institutions are invested in Rio Tinto, and the federal government's $60 billion Future Fund does not disclose what it is invested in whatsoever. The government decides what is a "good investment," and in the absence of transparency and accountability, Australians just have to trust that what the government is doing is ethical.

SUMMARY

Within days of the Norwegians' announcement, reports of homemade mortar bombs firing at the gates of the Grasberg complex rippled through world news media. For now, that was West Papua's response. Given that both Rio Tinto and Freeport have yet to accept their right of reply adequately, we hope the silence will be broken by other stakeholders who value what's important here: the Amungme and Kamoro people who just wanted their land but are left with this "red river."

NOTES

1. David Holley, 'A 'Red River' in Spain May Yield Clues to Life on the Red Planet,' *LA Times*, August 24, 2002, http://articles.latimes.com/ 2002/aug/24/world/fg-tinto24
2. Norwegian Pension Fund, "Recommendation of February 15, 2008, on Exclusion of Companies Rio Tinto Plc and Rio Tinto Ltd.," *Ethical Committee*, September 9, 2008, www.regjeringen.no/pages/2105350/ Recommendation%20RT%20final.pdf
3. Rio Tinto, "Norwegian Pension Fund," *Media Release*, September 10, 2008, www.riotinto.com/media/news_12275.asp
4. See for instance the history of discussion including Freeport-McMoRan and representatives of Rio Tinto who sat on the Freeport-Indonesia Board: Norwegian Pension Fund, "Recommendation of August 15, 2006, on Exclusion of FreeportMcMoRan Copper & Gold Inc," *Ethical Committee*, February 15, 2006, www.regjeringen.no/pages/1956975/F%20Recommendation%20 Final.pdf
5. Bob Burton, "BHP Admits Ok Tedi Mine is Environmental Disaster," *Asia Times*, August 13, 1999, www.atimes.com/oceania/AH13Ah01.html
6. Lindesay Parrott, "Dutch to Explore New Guinea area: Remote Section Disputed Territory will be Object of Intensive Research", *New York Times*, March 6, 1959, http://wpik.org/Src/NYT/19590306newExplor.pdf
7. *The Djarkta Times*, April 8, 1967, cited in Justus Van Der Kroef, "West New Guinea: The Uncertain Future," *Asian Survey*, Vol. 8 No. 8, August 1968.

8. Thomas Reynders, "Memo to Department of State" May 10, 1968, www.gwu.edu/~nsarchiv/NSAEBB/NSAEBB128/8.%20Airgram%20A-570%20from%20Jakarta%20to%20State%20Department,%20May%2010,%201968.pdf

9. UNESCO, "Lorenz National Park," *World Heritage List*, http://whc.unesco.org/en/list/955

10. World Bank, "Papua Public Expenditure Analysis: Regional Finance and Service Delivery in Indonesia's Most Remote Region," *Overview Report*, August 2005.

11. John Wing and Peter King, "Genocide in West Papua? The Role of the Indonesian State Apparatus and a Current Needs Assessment of the Papuan People," a report prepared for the West Papua Project at the Centre for Peace and Conflict Studies, University of Sydney and ELSHAM Jayapura, Papua, August 2005.

12. Freeport-McMoRan, "Media Release 10 March 1995," *Media Release*

13. Freeport-McMoRan, "Freeport-McMoRan Inc. to Sell Portion of its Shares in Freeport-McMoRan Copper & Gold Inc," *Media Release*, March 7, 1995, www.secinfo.com/dpBXk.ab.d.htm

14. Peter Waldman, "Hand in Glove: How Suharto's Circle, Mining Firm Did so Well Together," *Wall Street Journal*, September 29, 1998, interactive.wsj.com/articles/SB907020100505646000.htm

15. Lesley McCulloch, "*Trifungsi: The Role of the Indonesian Military in Business*, October 2000, www.bicc.de/budget/events/milbus/confpapers/mcculloch.pdf

16. As cited in Robin Osborne, *Indonesia's Secret War: The Guerrilla Struggle in Irian Jaya*, (Sydney: Allen & Unwin, 1985), p.120.

17. Joel Hefley and Tom Tancredo, "Representatives Write to Senate to Urge on IMET Ban," October 27, 2003, www.etan.org/news/2003a/10col.htm

18. Freeport-McMoRan, "Notice of Annual Meeting of Stockholders," *Media Release*, May 6, 2004, www.fcx.com/ir/AR/2003/pdf/fcx-proxy2003.pdf

19. Rio Tinto, "Rio Tinto Reaches Agreement to Sell Shares in FCX," *Media Release*, March 22, 2004, www.riotinto.com/media/18435_media_releases_3383.asp

20. Global Witness, "Paying for Protection: The Freeport Mine and the Indonesian Security Forces," July 2005, http://resources.revenuewatch.org/sites/default/files/Global%20Witness-Paying%20for%20Protection.pdf

21. Stephen Mayne, "Rio Tinto 2006 AGM Transcript," January 22, 2009, www.maynereport.com/articles/2009/01/22-1202-2283.html

22. Ibid.

23. As cited in AFP, "US Mining Giant Still Paying Indonesia Military," AFP, March 22, 2009, www.google.com/hostednews/afp/article/ALeqM5jJMKtoD9LnT34URkkkJmTjaSf8EA

24. Freeport-McMoRan, "2008 Working toward Sustainable Development Report," www.fcx.com/envir/wtsd/pdf-wtsd/2008/WTSD_2008.pdf

25. Amnesty International, "Amnesty International Report 2009—Indonesia," *Amnesty International Country Report*, May 28, 2009, www.unhcr.org/refworld/country,,,AMNESTY,,IDN,,4a1fade478,0.html

26. Jane Perlez and Raymond Bonner, "Below a Mountain of Wealth, a River of Waste," *New York Times*, December 27, 2005, www.nytimes.com/2005/12/27/international/asia/27gold.html?pagewanted=print

27. Norwegian Pension Fund, "Recommendation of August 15, 2006, on Exclusion of FreeportMcMoRan Copper & Gold Inc," *Ethical Committee*, February 15, 2006, www.regjeringen.no/pages/1956975/F%20Recommendation%20Final.pdf

28. Norwegian Pension Fund, "Recommendation of February 15, 2008, on exclusion of companies Rio Tinto Plc and Rio Tinto Ltd." *Ethical Committee*, September 9, 2008, www.regjeringen.no/pages/2105350/Recommendation%20RT%20final.pdf

29. Rio Tinto, "Norwegian Pension Fund," *Media Release*, September 10, 2008, www.riotinto.com/media/news_12275.asp

30. Rio Tinto, "Norwegian Pension Fund—Response Letter," *Media Release*, September 26, 2008, www.riotinto.com/media/news_12469.asp

31. Freeport-McMoRan, "2008 Working Toward Sustainable Development Report," www.fcx.com/envir/wtsd/pdf-wtsd/2008/WTSD_2008.pdf

32. Private correspondence made available by Robert A.G. Monks to the author.

33. Kevin Rudd, "The Global Financial Crisis," *The Monthly*, February 2009, www.themonthly.com.au/monthly-essays-kevin-rudd-global-financial-crisis–1421

CHAPTER 30

Sustainable Investing in Africa's Frontier Markets

Graham Sinclair and Roselyne Yao

Africa is a land of opportunity and struggle. Socioeconomic issues manifest themselves on this huge continent differently to those elsewhere, and imperatives that have come to the fore in the developed world seem very distant to those whose main goal is to simply get by. But new practices in sustainable investment are emerging in Africa in the 21st century. This chapter provides the view on the African opportunity, from Africa.

A frica may seem to be one consistent region to outsiders, but it has 54 separate nations with a range of socioeconomic issues that manifest differently by subregion and country and touch on ESG factors in ways different from many other parts of the world. The diversity of issues can be seen from the Twitter-fed revolutions of northern Africa, to food and water shortages, resource conflicts, and the emergence of South Africa from the grip of apartheid. The history of sustainable investing (SI) is also tied to Africa: fighting apartheid was a driver for the early years of socially responsible investment in the United States

SI in Africa is expected to grow. In 2011, SI is a niche in the investment field in Africa, but a substantial presence in the practice of ESG-integrated decisions with over US$ 125 billion in AuM, mostly from South Africa.[1] SI is a compelling investment approach to growing frontier and emerging markets using capital to drive economic development, applying an active ownership model of institutional investment. For SI to grow, companies must feel the influence of investors making the investment case for environmental, social and governance factors in the management of their businesses. Africa has about the same potential number of consumers as India or China. Analysts predict Africa's share of global GDP will rise from 4 percent in 2010 to 7 percent in 2030 and 12 percent in 2050,[2] putting "Africa back on the global investment radar."[3] The case for SI in Africa must connect to the economic development needs of growing economies from a small base.

Investment in emerging and frontier markets is driven mostly by the desire for new sources of returns and diversification benefits. Media have increased attention on the African opportunity: in November 2010, *Time* magazine posed the question: "Is This Time for Africa?"[4] In the competition with other emerging markets destinations to attract international investment, Africa has historically been seen as a less compelling proposition than markets such as Brazil, India, and China.

But investor appetite is growing. Investors and companies interested in long-term investment and joint ventures (especially those using locally available resources) may find opportunities in the large African markets. The investment opportunities, however, all need thorough due diligence and are enhanced by considerations of sustainability risk factors. Investors must educate themselves extensively on the specific socioeconomic, political, legal, business culture, infrastructure, and other country-specific contexts—the political turmoil in West and North Africa in early 2011 reminded investors of this.

STRONGER ECONOMICS: THE CASE FOR INVESTING IN AFRICA

Africa's nearly 1 billion inhabitants speak more than 2,000 major languages and dialects, and business is conducted in English, French, Portuguese, Spanish, Arabic, Swahili, and a variety of other local languages. Investors, both globally and in Africa, tend to divide the continent into three simplified country groupings: South Africa, North Africa (often grouped with the Middle East into MENA), and rest of Africa (an undifferentiated group of more than 40 countries covering sub-Saharan Africa outside South Africa).

Eight oil-producing nations, representing another 29% of the people, saw significant growth over the past decade.[5] These countries want to build on the social development foundation of the Millennium Development Goals, but the commodity is often a mixed blessing.[6] Africa needs low-cost, reliable, sustainable energy; infrastructure; regional integration with access to global markets; and stronger private sectors, without devastating its natural assets for future generations.

Despite the compelling numbers of the African consumer base, Africa must compete locally and internationally for investment capital. Africa is a fraction of world investment markets. As of December 2010, Africa accounted for just over 1% of global market capitalization in the MSCI All Country World Frontier Market index.[7]

In the next ten years, Africa is forecasted to have a collective GDP of $2.6 trillion, close to 50% urbanization, and 128 million households with discretionary spending. In the next 20 years, the continent's top 18 cities are expected to represent $1.3 trillion in consumer spending.[8] But the "frontier markets" tend to be riskier than emerging or developing markets, having weaker balance sheets, larger external deficits, and smaller foreign exchange reserves. They are also often reliant on a single commodity export while having higher external debt.[9]

Growth on the continent will continue to be underpinned by improved macroeconomic policies, lower public debt, and a reduction in political conflicts. According to the International Monetary Fund, African GDP per capita rates should continue to grow at around 5% per year on average through 2015. This translates into at least a 30% increase in spending power by 2015, which "also means that more consumers are making the transition from the very low levels."[10] In recent years, regional investment has increased, and pan-African initiatives do exist. For example, fund manager Harith established a $600 million Pan-Africa Infrastructure Development Fund in 2007 to support continent-wide projects in power generation, energy, telecommunications, transport, property development, water, and sanitation.[11] About 60% of these investments are in South Africa, Nigeria, Kenya, and Tunisia. International investor appetite has led to 2010 as a "record net buying of African equity, to the tune of $5.98bn."[12]

South Africa is the continent's largest economy and the SI pioneer in Africa. Most investment funds in Africa are either based or marketed in South Africa due to its relatively advanced capital markets, investment ecosystem, and established investor base. Growth rates as well as regional socioeconomic ties indicate that Egypt and Morocco on the north coast, Nigeria on the west coast, and Kenya on the east are critical areas for regional growth.

These economic hubs can also be recognized through the geographical clusters of venture capital (VC) and private equity (PE) activity. The 2011 Global Venture Capital and Private Equity Country Attractiveness Index report explains that the "well-established hubs of VC/PE activity [in Africa] are South Africa and Nigeria, often used as stepping stones into other regional markets."[13]

South Africa is perhaps better known to many in the SI field as a country target of ESG-screened portfolios in the 1970s and 1980s: Apartheid country screening was a cornerstone issue for the first wave of negative screen SRI funds during that period in the United States, Canada, and Europe. Michelle Joubert, head of investor relations, and Corli le Roux, head of the SRI Index at the Johannesburg Securities Exchange, explain:

> *The anti-apartheid movement positioned South Africa as a key hunting ground for values-based investors. The country's unique history in moving beyond this legacy has obliged companies to address labor, affirmative action and health related issues with much more urgency and vigor than elsewhere, so that today no business in South Africa can be divorced from the fact that sustainability and social responsibility is entrenched in the business landscape.*[14]

In the immediate post-apartheid era, South Africa sought private sector capital domestically from long-term investors in the private sector and pension industries. ESG-branded investment products were created to meet that need. In the 1990s, a range of investment products based on themes of Black Economic Empowerment, infrastructure, community development, and other ESG themes, but few became long-lasting investment industry successes.

Barriers to growth for the continent still remain. Investment barriers include limited information, small market sizes, lack of infrastructure and services, negative presumptions, and obsolete perceptions. In addition, the recent economic climate has added to such barriers.

Nevertheless, few investment advisors may be aware that the South African market has outperformed the U.S. market over the past five years: The five-year return and Sharpe ratio of the iShares MSCI South Africa Index exchange-traded funds are respectively +7.7% and 0.36; while the five-year return and Sharpe ratio of the iShares MSCI 500 Index exchange-traded funds are +2.28% and 0.13 respectively.[15] This fact contrasts with another key barrier—the so-called home-country bias—the common phenomenon globally of investors favoring their own domestic investment markets instead of diversifying geographically.

SUSTAINABILITY ISSUES IN AFRICA

Understanding the African economic landscape is not enough to fully grasp its investment risks and opportunities. Investors also need to be aware of continent-specific sustainability issues. Investors seek risk-adjusted performance: integrating ESG factors into the investment analysis offers a more accurate test of investable opportunities on the continent.

Sustainability issues in Africa include common worldwide issues, such as governance, corruption, climate change, water use and pollution, diversity, license to operate, human rights, and worker health and safety.[16] The challenges facing Africa and investors today range from a lack of access to clean water, poor road network infrastructure, unsecured supply of energy, lack of supply, and funding of affordable houses. Integrating ESG factors into investment is particularly important for developing countries, which have limited resources to mitigate or adapt to rapid urbanization, agricultural production swings, food price volatility, or the anticipated effects of climate change. In the African context, these broader systemic concerns may include the need for employee healthcare to cover a proactive HIV/AIDS policy that supplements public health services, or private sector water treatment systems that deliver treated water both as a factory input and as a public good.

Focusing on environmental sustainability, Africa is vulnerable to the impacts of a changing climate. Most of Africa reflects the conundrum of the developing world made evident at United Nations Climate Change Conference Communication on Progress (COP) 15 in Copenhagen in 2009: how to mitigate and adapt to a climate crisis from which Africa has not benefited, with the competing need to develop economies to lift populations out of poverty. The more developed Africa economies have the larger impacts: South Africa accounts for 38% of Africa's fossil-fuel CO_2 emissions total, and another 46% comes from Egypt, Algeria, Nigeria, Libya and Morocco combined.[17] Africa has a high degree of dependency on agriculture and extractable natural resources for jobs, incomes, taxes, exports, and foodstuffs. And Africa has smaller financial reserves. The continent is therefore more likely to be adversely impacted by raised temperatures and extreme weather events, inhibiting both economic development and the region's adaptive capacity. Mitigation costs for Africa are estimated at around $5 to $10 billion a year by 2030 to meet a 2°Celsius stabilization target.[18]

According to continent's largest institutional investor, the South Africa Government Employees Pension Fund (GEPF), "[C]limate change presents both risk—that needs to be managed in order to maintain the sustainability of our investments, and opportunity—for long-term investors such as the GEPF to invest in the new infrastructure required to shift to a low-carbon economy." The case for SI has a ready audience. More than half (52 percent)[19] of 160 respondents in the IFC-SinCo 2011 study think there is a strong case for SI. However, the SI case has been reinforced by local social and environmental crises, and corporate malfeasance.

The COP16 talks held in Cancun, Mexico, in December 2010 showed progress in favor of emerging markets, such as the creation of a new Green Climate Fund governed by an equal number of developed and developing countries administered by the World Bank.[20] Negotiations, however, have been unsatisfactory, which explains the announcement from the African Union regarding the creation of an Africa Green Fund administered by the African Development Bank.[21] COP17 is scheduled to be held in Durban, South Africa, in December 2011, and will act as a focal point for investors in Africa to address the growth path to a low-carbon, low-water, climate resilient economy.

In considering social factors, sustainability issues may be reflected through worker benefits, including healthcare covering a proactive HIV/AIDS policy to supplement limited public health services. Other social issues include diversity in the workforce, gender equality, labor conditions, access to healthcare, economic empowerment, housing, and education.

On the governance side, corruption can and will deter foreign investors as well as complicate international relations for years. In emerging markets, it is often said that politics are as important as economics for investors. The governance–growth connection in Africa is well understood but notoriously difficult to achieve, affecting large businesses and small entrepreneurs alike.[22] Interestingly, though, the comparison of a country's attractiveness based on the Corruption Perceptions Index places at least seven African countries ahead of the BRIC countries (Brazil, Russia, India, and China).[23] In South Africa, the leadership role of the King III Code of Corporate Governance[24] in raising standards of governance, and listing requirements of the Johannesburg Stock Exchange (JSE), has been important not only in Africa, but also in global emerging markets.

ROLE OF INDEXES

Indexes play the role of benchmarks in the SI world and generate a reference point for keeping score on ESG performance. In the new and emerging field of SI in Africa, sustainability indexes delineate the sustainability themes for a specific region against which investment approaches and performance may be measured. Investment in sustainability is a broad theme with many regional, issue, and implementation variations.

In two of the most mature economies in Africa—South Africa and Egypt—ESG indexes have been somewhat successful.[25] (For more on indexes in Africa, see Chapter 32.)

INTERNATIONAL EXPOSURE

African investor and business perspectives on ESG priorities are heterogeneous. As in other emerging markets, the private sector is expected to play a positive role in society. Public-private partnerships are also developing. But screening out exposure to a country based on norms of an international convention may be more of a compelling concern to investors in New York, Tokyo, or Zurich than to investors in Dakar, Nairobi, or Johannesburg. Local investors may rate the opportunity to grow the economy—and businesses that provide basic services to local communities—as the most important SI case.

In terms of Africa-specific ESG factors, analysts are increasingly looking at issues related to carbon emissions, conflict minerals, water scarcity, or supporting regulatory and governmental frameworks. ESG issues cross economic and investment themes and may be factored into the political economy. For example, through Section 1502, the Dodd-Frank Wall Street Reform and Consumer Protection Act addressed the issue of conflict minerals from the Democratic Republic of Congo.[26] Similarly, the Kimberly Process initiated in 2000 established an ethical basis for the diamond supply chain.[27]

Nongovernmental organizations (NGOs) play an important role in making the case for greater exposure on corporate ESG performance, arguing for higher quality of disclosure. Most recently, environmental NGOs, such as Centre for the Environmental Rights, the Endangered Wildlife Trust, and the Environmental Monitoring Group, have been pressuring the JSE SRI Index in response to the JSE SRI Index ranking eight firms that the NGOs consider not deserving a ranking on an ESG-branded index.[28]

All emerging markets seek to triumph in the new great game for Africa. In that regard, the Africa-China relationship is becoming one of the key trends to follow. It shows a new type of emerging to frontier market relationship: "China's approach to infrastructure is strategic and triangular: China invests in resources such as oil, coal, copper, etc., then it invests in energy to power-up the mines, thereafter it invests in the infrastructure to transport the resources to the nearest ports."[29]

According to official data from the China's Ministry of Commerce, Chinese companies signed $39 billion in labor service and construction contracts across Africa in 2008. While these contracts largely include funding from development agencies and African governments, in many cases China has financed major investments where traditional investors have failed to provide funding. At the forefront of Chinese investment into Africa is the China-Africa Development Fund, investing $5 billion into Africa: "There are currently thirty projects of the fund in various stages throughout Africa, ranging from power plants in Ghana and oil mining in Liberia, to car assembly plants in South Africa."[30] "African countries must implement meaningful structural and policy changes that could enable them to leverage China's involvement to enhance their development."[31]

While development financing institutions (DFIs) investing into Africa, for example the IFC or CDC,[32] have been at the forefront of encouraging local development of SI and ESG capabilities, the impact of BRIC-related investment on sustainability is unclear at present. Historically, the integration of environmental, social and governance (ESG) factors in PE has been driven mostly by client mandates, especially where development finance institutions (DFIs) such as the International Finance Corporation, CDC, FMO, Proparco, Norfund, or African Development Bank have been anchor investors.

FUTURE TRENDS: ESG, MEDIA COVERAGE, AND NETWORKS

Monitoring of ESG issues is fundamental for SI to spread beyond the major markets in Africa. Investment data in the region are patchy, but as investment activity increases, more data are being made available. The longer-standing markets, such as South Africa, Mauritius, or Egypt, have a better pool of data points and more sophisticated data flows, including companies with ESG data available through data providers. Regular, accurate investment information also depends on data providers making their research available. For example, Bloomberg has started tracking ESG data on a number of African companies.

Barriers to SI in the region are similar to obstacles faced elsewhere in the world. Such barriers include information gaps, lack of regulation, lack of ESG-related skills, lack of case studies in favor or evidence of risk-adjusted investment performance, and negative attitudes from the mainstream investment field. There is also outmoded thinking that equates SI only with ethical investment and negative screening. However, moving past blunt cynicism, the attitude of investors is shifting from "why?" to "how?"

On a continent with a vast range in literacy levels, the frank satire of cartoonists is an important tradition, playing a role in highlighting ESG issues and thus raising awareness of ESG risks to both African and international investors, for example Zapiro in South Africa or Kenyan Paul Kelemba ("Maddo").[33]

Networks have been important in developing an African approach to African sustainable development challenges, predating but emphasized by the World Summit on Sustainable Development in Johannesburg, 2002. Association-led initiatives such as the Extractive Industries Transparency Initiative (EITI)[34] are having a positive impact. In the realm of project finance, the Equator Principles[35], has attracted five African banks, including all four major South African banks. Eleven asset managers and banks signed on to the Carbon Disclosure Project 2010 and CDP Water 2010 Reports, covering South Africa's largest companies.

To develop local ESG knowledge in the investment value chain, there is the need to leverage country-specific networks, such as PRI South Africa (PRI has 33 signatories in Africa, mostly in South Africa[36]), as well as subject matter experts, such as the International Corporate Governance Network. pan-African initiatives such as AfricaSIF.org, launched in June 2010, with the mission to be a knowledge base, network, and advocate for SI on the continent.[37]

The IFC-SinCo Sustainable Investment in sub-Saharan Africa[38] highlighted significant growth in SI over the next five years, led by Private Equity (PE) funds, demand from asset owners, and new regulations that enable pension funds to both increase allocations to PE and/or enable ESG integration, notably in South Africa. The largest institutional investment market on the continent is South Africa which accounts for 95% of Sustainable Investment in SSA. In response to the report release in July 2011, Jim O'Neill, Chairman of Goldman Sachs Asset Management, commented that "With the economic opportunities and increasing investment in Africa, there is rising investor interest in the region. The concept of sustainable investing could also feature more prominently in African investment opportunities."[39] Using investor self-reported data, the study estimates US$125 billion of investment that integrates environmental, social and governance (ESG) factors in SSA which is set to grow significantly. At the same time, ESG-branded investment products represent less than 1% of assets under management (AuM) or US$5.5 billion. "The report's findings show how far interest has grown in sustainable investment and how much further it can go," according to Rod Evison, Acting CEO of CDC Group, which has over £1.1 billion committed to funds in PE in Africa.[40]

SUMMARY

Sub-Saharan Africa is developing an organic approach to SI, with a newfound positive attitude to tackling the development challenges in the subcontinent. As African infrastructure develops via roads, railways, airports, and water networks, the enormous SI opportunity in the next ten years is to meet increasing energy demands through alternative energy technologies, smart grid networks, and energy efficiency. These infrastructure decisions will have 50-year consequences. One may argue that any frontier market investment in Africa is in itself a type of ESG investment: deploying new capital in a cash-poor region needing sustained economic development is arguably much more material than a marginal dollar in stock markets of developed economies. Africa is still perceived as a very risky investment environment, but for pro-Africa investors, this constitutes an advantage, offering an effect barrier to entry.[41]

Africa is now one of the world's fastest-growing regions. Africa's economy is forecasted to grow at an average annual rate of 7% over the next 20 years, slightly faster than China's.[42] Africa has nearly 1 billion people, the fastest mobile phone penetration on the planet, and the seventh largest pension fund in the world, yet it is the poorest continent. Africa's sound growth prospects are underpinned by generally improved macroeconomic policies, lower public debt, and a reduction in political conflicts. But future investment will depend on a supportive environment with sound market regulation and institutions. Regulatory change is one of several drivers for the growth in sustainable investment in Africa in the major economies.

Sustainable development is a manifest challenge facing this generation of Africans: how to build capital for economic development through environmental impact risks, the socioeconomic challenges, and the threat of poor governance. SI is a long-term investment approach that best fits the opportunity for the future success of both investors and the African continent. The success or failure of sustainable development will define Africa's growth path. From a small but established base, an African interpretation of Sustainable Investment is growing. More work is needed, at policy, practitioner, and portfolio levels, to grow this investment theme.

NOTES

1. IFC-SinCo "Sustainable Investment in Sub-Saharan Africa" Report, Sinclair et al, IFC, July 2011. www.ifc.org/ifcext/sustainability.nsf/Content/Publications_Report_SI-SubSaharanAfrica
2. Citi: Investment Opportunities and the Expansion of the African GDP. Accessed May 2011.
3. "The Africa Factor: Challenges & Opportunities for European Companies," SG Research (November 2008). Société Générale Group, Sarbjit Nahal, cohead of SRI and Véronique Riches-Flores, Chief Economist Europe. www.sgresearch.socgen.com
4. Stephen Gandel, "Is This Time for Africa?" Time, November 3, 2010. www.time.com/time/magazine/article/0,9171,2026897,00.html
5. Robert Zoellick, "A Challenge of Economic Statecraft," April 2, 2008, Global Policy Forum. www.globalpolicy.org/socecon/bwi-wto/wbank/2008/0402statecraft.htm
6. The eight Millennium Development Goals—which range from halving extreme poverty to halting the spread of HIV/AIDS and providing universal primary education, all by the target date of 2015—form a blueprint agreed to by all

the world's countries and all the world's leading development institutions. www.un.org/millenniumgoals/

7. MSCI Global Equity Indices: www.mscibarra.com/products/indices/global_ equity_indices/

8. "MGI Lions on the Move: The Progress and Potential of African Economies," McKinsey (June 2010). www.mckinsey.com/mgi/publications/progress_and_ potential_of_african_economies/index.asp

9. UBS Investment Research, "Q-Series®: Global Emerging Markets," January 11 2011. www.ubs.com/investmentresearch

10. Africa's Development Prospects Remain Intact, Robert Ruttmann, Equity Research, Credit Suisse, January 11, 2011. https://infocus.credit-suisse.com/app/ article/index.cfm?fuseaction=OpenArticle&aoid=296391&lang=EN

11. Harith Fund Managers, www.harith.co.za/

12. Cameron Brandt, director of research at funds flow data provider EPFR Global.

13. Alexander Groh, Heinrich Liechtenstein, and Karsten Lieser, "Investing in Africa—Challenges and Opportunities," Global Venture Capital and Private Equity Country Attractiveness Index: 2011 Annual, www.iese.edu/research/ pdfs/ESTUDIO-143-E.pdf

14. World Federation of Exchanges, "Exchanges, ESG and Investment Decisions," September 2010. www.world-exchanges.org/files/statistics/excel/ WFE%20ESG%20publication%20.pdf

15. SinCo analysis, 2011 from Morningstar data.

16. IFC-SinCo "Sustainable Investment in Sub-Saharan Africa" Report, Sinclair et al, IFC, July 2011. www.ifc.org/ifcext/sustainability.nsf/Content/ Publications_Report_SI-SubSaharanAfrica

17. T.A. Boden, G. Marland, and R.J. Andres. "Global, Regional, and National Fossil-Fuel CO_2 Emissions," 2010. Carbon Dioxide Information Analysis Center, Oak Ridge National Laboratory, U.S. Department of Energy, Oak Ridge, Tenn., U.S.A. doi 10.3334/CDIAC/00001_V2010

18. African Climate Policy Centre (ACPC), "Global Context and Background," www.uneca.org/acpc/index.php?Page=global_context_background&Dir=back ground

19. This may, of course, reflect a sample selection bias but is higher than expected given the variety of inputs and diversity of interview candidates pursued by the SinCo+RisCura research team. IFC-SinCo "Sustainable Investment in Sub-Saharan Africa" Report, Sinclair et al, IFC, July 2011. www.ifc.org/ifcext/ sustainability.nsf/Content/Publications_Report_SI-SubSaharanAfrica

20. "Africa: Progress in Cancun, Work Begins on Durban," allAfrica.com/IRIN, December 12, 2010. http://allafrica.com/stories/201012120005.html

21. Statement by Donald Kaberuka, president of the African Development Bank Group at the High Level Segment, December 9, 2010. http://unfccc.int/files/ meetings/cop_16/statements/application/pdf/101210_cop16_hls_afdb.pdf

22. Steve Radelet, "Emerging Africa: How 17 Countries Are Leading the Way," Center for Global Development, September 1, 2010. www.cgdev.org/content/ publications/detail/1424378/ accessed July 2011. "Emerging Africa" describes the too-often-overlooked positive changes that have taken place in much of

Africa since the mid-1990s. In 17 countries, five fundamental and sustained breakthroughs are making old assumptions increasingly untenable: (1) the rise of democracy brought on by the end of the Cold War and apartheid; (2) stronger economic management; (3) the end of the debt crisis and a more constructive relationship with the international community; (4) the introduction of new technologies, especially mobile phones and the Internet; and (5) the emergence of a new generation of leaders. With these significant changes, the countries of emerging Africa seem poised to lead the continent out of the conflict, stagnation, and dictatorships of the past. The countries Radelet discusses are Botswana, Burkina Faso, Cape Verde, Ethiopia, Ghana, Lesotho, Mali Mauritius, Mozambique, Namibia, Rwanda, Sao Tome and Principe, Seychelles, South Africa, Tanzania, Uganda, and Zambia.

23. A higher score means less (perceived) corruption. Corruption Perceptions Index, Transparency International, www.transparency.org/policy_research/surveys_indices/cpi/2010

24. www.iodsa.co.za/en-us/productsservices/kingiiireportpapersguidelines.aspx

25. Apart from the two operational, investable indexes in Africa, media organization African Investor rolled out the AI SRI Index in September 2008. The SRI Index Series—the Africa investor SRI 50 and Africa Investor SRI 30 "aligned with the Millennium Development Goals and other internationally recognized ESG principles." Africa Investor was commissioned by the New Partnership for Africa's Development (NEPAD) and the United Nations to develop this pan-African SRI benchmark and attract global SRI flows to the continent.

26. Daniel Brooksbank, "SEC to Clamp Down on Extractive Payments, Mine Safety and Conflict Minerals," December 16, 2010. www.responsible-investor.com/home/article/sec_to_clamp_down_on_extractives_payments_mine_safety_and_conflict_minerals

27. www.kimberleyprocess.com/. The Kimberley Process Certification Scheme imposes extensive requirements on its members to enable them to certify shipments of rough diamonds as conflict-free. As of December 2009, the Kimberley Process has 49 members, representing 75 countries, with the European Community and its member states counting as an individual participant.

28. Ingi Salgado, "JSE'S Green Index Gets Red Light from NGOs," Business Report, December 23, 1010. www.iol.co.za/jse-s-green-index-gets-red-light-from-ngos-1.1004401

29. Deborah Brautigam and Adama Gaye, "Is China's Investment Good for Africa?" Council on Foreign Affairs Online Debate, February 20, 2007.

30. Princeton N. Lyman, "Senate Committee on Foreign Relations Subcommittee on African Affairs: Hearing on Strengthening U.S. Diplomacy to Anticipate, Prevent and Respond to Conflict in Africa," April 21, 2009 i.cfr.org/content/publications/attachments/Lyman_Testimony_April21.pdf

31. J. Ndumbe Anyu, J.-P. Afam Ifedi, "China's Ventures in Africa: Patterns, Prospects, and Implications for Africa's Development," *Mediterranean Quarterly*—Volume 19, Number 4, Fall 2008, pp. 91–110

32. www.cdcgroup.com

33. www.zapiro.com/ and http://afrikatoonz.blogspot.com/2006/10/paul-kelemba-maddo.html

34. www.eiti.org. The initiative aims to strengthen governance by improving transparency and accountability in the extractive sector.
35. Muziwandile Chonco, "Assessing the Adoption of the Equator Principles by financial institutions in South Africa." Gordon Institute of Business Science—University of Pretoria, November 11, 2009, http://upetd.up.ac.za/thesis/available/etd-04072010-154720/unrestricted/dissertation.pdf
36. www.unpri.org/signatories
37. One AfricaSIF supporter, for example, stated: "In order for sustainable investment to be a reality in Africa, transparency, collaboration and knowledge-sharing will be essential: This is what AfricaSIF offers. It is a multifaceted resource that clearly articulates the value proposition of investment in Africa." www.africasif.org
38. IFC-SinCo "Sustainable Investment in Sub-Saharan Africa" Report, Sinclair et al, IFC, July 2011. IFC, a member of the World Bank Group, has released the most comprehensive study to date of Sustainable Investment (SI) in Sub-Saharan Africa (SSA). The report is based on research by SinCo and RisCura including over 160 interviews of investors and advisors.
39. Goldman Sachs Asset Management comment to SinCo + RisCura media release, 19 July 2011.
40. CDC reaction comment to SinCo + RisCura media release, July 18, 2011.
41. Five answer options for each of the eight statements. Answer options: very/somewhat/marginally/not important/no idea. Most frequent five responses by quantity of "very important" answers. SinCo analysis based on SinCo and RisCura research, January 2010—April 2011
42. "A More Hopeful Continent: The Lion Kings?" *The Economist*, January 6, 2011. www.economist.com/node/17853324?story_id=17853324

CHAPTER 31

Evolution of ESG in India

Sumantra Sen

India, a country that is rapidly growing economically and emerging on the global scene, has largely avoided the recent financial crisis that has enveloped much of the rest of the world, especially in most of Europe and the United States. It has done so while not largely participating in the ESG movements that we have been discussing in this book. Natural resource issues, such as available fresh water, continue to be of strategic importance. Arguably, for Indian companies to succeed from here, they will need to begin demonstrating that they are not just pure growth plays; rather, that they compete globally with their peers using a sustainability lens.

India has recorded tremendous economic growth in recent years. A large share of this growth can be attributed to the burgeoning services sector. Rising education levels and a competitive environment have led to the development of skilled Indian workforce, which has facilitated growth in information technology and enabled services.

SUSTAINABILITY ISSUES IN INDIA

Almost in line with the economic growth Indian equity markets have become the most vibrant markets in the world with both major stock exchanges, the National Stock Exchange (NSE) and the Bombay Stock Exchange (BSE), witnessing remarkable growth in the last decade. The BSE, with a market capitalization of $1.55 trillion, is the fourth largest exchange in Asia and eleventh largest in the world. The NSE has become the country's largest stock exchange in terms of number of trades and has grown more than 15-fold in the last 15 years to reach $1.3 trillion. This statistic indicates the key role that primary and secondary markets have played in providing access to capital for Indian corporates.

However, in the midst of positive economic developments, social and welfare issues concerning poverty, illiteracy, and poor health services to a large part of the population continue to drag overall economic performance and raise questions regarding the sustainability of developments to date. A large part of the Indian population dwells in rural areas, most of which lack basic amenities. Even though the state has taken a number of steps to target these issues, they continue to persist, thereby compelling policy makers to draft an economic policy that targets basic infrastructure development.

Among all these issues, absence of inclusive growth is most critical. Although India has been growing in terms of population and economy over the years, its benefits are concentrated in a small percentage of population. In the long run, this fact is likely not only to have broad political and social implications but also to result in a saturated market inhibiting business and economic growth. The impact of this unequal opportunity is already visible in rapidly expanding urbanization, as large numbers of people from rural areas are migrating to towns and cities in search of better employment. Urbanization is an integral part of economic growth, but it raises challenges to infrastructure, housing, and natural resources in the long run. The widening gap between demand and supply of infrastructural services negatively impacts access to basic services, such as drinking water, sanitation, education, and healthcare.

Another concern that has attracted immense attention in India and globally is global warming and climate change. India is ranked as the third largest emitter of carbon dioxide after the United States and China, with vehicular exhausts and industry being the key contributors. As the country's carbon footprint has grown, the attitude of the business community toward pollution has resulted in the depletion and contamination of the natural resources. By some estimates, the country may have losses of around 5% of gross domestic product simply on account of climate change. As the natural disasters become more frequent and devastating, the climate change issue will seriously challenge decades of good work done in the vulnerable emerging markets.

The National Action Plan on Climate Change under the leadership of the prime minister has been initiated to identify eight core national missions running through 2017 that promote the development objectives while yielding co-benefits for addressing climate change effectively. The plan directs the ministries to submit detailed reports on the implementation of such plans to the prime minister's Council on Climate Change by December 2008. The plan further recommends specific energy consumption decreases in large energy-consuming industries; energy incentives; financing for public-private partnerships to reduce energy consumption; greater emphasis on urban waste management and recycling, including power production from waste; and strengthening the enforcement of automotive fuel economy standards and using pricing measures to encourage the purchase of efficient vehicles. With water scarcity projected to worsen as a result of climate change, the plan sets a goal of a 20% improvement in water use efficiency through pricing and other measures.

OPPORTUNITIES IN INDIA'S SUSTAINABLE INVESTING MARKET

Under the backdrop of these negative externalities, strong governance standards and corporate social responsibility become imperative. Indian corporations have began to include the best practices in their governance and to adopt strong corporate governance standards in the listing agreements that all publicly listed companies execute with the stock exchange where their shares are traded. The Indian Companies Act, 1956 lays out the principles of corporate governance, highlighting the duty of boards of directors to adopt the accounting standards stipulated by the Indian Chartered Accountants Institute, to maintain proper books of accounts and prepare financial statements. The Satyam Computers episode involving a US $ 1 billion accounting fraud in 2009 further turned out to be an eye opener for investors and regulators and raised questions on the accounting and auditing standards followed in general. Regulators have since tightened corporate governance standards seeking more transparency from companies. Investors and investment managers have also begun to view governance standards as an overall reflection of a company's business model and management quality. While such corporate governance standards will continue to evolve for a developing country like India, recent scams continue to challenge the nation to build the right framework and to implement it rigorously.

As India integrates with international economies and attracts increasing global investors, interest in critical sectors such as infrastructure, environmental, social, and governance (ESG) factors will continue to play a larger role in providing opportunities. In accordance with the growing demand of extrafinancial information disclosure and higher standards in managing ESG issues, Indian companies' nonadherence to such benchmarks may inhibit the availability or raise the cost of capital significantly. The growing awareness among the domestic institutional or private investors and other stakeholders will keep bringing ESG-related issues into the mainstream, which will impact the overall valuation, ability to raise capital, and long-term stakeholder wealth.

CONSIDERING THE INTEGRATION OF ESG FACTORS

The integration of ESG factors into extrafinancial disclosures has begun. In 2000, serious efforts to promote sustainability reporting guidelines were taken up by the Global Reporting Initiative. According to its recent report, 56 leading companies from diverse sectors, such as construction; computers; mining; chemical; health products; energy; oil and gas; banking; automotive; and the food and beverage sector in India have taken voluntary steps to publish sustainability reports or include the ESG disclosure in their annual reports. Although several large companies have been publishing the reports over the last six or seven years, the reporting quality is still not at par with the international peers.

Further, to gain interest at the institutions associated with capital markets in India, the sustainability index sponsored by International Finance Corporation and executed by CRISIL and KLD was launched in 2008. The index measures and ranks 50 NSE-listed companies on their ESG performance.

Key steps to galvanize participants toward extrafinancial disclosures include the issuance of a circular by the Reserve Bank of India in 2007 communicating its expectations that major banks participate in mainstreaming sustainability issues and the release by the Ministry of Corporate Affairs in 2009 of "Corporate Social Responsibility Voluntary Guidelines" encouraging companies to adopt guidelines to manage the ESG issues.

The investment management community has a general awareness of ESG issues, but it has not yet structured an approach to streamline the issues in its main decision-making process. In investment decision making, commonly managers look for companies with sound governance practices but ignore any objective ESG information. Even though these preliminary steps are noteworthy, integration of ESG in India is lower than in the global market, including other emerging markets. This state of low demand and adoption of ESG issues in India is reflected in the slow development of responsible investment products in the country. ABN AMRO India was among the first to launch a three-year close-ended Sustainable Development Fund in March 2007, benchmarked against the BSE 200. At the launch, the fund managed to raise Rs. 60 Crores (approximately US $ 13 million); since that time, however, it has been under constant redemption pressure.

Investment practitioners have an extremely low awareness of tools, best practices, and even the dedicated index, which could be why they have not bothered to include them in the decision-making process. However, a company's track record in matters related to corporate governance is a very important part of investment decision. The growth of the Indian economy and its capital markets has brought with it social and environmental pressures and a need to raise the standards of corporate governance. As a voluntary guideline, the Confederation of Indian Industry developed a Code for Desirable Corporate Governance in late 1990s. The fraud by the promoters of Satyam Computers in 2009 highlighted the flaws and accelerated the adoption of stringent governance standards. There has been a sharper response to building regulatory frameworks, reporting mechanisms, and audit procedures to ensure that corporate governance standards of companies are aligned with the objective of investor protection.

Fund managers' thorough analysis of the quality and ability of management, financial disclosures, and robust business models ensures that there is a holistic scorecarding and ranking of companies on diverse parameters. Managers feel that very few companies disclose complete information on ESG; even if data are available, they may not be presented in ways that allow comparison. Further, investment managers have made no significant effort to communicate the requirements of ESG-related disclosure from investee companies.

SUMMARY

ESG factors play a crucial role in generating sustainable long-term returns. The relative recovery and performance of some companies since the recent global crisis has been tracked by most managers. Even without an objective score on ESG parameters, they recognize that the leaders have stronger extrafinancial performance. The best practices adopted by select managers indicate that integration of ESG factors can build a business case for some Indian companies among their emerging market peers, which can be useful for sectors like infrastructure. In spite of these trends, the demand for nonfinancial information from the investors in India, however, has not reached a maturity level. The lack of awareness and collective thought around integration of ESG factors can be attributed to the absence of institutional investors, such as the domestic pension fund, in this space.

Therefore, at this stage, even though corporate governance standards and management capability are constantly tracked in the securities' selection process, the short-term investment horizon of the investors does not allow long-term strategies like environment and social issues to act as differentiators. The acknowledgment of the need for transparent disclosure and of the value ESG factors can create in the long term are some encouraging signs that should serve as key drivers to take the mainstreaming of responsible investing forward.

REFERENCES

Ritu Kumar and Dan Siddy, "Sustainable Development in India 2009," TERI-Europe report, IFC.
"Sustainability Reporting Trends," Global Reporting Initiative, 2010.
Sean Gilbert and James O'Loughlin, "Reaching Investors," Global Reporting Initiative, 2009.

CHAPTER 32

Indexes

Graham Sinclair

Indexes have the potential to play a greater role in sustainable investing. Sustainability indexes can provide a benchmark; a reference point against which the progress of sustainable investment can be measured globally by specific regions and across asset classes.

Indexes provide a signal for the viability and feasibility of sustainability. Equity portfolios typically are measured against a standard benchmark of some sort, which often acts as the implied measure of how well an investment strategy performs. Sustainability indexes have proven useful over decades by presenting data and reference points for debate on performance and on material ESG issues, attempting to demonstrate both the risks and the opportunities of sustainable investment.

Sustainability indexes have acted as benchmarks for new investment in developed economies and emerging markets. Thematic indexes ranging from clean tech to green real estate or sustainable lifestyles have introduced a next generation of benchmarks. The company constituents in sustainability indexes have exhibited a range of reactions, including a positive demand for inclusion in certain sustainability indexes seeking the halo effect of a positive ranking.

Sustainability indexes have the potential to improve and mature. However, the question remains: In a volatile world of innovation, can passive investment of any kind capture the winners of the future? However, the changes to institutional asset management imply that a large percentage of assets are—and likely will be—passively managed to increase diversification and drive down costs. The shift of new asset flows into indexed investing creates a large opportunity not currently seized by sustainability indexes. Such indexes enable institutional investors, especially "universal owners," to track the market with the added benefit of ESG factors. This chapter looks at sustainability indexes and their potential impact.

Passive investment represents an important part of the investing landscape. Indexes are often both an investment signal and an investment strategy. Indexes frame complexity, acting as benchmarks and tools for stakeholders. As investors seek risk-adjusted returns over an investment horizon, indexes provide a means to understand how investments are performing—keeping score; they act as investment propositions to follow a particular market or investable theme.

Sustainability indexes are a potentially important but often overlooked component of the investment marketplace, where asset owners often feel compelled for cost reasons, among others, to invest passively a good percentage of the time. An index that ranks major companies across the globe, a region, or a country may be a useful tool for measuring company efforts in sustainability. Sustainability indexes build the sustainable investment brand, increasing advocacy, engaging the private sector, inviting increased effort by ranked firms, and helping attract new fund flows to best-performing companies or business units in the medium term.

Nonetheless, not all sustainability indexes are credible, and some deserve to be short-lived. Noncredible or nonflexible indexes cannot withstand scrutiny or adapt to changing trends in sustainability and/or investment practice while preserving their core mission focused on sustainable long-term investment performance.

THE "WHAT" AND "WHY" OF INDEXES

An index describes and simplifies a part of the investment universe, aggregating and simplifying, which is both a strength and weakness. For example, how do you describe the activities of the busy marketplace in a singular way for interested observers? The "Dow 30" is a stock market index created in the nineteenth century by proprietors of what would later become the *Wall Street Journal*. The Dow Jones Industrial Average established an index of 30 of the largest and most widely held public companies in the United States as a proxy for the activities of the stock market.[1] This one index was able to communicate some meaning to the myriad individual company movements at any point in time and has become part of the investment ecosystem, a benchmark for stock market activity.

Indexes have a long history of leveraging change. They provide a reference point when investors seek to understand new themes (such as nanotechnology) or regions (such as frontier markets). For example, the MSCI Emerging Markets Index has become the foremost benchmark for investing in emerging markets (EMs) and was established by the work of the IFC in the early 1980s, which invested money into the theme. As more investors better understood the grouping of countries and tracked the performance by tracking the index, they came to better understand these markets at a time when they were new for many.

Sustainability indexes have emerged alongside demand for strategies integrating environmental, social, and governance (ESG) factors. Leading countries and investors have established ESG-issue and sustainable investment indexes for some years now, including in major emerging markets Brazil (2005) and South Africa (2004). The index may be designed to recognize companies with existing sustainability practices and to encourage those that may have neglected these responsibilities.

Sustainability indexes benefit the marketplace by establishing a practical outcome of ESG thinking in a given theme or region. The sustainability index series may crystallize debate around sustainability and provide incentives for companies to incorporate ESG criteria into their everyday business activities. They also provide investors across asset classes with tools to assess and value company performance sustainability. If successful, a ranking or index then becomes a core part of the investment lexicon. The benchmark of investable companies, whether through equity, fixed income, and/or price/earnings asset classes, acts as a model to frame debate, serves as a touchstone across countries and asset classes, and promotes the development of new investment portfolios and products that explicitly integrate ESG factors.

Index success may be as an instrument or tool for:

- Analysis for investment (e.g., Dow Jones Sustainability Index[DJSI])
- Awareness impacting reputation
- Establishing a new ESG factor as investment theme
- Advocacy and engagement (e.g., Johannesburg Stock Exchange [JSE])
- Driving net new cash flow to new research and development and projects (e.g., Global Climate 100)
- Measurable progress advancing the sustainability mission (e.g., BOVESPA)

Most important, an index helps rank winners and losers. An index is able to segment over- and undersustainability performance by companies, recognizing that one company may be higher or lower than another in some criteria and not in others. The equilibrium chosen for the rating and weighting must be decided, balanced with the overall sustainability index goal of dealing specifically with one ESG factor or many.

The purpose of a sustainability index must be clearly defined for stakeholders in order to create focus. The rank or index description must be succinct, such as "an index of companies actively leading in sustainability globally." Many interesting variations will emerge in the design, development, and ongoing execution of an index. In our experience, key components of a sustainability index include focus (the need met, including the aim of an index as "a tool for a more effective carrot for companies," to quote a colleague), objectives, logic model, governance, decisions on employing to index vendors/partners, criteria to select companies into the index, sponsors for the governing entity, and the process employed to develop it.

For the sustainability index, definitions are the key. Sustainability is both global and local, with both elements essential. ESG issues in each region/country/sector need to be assessed and the working definition generated from in-depth stakeholder consultation.

Indexes also offer investors an opportunity for exposure and transparency to remote regions of the world. Dow Jones has revealed plans for a new country classification system that will include frontier markets as a separate category for the first time. Seventeen of the 35 countries currently classified as emerging markets will join the new frontier markets list, which will have a total of 20 countries. The construction of such cutting-edge indexes presents real challenges, especially with respect to liquidity and accessibility. Frontier markets are typically much less accessible to foreign investors than other markets, exhibit notable limitations in their regulatory and operational environments; and have smaller investment landscapes than other markets.

Companies included in indexes have the potential for preferential access to capital, receive significantly greater research coverage in the investment community, and benefit from higher liquidity. In addition, index inclusion can increase a company's stock price. Firms excluded from indexes typically lose institutional investment and can experience considerable stock price declines, especially in the short term; longer-term effects remain unclear.[2] Inclusion in indexes oriented around ESG issues—ranging from the Domini 400 Social Index to the more recent DJSI (since 1999) or the JSE SRI Index (since 2003)—can improve a company's reputation. Therefore, firms are willing to allocate resources to complete questionnaires required by some index providers.

When Is a Ranking an Index?

"Index" is a term applied to lists, ratings, rankings, and investable indexes. For sustainable investment, not all rankings are useful indexes. Benchmarks are basically reference points against which the performance of a financial strategy, instrument, or idea may be compared.

Index architecture must map to the investment case and the index proposition. Indexes (and indexed portfolios) are actively managed investment instruments that are constructed according to objective criteria and are compiled and marketed by financial services firms, such as FTSE Group/Financial Times (www.ftse.com/Indices), Morgan Stanley Capital International Indexes (www.msci.com), Standard & Poor's Indexes (www.sandp.com), and Dow Jones Indexes (www.djindexes.com/).

As shifts in institutional investment management affect philosophy and strategy about the best sources of alpha- and beta-driven returns, so the opportunity opens up for more passive investment products built from an underlying index. Index funds are often preferred to active funds for reasons of diversification but mostly for the lower fees they offer. Performance to the end investor is always net of fees, so the net-of-fees performance impact of passively tracking an index can be a compelling proposition for many.

INDEX ARCHITECTURE

Index architecture is often delivered as one of two models: (1) a broad universe filtered for high/low on ESG ratings, or (2) a theme index ranking a narrower cohort of firms according to a particularly segment of the business world.

Two main categories of index dominate.[3]

1. Some indexes of listed equities are designed to be broad, using ESG criteria and scoring systems to select companies that are "leaders" in social and environmental responsibility. Examples include the FTSE4Good series, the BM and FBOVESPA Corporate Sustainability Index (ISE), the Johannesburg Stock Exchange Socially Responsible Investment Index, and the Wiener Börse VÖNIX Sustainability Index.
2. Sector-specific indexes offer a spotlight for a narrow section of investable firms filtered for ESG performance, typically in relation to clean technology, sustainable energy, and environmental services. Successful development and market acceptance leads to index licensing for the creation of exchange-traded funds (ETFs). Such indexes include Deutsche Börse's DAXglobal Alternative Energy Index and the Nasdaq OMX Clean Edge Global Wind Energy Index.

Strategic design decisions will improve the attractiveness to buyers or licensees. Index design must cover a basic understanding of legal and compliance requirements where investment products are to be licensed. The purpose of the vehicle is to balance the trade-off between building a sophisticated infrastructure and keeping costs of ongoing maintenance and marketing low to generate a high return on effort invested.

Differentiation: Importance of the Right Criteria

The criteria are the greatest source of differentiation but also create tensions and ongoing costs of production. For example, quality research based on extensive criteria is not an inexpensive proposition. In a sustainability index that addresses a specific theme, the criteria selection and index weightings are based on the index provider's unique methodology and skill set for calculating sustainability scores. Strategic design decisions affect the attractiveness of indexes for buyers or licensees.

Criteria should allow for best practice of both large and small companies, with many smaller companies not having the same lens on them historically. In order to concentrate on impacts, not inputs, and perhaps most controversially, the index criteria should attempt to focus on what the performance actually is versus what companies say, for example, about sales in target populations in target countries.

The JSE SRIX in 2010 attracted negative attention for application of criteria. Environmental nongovernmental organizations (NGOs), such as the Centre for Environmental Rights, the Endangered Wildlife Trust, and the Environmental Monitoring Group have been pressuring the JSE SRI Index based on their rankings of eight firms that the NGOs consider not worth a ranking on an ESG-mandated index. The JSE SRIX listed eight companies that had transgressions reported in the South African Department of Environmental Affairs' National Environmental Compliance and Enforcement Reports.[4]

Importance of Securing Stakeholders

Any individual, group, or business with a vested interest (a stake) in the success of an organization is considered to be a stakeholder. In general, a stakeholder can be one of two types: internal (from within an organization) or external (outside of an organization). Examples of stakeholders are owners, managers, shareholders, investors, employees, customers, partners, and suppliers, among others.

The ability to bring different stakeholders together is often demonstrated in the convening partners' ability to draft agreements for the index criteria.

The ranking of companies may be based on a methodology and criteria developed by subject matter expert partners, delivered by professional ratings agencies and academic institutions, and with index provider partners providing technology and administration. Clarifying the objectives of stakeholder consultation will ensure that the engagement process is the most effective at garnering the information needed to finalize the methodology.[5] The objectives of the stakeholder consultation include gathering stakeholder feedback and generating buy-in for the methodology (criteria, weights, indicators, and evaluation/scoring guidance, etc.)

Typical index stakeholders include:

- International organizations (e.g., the World Business Council for Sustainable Development [WBCSD])
- International and/or national not-for-profit organizations (e.g., World Wildlife Fund, Global Fund)
- Financial services institutions (e.g., PricewaterhouseCoopers)
- Sustainable investment-related not-for-profit organizations (e.g., Carbon Disclosure Project, Global Compact, PRI, Global Reporting Initiative)
- In-country stock exchanges (e.g., the Istanbul Stock Exchange)
- Media, especially business media online and hardcopy, television (e.g., *Newsweek*).
- ESG research vendors (e.g., EIRIS for JSE SRIX)

Unfortunately, many stakeholders rush to "build" a sustainability index without some important design thinking. A weakness, either in the initial index or observed later in its life cycle, may be the result of the rush to build a complex, multistage, multistakeholder index without careful consideration. Better indexes seek representation of reputable players in a consortium with a strong recent history in the sustainability subject area and proven ability to engage. The index stakeholder consortium will seek some mainstream representation from major investors in developed and emerging economies, issue experts in the particular sustainability area, and index engineers. To improve rigor and authenticity, indexes and their stakeholder processes link themselves to academics at business, policy, and scientific research institutions and universities.

A successful index will need stakeholder goodwill and convening power to establish a workable consensus. Representation by industry is critical in at least two different contexts—investors and research providers—but the players may be different and even competitive. Representation should cover both the potential users of the index (investors, asset owners, companies, and others in philanthropy, policy, academic, and NGO circles) and contributors to the quality of the ranking and criteria (NGOs, academics, media, foundations, and companies). A key to success is having the skill and energy to design then build this multistakeholder initiative leading up to the launch. More funding will ensure better accountability and probably better architecture and methodology. Finally, index administration vendors (FTSE, Dow Jones, Standard & Poor's, and MSCI) play a small mechanical role in calculating and operating indexes but a larger and potentially important role as distributors and marketers of indexes. As index specialist providers, these organizations are important partners to the success of many indexes. Other major roles for institutionalizing, researching, and marketing the index range from international and not-for-profit organizations, to stock exchanges, banks, and investment managers.

Examples of index roles include:

- *Investment data providers.* Investment and company-comparative data (e.g., Bloomberg, Morningstar, INET, Reuters)
- *Research and analysis firms* (e.g., MSCI ESG, Sustainalytics, Trucost, EIRIS, Glamis, Solaron, ThomsonReutersAsset4)
- *Index marketing organizations* (e.g., Dow Jones, FTSE, MSCI, S&P)
- *Index operations and calculations* (e.g., MSCI, Dow Jones, FTSE, S&P)
- *Index overall management.* Universities, industry associations, stock exchanges, or special-purpose not-for-profit organizations

RESEARCH QUALITY AND INDEPENDENCE

Research providers should be sourced from commercial, NGO, and academic worlds with sustainable revenue and/or funding models to ensure that quality research grows over time. With free research, you typically get what you pay for. Core research providers may include a model supplementing for-profit research with not-for-profit or academic input, which avoids a weakness in verifying data and analysis that does not have academic or third-party rigor. The criteria may be dependent on the skill and quality of research providers: for example, on a new theme or in a new geography, where no current detailed coverage of company sustainability efforts is currently covered by research houses.

Another example of ESG coverage models is EIRIS (www.eiris.com), the not-for-profit ESG research firm based in London. In August 2010, EIRIS partnered with the South African University of Stellenbosch Business School to conduct research underpinning the JSE SRI Index, reviewing 143 companies. Less research makes for cheaper operations. More research leads to more rigor and better impact. Indexes need to be reliable, and reliability is a function of the criteria and the adjudication process and the mechanics of ensuring that the data points are filtered through various stages to deliver the ranking results. Data, criteria, and judges form the crucial triumvirate. Reliability of the underlying data from companies through, for example, external verification or certification (in 2009, the JSE SRI observed 20/60 companies using verification of some sort) is one useful mechanism. As more than one paper has expressed, only a few raters provide sufficient disclosure for stakeholders to understand how the ratings are constructed; those that are most transparent have the best potential to take hold and garner credibility, and therefore both corporate and investor confidence.

Just as credit ratings agencies have been compelled to be more transparent about their process in the United States and elsewhere, so one may expect that sustainability ratings will need to be more transparent even where the actual methodology "black box" is some kind of competitive advantage. Compared to a simple ranking, more substantial and investment-ready indexes developed by index vendors require rigorous methodologies and assessment of their value and development costs. (For instance, compare the complex committee structure and seven-factor criteria for selecting for the Domini 400 versus the ranked, self-recommended companies of the *Fortune* 100 Best Companies to Work For.)

LESSONS FROM THE LEADING SUSTAINABILITY INDEXES

Building sustainability indexes is complicated. Indexes must be clear in order to create focus. Criteria matters, as do longevity and consistency. The next sections describe a variety of indexes in detail.

General ESG Indexes

Indexes taking ESG factors and criteria into account are discussed next.

KLD 400 Social Index   The KLD 400 Social Index has been in existence since May 1990. It selects large U.S. companies using ESG criteria while seeking maximum performance and underlies the ETF known as iShares FTSE KLD 400 Social Index Fund. Over the years, the KLD 400 has come to send many other messages and has used primarily backward-looking criteria (e.g., company violations filed with the Securities and Exchange Commission), but it is one of the two most invested-against indexes using ESG criteria in the United States.

The KLD 400 has presented an opportunity to observe ESG factors at play in decisions regarding major U.S. listed equities. For example, many of the studies on the impacts of ESG factors in investment in whole or part reference the performance of the index and the investment vehicles that were licensed against it. Investment firms can purchase the index list as a "buy list" or a license to the entire index to build their own investments products. At present, Green Century has licensed the KLD 400 for a mutual fund, while iShares offers an ETF. One of the largest U.S. asset owners, TIAA-CREF, has long relied on KLD data for investment as a way of keeping its costs low.[6] KLD has had its critics over time but has long been a leader in the field. Criticism has included having decent policy and procedure analysis, however inconsistent environmental impacts data.[7] Since MSCI acquired RiskMetrics in June 2010 (and in the process, acquired legacy SRI data providers KLD and Innovest which had been previously acquired by RiskMetrics) the future for its ESG research, and therefore its indexes, will be interesting to watch.

Dow Jones Sustainability Index   The other most invested-against source of ESG data is that which backs the Dow Jones Sustainability Index (DJSI), as researched by Sustainable Asset Management (SAM). (For more on SAM, see Chapter 6.)

FTSE4Good Index Series   The FTSE4Good Index Series was designed to measure the performance of companies that meet globally recognized corporate responsibility standards and to facilitate investment in those companies. FTSE4Good sells the Index Series as an ideal basis for "retail socially responsible investment products and for fulfilling institutional mandates."[8] As with all FTSE indexes, FTSE4Good has transparency, clarity, and independence. The FTSE4Good Index Series was launched in 2001 from the London Stock Exchange. Currently, about 40% of all eligible companies worldwide meet the FTSE4Good criteria, which broadly indicate that the criteria require a level of corporate responsibility practice that may be challenging but can certainly be attained.

FTSE4Good criteria have encouraged a significant improvement in human rights and environmental policy and management system transparency across a wide range of sectors. All revenue from license agreements is donated by FTSE to UNICEF. To date, FTSE has already raised over $2.5 million for UNICEF. The FTSE4Good Policy Committee's role is to:

- Act as an independent judge of the ability of constituent companies to meet the FTSE4Good Index Series criteria.
- Oversee the consultation process undertaken to develop criteria.
- Approve criteria revisions or new criteria.

Since the index series was launched, the environmental criteria and human rights criteria have been strengthened. The FTSE4Good inclusion criteria are designed to be challenging but achievable in order to encourage companies to try to meet them. For companies, FTSE4Good positions the benefits of index membership as:

- Managing environmental and social risk
- Reputation
- Cost savings
- Brand marketing
- License to operate

Country-Level ESG Indexes

Sustainability indexes have acted for years as a signal regarding a universe of companies, typically in more developed countries, such as the United States and the United Kingdom. As EMs became more interesting destinations for institutional investors in the last decade, the interest of investment stakeholders in raising the sustainability issue to investors and growing institutional investors' appetite for new investment themes in remote countries helped create the context for the development of country-level indexes for frontier and emerging markets.

The World Summit on Sustainable Development in Johannesburg 2002, the ten-year anniversary of the watershed Rio 1992 Summit that among other things introduced the Kyoto Protocol, created the impetus for the first-ever emerging markets index, the JSE SRI index. Other country ESG indexes followed that development in 2004, including those in Brazil, South Korea, Egypt, Malaysia, China, and India. Others continue to be added; for example, the Istanbul Stock Exchange Sustainability Index is scheduled for launch in December 2011.

A country index considers the appeal to regional and global sustainability investors and stakeholders and may consider, for example, how it may be combined as a composite of global regions using a construction mapped from the most commonly used investment indexes (e.g., DJ Global, FTSE Global, MSCI Emerging Markets).

South Africa: JSE SRI Index   The JSE SRI Index has been a catalyst for debating how and in what form ESG can be implemented in equity investment in South Africa. The reaction in the investment ecosystem may be mixed and sometimes difficult to attribute beyond anecdotal evidence. In the two-year engagement the JSE has pursued with JSE-listed companies, increased ESG disclosure from these companies has been experienced. At a very basic level, this alone has forced people at these companies to grapple with the question of what exactly is sustainability. Many of the JSE-listed companies targeted are in sectors that have major social and environmental effects, and as a result, they are subject to greater scrutiny.

Brazil: Índice de Sustentabilidade Empresarial   Launched with International Finance Corporation (IFC) funding in December 2005 at the International Conference on Sustainable Finance in Emerging Markets in São Paolo, Brazil, the Bovespa Corporate Sustainability Index (Índice de Sustentabilidade Empresarial [ISE]) is the first index tracking the economic, financial, corporate governance, environmental, and social performance of leading companies listed in the São Paulo Stock Exchange (BOVESPA). BOVESPA became the first stock exchange to join the signatories of the United Nations' Global Compact. As part of this process, and due to the lack of a benchmark for SRI funds, a working group was created to develop a sustainability index for the Brazilian stock market.

Developed by the Center for Sustainability Studies of Fundação Getulio Vargas, a leading business school in Brazil, the ISE seeks to include up to 40 companies that strive for excellence in managing sustainability. By rewarding companies that deliver solid economic results and incorporate ESG elements in their business model, this index, if successful, will encourage other companies and exchanges to follow its example in the race for capital. The BOVESPA Corporate Sustainability Index is revised annually to ensure that it reflects the real business sustainability level of listed companies and incorporates the evolution of sustainability practices and theoretical benchmarks. In launching the ISE, BMandF BOVESPA and the Fundação Getúlio Vargas sought to develop an investment product that could be used by responsible investors to facilitate the investment process, either by buying securities issued to track the ISE or by using the analysis performed by the index managers as proxies in their own investment decisions. The ISE was designed "to create an efficient investment mechanism to group companies with superior performance that manage environmental, social, and governance risks and opportunities."[9]

Thematic Indexes

General country or issue-level benchmarking exercises, such as the Transparency International Corruption Perceptions Index, Carbon Disclosure Project Leadership Index, and the Ease of Doing Business, are useful tools, but investors often need more detailed and company-specific coverage. Newer thematic indexes include those presented next.

Healthy Living Index: SAM Sustainable Healthy Living Fund The SAM Sustainable Healthy Living Fund is designed to invest from the global stock universe in the most attractive enterprises along the health value-added chain. For this purpose, those trends that influence the Healthy Living sector are investigated in the first step by means of macroeconomic analysis.

Carbon Leaders Index: CDLI (CDP/Innovest) The CDLI scores for the Global 500, Europe, FTSE 350, and S&P 500 companies are used by index provider Markit to create a family of equity indexes.

Access to Medicine Index: ATMI Companies ranked on eight criteria (e.g., pricing, research and development) by awarding 5 points for best practices in data collected through publicly available sources and interviews with company executives and stakeholders. The objective is to supply stakeholders with independent and reliable information on the efforts of individual pharmaceutical companies to improve global access to medicines and to provide pharmaceutical companies and the public a transparent means to assess, monitor, and improve their performance.

***Newsweek* Green Rankings** The *Newsweek* Green Rankings are data-driven assessments of the largest companies in the United States and the world. The goal is to cut through greenwashing and quantify the actual environmental footprints, policies, and reputations of the largest 500 U.S. and global 100 companies. To do this, *Newsweek* teamed up with three leading environmental research organizations to create what it calls the most comprehensive rankings available. MSCI ESG Research, formerly KLD, performed a policy and procedure analysis; Trucost performed a quantitative measurement of environmental performance assessment; and CorporateRegister.com performed an informed reputational survey. The Green Rankings methodology was created in consultation with an advisory panel convened by *Newsweek*.

S&P IFCI Carbon Efficient Index The S&P/IFCI Carbon Efficient Index[10] measures the performance of investable emerging market companies with relatively low carbon emissions while closely tracking the returns of the S&P/IFCI Large MidCap Index. All constituents are ranked within their respective GICS®. The S&P/IFCI Carbon Efficient Index retains many of the same constituents as the S&P/IFCI Large MidCap Index, but with index weight adjustments made due to comparisons among companies within the same global sectors, utilizing the Carbon Footprint metric. The Carbon Footprint is calculated by Trucost and is defined as the company's annual greenhouse gas emissions assessment, expressed as tons of carbon dioxide equivalent, divided by annual revenues. Through a set of well-defined rules, the index seeks to closely track the return of the S&P/IFCI Large MidCap Index while lowering the total carbon emissions of the index portfolio as a whole.

COMPANY REACTIONS TO INDEXES AND THEIR IMPACTS

Measuring performance is intrinsic to investment. Index membership literally confers "investment grade" on firms because numerous managed funds are benchmarked to or directly invested in these indexes. Where the index is themed, selection into the club confers a certain halo effect or positive association for that company because there has been a dramatic increase in the scale of funds that directly track market indexes. Gaining and maintaining membership in an index club is often a critically important goal for company executives.

A driver for company and investor action is competition, leveraging the competitive nature of the market and how companies rate and rank against each other. As with any differentiating characteristic, companies seek to gain competitive advantage with investors, prospective employees, and other stakeholders, and a high ranking in an index can give them such an advantage.

Company characteristics must be clear about publicly listed versus privately held or illiquid securities. When a company is ranked or included in an influential or prestigious index, it will refer to that fact, especially when the firm is looking to present credentials for its own credibility. For example, Brazil petroleum major Petrobras lists five accreditations on a full-page color advertisement in a magazine targeted at investors and company executives, including membership in the DJSI.[11] Exclusion from an index can encourage companies to pledge changes or otherwise raise their game. Positive impacts of indexes ranking companies includes company changes in behavior, organizational structure, establishing new lines of business or acquisitions, increased reporting, and reduced negative impacts.

One of the best examples of testing for impact is the study by IFC on the BOVESPA ISE. Conducted in 2010, it tested the ISE's impact on strengthening sustainability practices of member companies. Findings and conclusions were based on over 40 key performance indicators over time. Firms report valuable benefits in terms of improved sustainability practices, better reputation, and, to some extent, positive impacts on their stock price, access to capital, and liquidity in the stock market. The major benefits seem to be in terms of the companies' own review of their sustainability practices, leading to increased competitiveness, satisfaction of being a responsible company, and improved reputation.

Matching Desired Impact with Index Construction

Sustainability indexes have provided a signal for the viability and feasibility—both the "why" and the "how"—of making sustainable investment happen. Many indexes fail to generate the impact expected or are merely marginally effective. Sustainability indexes should identify types of companies, in target regions, that will generate the positive impact toward alleviating sustainability required.[12] The need must be explicit and measurable. Index construction must match the desired impact.

Of course, change is to be expected, and indexes must be expected to change too. Of the 108 ratings in the "Rate the Raters" project,[13] only 21 existed in 2000; the vast majority have emerged only within the last decade. Even established indexes cannot avoid serious criticism (e.g., DJSI attracted a debate in 2009 in "Is the Dow Jones Sustainability Index Worth a Damn?"[14]), The outcomes of the index may determine its utility, and every index will attract naysayers. An ignored index is the weakest of all. For example, when Halliburton was named in September 2010 to the DJSI as both a North American and a world leader, meaning that it was considered to be in the top 10% among companies in the oil field services sector, the sustainability blogosphere lit up.[15]

Sustainability indexes have positive and negative attributes.[16] Proprietary screening/ranking tools and investment-driven screening and rating systems:

- Use clear-cut methodologies to evaluate company practices or create indexes of socially responsible companies.
- Help to assess basic indexes, creating a list of "socially responsible companies" that excludes "sin stocks" (tobacco, nuclear power plant owners, weapons manufacturers).
- Collect and analyze data to rank companies according to social practices.

There are trade-offs to sustainability indexes. Advantages include that they:

- Help investors make informed choices on companies to invest in and support based on company's ESG performance.
- Contribute new knowledge on company practices through surveys and other data gathering.

- Help identify risky behavior and relative performance across ESG topics (environment and governance).
- Simplify investment selection choices.
- Also pay some limited attention to potential upsides (e.g., part of MSCI's environmental score is tied to whether a company has upside exposure to the green megatrend).

Disadvantages include:

- Low company response to surveys (around 25%), thus leaving much research without any formal company input.
- "Survey fatigue" among companies results in poor-quality data.
- Most effective in area of risk management. Indexes are only about "avoiding bad," and rankings focus on responsibility without thinking about a link to value.
- Lack appropriate models to truly evaluate upside from ESG actions.
- Frequency of ESG reviews and costs associated with large company universes result in a lag factor to ESG changes.
- Black box orientation of indexes with intellectual property barriers reduces clarity and confidence in operations of index rules.

SUMMARY

A key driver for company and investor action is competition: leveraging the competitive nature of markets, how companies rank against one another, as well as how investment portfolios compare to benchmarks. Competition is fierce, and likely to become fiercer, in the investment index marketplace with new indexes launching often. As the sustainability theme becomes less about a niche and more part of business as usual, both companies and investment firms must keep demonstrating their innovation or differentiation.

Ratings, rankings, and indexes are useful for promoting sustainable investment, but the common view is that "most existing sustainable indexes are the result of a partnership between CSR rating agencies and index providers." In 2010, the IFC engaged Esty Environmental Partners to research EM sustainability indexes. The project built on the boom in the number of such indexes being launched over the past decade. Esty Environmental Partners (EEP) identified 17 emerging markets indexes, with the vast majority being introduced in 2009 and 2010. Efforts are under way to develop two additional EM indexes in 2011, in Mexico and Turkey.

A sustainability index is a sustainable investment product that is inherently scalable; by incorporating ESG factor analysis into its design and execution, the index may significantly reduce the transaction costs for investors to access sustainable investment. A sustainability index creates an important benchmark for investors and companies, sending a powerful signal to companies about sustainability best practices and clarity on sustainability when dealing with investment decisions. In the past decade, there has been "a proliferation of initiatives to create sustainability indexes in a number of emerging markets ... however, to date these indexes have yet to deliver on their potential."[17]

At thematic and country levels, the opportunity for sustainability indexes to present sustainable investment entry points to global emerging markets investors is only slowly being taken up. Some argue that indexes are a feature of mature markets with less inherent risk and volatility, while sustainability is a new and emerging theme. But perhaps it is exactly because there is a need for an interpretation of the new sustainability theme, that the bundled solution of an index has a role to play. For example, sustainability indexes have acted as benchmarks in both developed economies and emerging markets. Thematic indexes, ranging from clean tech, to green real estate, to sustainable lifestyles, have introduced a next generation of benchmarks. The company constituents in sustainability indexes have exhibited a range of reactions, including a positive demand for inclusion in certain sustainability indexes as companies have been seeking the halo effect of a positive ranking. Sustainability indexes retain the potential to improve, to mature as investment structures, and provide utility to sustainable investment practitioners, stakeholders, and marketplaces.

NOTES

1. money.cnn.com/data/dow30/
2. Martin Gold, "The Impact of Index Trackers on Shareholders and Stock Volatility," 2009. www.qfinance.com/investment-management-best-practice/the-impact-of-index-trackers-on-shareholders-and-stock-volatil?full
3. Dan Siddy, Delsus Limited, "Exchanges and Sustainable Investment," report prepared for the World Federation of Exchanges, August 2009. http://delsus.com/
4. "JSE'S Green Index Gets Red Light from NGOs." www.iol.co.za/jse-s-green-index-gets-red-light-from-ngos-1.1004401
5. Terrence Guay, Jonathan Doh, and Graham Sinclair, "Non-Governmental Organizations, Shareholder Activism, and Socially Responsible Investmetns," *Journal of Business Ethics* 52 (2004): 125–139.
6. Scott Budde, *Compelling Returns* (Hoboken, NJ: John Wiley & Sons, 2008).
7. www.hks.harvard.edu/m-rcbg/CSRI/publications/workingpaper_33_chatterjie tal.pdf

8. www.ftse.com/Indices/FTSE4Good_Index_Series/Information_for_Investors/ Investors_information.jsp

9. "BM and FBOVESPA Sustainability Index and the Responsible Practices of Brazilian Corporations," IFC Issue Brief, February 2011. www.ifc.org/ifcext/ sustainability.nsf/AttachmentsByTitle/fly_BovespaBrief/$FILE/fly_BovespaBrief .pdf

10. www.standardandpoors.com/indices/sp-ifci-carbon-efficient/en/us/?indexId= sp-ifci-carbon-efficient

11. *Bloomberg Markets*, December 2009.

12. Lucian Bebchuk, Alma Cohen, and Allen Ferrell, "What Matters in Corporate Governance?" *Review of Financial Studies* 22, No. 2 (2009): 783–827. www.rfs.oxfordjournals.org/cgi/content/full/22/2/783

13. www.sustainability.com/library/rate-the-raters-phase-three

14. www.grist.org/article/2009-09-14-dow-jones-sustainability-index-worth-a-damn/

15. R. P. Siegel, "When Pigs Fly: Halliburton Makes the Dow Jones Sustainability Index," September 24, 2010. www.triplepundit.com/2010/09/when-pigs-fly-halliburton-makes-the-dow-jones-sustainability-index/?utm_source=feedburn erandutm_medium=feedandutm_campaign=Feed%3A+TriplePundit+%28 Triple+Pundit%29

16. Marla Brill, "Sustainability Indexes: Pros and Cons: Environmental, Social and Governance Criteria Are the Basis," FA Green September 2009. www.fa-mag.com/component/content/article/14-features/4445.html?Itemid=131

17. IFC Request for Proposals #09-CSB–04082010, Sustainability Index Study/ Instruments for Sustainable Investing, Date of Issuance April 12, 2010.

CHAPTER 33

How Asset Owners Can Achieve a Sustainable Investing Framework

Roger Urwin

In this chapter, industry thought leader Roger Urwin shares his perspective on asset owners and how they should, in many cases, seek and achieve a sustainable investing perspective to their modeling and asset allocation.

Sustainable investing (SI) and its cousin, responsible investing (RI), have a growing footprint in the institutional investment world. But it would be wrong to say they have yet had a major influence on the allocations of institutional investors. This is not surprising as innovations go. Whenever there is new investment thinking, it takes a while to become mainstream. The RI/SI industry has the additional obstacle of the confusing legal context of fiduciary duty to overcome, particularly where pension funds are concerned. It follows that RI/SI strategies have to be seen as *better than* traditional strategies to establish their credibility. Asset owners need strong and coherent investment beliefs to overcome this hurdle.

This chapter focuses on SI as encompassing long-term, returns-driven strategies that integrate environmental, social, and/or governance factors in investment decision-making. The result is long-term investing that is efficient and fair in intergenerational terms, positioning SI in line with fiduciary principles of loyalty to all beneficiaries without undue bias to any one segment.

IMPORTANCE OF VALUES AND BELIEFS

The SI proposition can be presented in a matrix of sorts comprising values (from which the mission is derived) and beliefs (from which the investment strategy is derived).

Where a fund is positioned on this matrix is central to the SI debate. To date, funds have found strong reasons to adopt a values-based position, and this correlates with the opening observation on limited allocations to SI or RI.

Funds have clustered in the traditional socially responsible investment mission, and the vast majority of institutional funds have a finance-driven mission, making the dual mission seemingly inappropriate. But it is perplexing why more funds don't think more positively about their sustainable mission. My experience has shown that this "mission" often has not been thought through, and when funds do address it, they often benefit. This mission conforms to legal imperatives, seems to do a better job with the reputational issues in the environmental, social, and governance (ESG) area, and arguably has more legitimacy with members and other stakeholders.

Further movement toward SI often emerges from investment beliefs. Beliefs encompass the principles and high-level thinking about how the investment world works and how to achieve investment success. Developing effective beliefs is time consuming and challenging but yields considerable financial benefits. It has become an investment approach that is increasingly practiced by institutional investors.[1]

The process of specifying beliefs allows investment committees to be more coherent and logical when making decisions. Given the large amount of information potentially relevant to investment decisions, the discipline of inserting beliefs in the decision-making process allows fiduciaries to avoid information overload and concentrate on key issues. Furthermore, by making investment thinking more transparent, there is greater clarity for all interested parties as to the arguments embedded in the funds' investment decisions.

But there are three problems with applying to beliefs to SI strategies:

1. Historical results for SI do not go back that far in time, with the consequence that past results cannot be relied on to inform assumption setting with regard to other investment opportunities.
2. Given the dynamic external environment, there will likely be significant differences between past and future results.
3. The subject requires an expanded frame of reference to consider results both in financial terms, and also with respect to extrafinancial factors.

There is one further critical consideration. Fiduciary boards are rightly concerned to make decisions that are in keeping with the high standards expected of them and not tainted by any possibility of bias. This raises the bar for validating SI strategies with increased requirements for transparency.

So beliefs are a problem. But then they are very much the solution as well.

INTEGRATED ALLOCATIONS AND TARGETED ALLOCATIONS

Institutional investment at its core is a two-level decision. The hierarchy starts with *asset allocation*, how much will be allocated to the major investment groupings: equities, bonds, real estate, and so on. The strategy is completed with *mandate allocation*. The managers who have been delegated portfolio responsibilities are given asset allocation benchmarks that, when aggregated across all mandates, ensure overall conformity with the target asset allocation.

We see two distinct approaches to SI. There is the integrated approach, where ESG and active ownership are key elements of the mandate. Then there is the targeted approach, which focuses on asset allocation, where specialist investment is allocated into ESG-related themes such as clean tech, renewable energy, and water.

The key characteristics in an integrated ESG mandate are the obligations on the manager and the asset owner, which can be summarized this way:

- The manager should assess ESG factors in the investment process, take an active ownership role, and report on the ESG and active ownership role and actions.
- The asset owner should describe expectations for the manager to account for ESG factors in the mandate and undertake monitoring of the ESG processes and actions of the manager.

Decisions to use this integrated ESG approach flow from the investment belief that the approach is value enhancing, producing higher returns, lower risks, or some combination of the two.

These beliefs are contextual to the fund's circumstances including:

- The fund's governance capabilities or governance budget for these activities
- The form of delegation adopted by the fund that respects its investment mandates

- The capabilities of the fund's managers in undertaking ESG or active ownership work
- The effectiveness of the implementation of ownership actions through the fund's custodian
- Whether the fund's oversight of its managers' actions adds value on a net of costs basis

While these arguments have merit, and integrated approaches to SI are a growing force, more impact will occur through targeted approaches. Such approaches encompass mandates holding assets that will more directly benefit from ESG and sustainability trends such as the transition to a low-carbon economy and increased environmental regulation and natural resource efficiency. This area covers energy efficiency, renewable energy, clean tech, water, and waste and extends to human/labor rights. These investment themes can be applied to equity, private equity, infrastructure mandates, and also bonds and commodities, including carbon.

Asset allocation decisions generally employ various optimization methods to identify strategies that are optimal, or close to optimal, in having higher expected return per unit of risk. Applying this approach to sustainable strategies struggles with the data inputs where quantification of various parameters is required: beta-related items, such as expected returns, risks, and correlations; and alpha components, including, risks, and tracking error for mandates in each asset class.

With limited empirical data on which to base assumptions, the allocation process has had to work with other methods, the most important of which is the use of risk factors.

RISK FACTORS AND ESG BETA

While the inclusion of SI mandates is strategic in nature, ESG does not constitute a normal "asset class." Instead, the strategy is best seen as a form of overlay to existing asset classes, introducing an exposure to a particular type of risk with an associated return. The modern term for an overlay of this sort is "risk factor."

The use of risk factors is a new but growing method for adding sophistication to strategy. A common subdivision uses eight factors: equity, credit, illiquidity, insurance, skill, interest rates/duration, inflation, and currency. But the subdivision could be extended to include ESG.

This discussion is helped by first considering equity beta. This is the systematic and nondiversifiable risk source that produces sustainable returns in excess of the risk-free rate in return for the risks taken. The equity beta is made up of some fundamental components, including an ESG element—the ESG beta. ESG beta is essentially an aggregation of companies' financial exposures to environmental and social factors, the costs and benefits of dealing with these factors, and how these are changing. This exposure has an associated investment risk and return derived from systematic changes in these ESG costs and benefits.

The key step in using the ESG factor is building a view about its return potential. This comes down to a belief about whether investments that are favorably positioned on ESG will outperform those that are not. Such a belief is best approached using the technique of scenario analysis.

Scenario Analysis

The central principle of scenario analysis is building a number of possible alternative future versions for the investment landscape. Each alternative can be matched to an investment strategy that would be expected to perform robustly if those conditions were to occur.

By way of illustration, we can consider the domain of climate change and resource depletion. Scenarios for the future would address a number of areas, including:

- *Climate/resource impacts.* The progression of climate change and resource depletion and the associated impacts that would accompany them, particularly with respect to mitigation and adaptation
- *Public policy and carbon pricing.* The extent to which governments will support the science, technology, and infrastructure issues to address climate change and resource constraints using incentives and taxes (including one of the most significant: carbon pricing)
- *Technology impacts.* The impact of technologies in bringing about transitions to a lower-carbon, energy-efficient, more sustainable economy
- *Sustainable investment rent capture.* The extent to which investors are able to extract an appropriate profit or rent for their risk capital, risk exposure, and endeavor through mandates and managers and asset owner governance
- *Sustainable investment flows and pricing.* The extent to which companies or enterprises in this space, particularly those with effective management of sustainability issues, will attract growing investment flows affecting future valuation and relative cost of capital

The use of scenarios can deal with both subjective and objective inputs and so is well suited to the sustainability area. This list must be assessed carefully, given the interconnectedness and the specialized nature of these elements. But most asset owners and asset managers would be prepared to commit relative statements of conviction to each point and reach an overall conclusion as to the direction and significance of any factor.

A more expansive view of sustainability takes into account two other aspects of an institutional fund's mission: the comparative advantage in respect to its long time horizon and the intergenerational equity issue. Investors have different time horizons, with different attendant pressures to perform in both the short and the long term. Many institutional investors have a natural long-term orientation; this is certainly the case for most pension, sovereign, and endowment funds. Such funds can consider the merits of various strategic choices to exploit pricing that may well be dominated by short-term investor risk aversion. The extent to which longer-term issues, such as climate change and resource depletion, are priced into current asset prices is a contentious point.

The idea of universal ownership is relevant in this regard.[2] The holdings of many institutional funds are highly diversified across the global market and the global economy. The performance of such funds, therefore, is much more heavily dependent on the long-term progress of the economy and the global market than on individual companies.

The global nature of their holdings provides incentives for investors to use their ownership influence to produce system-wide benefits. It can also affect the magnitude of the exposure that funds might want to have to ESG-sensitive investments, which can provide a form of hedging against climate change. If widespread environmental degradation continues, a relative decline in the economic growth and performance of corporations, arising from the increases in the costs of mitigation and adaptation, would be expected. The poor financial returns that would arise in such a scenario would be offset by investments in environmental opportunities and clean technology.

QUANTITATIVE METHODS OF RISK AND RETURN

This is not to argue for a completely qualitative process. The link between qualitative beliefs and quantitative assumptions about risk and return is a critical part of most investment processes. In SI, though, there is the problem of uncertainty, which gives rise to difficulties with setting assumptions for sustainable mandates. It is worth differentiating between risk and return estimates—the principal problem lies with return estimates. To contrast, risk estimates in many sustainable mandates can be obtained by reference to assets that have had reasonably long price histories. It follows that the allocation discipline will rely more substantially on the quantification of risk than of return.

TABLE 33.1 Sample Description of Targeted Sustainability Mandate Investing in ESG Themes across Public and Private Markets

Asset types	Listed equities, private equity, infrastructure, green property, carbon credits/offsets	
Universe	Any business with >20% of revenue/capital coming from environmental technology; maximum of 70% in private markets	
Performance benchmark	Composite Index from underlying pieces	Consumer Price Index (CPI); comparison also with World Index
Performance and risk targets	Index + 1.5% per annum Tracking error of 8% per annum 3-year shortfall risk	CPI + 5% per annum over 10-year period Volatility 15% per annum 3-year shortfall risk

The process starts with a specimen of the mandate. Table 33.1 offers examples of suitable parameters.

The narrowing of the opportunity set of sustainability mandates leads to the need to consider its tracking error relative to a mainstream benchmark index.

The critical point is to give an influential position to risk control considering downside risk relative to the benchmark. This measure of "tracking error risk" can be seen as a form of regret risk. This discipline provides some control over the sustainability of the mandate through periods of underperformance.

The likely results of the process are given in Table 33.2, considering a range of different institutional funds.

While mostly based on beliefs and downside risk, any new allocation should also consider the overall risk budget, management costs, and liquidity. An important measure will be the overall risk for the whole fund with and without the sustainability element.

In summary, the process of deciding sustainability allocations cannot be a precise one; the limited empirical baseline for assumption setting and the newness of current strategies makes this inevitable. However, a pragmatic process can be followed successfully by combining a robust set of beliefs with a downside risk discipline.

MONITORING FRAMEWORK

It should be noted that this is an iterative process involving a monitoring framework. This monitoring involves reviewing the experience and

TABLE 33.2 Likely Results

Fund Characteristics	Allocations of Assets to Integrated ESG	Allocations of Assets to Targeted ESG
Corporate pension fund with midlevel governance	Nil	Nil
Corporate pension fund with strong governance and beliefs in ESG	Up to 50%	Up to 4%
Public pension fund with dual mission	Up to 75%	Up to 6%
Sovereign wealth fund	Up to 75%	Up to 8%
Defined contribution fund choice based on member wishing to invest in line with certain values in sustainability	Up to 50%	Up to 8%
Endowment fund with sustainable mission and ESG beliefs	Up to 50%	Up to 8%

Source: Adapted from R. Urwin, *Allocations to Sustainable Investing*, Towers Watson Technical Paper 165695, PRI Academic Conference, Copenhagen, 2010. www.unpri.org/academic10/Copenhagen_v5.pdf

outcomes of the allocation process and making periodic adjustments. Part of the process will involve revisiting beliefs that are convictions of relative likelihood rather than absolute certainty. This process of revision is essentially Bayesian, adjusting assumptions to reflect new experience. As the sustainability field is still developing, the influence of new experience is likely to be more influential over time than in other areas, where a greater body of empirical results and experience can be drawn on. The influence of feedback is particularly important, as these decisions need greater justification in pure financial terms. Effective monitoring would quantify both financial and extra-financial outcomes. The most critical function of monitoring is that funds assess the performance potential of an effective long-term strategy, irrespective of any possible short-term underperformance.

There is growing evidence of SI through funds and managers becoming part of the United Nations Principles of Responsible Investing (PRI). Funds that adhere to these principles undertake, consistent with their fiduciary duties, to commit to six principles including these two:

We will incorporate ESG issues into investment analysis and decision-making processes.

We will be active owners and incorporate ESG issues into our ownership policies and practices.

The processes in this chapter should help with the monitoring of PRI adherence. The allocation framework helps funds with the implementation issues with these two principles, while the framework helps both funds and investment managers to demonstrate their adherence to these principles.

SUMMARY

There is one further area of beliefs to consider relating to the governance of individual funds: The challenges of dealing with sustainable strategies are considerable, and it follows that successful implementation of such strategies will be correlated with strong governance.

Sustainable investing continues to suffer from three obstructions:

1. The newness of this investment thinking and practice, which, in a conservative industry, takes a while to become mainstream
2. The stringent requirements for "pure finance" support for the strategies
3. The lack of accepted process for its adoption, given limited empirical data

The SI model advocated in this chapter is financially superior to traditional investment models. It has the support of solid finance standing behind it. It has the collateral support of certain critical benefits that it delivers to society. The fact that it is difficult to implement is the only thing that stands in the way of its widespread adoption. It can be made simpler if funds work toward a better framework.

The information in this chapter attempts to set a clearer framework for making progress with SI strategies by concentrating on two components: investment beliefs and downside risk control relative to the mainstream market. The central discipline in allocations to sustainable mandates covers these four points:

1. All allocations require the articulation of investment beliefs that present the performance case after risks and costs are taken into account.
2. Quantification of return estimates is too uncertain for direct use in the allocation process, but quantification of risk estimates can be used.
3. The allocation should be scaled by reference to conviction reflecting beliefs, governance, and mission considerations.
4. The target limit to the allocation should reflect the ability of the asset owner through a stress test of expected performance cycles, hence the use of discipline measuring risk relative market benchmarks.

This chapter also promotes the significance of the monitoring process that informs future iterations of the process and reports on the return on both the pure financial mission and the extrafinancial mission. The opportunities for such an expanded monitoring model will play a considerable part in increasing the influence of PRI. There is considerable work ahead in the industry to provide the tools necessary to support this extrafinancial accounting; more measures, benchmarks, and decision tools are required.

It appears inevitable that sustainability will have a major influence on the shape of economic and financial markets over the coming decades. Given the twin pressures of environmental and social change, SI will take a steadily increasing profile in the institutional funds area, provided it gets the support of a stronger investment framework.

NOTES

1. G. L. Clark and R. Urwin, "Best Practice Investment Management," *Journal of Asset Management* 9(1): 12–21 (2007).
2. A. William and J. Hawley, "The Emergence of Universal Owners," *Challenge, The Magazine of Economic Affairs* 43 (4): 43–61 (2000).

CHAPTER 34

On Performance

Bud Sturmak and Cary Krosinsky

As mentioned frequently throughout the book, sustainability issues have been increasing in relevance over time and are now perhaps more relevant than ever. Measuring a corporation's ESG performance is crucial to understanding how it operates and provides a far more complete picture than financial statements alone. Ongoing research and industry developments continue to demonstrate the financial materiality and opportunities presented by the more positive strand of sustainable investing. The evidence is becoming undeniable: Companies with strong and positively focused ESG profiles are outperforming traditional rivals.

In many ways, the first wave of socially responsible investing (SRI) has become a stumbling block that sustainable investing must overcome on the path to becoming a mainstream investment strategy. SRI is generally defined as a values-based strategy that can be restrictive in nature. SRI mutual funds are not universally appealing, as many necessarily focus on different mandated sets of stringent values that can be ethical and/or religious as well as socially and/or environmentally focused.

By contrast, issues concerning sustainability and the environment should be universally appealing. Sustainable or environmental, social, and governance (ESG) integrated funds offer a unique and distinct approach from traditional SRI funds and are focused on forward-looking issues and opportunities that can drive investment performance.[1] By seeking to identify industry leaders with competitive advantages, sustainable investing is a long-term strategy that is designed to outperform. Additionally, the sustainable approach to investing utilizes metrics that were not previously material to most company's share prices. In examining performance, one must take into account the fact that sustainable investing and ESG analysis were not mature fields until the last decade, perhaps even more recently than that. In fact, the ESG data industry is still maturing and evolving as we speak, as are investment methodologies.

SRI TECHNIQUES

Techniques vary widely within SRI, from investing in a benchmark index that excludes alcohol, tobacco, firearms, and gambling to investing in clean tech. As noted, some of these core SRI approaches are distinct from sustainable strategies that focus on ESG analysis. Therefore, when examining performance, it is crucial to separate studies that focus on the older forms of SRI investing from more recent studies that are focused on the more positively defined form of sustainable investing. One must be cautious regarding studies that don't make this differentiation.

In the fall of 2007, one of the more widely regarded performance studies, "Demystifying Responsible Investment Performance," was released by Mercer and the United Nations Environmental Programme's Finance Initiative (UNEP FI). This study of studies examined 20 key academic studies focused on SRI and investment performance and concluded, "There does not appear to be a performance penalty from taking ESG factors into account in the portfolio management process."[2] There are several key problems with this study. The majority of the studies included in this analysis are quite dated, with most of the data focusing on the period of 1990 to 2003. The mutual fund studies in particular are almost entirely focused on the performance of ethical and religious-based strategies. The world has changed significantly over the last eight years, with ESG issues becoming more relevant by the day. ESG as we know it today arguably did not even exist for the period covered by these studies, certainly not in a robust manner. It is likely that several key SRI investment managers had not even started evolving their thinking out of their original purely negative approach during the period covered by these studies. Since the majority of these mutual fund strategies were focused on negative screens and exclusionary processes, it would be extremely difficult for them to outperform, as many studies show. None of these studies includes any of today's more sustainability focused or ESG integrated strategies.

A closer look at the Mercer/UNEP study reveals other interesting conclusions. We divided the 20 different academic studies into two groups, one focused on general ESG issues and stock performance and another group focused on SRI mutual fund performance. There are 12 studies focused on general ESG issues and stock performance, and there are eight studies specifically focusing on SRI mutual fund performance. Of the 12 studies in the first group, nine show a positive correlation between ESG and investment performance, far greater than the overall UNEP study suggests. Of the eight studies focusing on SRI mutual fund performance, one shows a positive correlation, two are neutral-positive, three are neutral, and two are negative. The studies focused on mutual fund performance fail to match the positive correlation so clearly established by the other group, which is not surprising based on the problems with SRI mutual fund strategies outlined earlier.

ESG AFFECTS INVESTMENT PERFORMANCE

An examination of more recent studies reveals far more compelling evidence that ESG factors can materially affect investment performance. The Moskowitz Prize is awarded annually for outstanding quantitative research in the field of SRI. Alex Edmans, the 2007 Moskowitz prize winner, conducted a study on the *Fortune* 100 Best Companies to Work for in America, which has been published annually since 1998. The study showed that the companies named to *Fortune*'s list consistently outperformed both the Standard & Poor's (S&P) 500 and the Russell 3000 Index by a wide margin. From 1998 to 2009, the average annualized return of the *Fortune* 100 Best Companies was +7.35% better than the S&P 500 and +7.03% better than the Russell 3000 Index. Interestingly, in the severe market downturn in 2008, the average return of the *Fortune* 100 Best was −32.70% versus −37.00% for the S&P 500 Index and −37.31% for the Russell 3000 Index. In the 2009 market rebound, the *Fortune* 100 Best Companies rebounded far more strongly than the broader markets, up +57.32% versus +26.46% for the S&P 500 and +28.34% for the Russell 3000. In 2005, the San Francisco–based fund manager Parnassus Investments created a mutual fund based on the *Fortune* 100 Best list called the Parnassus Workplace Fund. The fund has outperformed the large-cap growth median peer group by +10.98% over a three-year period and +6.64% over a five-year period ended December 31, 2010. The Parnassus Workplace Fund is ranked in the top 1% of all large-cap growth funds (a category with 1,314 funds over the three-year period and 1,108 over the five-year period).

While it may appear that the Edmans study and the *Fortune* 100 Best list are somewhat narrowly focused, a great workplace can be a proxy for a company's overall ESG performance. The *Newsweek* Green Rankings, which look through a much wider lens, examine the quantitative environmental impacts, sustainability policies, and procedures that are in place as well as an informed reputation of the largest 500 companies in America. The largest companies that were named to the *Fortune* 100 Best list and were also ranked by *Newsweek* scored quite well. Twenty-six of the 100 companies on the *Fortune* 100 Best list were ranked by *Newsweek*, with an average ranking of 126 out of 500 and an average Green Score of 77.20. This seems to suggest that companies that treat their workers well may also have higher standards with regard to the environment and corporate governance, which also suggests that corporate performance in key areas such as workplace, environmental impact, and corporate governance are not mutually exclusive of one another. Noted economist and Goldman Sachs strategist Abby Joseph Cohen recently noted, "Not surprisingly, there's a very high correlation between companies that score well on governance issues, and those that score well on sustainability, climate stewardship and community engagement."[3]

TRENDS FROM PERFORMANCE REPORTS

The performance of the companies named in the *Newsweek* Green Rankings, which have been published in 2009 and 2010, reveal a similar trend. As Marc Gunther noted in a recent article, "It turns out that over the past year, the top 100 companies in the 2009 Newsweek list outperformed the S&P 500 by 6.8%."[4] A more detailed analysis of performance of the *Newsweek* list was performed by Tom Konrad of Seeking Alpha, who concluded that greener companies outperform their brown counterparts. Konrad's research concluded that "in brown sectors, the greenest stocks strongly outperformed the brownest stocks."[5] To further explain, in more industrial sectors such as oil and gas, food and beverage, utilities and basic materials, companies that had stronger environmental performance had far superior investment performance. This outperformance may be indicative of the competitive advantage gained by those companies that are more sustainable and also the risks that may be present for companies that have poor environmental performance.

In 2010, the Moskowitz prize-winning study, "Corporate Environmental Management and Credit Risk,"' showed that companies with strong environmental track records paid lower costs for debt.[6]

Companies with poor records paid higher costs for debt and experienced lower credit ratings. The study examined data from 1995 to 2006 and found that by dividing the sample in two periods, 1995 to 2000 and 2001 to 2006, the link between a company's environmental track record and debt costs is even stronger in the more recent period. The study shows that a company's environmental track record has a direct and measurable financial impact.

Those pondering the financial materiality of sustainability, and its potential impact on investment performance should examine the activities of Goldman Sachs in recent years. In 2007, Goldman Sachs created an entirely new equity strategy incorporating ESG analysis called GS SUSTAIN. Goldman created the GS SUSTAIN Focus List, which names the companies Goldman believes are the best-positioned sustainable companies across different industries. In a 2009 Goldman Sachs report, the firm noted, "We believe the equity market is only beginning to recognize the magnitude of impact the transition to a low-carbon economy will have on companies' competitive positions and long-term valuations."[7] As noted in the *New York Times* in November 2010, "Goldman Sachs says the GS SUSTAIN Focus List, an index of the top tier of the 1,000 companies tracked, has outperformed the more generalized MSCI All Country World Index by 39.9 percent since the unit's creation in June 2007."[8]

A recent study focusing on mutual fund performance showed a strong correlation between ESG integration and outperformance, increased alpha, and lower carbon footprints. The November 2010 joint study by Trucost and RLP Capital sought to examine the affects of ESG analysis in U.S. equity mutual funds. The study measured the carbon footprints, performance, and risk of the largest ESG funds by asset size and compared the data with the largest traditionally managed funds and their median peer group data. The study showed that ESG integration led to a significant increase in alpha over traditional financial analysis. Additionally, all eight of the funds incorporating ESG analysis outperformed their Median Peer Group over a one-year period, with seven out of eight outperforming over a three-year period and five of eight outperforming over a five-year period. This study referenced data as of June 30, 2010; more recent data, as of December 31, 2010, showed that all eight of the ESG funds outperformed their Median Peer Group over the three-year period, with six out of eight outperforming over a five-year period.

Additionally, Trucost measured the carbon footprints of all funds in the study as well as those companies specifically in the S&P 500. The carbon footprints of the ESG funds were 46% smaller than those of funds in the S&P 500. In comparison to the traditional funds in the study, the funds integrating ESG analysis were on average 40% less carbon intensive. The alpha data revealed that all eight ESG funds included in the study had a three-year alpha that scored in the top quartile versus all other funds in their peer group. The average alpha percent rank for the ESG funds was 13, which translates to an alpha that is better than 87% of all other funds.

SUMMARY

We can draw three conclusions from the material presented:

1. There is a growing correlation between the best-run companies and those taking action to address ESG risks and opportunities. This correlation is now showing up in stock performance.
2. The classic SRI funds do not outperform, hence our urgency at stressing the sharp distinction between these positive and negative approaches. We do not disagree with the mantra that you have not outperformed when investing solely to your values; in fact, the studies presented here reinforce that. Separately, as we demonstrated in our first book and subsequent paper released at the UN Academic Network Conference in Ottawa[9] as well as the more recent studies referenced in this chapter, the more positive approaches can lead to outperformance.
3. Studies that do not separate out the various strands of SRI remain dominated by negative approaches that fail to outperform, drowning out the potential impact of the positive approaches. Worse, these studies hide the opportunities that sustainability offers for investors, opportunities that leading corporations are now actively and robustly pursuing.

In a changing world, companies face both increasing risk and opportunities and the likelihood of a greater performance disparity separating the laggards from the embracers. At minimum, given constrained resources, climate change, and potential regulatory impacts, business as usual seems to be the only impossibility. The opportunity to address this change in a positive way via sustainable investment strategies remains.

NOTES

1. Cary Krosinsky and Nick Robins, eds., *Sustainable Investing: The Art of Long-term Performance* (London: Earthscan, 2008), p. 21.
2. UNEP Financial Institute, "Demystifying Responsible Investment Performance" (October 2007). www.unepfi.org
3. Abby Joseph Cohen, "Perspectives on Sustainability," Ford Sustainability Report 2009/2010.
4. Marc Gunther, "Can Sustainable Investing Beat the Markets?" October 10, 2010, GreenBiz.com. www.greenbiz.com/blog/2010/10/21/can-sustainable-investing-beat-markets
5. Tom Konrad, "Buying Green Stocks Pays, But Finding Green in Brown Stocks Pays More," Seeking Alpha, October 25, 2010. http://seekingalpha.com/

article/231918-buying-green-stocks-pays-but-finding-green-in-brown-stocks-pays-more

6. http://responsiblebusiness.haas.berkeley.edu/MoskowitzPrizeWinners.html
7. Goldman Sachs, "Change Is Coming: A Framework for Climate Change—A Defining Issue of the 21st Century," GS SUSTAIN, May 21, 2009. www2.gold mansachs.com/ideas/environment-and-energy/goldman-sachs/gs-sustain/climate-change-research.pdf
8. Nathaniel Gronewold. "Corporate 'Sustainability' Push Flowers in Sluggish Economy," *New York Times*, November 17, 2010.
9. Krosinsky and Robins, *Sustainable Investing*, Chapter 2. www.unpri.org/academic09/agenda.php

CHAPTER 35

Private Equity

Graham Sinclair

Private equity (PE) is a small but strategic investment discipline with the opportunity to be an ideal fit for sustainable investment over ten-year investment horizons. Action since 2008 has seen some major new ESG initiatives in PE. The new themes emerging present promise for further interpretation and implementation of ESG in PE asset management in progressive ways.

The best-practice PE firms are active in determining risk through enhanced due diligence. Beyond the common long-term time horizon, investee companies and PE firms both have a vested interest in building firms with lower risks, higher potential returns, and better corporate governance.

The future is positive for PE, perhaps especially in sustainable investment, where investors offer longer-term capital and where more exhaustive analysis of all factors impacting company performance is the norm. In new emerging and frontier markets, the opportunities for PE and sustainability may be the greatest of all.

S ustainable investment (SI) is a fundamental investment theme that explicitly integrates environmental, social, and governance (ESG) factors in investment decisions with a view to long-term sustainable performance. This philosophy is practiced in the private equity (PE) asset class today and has continued to evolve over the past five years with an increased awareness and increased activity by PE investors and fund managers. The sustainable PE investment field has now advanced from the "why" to the "how" stage, looking into strategies to integrate ESG factors into all four stages of the

PE investment life cycle. Of the two models of investment typically used by PE firms, the fundamental active ownership model is the one that fits the SI theme; the financial engineering/governance modification model may be more problematic for the sustainability ethos.

With its unique investor-investee nexus, PE funds have the opportunity to allocate capital to tomorrow's most promising sustainability companies, products, and services. This chapter presents existing approaches, some drivers for the increase in ESG, new themes, and points to some conclusions on where the PE asset class is moving.

PRIVATE EQUITY AS A NICHE OF GENERAL ASSET MANAGEMENT

PE is a specialist discipline within the field of investment. PE funds can have geographic, business stage, balance sheet type, business size, or sector focus. Often grouped together as "alternative asset" classes with hedge funds, PE and venture capital (VC) are recognized as having a greater influence than their asset size suggests due to media interest, investment talent that migrates to their higher-fee operations, and direct involvement with investee businesses. Since the drama of barbarians at the gates of Nabisco in the 1980s, PE has remained media-worthy, especially in the developed markets where financial engineering and billion-dollar payouts have made front-page and business-page news. PE relies on sharp investment acumen and insights into business through networks and demonstrated track records, so it is not surprising that first movers have established a commanding role in the industry: The top ten firms controlled 30% of the sector's capital in 2008, just as they did in 1998.[1]

Can a niche of the asset management industry have a leveraged role for SI? The underlying models employed by PE funds, and the stakeholder reaction to the investments, present the opportunity. A comprehensive analysis[2] of PE management models outlines two distinct PE models: (1) a traditional financial investor with focus on financial engineering and selective changes in the governance model of portfolio companies and (2) a modern form of PE seeking value creation through active ownership.

Active investors are able to outperform more traditional financial investors significantly by realizing the proceeds of intervention in strategic decision making while avoiding the costs of "corporate infrastructure." In developing countries, PE investments tend to operate with relatively little corporate restructuring, such as leveraged buy-outs or more financial engineering strategies seen often in North America and Europe.[3]

PE is a relatively small but strategic investment discipline with an influential role to play in SI. PE has influence beyond its size, especially in frontier and emerging markets, because it makes a broader social and economic impact developing small growing businesses (SGBs). It does so mostly by offering capital to small and mid-tier firms expanding beyond debt financing. PE provides the opportunity to add reputation, intellectual, relationship, and financial capital to SGBs. For small, medium, and micro enterprises that survive the startup phase but are confronted with financing crunches as they grow, first venture capital and later PE are the only source of financing available beyond family and friends and the constraints of debt financing.

For the most part, PE portfolio companies have weathered the economic downturn triggered by the global financial crisis through a combination of revenue protection, production efficiencies, cost cutting, and careful working capital management. Globally, PE firms made 1,612 acquisitions in 2009, a 36% decrease from 2008.[4]

Similarly, the trendy theme of clean tech in PE has experienced some restructuring. Major asset flows into PE clean-tech funds and portfolio companies from 2004 to 2008 may have created a bubble. The global financial crisis in 2008 led to an urgent need from private equity general partners (PEGPs), and the clean-tech portfolio companies they owned, to take a critical look at the available capital and their own cost structures. Clean-tech companies, such as Tesla (before its successful NASDAQ initial public offering in 2010) and SunTech, moved to down- or right-size their operations, The fundraising boom through 2008 for clean-tech companies did insulate some firms. In the short term, the PE clean-tech funds themselves had the benefit of a large amount of capital through new funds, such as Element Partners, RockPort Capital, Kleiner Perkins, and VantagePoint. Capital was still available, but further cash calls from limited partners (LPs) were uncertain. The field of PEGPs and available clean-tech companies for positive exits has diminished, with more pain to come as PEGPs aim for exits and may be forced to take a haircut.

Investors and analysts, however, expect that the pace of deals can only increase in 2011 and beyond, such as in frontier countries including those in Africa, as more overseas corporates and banks target rapidly expanding economies, growing middle classes, and rising trade.[5]

There are the following major industry segments in private equity:[6]

1. *Venture capital.* Typically, investment at the early stage of a business. VC investors finance companies that bear risk but promise high growth thanks to the innovative nature of their technologies, products, or services. This category is sometimes broken down further: Capital prior

to VC is seed capital, which is used to finance the development of new technologies or products.

2. *Growth capital.* A stake in developing a company with a firm foothold in its market and a high-growth outlook. The purpose of this type of investment is to guide the director in devising the company's development strategy in order to create value and a strong cash position in the medium term.

3. *Distressed capital.* Funding the capital of distressed companies for which measures have been identified and implemented in order to turn the company around.

4. *Buyout.* Investment in capital to finance the acquisition of an unlisted company.

5. *Leveraged buyout (LBO).* Acquisition of a company by capital investors, in association with management of the company purchased, by using varying levels of debt that will be repaid through future cash flow. This type of deal is used to take advantage of a significant leverage effect in periods of growth.

PE'S FIT WITHIN SUSTAINABLE INVESTING

SI is practiced in the PE asset class today, and it has evolved over the past five years with an increased awareness and increased activity by PE investors and fund managers.

As a result, the PE business model—a long-term mission of supporting the development, profitability and sustainability of the investee companies in order to sell them on—fits the sustainability theme.

Beyond the common long-term time horizon, investee companies and PE firms both have a vested interest in building a firm with lower risks, higher potential returns, and better corporate governance. Their common end goal is to sell to prospective buyers or portfolio investors. This investment philosophy motivates the integration of ESG issues, both to ensure long-term returns for investors with the most complete risk/return trade-off and also to maximize positive economic impact in markets where money is invested.

The pressure for better sustainability performance by companies also has increased the demand for ESG skills as they fulfill a need to reinforce the license to operate, deal with an increased social scrutiny of how business is conducted, and deal with greater media scrutiny with higher awareness on ESG issues or increased potential impact from social media. PE firms consider that integrating ESG factors in the investment model is a way of doing business that allows a fuller appreciation of the long-term, ongoing context of the investee company.

[PE investors are] highly influential as opposed to a minority share-holder in a listed corporate. You have no liquidity so you can't just sell if you are unhappy. You need to make it work and you need to make it a better business and a more sustainable business is a better business that will command a higher multiple when one does sell. So sustainable investing makes business sense from a PE perspective.[7]

The PE sustainable investment case is still relatively new. There are barriers tied to a lack of data, lack of track records, and quite a bit of uncertainty. These barriers will be overcome by those PE leaders who see the opportunity and are willing to commit the resources to unpack it.[8]

PE firms are ready to adopt ESG principles,[9] are increasingly conscious of the principles, and are ready to develop and implement them. They increasingly consider that there is a positive link between better ESG performance and investment outcomes, despite the fact that many are unsure of how to articulate the case.

For example, the PE firm KKR states: "Early assessment of ESG issues can help in two ways. First, it can identify risks that can materially impact company value. Second, it can uncover potential areas of improvement that can enhance the success of an investment."[10] Similarly, the Carlyle Group considers that there is no conflict between incorporating ESG principles into investment decision making and generating financial returns; for Carlyle, it is rather a question of identifying "the right ESG issues [within a portfolio company], monitoring them and driving performance."[11]

Making the SI case—highlighting financial returns and/or articulating the ESG impact—is a major driver for future asset flows, products, and intellectual development in PE.

DEVELOPMENT FINANCE INSTITUTIONS LEVERAGE OF EMERGING MARKETS PRIVATE EQUITY

In actively seeking to invest in frontier markets and to promote investment marketplaces, development finance institutions (DFIs) in frontier and emerging markets have played an important role in the evolution of PE and venture capital. DFIs have been enablers, and remain important anchor investors, in PE funds managed by local and global PEGPs. It is possible therefore to find a greater proportion of PEGPs operating in emerging markets while employing some form of integrated SI/ESG process to fit client mandates. Indeed, DFI mandates often include ESG standards.

In Latin America, Africa, and some parts of Asia, most PE firms/funds are currently managing (or have managed) assets for clients with explicit

ESG mandates, such as international or regional DFIs including the International Finance Corporation (IFC) or African Development Bank. For example, in the African market, at least 15 PE fund participants—with more than $9 billion in assets under management in 2010—have a strong DFI LP base.[12] A high-profile DFI driving PE industry activity is the IFC. The IFC SI team's overall objective is to increase the quality and quantity of sustainable private equity and portfolio investment in emerging markets. IFC tools and programs supporting SI in PE include the environment and safety assessment tool for general partners (GPs), cleaner production audits of portfolio companies, and sustainability guidelines for LPs.

The positive impact of DFIs has a longer-lasting effect. Many PE funds that either have or have had mandates from DFIs continue to "slipstream" behind the methodology the DFIs use. They have ESG frameworks mapped to DFIs, such as the IFC Social and Environmental Management Systems. This is in effect a filter to help PE firms execute their ESG approaches on an annual basis and encourages investment agreements to contain appropriate environmental representations, warranties, and covenants such that projects are in compliance with host country environmental, health, safety and social requirements.[13] Similarly, the Swedish DFI Swedfund takes ESG factors into account when deciding which fund managers to invest with and monitors fund managers during the funds' life. Thirteen of the 15 funds in which Swedfund invests have signed up to ESG standards from a DFI.[14]

PE-SPECIFIC ESG METHODS

The investment committees of PE funds work through stages in assessing investment opportunities. The best approaches have an integrated strategy that leads to risk mitigation and value addition. A 2010–2011 IFC-commissioned study on sustainable investment in sub-Saharan Africa showed that Stages II and III are those during which ESG integration is the most critical.

At the preinvestment stage, there may simply be exclusions based on client mandates or the house view of the PE fund, such as on defense, tobacco, hard liquor, pornography, or political country screenings.

PE firms have developed a practical awareness of the importance of ESG issues in emerging markets for assessing management and/or business quality linked to:

- Limited resources and stakeholder reputation in public and private sectors
- Demand for skilled labor
- Need for the license to operate

- Social scrutiny and media attention in an Internet and cell phone–enabled era
- Opportunity for new markets and/or new consumers of products and services

The focus on what ESG is, and how it impacts investment decisions, is reflected in regular risk management processes. These processes address a number of sustainability issues, but the ESG factor cited the most by PE practitioners today is corporate governance. PE funds describe corporate governance as an easy win and as adding value.

The hypothesis that ESG benefits PE investors is partly borne out by the use of corporate governance. PE investors speak of corporate governance as a binary hygiene factor: Either the investee company has corporate governance that is good and/or fixable, or the company is not investable. PE investors make big bets and cannot easily extract their capital. So the binary decision is this: Invest or do not risk capital. The case for using ESG factors to explore the opportunity side of the equation is less developed, and this is where innovation can be driven going forward.

In addition, apart from country- or company-specific issues, there are sector-specific issues, such as pharmaceutical animal testing.

In the end, PE investors tend to "place value in honesty between executives and being up front and transparent, which leads to PE trusting relationship with a person."[15]

In terms of exit strategy, both the recent IFC/SinCo study in sub-Saharan Africa and the CDC/Oxfam study on PE in Africa found that exit strategies for PE in sub-Saharan Africa are different from those in developed markets:[16] With fewer opportunities for IPOs due to under-developed stock exchanges, sub-Saharan Africa PEGP exits usually will be via company sales to other PE funds or funds of funds, management buyouts, and/or sales other companies as strategic buyers.

PE funds thrive in some respects by keeping critical investment and company information from their competitors—including when it comes to reporting on ESG advantages. And in a hypercompetitive context, why should they disclose valuable information unless they are required to, one might suggest, even if that is counterintuitive from a larger sustainability construct perspective. Beyond the low-hanging fruit of industry-wide frameworks and policy statements, it is unreasonable for PEGPs to actively share intellectual property about their proprietary ESG approaches.

Initiatives, networks, and collaborations are the better way to help PE firms contribute, without exposing too much information on their competitive advantage in processes or philosophy, by driving the leaders (whether measured by asset size, influence, effort, or coverage) to increase the industry activity.

PE BEST PRACTICES AND ESG CASE STUDIES

It is unclear how many PEGPs are fully committed to a sustainable investment philosophy. Practitioners, or their institutions, may be nonspecific about actions on ESG/SI, and returns are probably a greater priority. Research in Europe, however, confirms that PE firms are seeking to adopt ESG principles. The 2010 Ethos survey[17] describes that while PE investment houses remain unfamiliar with the practical implications of responsible investment, they are increasingly conscious of the principles and ready to develop and implement them. The majority of the 21 survey respondents said they took ESG issues into consideration for investment decisions, although just eight had adopted management procedures to guarantee that process. The gap between policies and actions is worrying and the target for further action. It is also the opportunity for market leaders. Additionally, 18 of these respondents said they had regular ESG dialogs with their portfolio companies, with 16 willing to publish an ESG report for their investors alongside financial reporting. Voluntary reporting of ESG is not an option for DFI-led mandates or mandates from institutional investors, such as the $64 trillion investor-led Carbon Disclosure Project.

The best practice PE firms are active in determining risk through enhanced due diligence. For example, PEGP Actis[18] uses a five-factor risk rating in health and safety, social, environmental, climate, and "business integrity" through three levels of risk:

1. *Low.* Using a comprehensive ESG manual integrated into investment process
2. *Medium.* Covers commodity-style environmental impact assessments
3. *High.* Involves two-person onsite team visits (e.g., in the Niger delta for oil and gas, where risks are easier to explain when one has been on the ground)

After the tough past few years, and as mergers and acquisitions activity increases, a new emphasis on sustainability footprints and impacts is expected. For example, the Carlyle Group states that "through a partnership with Environmental Defense Fund, we developed EcoValuScreen, a due diligence tool that identifies operational changes to improve a company's environmental footprint and bottom line."[19]

While coverage of ESG issues exists, how different investors in/into sub-Saharan Africa approach sustainability is reflected in the diversity of definitions used in interviews and fund marketing materials. Streamlining themes, definitions, and criteria for measuring ESG factors will improve the opportunity to increase PE and the general asset management supply of SI products and/or reporting of existing products.

Case stories are being collated globally to track best practices to help present a fuller picture of ESG factors in PE today and offer examples of how PE firms are thinking about SI impacts and opportunities in the funds and companies they invest with. A famous ESG example is the Celtel/Zain corporate governance case. Mo Ibrahim, the founder of Celtel, claimed never to have given or taken a bribe and now promotes better governance in Africa.[20]

CONTRASTING PE AND LISTED EQUITY INVESTORS

SI approaches and ESG integration by PE and general asset management firms differ. Analysis from investment practitioners suggests that the (smaller) PE investment community is more active than the (larger) general asset management community in driving sustainable investment practices regionally. Indeed, the 2011 IFC/SinCo sub-Saharan Africa report suggests that PE investors have something to teach general asset management practitioners based on their PE experiences with ESG-integrated investment processes and ESG impact reporting expectations.

PE is arguably "a better form of ownership than listed equity, as it has a better alignment of stakeholders' interests."[21] Strong evidence supports the argument that PE is a better platform to drive sustainability forward compared to listed equity managers. PE firms offer influence to drive the agenda toward sustainability.

As a result of the key differences between PE and listed equity companies, portfolio companies from PE funds (compared to investee companies from general asset management investors) may come to recognize and appreciate the strategic value addition, financial acumen and patient capital that come with PE and VC firms in the shareholder base.[22]

In addition to the differences in relationship with tier investee companies, PE firms have fewer staff and a smaller publicity profile than general asset management firms. Moreover, as mentioned, a counterintuitive finding from the IFC-commissioned SinCo/RisCura 2011 study is that more SI is being conducted by PE funds than by major asset management houses. This assessment is based on the significant role of DFI investment in PE funds in emerging markets.

NEW SI ACTIVITY IN THE PE ASSET CLASS

In 2008, the Environmental Defense Fund (EDF) began a pilot project to identify operations in three KKR portfolio companies that could benefit from environmental tweaking. EDF states that, during the first year, the exercise resulted in more than $16 million in savings and reduced greenhouse gas emissions by 25,000 tons. KKR followed by launching its first-ever ESG report. In 2011, Carlyle released its inaugural Citizenship Report, a 23-page compendium of the firm's attempts "efforts to incorporate environmental, social and governance considerations into its investment practice and into its own daily operations.[23]

On the networking side, the industry body International Limited Partners Association (ILPA), with over 240 institutional member organizations collectively managing approximately $1 trillion of private equity assets, now references ESG in its Private Equity Principles Version 2.0.[24] Work continues in 2011 with three guiding principles forming the essence of an effective private equity partnership: alignment of interest, governance, and transparency. ILPA also published an update to the PE principles and the first standardized reporting industry template to help enhance the PE asset class globally in January 2011. ESG issues are a part of that framework.[25]

In February 2009, some of the world's biggest private equity firms signed a set of voluntary ESG investment standards drawn up by the Washington-based U.S. Private Equity Council (PEC), a trade group representing 13 of the largest PE firms. PEC ESG guidelines incorporate ESG issues into investment decision-making decisions and ownership activities. The responsible investment guidelines were created with support from some of the world's largest pension funds.

PE ALLOCATIONS INCREASE

Long-term savings vehicles such as pension funds are uniquely positioned to manage the long investment term and limited liquidity of PE investment, thus capturing what appears to be a significant performance premium and diversification benefits.[26] Through 2020, continued growth in PE allocations is expected, with standouts including many Ivy League endowments allocating growing percentages of their investment to PE. (For example, Yale University PE investment rose from 14.8% in 2005 to 24.3% in 2009.)[27] Similarly, emerging markets, such as South Africa, have doubled the allowed allocation to PE from 5% to 10% on pension fund assets. Sustainability will almost certainly grow as a factor within this larger PE market, perhaps especially as it pertains to innovating companies. Large pension funds are also participating more. For example, since 2004, CalPERS, the largest public pension fund in the United States with $205 billion in assets, has committed $1.5 billion of capital to clean-tech investments, as part of $48 billion of total invested and committed PE capital. CalPERS had a strategic priority for 2010 to integrate ESG factors into the formal due diligence process for all traditional and PE investments. This is a significant shift, with implications for PEGPs not just in the United States but globally, given CalPERS' global presence and its emerging markets principles, launched in 2007.[28]

INCREASED PE FUNDS FOCUSED ON EMERGING MARKETS

PE is a good fit with SI, especially in emerging and frontier markets. Unlike general asset management, PE works in markets where only basic elements of the investment ecosystem exist. As it can operate with less investment infrastructure, PE is able to provide capital in frontier markets and across large, medium and small firms.

Beyond the economic development benefits of PE by making new capital available, this form of financing and investment is by nature supplemented by assistance in business operations, thereby contributing to economic efficiency and innovation.[29] PE investors are hands-on with a vested interest in good management and governance of their investee companies, which is especially also useful as these companies grow.

Bucking global trends, 210 PE funds focused on emerging markets raised a record-breaking $66.5 billion in 2008, a 12% increase over the $59 billion raised in 2007, according to new research from the Emerging Markets Private Equity Association (EMPEA). In addition to the continued prominence of Asia, there was a significant rise in the number and size of funds targeting multiple regions or global emerging markets (EM) opportunities. The PE model in EM is more about equity investments in growing companies and less about leverage.[30]

LPs view EM PE opportunities as attractive both in their own right and relative to PE opportunities in developed markets, in the following respects:[31]

- The EM share of new PE commitments will continue to grow as LPs seek exposure to high-growth markets.
- Investors with existing exposure to EM PE plan to grow their exposure from 6% to 10% of total PE commitments in 2010 to 11% to 15% over the next two years.

- LPs expect their new commitments to EM PE to accelerate over the next two years.
- The majority of LPs expect EM PE funds to outperform PE as a whole.
- Seventy percent of LPs are either satisfied or very satisfied with the performance of their EM PE portfolio relative to their listed equities in EMs.
- Sixty-one percent of LPs consider themselves to be just as aligned with their EM PE managers as with their developed market GPs, while an additional 23% of LPs consider themselves to be more aligned with their EM GPs.

China, Brazil, and India remain the most attractive emerging markets for GP investment. Political risk and inexperienced GPs are the main barriers to first-time PE investment in Africa and Latin America.

An additional strategic fit between the PE theme and EMs is that PE funds benefit from the strategic role they play in frontier and EMs providing liquidity, business acumen, and frontier capital in less sophisticated investment ecosystems, such as relatively illiquid, smaller public equity markets without adequate disclosure rules or exchange requirements. As a result, midsize buyout, distressed debt, secondary, and EM funds focused on China, India and Brazil may garner increased interest.[32]

Despite this uptake in the PE EM theme, EMs primarily presents minority investment opportunities for growth capital: For example, two-thirds of the 2010 investments in Brazil, China, and India were minority stakes. In addition, EM deals typically are small by western standards and more laborious to negotiate.

FUTURE SUSTAINABILITY THEMES IN PE

Increased pressure from strategic buyers and institutional investors will continue the pressure on PE funds to be proactive in their approach and transparent in their impact. The PE exit decision is facing more scrutiny for ESG issues, not only from strategic buyers but also from the new and increased pressure to make ESG disclosures in listing requirements and/or deal frameworks.

Coming off the tough years of 2007 to 2010, the future of PE is still reconfiguring with some mid-market deals and fewer mega-deals at least until the credit and asset-gathering pictures settle. From a portfolio management perspective, there will be increased attention to making strategy and operational improvements to generate increased valuations. PE firms are also increasingly looking at more basic industries, including industrials/infrastructure, consumer products, materials, and energy and power, as these industries tend to be more recession resistant and have high potential for value creation from an operational standpoint.[33]

As the PE in Ems matures and grows, capital will be flowing in from both domestic and foreign institutional investors looking to invest with proven PE skills and in new themes best accessed by PE in frontier markets. In a similar vein, a purist trend in PE has emerged with a focus on a single type of investing (in a single thematic or regional focus).

Allocating capital to the most promising companies and sustainability technologies will be crucial at a systemic level going forward. Not every clean-tech deal is a good idea. And of course the industry will face challenges from disintermediation, for example, by sovereign wealth funds.[34]

Region-specific ESG guidelines present a promising approach to balancing the generic nature of global approaches with the locality of investments in business located in time and place.

At the thematic level, infrastructure opportunities abound and will likely continue to experience better opportunities and increased deal activity from 2010 onward as the global economic recovery continues and the effects of infrastructure-focused stimuli in China, the United States, and EMs begin to take hold.

In Latin America and Africa, the new agriculture theme has attracted strong asset flows. For example, Phatisa's African Agriculture Fund, with a $300 million target, included a coordinated pool of European DFIs[35] as well as African DFIs as limited liability partner investors. But agriculture is a double-edged sword: "[R]ising levels of international investment capital in African agriculture and agribusiness have taken the investment thesis directly into the intensely political arena of global food security and land rights."[36] PE funds need to establish bona fides in this politically sensitive, high-impact SI theme.

SUMMARY

SI in the PE asset class has evolved over the past five years with increased awareness and activity by private equity limited partnerships (PELPs) and PEGPs (investors and fund managers).

Skills and information gaps persist, but some of this may be the opacity of the asset class and sheltering competitive advantage. As the assets apportioned to PE grow, the opportunity for positive impact and the importance of this type of asset class will increase.

Despite the rough few years, the proposition for PE remains positive. With structural and capital markets changes, PE remains an important asset class for growing businesses and capital efficiency. The future is positive for PE,[37] and perhaps especially in SI, where investors offer longer-term capital and where more exhaustive analysis of all factors impacting company performance is the norm.

The importance of ESG factors in PE is becoming more substantively understood, and appreciated, but greenwashing of existing and future PE funds activity is possible. Best practices are emerging from PE firms that are seeking positive outcomes from ESG integration and sustainability themes. These market leaders are exploring risk mitigation as well as new opportunities.

PE is a specialized form of investment that benefits from proactive fundamental due diligence and active stewardship of investee companies with the aim to be sold at a higher exit valuation after five to ten years. With its unique investor-investee nexus, PE funds are able to allocate capital to tomorrow's most promising sustainability companies, products, and services. The PE industry's resilience and agility in adapting to the adverse market conditions of the years from 2007 to 2009 will serve it well as the market continues to recover and ESG factors become more relevant in asset gathering, due diligence, and company exits. But the proof is in the portfolio company exits—and therefore in the performance.

NOTES

1. Conor Kehoe and Robert N. Palter, "The Future of Private Equity: These Funds Face a Credit-Constrained World; They Must Adapt to Thrive," *McKinsey Quarterly* (April 2009).
2. Daniel O. Klier, Martin K. Welge, and Kathryn R. Harrigan, "The Changing Face of Private Equity: How Modern Private Equity Firms Manage Investment Portfolios," *Journal of Private Equity* 12, No. 4 (Fall 2009): 7–13.
3. Oxfam, CDC, the Church of England—Ethical Investment Advisory Group, "Better Returns in a Better World: The Role of Institutional Investors in Private Equity Investing in Developing Countries," April 2010.
4. Ernst and Young quoting Dealogic, "2010 Global Private Equity Watch: New Horizons Emerge," April 2009. Among the acquisitions, there were 956 where the value was disclosed and 656 where the value was not disclosed.
5. David Dolan, "Africa M&A Surges to Record $44 bln in 2010," January 19, 2011. http://af.reuters.com/article/investingNews/idAFJOE70I0IZ20110119?sp=true
6. According to Cora Fernandez, Sanlam PE and SAVCA chair: "Portfolio companies will come to recognize and appreciate the strategic value-addition, financial acumen and patient capital that come with PE and VC [venture capital] firms in your shareholder base." 2011

7. Sean Dougherty, Brait PE, personal communication with the author, August 4, 2010.

8. CFA Institute, "Environmental, Social, and Governance Factors at Listed Companies: A Manual for Investors," May 2008. www.cfapubs.org/doi/pdf/10.2469/ccb.v2008.n2.1

9. Hugh Wheelan, "Ethos Survey Report Follows Launch of SRI Private Equity Fund-of-Funds," May 6, 2010. www.responsible-investor.com/home/article/private_equity_firms/

10. www.kkr.com/company/our_business.cfm

11. Quoting Andrew Marino, principal, U.S. buyout industrial team at the Carlyle Group, at the Responsible Investment Forum, hosted by Private Equity International in London, 2010.

12. DFI LPs include, for example, CDC Group Plc, the European Investment Bank, the African Development Bank, the International Finance Corporation, and the Development Bank of Southern Africa. Norfund, a Norwegian government agency, has 59% of primary investments that currently are in Africa, opened offices in South Africa and Kenya, and planned commitments to up to 10 PE funds during 2010, with Africa remaining a preferred region. The French DFI Proparco expects to commit up to $43 million to PE funds focused on Africa over the next 12 months Export Development Canada is finalizing a commitment to a mid-market Africa-focused buyout fund. Reported in Preqin Special Report, "The Private Equity Market in Africa," October 2010. www.preqin.com

13. SEMS for Private Equity Template, www.ifc.org/ifcext/sustainability.nsf/Content/FinancialInstitutions_PrivateEquityFunds

14. Swedfund, "Swedfund's Investments through Funds—Capital for Economic Growth and Development Driven by Local Businesses," 2010. www.rosencrantzandco.com/Swedfund_fund_report_2009_final.pdf

15. Dougherty, personal communication.

16. Oxfam et al., "Better Returns in a Better World."

17. Wheelan, "Ethos Survey Report."

18. www.act.is

19. The Carlyle Group, "Corporate Citizenship 2010: A Progress Report to Our Investors, Our Partners, and Our Communities."www.carlyle.com/Company/item11840.pdf

20. www.moibrahimfoundation.org/en/section/the-ibrahim-index

21. Dougherty, personal communication.

22. Cora Fernandez, "SAVCA Foreword," May 22, 2009. http://free.financialmail.co.za/projects09/savca09/savcaa.htm

23. www.carlyle.com/Media%20Room/News%20Archive/2011/item11846.html

24. http://ilpa.org/principles-version-2-0/

25. "Is Private Equity a Suitable Investment for South African Pension Funds?" www.actuarialsociety.org.za/Portals/1/Documents/2aa46ca0-9dd5-4da3-bebb-ef6dfad87109.pdf

26. www.yale.edu/investments/Yale_Endowment_09.pdf

27. www.calpers.ca.gov/eip-docs/investments/policies/inv-asset-classes/equity/ext-equity/emerging-eqty-market-prinicples.pdf. See Gabriel A. Huppé and Tessa Hebb, "The Virtue of CalPERS' Emerging Equity Markets Principles," *Journal of Sustainable Finance and Investment* 1, No. 1 (February 2011): 62–76. CalPERS' new principles-based approach to investing in emerging markets stands at the midpoint between its previous alpha-generation policy of complete country-level divestment and its beta enhancement associated with universal investing in its domestic and developed markets.

28. DBSA and SAVCA, "Economic Impact of Venture Capital and Private Equity in South Africa 2009 Study," *SAVCA* (October 2009). www.savca.co.za.

29. Jennifer Alexander quoted in EMPEA media release, "Emerging Markets Private Equity Funds Raise Record Amount of Capital Despite Global Slowdown," February 9, 2009.

30. EMPEA/Coller, "Capital Emerging Markets Private Equity" survey, April 2010. Investors' views of private equity in emerging markets.

31. John Harley, "2010 Global Private Equity Watch: New Horizons Emerge, Ernst and Young, April 2010.

32. Howard Sun, "The Future of Private Equity," *Seeking Alpha*, March 5, 2010.

33. McKinsey Quarterly (April 2009).

34. KPMG/Preqin, April 2010.

35. "African Agriculture Fund First Closes on US$135 Million," December 9, 2010.www.africa-investor.com/article.asp?id=8066

36. http://blogs.reuters.com/africanews/2010/08/24/african-agricultural-finance-under-the-spotlight/

37. Kehoe and Palter, "The Future of Private Equity."

CHAPTER 36

Blue Wolf

Implications for Private Equity

Adam Blumenthal and Michael Musuraca

While we have been focusing primarily on public equity, there are major implications for other asset classes as well. Creative ways are emerging within private equity, for example, that use sustainability, even labor, as a way of maximizing value. KKR and the Environment Defense Fund (EDF) have expanded their successful cost savings initiatives within their vast portfolio, as can be seen from the demonstrations listed at the EDF Web site. Most observers may think that using labor of a way of finding value within sustainability is a nonstarter. However, as you'll soon see, Adam Blumenthal and Mike Musuraca have been doing just that. Here's a specific case on how Adam and his colleague and partner Mike have managed to achieve this success.

Finch, Pruyn and Company was a cornerstone of the Glens Falls, New York, economy when Blue Wolf Capital Partners and its partner, Atlas Holdings, purchased the company in June 2007. Established in 1865 as a sawmill, lumberyard, and quarry operation, Finch had converted to papermaking in 1905 and built a small (2%–3% market share) but national presence in the uncoated freesheet market from its single mill, in large part because of the firm's vaunted customer service and the fact that the company's paper was considered to provide for superior print reproduction.

By 2007, Finch was the leading private sector employer in the Adirondack region of New York State as well as a major philanthropic contributor to the larger community. The company had also developed a well-earned reputation for practicing responsible forestry and was the largest private landowner in the state, with more than 160,000 of forestland managed in a sustainable manner for wood production, recreation, and as a wildlife habitat. The company's forestry practices carried certifications from both of the leading third-party sustainable forest certifiers, the Forest Stewardship Council and the Sustainable Forestry Initiative.

Yet all was not well at Finch in 2007. The company's ownership was comprised of over 100 family members, all descendants of the original founders. While they had little to do with the company's day-to-day operations, the ownership was a deeply divided group, and one that often engaged in protracted quarrels during which lawsuits were frequently threatened and sometimes filed.

In addition, the company's relationship with its unionized workforce was severely strained (over two-thirds of the company's workforce is unionized and represented by seven different local unions), at a time when increased competition in the paper industry made it increasingly difficult for Finch to maintain its market position. There had been two strikes since 1996. The first was a two-week walkout, but the second was a bitter six-month battle during which the company hired nearly 500 permanent replacement workers. Although Finch did gradually recall many of the striking workers as vacancies came open in the months after the strike, the scars from the strike ran deep within the hourly workforce. Finch's management style had also not adapted to the new world of manufacturing, one in which many of the most successful companies had moved from a centralized top-down approach where a small group of senior managers made all major decisions to one where line managers and workers had greater control and accountability for their work as a way of increasing productivity and encouraging innovation.

Finally, while the company had made some capital investments, primarily in papermaking and environmental remediation projects, long-term capital planning and investment had lagged, and much of the mill's physical plant and supporting technology was in need of maintenance and upgrading. The same was true when it came to strategic planning about the changing nature of the paper industry and whether Finch needed to revise its core product mix and marketing strategy. In the midst of a booming economy, the challenges facing Finch would have been difficult to overcome; coming during a protracted slowdown in the world's economy that had reduced the demand for printing paper, it became clear to the owners that change were needed.

CHALLENGES AND OPPORTUNITIES

Despite the challenges, Blue Wolf identified a number of reasons that Finch was an intriguing investment opportunity besides its brand name. The first was that the company is an integrated manufacturing operation, producing three-quarters of the pulp it consumes and more than two-thirds of its own energy. This makes the company less prone to shocks coming from changes in the market price for pulp and energy. The second was Finch's national reputation as a responsible forestry manager.

Moreover, the partners at Blue Wolf had developed a deep relationship with officials in the United Steelworkers (USW), AFL-CIO, the labor union representing the bulk of the hourly workforce at Finch. Recognizing that union cooperation would be essential to achieving the improved operating efficiencies necessary to keep the mill competitive, the partners at Blue Wolf reached out to the USW to discuss the parameters of the changes envisioned and to ensure that the union was willing to be a partner in stabilizing and growing the company. Assured that the USW was interested in engaging the new owners, Blue Wolf and Atlas completed the purchase of Finch, Pruyn and Co.'s assets in June 2007 and renamed the company Finch Paper, LLC.

On the same day they took ownership, Blue Wolf and Atlas announced the sale of 160,000 acres of Adirondack forestland. A number of weeks later, they sold the on-site hydroelectric plant. In each instance, the sales represented a strategy in Finch's lasting interest—reducing the company's long-term debt while maintaining the benefits that both the forestland and the hydro facility provided to the company's operations.

The forestland was sold to the Nature Conservancy, one of the leading environmental organizations in the world. The transaction kept the land with owners that shared the company's desire to preserve the land as open space but also knew the value that responsible timber harvesting had in safeguarding the health of the forest, in the local economy, and in maintaining a renewable supply of wood to meet society's needs. Finch and the Nature Conservancy also signed a 20-year agreement under which the Conservancy would continue to supply wood for making Finch Paper. Despite the sale of the forestland, the new owners also decided to retain its entire forestry staff as well as to offer consulting services for forest management to public and private forest owners, including the Conservancy. Finch also signed a long-term supply contract with the new owner of the hydroelectric plant, thereby locking in an affordable supply of green energy for years to come with the operational and maintenance costs.

GENERATING RESULTS

One of the principles guiding Blue Wolf's strategy is investing for the long-term, and the firm makes clear to its operators and investors that environmental stewardship and conservation are core components of its strategy, because building companies that achieve healthy growth and are sustainable over the long term means being industry leaders in quality, workplace safety, and environmental stewardship. Blue Wolf also knows that attaining best-in-class status means creating a workplace culture where workers are committed to the vision and empowered to help lead.

The effort to change the workplace culture at Finch began with the former chairman, president, and chief executive officer, who had been with the company over 50 years and who helped stabilize the new company and begin the transformation over the first year and a half. Yet it was under the new president and chief executive, Joseph F. Raccuia, that major changes began to take place. Upon assuming control, one of Raccuia's first actions was to invite the leaders of all seven local unions representing workers at the company to meet and discuss ways of improving communications between management and labor. Shortly after, the company created the Finch/All Unions Joint Steering Committee, which brought together hourly workers and salaried employees to flesh out key areas of workplace concern and establish a forum for addressing the concerns. One of the committee's first initiatives was to form the Joint Safety Leadership Team, a labor/management committee that reviewed existing safety protocols and devised new protocols and initiatives. Raccuia and his management team then rolled out their mill-wide Continuous Improvement Initiative, an effort to achieve efficiencies, reduce expenses, and fortify the company's economic health.

The success of these programs can be seen across the company's operations, from workplace safety to product quality; from environmental protection and energy usage; and from improved productivity to an improved bottom line.

Making paper is an energy-intensive business. The combined value of the power made or purchased by Finch is $50 million. Even though two-thirds of the energy produced by Finch comes from nonfossil fuels—hydropower and the burning of biomass—management sought to further reduce the use of fossil fuels and started a project to maximize energy efficiency. The result was the Finch Paper Energy Initiative, a company-wide effort to have hourly and salaried employees document and report energy-wasting leaks of steam, water, or air. Over the first year, employees reported such events at the rate of five per week, leading to the correction of many of the leaks within 24 hours. At the same time, Energy Action Teams, comprised of hourly and salaried workers throughout the manufacturing departments, were also identifying new conservation projects with the aid of an in-house energy model that allowed for employees to project and monitor energy use. The implementation of the conservation projects achieved a reduction of $3.1 million in the first year. All told, after one year, the programs had led to a 10% reduction in purchased energy use, a 4% reduction in overall energy use from the previous year, and an estimated 14% reduction in greenhouse gas emissions measured against a three-year baseline average. As a result of these efforts, Finch Paper received the *Pulp and Paper International* magazine award for Energy Efficiency in 2009, and the American Forest and Paper Association conferred its award on the company in 2010.

The effort to reduce energy consumption was matched in the area of workplace safety, a cornerstone of Blue Wolf's efforts to build world-class companies. From all levels of the company, the mantra that all tasks needed to be done safely is constantly reinforced, and standards are communicated to all employees daily. The company strictly enforces a policy that all injuries and near misses to be reported and thoroughly investigated so that corrective action can be taken. Daily before work begins on every shift, supervisors conduct safety meetings with their work crews to share information and remind workers of what is expected of them in terms of safety. Safety audits are also performed regularly by employees, including senior management, and the company's Safety Plan was mailed to each employee's home to reinforce the message. The company also instituted a Safe Choice rewards program for employees that allowed for them to earn points for engaging in safety programs, such as participating in safety meetings and filing safety analysis reports, that can be exchanged for gifts.

The results of the various safety programs have been impressive. Using U.S. Occupational Safety and Health Administration Standards of Recordable Incident Rate (RIR), less than 1.0, and Lost Time Incident Rate (LTIR), less than 0.5, the company has made tremendous strides, as RIR rates have fallen from 3.22 in September 2009 to 0.97 in September 2010 and LTIR rates have fallen from 1.40 to 0.41 over the same time frame. The drop in costs associated with workplace injuries has been substantial as well, as medical expenses and lost-wage payment fell from nearly $1.4 million in 2009 to under $200,000 in 2010, not including the savings from the reduction in overtime paid when workers need to cover for a colleague's absence.

LABOR RELATIONS CODA

Prior to Blue Wolf's investment in Finch Paper, contentious contract negotiations between the company and its unions had been the order of the day, which included two strikes over an 11-year period, the second of which, in 2001, had resulted in a bitter six-month struggle that saw the company hire permanent replacement workers. In the fall of 2009, Finch and the Steelworkers (the largest of Finch's unions) began negotiations on a new collective bargaining agreement. What had taken five months to complete when the contract was last negotiated in late 2006 and early 2007 took one week to settle in 2009. A large part of the reason for the swift conclusion of negotiations was the trust that had been built between the new owners and managers and the workers represented by the Steelworkers. This trust allowed for each side to achieve a settlement that benefited both sides.

The new agreement called for general wage increases and a reduction in the workers' share of health insurance premiums, from 35% to 20%, at a time when most American workers were paying a larger share of their health insurance premiums. The agreement also restored language requiring union membership for nonsalaried employees, which had been eliminated in 2001. In exchange, the Steelworkers agreed to changes in holiday pay and to allow the company the ability to contract out the modernization and operation of the Finch woodyard, which both management and the union saw as in their best long-term interests.

SUMMARY

Contract negotiations represent a tip of the iceberg when it comes to labor relations. Union grievances fell 44% from 2008 to 2009 and are on course to drop by an additional 33% in 2010, and absenteeism has plummeted, in large part due to the efforts of the Finch/All Unions Joint Steering Committee that urged union members to be cognizant of the impact an unscheduled day off would have on their colleagues.

Three years after Blue Wolf purchased Finch, it is thriving despite one of the worst recessions in the last 70 years. The decisions to shed noncore assets, reduce costs, and invest in new technology and products have been vital to the company's success, but equally important have been the cultural shifts in how the company conducts its labor relations and environmental conservation efforts. The bottom line is that Finch is now in a position to grow in a sustainable way, the hallmark of a truly responsible investment.

CHAPTER 37

New Business Models, Measurement, and Methodologies

Howard Brown

As we move forward in this age of increasing population and dwindling resources, there is a growing awareness that we need new ways to pursue and measure business success. There are different categories of possible solutions.

Tim Jackson, in his book *Prosperity Without Growth* (Routledge, 2009), advocates a three-day workweek as a way out of this global resource crunch and to deal with the arguably unsustainable American style of overwork and stress that doesn't lead to increased happiness. B Labs has created an increasingly accepted new social impact business model, potentially changing the ways of measuring corporate success. Companies such as Zipcar encourage shared use of resources, which will decrease the need for everyone to own one of everything, especially in large cities, which now represent roughly half the global population (a demographic shift that also marks a sea change, according to Stewart Brand in *Whole Earth Discipline*.) The old, negative, backward-looking environmental, social, and governance metrics fail to achieve success, and are of decreasing relevance, as they do not, and cannot, capture the dynamic shifts and opportunities that are well under way in the corporate world.

New ways of measuring impacts and opportunities are emerging. The quality of supply chain management is but one such new category for measuring the quality of business operations. Innovation, both actual and potential, has become a significant driver worth measuring as well. In this chapter, we read about dMass, a concept that encompasses a number of innovative strategies all aimed at delivering more benefits to people using fewer resources. It is proposed as a way to align business and environmental performance by measuring how well resources are being invested.

---

dMASS:

verb 1. The process of reducing the mass of material resources required to produce wealth (or well-being) through improved design and applied science.

noun 1. The mass of material resources eliminated or that can be eliminated in the production of a given amount of value.

2. A strategy that leverages intellect to deliver more wealth or benefits using less resource mass.

3. A path to a sustainable future based on improving resource performance.

The *d* in dMASS stands for reduction through design.

It's no coincidence that resources are becoming more central to disparate strategies in design, business, and environmental management. Resources are at the heart of virtually every problem businesses and governments are facing, from the costs of operating to debt and risk. The way we use resources matters now more than ever.

Economic activity involves using material resources to make tools that deliver useful functions (or benefits) to customers. Tools can range from cups and stoves, to medicines and medical instruments, lighting and plumbing, and even houses and cars. To be sure, these things contribute to our wealth. But in a resource-constrained world, we have to be very clear about the difference between the physical products themselves and the wealth they help deliver.

Wealth is not the same as resources or the things made from them. Wealth is the *capabilities* or *benefits* that result from using tools or products. Owning any particular object doesn't in itself make us wealthier; it's the function of an object that matters, not it's mass. The value of toothpaste is in maintaining healthy teeth; the value of a washing machine is in providing clean clothes; the value of a jacket is in keeping your body warm; and the value of a refrigerator is in safely storing food. Wealth, much like biological adaptation, ultimately is about enhancing one's security, health, and well-being. People buy products to harvest benefits that increase their wealth.

Economists describe the tools we use to create wealth as products that companies *produce* and people *consume*. Yet we know from physics that nothing is really ever produced or consumed. When we "produce" something, we are really rearranging our environment (Earth's crust). We mine resources and then shape them into useful tools. In that sense, we're much like birds building nests or bees building hives, but on a grander scale. When we "consume" something, it does not go away. We temporarily tie up those resources for a particular use, then release them back into our environment in an altered form. Resource mass that is processed by a company but never becomes part of a product is called waste. But waste (or pollutants) is actually made up of valuable resources that were mined, refined, moved around the planet, and then lost from an economic process and released in a form and place where they are counterproductive (they diminish wealth). Waste is a resource that we could have used to increase wealth, if only we were better at design and management and at applying our knowledge of how nature works to economic activity.

RESOURCES AND PRODUCTS VERSUS WEALTH

Over time, we've confused resources and products with wealth itself. We forgot that they are the *means* to achieve wealth. As a result, both manufacturers and buyers tend to measure and place emphasis on the amount of things we manufacture and buy rather than on the function of those things and the benefits that they deliver. Businesses and investors often associate success with selling the most stuff at the highest price customers will pay; economists measure collective success by an increase in the total price all customers pay for everything (gross domestic product).

We also tend to think that innovation stems from individuals making somewhat random discoveries. The truth is, there is a powerful pattern to useful discovery, an underlying trend or direction to real wealth-producing innovation that has occurred largely below the radar screens of media and investors. Now there is an explosion of scientific knowledge that will reinforce this trend and make it a dominant factor in shaping business. That trend is *humanity's progressive ability to do more with less*—to generate more wealth-producing benefits for more people with fewer resources per capita. dMASS encompasses many different methods for eliminating resources used in delivering value to people. It is the key to successful design, to innovation and to business strategy as well as to environmental management.

TREND OF DOING MORE WITH LESS

You've probably noticed the trend toward doing more with less in certain industries, such as information technology and aerospace. (We're all familiar with the story of the room-size mainframe computer morphing into the tiny tablet.) But improving performance per ton is a much bigger trend in our economy, and it started long ago.

In bridge design, you can see how our ability to do more with less has been developing over a long time. People have built bridges to create wealth—to access resources, to trade with others, to enable migration—for millennia. During this time, we've found ways to build longer and stronger bridges that require fewer tons of material resources relative to the area they span and the weight they can support. What started as a pile of stones filling a waterway became an arched bridge, a suspension bridge, and someday a bridge suspended by barely visible nanowires. In other words, we've been able to progressively deliver more function with fewer resources.

Today we are seeing more and more innovative designs that are explicitly intended to do more with less. This dMASS activity reflects the beginning of a shift toward dramatically higher resource performance. The shift needs to happen swiftly and in every corner of the economy. For companies and people to adapt and prosper, resource performance should be at the center of business strategy and metrics.

Metrics are particularly important because they drive behavior. They create incentives, both ones you intend and ones you don't. In short, *you get what you measure.*

I learned the truth in this adage when I was the chief executive of a business that helped companies connect environment and business metrics. There was one manufacturing client, a battery company, that sought my advice as it launched a new initiative to measure environmental performance. The client was concerned about the large amount of scrap being produced and wasted at plants, so it began tracking tons of scrap recycled. When scrap recycling grew, executives thought they had a success on their hands. But the tons of recycled scrap continued to grow month after month. Eventually it became clear that plant managers, aware that they would be rewarded by recycling more scrap, were paying too much attention to recycling and too little attention to minimizing scrap production in the first place.

IMPROVING OVERALL PERFORMANCE

I approached the problem from a new angle, reflected in this simple principle: *If you don't use it, you can't spill it.* My advice to executives was to look at the total resource inputs (in tons) required by their manufacturing and delivery processes in relation to their output, or the product they delivered to their customers. If my client could reduce the mass of resources at the front end without compromising the value it delivered, the company not only would realize a reduction in scrap and improve overall environmental performance (due to fewer spills and emissions), it also would:

- Reduce its purchasing, production, and warehousing costs;
- Reduce the fuels used in manufacturing, transport, and throughout the entire supply chain;
- Reduce the potential for fines related to environmental impacts;
- Reduce its carbon footprint.; and
- Ultimately enhance its brand value.

One of the key aspects of this advice was to look at the product the company was delivering to customers. Remember the point I made earlier about wealth: Wealth is not the same as resources or things but is rather the *capabilities* or *benefits* that result from using specific tools or products. A company's real products are *not* the physical items it sells. A company's outputs are the function or benefits it delivers to its customers. That's what customers pay for; that's what they want. People do not want batteries; they want portable energy. The important relationship for this company, from both an environmental and a long-term business strategy standpoint, was that between the amount of energy delivered to customers and the mass required to deliver it. The company's future might be in energy-harvesting technologies or something else that can deliver portable energy without batteries that need to be replaced frequently. It should be measuring the benefit it actually delivers to customers and working to reduce the mass required to deliver it.

SUMMARY

dMASS describes a path to a sustainable future based on improving resource performance. It involves leveraging intellect and using improved design and applied science to reduce the mass of material resources required to produce wealth. It places emphasis on outcomes (on improving human well-being) and shifts the focus away from standard measures of output toward measuring actual benefits delivered.

In the case of the batteries, dMASS thinking moves the focus from the means (batteries) to the ends (portable energy). Truly innovative change that brings about a fundamental alteration in how something works requires asking "How can we do this better?" rather than "How can we make this thing better?" With a focus on function, or the desired outcome, rather than the material object, we can find ways to eliminate mass.

Resources are metals, minerals, fuels, water, and all material things that can be measured by their mass (weight). Mass serves as an indicator of all resources, including those lost as pollution. In a business environment where the supply of material resources and fuels is becoming tighter, costs are more volatile and supplies are more at risk. Companies that can deliver more with less win, as they are less influenced by these factors. By measuring and improving resource performance, companies also increase their environmental performance, reduce the potential for environment-related fines, and ultimately can increase their value by lowering the cost of sales and reducing risk to their brand's reputation.

Environment is not a cost to business. It is integral. Any metric that endeavors to measure environmental performance should reflect this; it cannot be tangential to other business performance metrics. A metric should be fundamental. That is, it should not be focused on one or another distinct factor and therefore subject to a costly overhaul when the "next big thing" comes along. It should be simple and based primarily on data already being collected by companies. Most important, it should help drive desired outcomes. It should help companies manage risk and increase both environmental and financial performance.

A metric based on resource performance, one that measures the relationship between the benefits a product delivers and the mass required to produce those benefits, would offer an opportunity to align environmental and business performance. Investment in dMASS strategies and innovations that succeed in reducing the materials needed to produce wealth offer the best potential for creating sustainable businesses.

CHAPTER 38

Terminology and Intention

Lloyd Kurtz

One of the very first researchers in the field of socially responsible investment (SRI) is Lloyd Kurtz, who was hired in the early days by Boston-based KLD, and has subsequently pursued a career in asset management. In 2005 he also became affiliated with the Center for Responsible Business at Berkeley, and remains an eminent thinker in the field in the United States. With our review of the state of play now almost complete, Lloyd now gives us a final perspective on the evolving terminology that has emerged. We have left this discussion for last intentionally, as the ongoing terminology war can be a distraction with differing factions emphasizing subsections of environmental, social, and governance factors, at times claiming to do more than they actually do. An example would be "SRI" funds that had oil drilling companies involved in the Deepwater Horizon incident as their largest holding. Sadly, there are many similar stories, but this book is an effort to point out investment practices that are working. New forms of investment strategy have emerged, especially in the realm of impact investing, which seems to be carving out a useful niche, but does not, and perhaps cannot, touch the larger picture. Ethical, social, sustainable, responsible, and so on—we have avoided dwelling too much on this topic of terminology, as it distracts from practical application, but it is a critical subject to investigate and clarify. In this chapter, Lloyd parses this out for us across the various categories that have emerged.

At a recent conference, behavioral finance theorist Hersh Sheffrin asked investors: "What is your objective function?" In other words, what are the intended outcomes of your investment strategy? Answering this question requires that investors carefully and honestly examine their motivations.[1]

Socially responsible or environmental, social, and governance (ESG) investing has been aptly described as a container concept—one encompassing a very broad range of activities. This diversity is the product of success: The past ten years has seen significant growth and innovation in the field. But success brings new challenges. We may have reached the point where the diversity of practice is so great that there is no longer any *essential* feature, although many family resemblances remain. It is harder than it used to be to say what socially responsible investing *is*.

This creates problems as we try to frame investment objectives. ESG investors agree that a focus on financial risk and reward using conventional methods is insufficient, but they do not always agree on what additional elements should be emphasized. We all want to own companies meeting our standards, some want to actively promote change and influence corporate behavior, and no one wants to underperform, of course. But if one must choose—*and sometimes we must*—which should take precedence?

We suggest that all ESG strategies embed some combination of four motivations. These categories owe a great deal to prior work, notably Peter Kinder's 2005 taxonomy of social investors:[2]

1. Values
2. Financial performance
3. Fiduciary duty
4. Impact

Some investors focus on just a single one of these motivations, and in this chapter we will describe them individually. But ESG strategies often embed multiple motivations. Some U.S. mutual funds seek to appeal to all four, simultaneously employing portfolio screening, ESG integration techniques, shareholder activism, and direct investment in vehicles designed for social and/or environmental impact.

VALUES

The simple and powerful premise of values-based investing is that if you have values, you should act on them. U.S. practice is particularly identified with values-based investing, but it is by no means an exclusively American phenomenon. Islamic investors throughout the world invest according to Sharia law, for example. Nor are all values-based investors exclusively motivated by religion. In 2010, the Norwegian Ministry of Finance announced that, for ethical reasons, it would exclude 17 tobacco companies from government pension funds.

Part of the creative tension of ESG investing arises from the simple fact that the industry is highly innovative, but in many cases values do not change much over time. Most religious organizations have the same values they had 20 years ago. Environmentalists who didn't like polluters over the past two decades or more still don't like them.

But while the underlying values of most investors are relatively stable, considerable progress has been made in the management of their portfolios. In many cases, the challenges of values-based investing reduce to tractable problems in portfolio construction.

Studies of traditional values-based indexes have consistently found that return differences compared to the broad market were driven to a great degree by differing risk profiles—and that the risk profiles of these indexes could be brought more in line with the market through the use of optimization techniques.[3] Forthcoming research extends these findings into the 2000s.[4]

This is a good result for values-based investors. It suggests that for the last 20 years, their universe has had close to zero alpha. It follows that with good risk management, values-based investors should be able to expect, on average, average performance, plus or minus the impact of active management strategies and fees. And so there has been no observable performance penalty for values-based investing.

A real-time experiment supports this view. The MSCI USA ESG Select Social Index (formerly the FTSE KLD Select Social Index) is an optimized social investment benchmark. Its risk characteristics are matched to those of a broad market index using optimization techniques while maximizing exposure to positive social and environmental characteristics. Table 38.1 shows the performance from the product's launch in June 2004 through the first quarter of 2010 (when the operator of the index was acquired), compared with an unscreened broad market benchmark.

In this case, maximization of exposure to the social factor had no observable impact on risk-adjusted returns.

Not all values-based strategies have this property, however. Investors who exclude entire sectors—for example, Islamic investors (sin and financial

TABLE 38.1 Performance of a Risk-Managed Social Index

	Annualized Return	Standard Deviation of Returns
FTSE KLD Select Social Index	3.16%	15.19%
FTSE US 500 Index	3.09%	15.19%

Source: KLD Research and Analytics, FTSE KLD Social Select Index Fact Sheet, March 31, 2010. www.kld.com/indexes/data/fact_sheet/KLD_SSI_Fact_Sheet.pdf

stocks), Christian Science organizations (healthcare stocks), and progressive environmentalists (energy, materials, and other extraction-related stocks)—may find that even with state-of-the-art risk management tools it is not possible to fully diversify portfolios when compared to a broad market benchmark.

Although there is considerable evidence that traditional values-based investors have earned competitive returns, there remains a strong temptation (for both advocates and critics) to argue otherwise. In January 2010, the U.S. Social Investment Forum issued a press release with the headline "Two Thirds of Socially Responsible Mutual Funds Outperformed Benchmarks during 2009 Economic Downturn."[5]

The funds reviewed appeared to be primarily values-motivated. According to the accompanying tables, the most prominent negative screens were tobacco (excluded or restricted by 95.6% of the funds), defense and weapons (91.3%), alcohol (83.8%), and gambling (79.4%).

The lead paragraph said:

> *The verdict on SRI mutual fund performance is in: A review of 160 socially responsible mutual funds from 22 members of the Social Investment Forum (SIF) finds that the vast majority of the funds—65 percent—outperformed their benchmarks in calendar year 2009, most by significant margins.*

Apart from the short-term nature of the analysis, no adjustments were made for risk, nor was there any attempt to deal with survivorship bias or other potentially important factors. Studies that make these adjustments find that U.S. social funds perform about in line with their non-ESG peers, just as the underlying investment universes do.[6]

It would be newsworthy if a particular set of values happened to translate into a consistently superior investment strategy, but there is scant evidence for this. But if values are paramount, this should not matter. Values-based strategies need not turn in world-beating performance to fulfill their objective function.

FINANCIAL PERFORMANCE

Of course, not all ESG investors are values-driven. In 2008, the research firm Innovest (since acquired by MSCI) sought to differentiate its work from that of more values-oriented services (emphasis added):

> *Innovest's research is focused on those "intangible" factors which contribute to financial performance. Environmental, social, and*

> *governance performance are regarded as investment risk factors and as leading indicators for management quality and long-term financial performance. With most other contemporary analyses of companies' ESG performance, financial returns remain a secondary consideration, behind what are often ad hoc "ethical" judgements.*[7]

Many practitioners have embraced this model, discarding traditional values-based methods as overly restrictive or misaligned with client objectives. David Blood of Generation Investment Management told the *McKinsey Quarterly* in 2007 that values-based screening strategies "remained niche; returns were lackluster due to the fact that your investment opportunity set was limited."[8]

The argument for ESG alpha has gathered force over the past ten years as new studies documented strong returns for companies with good environmental and employee relations records. There has also been considerable progress toward a theoretical explanation of why ESG factors should matter for investment performance. In his excellent study of *Fortune*'s Best Companies to Work For, Alex Edmans argues that "the stock market does not fully value intangibles, even when independently verified by a highly public survey."[9]

These findings come at a time when traditional quantitative approaches appear to be losing efficacy. Each year computing power gets cheaper, and the supply of financial engineers increases. It is at least possible that some long-standing effects are finally being arbitraged away. Vadim Zlotnikov documents a loss of efficacy in widely used quantitative factors and proposes a model that identifies the level of crowding associated with particular quantitative strategies.[10]

It may be that research into ESG factors will yield a higher relative payoff than in the past. Researchers have now documented positive return impacts from both superior employee relations (Edmans) and superior sustainability performance (Derwall et al.).[11] No one knows how many others may remain in the wild, and the race is on to identify them and incorporate them into alpha strategies. Whether the resulting portfolios will retain any appeal for values-based investors is anyone's guess.

In any case, ESG alpha is like any other kind of alpha: Many seek it, and the results are easily measured.

FIDUCIARY DUTY: UNIVERSAL OWNERSHIP

For some observers, fiduciary duty is the primary reason *not* to use ESG factors in investment analysis.[12] John Langbein and Richard Posner's seminal critique argued that that screening portfolios could impose unacceptable diversification costs, and that large institutions had a duty to frame their investment objectives solely on the basis of financial risk and return. As described earlier, the first objection has been largely addressed by the finding that social investment universes have had competitive performance over time.

Major efforts were made in the 2000s to address the second objection. In their 2000 book, *The Rise of Fiduciary Capitalism,* James Hawley and Andrew Williams make the case for a fiduciary approach to the incorporation of ESG factors.[13] Rather than appealing to a particular values system or the profit motive, they argue that institutional investors are bound to look out for the well-being of their beneficiaries and ought to use their influence as owners' agents to promote it.

Hawley and Williams argue that fiduciary investors must have a broader objective function—their definition of success must include not only the financial returns from the portfolio, but also the real social and environmental impact of the enterprises in which they invest. Unlike values-based and financial performance-seeking social investors, large institutions are less able to pick and choose their holdings. Because of their size, they cannot substantially modify their portfolios without having to accept liquidity costs and risking market disruption. Therefore, Hawley argues, "since they cannot sell they must care."[14]

This argument strongly implies that large institutions should engage with corporate management on social and environmental issues, and has gained support among important international players. In 2005, the United Nations (UN) Environment Programme's Finance Initiative sponsored a major legal study arguing that arguing that ESG investment did not conflict with fiduciary duty and that it "is clearly permissible and is arguably required in all jurisdictions."[15] In 2010, the same organization built on this work with a report entitled "Universal Ownership: Why Environmental Externalities Matter to Institutional Investors."[16]

Launched in 2006, the UN's *Principles for Responsible Investment* includes extensive language on how investors can monitor and engage managements of the companies in their portfolios.[17]

> *We will be active owners and incorporate ESG issues into our ownership policies and practices.*
> *Possible actions:*
> *Develop and disclose an active ownership policy consistent with the Principles*
> *Exercise voting rights or monitor compliance with voting policy (if outsourced)*

> *Develop an engagement capability (either directly or through outsourcing)*
>
> *Participate in the development of policy, regulation, and standard setting (such as promoting and protecting shareholder rights)*
>
> *File shareholder resolutions consistent with long-term ESG considerations*
>
> *Engage with companies on ESG issues*
>
> *Participate in collaborative engagement initiatives*
>
> *Ask investment managers to undertake and report on ESG-related engagement*

These goals are ambitious and may appear idealistic to some, but they also address the most basic aspects of corporate governance. The Principles correctly recognize that owners that wish to retain their rights must exercise them, and insist that they be respected.

This cannot be taken for granted. The first decade of the new millennium, which began with Enron and ended with Lehman and AIG, was surely the worst for corporate governance in modern history. Multiple layers of oversight failed, including mechanisms introduced with the 2002 passage of the Sarbanes-Oxley Act. Despite the presence of a dedicated regulator, Fannie Mae and Freddie Mac engaged in, in the words of Warren Buffett, "two of the greatest accounting misstatements in history."[18] According to *Washington Post* columnist Mike DeWine:

> *A 2006 examination conducted by the Office of Federal Housing Enterprise Oversight . . . concluded that Fannie Mae portrayed itself "as one of the lowest-risk financial institutions in the world and as 'best in class' in terms of risk management, financial reporting, internal control, and corporate governance"—all while it was cooking the books, smoothing out earnings and violating 30 generally accepted accounting principles.*[19]

Most forms of ESG investment depend on good faith and appropriate disclosure from the enterprises in which investments are made. All ESG investors, but particularly universal owners, must therefore be deeply concerned with the reform of basic governance.

IMPACT

While worthwhile in themselves, the motivations just discussed do not directly address a primary objective of many investors: *change*. Avoiding polluters may ensure that an environmental groups' portfolio is consistent with its mission, but it also forgoes the opportunity to use the rights and influence of a shareholder to work for change. Investing primarily in publicly traded stocks and bonds may offer liquidity and diversification, but it may also dilute the potential positive impact of the capital employed.

The desire for greater social impact has led to rapid innovation in private equity and venture vehicles targeted at specific social and environmental problems. Some of the impetus for this has come from dissatisfaction with traditional philanthropic models. Antony Bugg-Levine and John Goldstein argue that traditional philanthropy cannot be the whole answer: "[T]here is not enough charitable and government capital to meet the social and environmental challenges we face. Where, then, will we find the money to complement charity and government to bring solutions to scale?"[20]

From a financial perspective, people of goodwill can disagree about whether a venture that is socially motivated is at a disadvantage to one that is not. But when we focus on social impact, it is apparent that there are many opportunities to create social benefits more efficiently than the traditional philanthropic apparatus allows.

From an investment perspective, a grant is simply a very bad investment. It has a −100% return, with zero volatility. The only justification for it is that it entails some positive social effect. But mightn't there be ways to achieve similar social impact while recovering a portion of the capital? Even a money-losing investment, in this context, would be better than a grant. In a world where most investors are accustomed to ignoring opportunities with returns below the risk-free rate, this type of analysis requires significant mental adjustments.

The broad implementation of impact investing will be challenging because most nonprofit organizations separate the allocation of grants from their investment decision making. The investment side doesn't like illiquid investments that might well be suboptimal in conventional frameworks. The grant-making side may not wish to modify long-standing practices in which considerable competence has been developed. But the opportunities are so numerous and potentially beneficial that further innovation and widespread adoption are inevitable.

MAPPING TECHNIQUES TO MOTIVATION

ESG investors need to work hard to clarify their objective function. They must be as honest as possible, with both their constituencies and themselves, about what they hope to accomplish. Appropriate techniques differ according to the investor's motivation—although each technique could *conceivably*

	Engagement	Negative Screening	Positive Screening	Specialized Venture/Private Equity Vehicles
Values	✓	✓	✓	
Financial Performance			✓	✓
Fiduciary Duty	✓	*		
Change	✓	*	✓	✓

FIGURE 38.1 Investor Motivations and ESG Techniques

be used for each motivation, Figure 38.1 roughly illustrates the features of current practice.

Values-based investors historically have emphasized negative screening because it is the most efficient way to ensure that they do not own investments conflicting with their beliefs.

Investors motivated by fiduciary considerations are often limited primarily to engagement—large pension funds, for example, may rule out screening strategies altogether on the grounds that even very small diversification costs would be unacceptable. We mark negative screening with an asterisk in this case, however, because the threat of exit tends to improve the prospects for successful engagement.[21] The same is true for change-motivated investors.

Both financial performance–motivated and change-motivated social investors may invest in thematic or special purpose investment vehicles targeted at a particular opportunity or issue area. In these situations it is particularly important to be clear about which motivation takes precedence. In a broad review of community development venture investments, Anna Kovner and Josh Lerner find that they have been "less likely to go public or be acquired than . . . comparable investments by traditional VCs [venture capitalists]," but also note that these investments are likely to have a "positive return to their community."[22] Whether that's a desirable combination of attributes depends on what kind of investor you are.

SUMMARY

ESG investment is a complex and challenging field, so it is not surprising that we encounter challenges of terminology and intention. This is particularly true when discussing financial performance. Financial performance is, of course, a primary objective of any investment—why bear risk if there is no prospect of return? Sometimes, however, the discussion of performance obscures more important messages.

Brad Barber offers the example of the divestment of tobacco stocks from California's employee retirement funds. Although the decision was framed mainly in financial terms, it was, in fact, primarily values-based.[23]

A 2005 report by the UN Environmental Programme bases its arguments primarily on fiduciary considerations ("quality of life and quality of the environment are worth something, even if not, or particularly because, they are not reducible to financial percentages") but also asserts that "the integration of environmental, social and governance (ESG) issues into investment analysis, *so as to more reliably predict financial performance*, is clearly permissible and is arguably required in all jurisdictions"[24] (emphasis added).

In their excellent 2009 review of impact investing, Bugg-Levine and Goldstein ask: "must we sacrifice return in order to generate impact, or conversely, must we dilute impact to gain additional financial return? . . . Or can pursuing both objectives result in *enhanced financial returns* with a meaningful impact?"[25] (emphasis added).

In some cases, such as organizations governed by the Employee Retirement Income Security Act, a primary focus on financial performance is mandatory and it may not be possible to fully incorporate other motivations. But in many other situations financial and extra-financial motivations can be combined into a richer and more beneficial objective function.

That is the promise of ESG investment: By broadening and clarifying the objective function, we seek to deploy capital in a way that better meets the needs of the investor, and of society.

NOTES

1. Hersh Shefrin. "Impact Investing and Behavioral Finance." Value of Values conference, Leavey School of Business, Santa Clara University, Santa Clara, California. May 14–15, 2010.
2. Peter Kinder, "'Socially Responsible Investing': An Evolving Concept in a Changing World," KLD Research and Analytics, 2005. I deny that I am stealing Kinder's work because stealing is an art requiring craft and ingenuity and some of this is a direct lift. Anyone interested in this topic should read his entire essay.
3. Christopher Luck, "Domini Social Index Performance," The Investment Research Guide to Socially Responsible Investing, Colloquium on Socially Responsible Investing, 1998. Dan DiBartolomeo and Lloyd Kurtz, "Managing Risk Exposures of Socially Screened Accounts," Northfield Working Paper, 1999. www.northinfo.com/documents/63.pdf
4. Lloyd Kurtz and Dan DiBartolomeo, "The Long-Term Performance of a Social Investment Universe," *Journal of Investing*, Fall 2011.

5. www.socialinvest.org/news/releases/pressrelease.cfm?id=151

6. There are many such studies, but these three are representative: S. Hamilton, H. Jo, and M. Statman, "Doing Well While Doing Good? The Investment Performance of Socially Responsible Mutual Funds," *Financial Analysts Journal* (November/December 1993); pp. 62–66.

   Rob Bauer, Kees Koedijk, and Roger Otten, "International Evidence on Ethical Mutual Fund Performance and Investment Style," University of Maastricht Working Paper, 2002. http://papers.ssrn.com/sol3/papers.cfm?abstract_id=297882

   Luc Renneboog, Jenke ter Horst, and Chendi Zhang, "The Price of Ethics: Evidence from Socially Responsible Mutual Funds," ECGI Working Paper No. 168/2007, European Corporate Governance Institute, 2007. Available for download here: http://papers.ssrn.com/sol3/papers.cfm?abstract_id=985265

7. Innovest Strategic Value Advisors, 2008. www.innovestgroup.com/images/pdf/isva_differentiation.pdf

8. "Investing in Sustainability: An Interview with Al Gore and David Blood," *McKinsey Quarterly* (May 2007). www.mckinseyquarterly.com/Investing_in_sustainability_An_interview_with_Al_Gore_and_David_Blood_2005

9. Alex Edmans, "Does the Stock Market Fully Value Intangibles? Employee Satisfaction and Equity Prices," *Journal of Financial Economics* (in press).

10. Vadim Zlotnikov, "Quantitative Research: When Should We Follow the Herd or Go Against It? Examination of Factor Timing Strategies," Bernstein Research, 2010.

11. Jeroen Derwall, Nadja Guenster, Rob Bauer, and Kees Koedijk, "The Eco-Efficiency Premium Puzzle," *Financial Analysts Journal* (March/April 2005). pp 51–63

12. John H. Langbein and Richard A. Posner, "Social Investing and the Law of Trusts," Yale Faculty Scholarship Series, Paper 490, 1980. www.law.yale.edu/documents/pdf/Faculty/Langbein_Social_Investing_Laws_and_Trusts.pdf

13. James P. Hawley and Andrew T. Williams, *The Rise of Fiduciary Capitalism: How Institutional Investors Can Make Corporate American More Democratic* (Philadelphia: University of Pennsylvania Press, 2000).

14. James P. Hawley, "Universal Owners, Fiduciary Capitalism and Responsible Investment: Challenges and Opportunities," Presentation for Netspar-UMBS Academy, Saint Mary's College, Moraga, CA, 2008.

15. United Nations Environmental Programme, "Spotlight on Investors' Environmental Responsibility," 2005. www.unep.org/Documents.Multilingual/Default.asp?DocumentID=455&ArticleID=5015&l=en

16. www.unpri.org/files/6728_ES_report_environmental_externalities.pdf

17. UN Global Compact, 2011. www.unpri.org

18. Transcript of television interview "Three Hours with Warren Buffett—Live from Omaha." CNBC'S *Squawk Box* with Becky Quick, Friday, August 22, 2008. www.cnbc.com/id/26337298/site/14081545/

19. Mike DeWine, "Fannie Mae, Wasting Taxpayers' Money and Time," *Washington Post*, February 18, 2011.

20. Antony Bugg-Levine and John Goldstein, "Impact Investing: Harnessing Capital Markets to Solve Problems at Scale," Community Development Investment Review, Federal Reserve Bank of San Francisco, 2009. www.frbsf.org/publications/community/review/vol5_issue2/bugg_levine_goldstein.pdf

21. For a deep analysis of this logic, see Albert O. Hirschman, *Exit, Voice, and Loyalty: Responses to Decline in Firms, Organizations, and States* (Cambridge, MA: Harvard University Press, 1970).

22. Anna Kovner and Josh Lerner, "Doing Well by Doing Good? Community Development Venture Capital," Federal Reserve Bank of New York, Working Paper 2010.

23. Brad Barber, "Is Good Governance Valuable?" Presentation to the Value of Values conference, Leavey School of Business, Santa Clara University, Santa Clara, CA. May 14, 2010.

24. UNEP Finance Initiative, "A Legal Framework for the Integration of Environmental, Social, and Governance Issues into Institutional Investment," October 2005. www.unepfi.org/fileadmin/documents/freshfields_legal_resp_20051123.pdf

25. Bugg-Levine and Goldstein, "Impact Investing." www.frbsf.org/publications/community/review/vol5_issue2/bugg_levine_goldstein.pdf

Conclusion

Cary Krosinsky

L ooking back on all that we have discussed, we see an impossible-to-deny trend towards sustainability having now emerged as a key "survive and thrive" criteria and a positive driver of value for corporations. Investors are beginning to apply these same positive methodologies and considerations with success. We have reviewed many leading investors and their approaches, as well as those who are starting to lean more towards our opportunities-driven way of thinking. We've heard from a myriad of respected thought leaders, from Dan Esty to Paul Hawken, Roger Urwin to Matthew Kiernan, to the largest hedge fund manager in the world and back to one of the first socially responsible investment researchers in the field. We've explored the specific regional issues that are emerging as well as the criticality of data, barriers, and other challenges and opportunities for new ways of thinking and analysis.

What haven't we covered?

Asset owners, for starters—although this book should be of interest to any investment novice or professional who wants to better understand the nuances in the field as they consider their choice set. Any asset owner can and should ask their advisors if they are truly factoring in the opportunities and risks that emerge from applying this vital lens of sustainability trends. European pension funds, especially those in Scandinavian countries, take sustainability as an opportunity very seriously; however, most global asset owners still do not, even though momentum is certainly building. First movers in California among U.S. pension funds lead the way, with the rest of U.S. states and cities not quite seeing this light. Endowments like Yale's have started to factor in their sustainability-related efforts and investments in their most recent reports,[1] but most endowments still do not see these opportunities or, if they do, know how to leverage them with success. Universities are competing on the basis of their sustainability programs; it would be exciting to see them start competing on the strength of their investments in this area as well. And so, this is also a book for students, those looking not only to learn how they can apply sustainability to investing, but to also demand that their own institutions understand the nuances, and practically consider and invest accordingly.

And mostly, this is a book for the interested investment professional and individual investor. The majority of mutual fund assets and related providers and distributors certainly do not consider sustainability as an opportunity. Arguably, the largest opportunity of all is for one of the largest fund managers in the world to embrace this way of thinking, which would be unique as of this writing none of the very largest equity fund managers use sustainability as a lens as of this writing.

All too often, corporate pension funds and 401(k) plans also do not factor in our way of thinking, even if their own organizations have sustainability completely embedded in their strategic planning. Aligning their investments with their strategy would be the next logical step, and another opportunity unto itself.

Likewise, foundations, even those in the environmental field, tend to look the other way and rely on "experts," usually because they don't understand markets themselves and figure someone else can best figure out how to squeeze another dime out of their dollar, even if against their core belief set—and hence Urwin on a framework they should apply (see Chapter 33). These are slow-changing institutions with relationships that have built up over time. Assets are sticky, and it takes a generation, but do we have that amount of time to spare?

And so we have focused on fund managers, and how they get this right, to help any asset owner, consultant, pension fund trustee, 401(k) plan trustee, or individual investor understand that there is indeed a way to marry sustainability and value and that, in fact, doing exactly that may well be an investor imperative, as it is a corporate imperative. It is arguably already the fiduciary duty of any asset owner today to factor in the clear trends that are emerging, even if the legalities remain to be sorted. In many ways, this is a book about how things have been done and how much more there is to do.

We also haven't covered the state of the data industry, as it is in a major state of flux, with the largest players having announced rethinks of their strategy and few having ever turned a profit. The fear is that by the time you read this, the players and metrics will be different. For this reason, we have created a Web site at www.sustainabilityandinvesting.com to provide updates to the field and a community of resources and discussion. We hope you will participate in this evolving, positively focused field of opportunities.

There are also a number of socially responsible investment managers not covered in this book, partly due to space considerations and partly due to the fact that most such assets do not look at sustainability as a positive driver of value.

Regardless of who is actually doing what within the ESG space, there is not only room for all to participate, but this cooperation and active participation is essential and helpful in encouraging the sort of macro changes that the world likely requires. In effect, a global effort is required for all players—investors, corporates, academics, governments, and civil society alike—to find common ground and solutions. Those who choose to point fingers without offering alternatives aren't solving the problem and may be making matters worse.

This book has attempted to tease out tensions between approaches and, while doing so, to show that there is much more common ground than disagreement at the end of the day and that together, as constituents and interested parties, we are all stronger: corporates and investors alike—all stakeholders, in fact.

It is also very much the time for all parties to come together to solve our problems constructively: Values-based investors need to find common ground with companies, governments, academics, and civil society to find the solutions we require, both within investment houses and in corporations. Again, refer to our Web site for write-ups on managers we didn't have space for here and for what we hope will be an active community where these issues can be discussed. Likewise, see the appendices and the book's Web site for lists of leading nongovernmental organizations in the field, leading research being published, and curriculum that is taught on this subject today. These are ever-changing, evolving categories of interest, and listing them in print would be to mark a point in time, when such things are necessarily fluid.

We also have not discussed in great detail issues such as ecological economics, measures such as distance from target and tipping points. These are vital, essential, critical things that we cannot know, although we can know what damage we are doing and that we are approaching the edge of a cliff whose edge we cannot necessarily see. For more on this, see the excellent video of Robert Costanza speaking at Yale in 2010 as part of the Visions of a Sustainable World series.[2] Also, see the recent work on limits performed by the Carbon Tracker Initiative, at www.carbontracker.org.

There are also additional issues of import surrounding sustainable agriculture and infrastructure that we were only able to touch on here briefly. The capacity for efficiencies in buildings, provides an opportunity to reduce a large percentage of our global footprint, and this was covered extensively in our first book, as were other topics across the field.[3]

There remains much uncertainty in the sustainability measurement practice and in investing in general. Mainstream investors who pretend to have everything down pat as a science are arguably being willfully misleading. A more sophisticated perspective is to recognize the flaws inherent in all forms of investment: Know what you don't know, in other words. Why do finance and the investment world rely so much on models that attempt to encompass everything, when there is so much we don't know and so many recent examples of crises which these models failed to capture? We also operate with certainty in a world where science can only take us so far. How can time extend back forever in infinitum as well as forward infinitely? Understandably, our minds cannot wrap themselves around some things. Yet we approach the field of investing as if there are tenets written in stone. There are no such things.

Even the history of investing is hardly taught. At most, we look back 50 years when considering the behavior of markets; 100 years at the very most with rare exception. The crashes of the 1800s in the United States are hardly well understood. The British East India Company—the first ever publicly traded company—raped and pillaged its way through crashes and burns while compiling vast wealth, but not for the long-term shareholder. For more on this story, see the excellent book by my coauthor and friend Nick Robins, *The Corporation That Changed the World*.[4] Yet we assume that successful mainstream financial strategies of the 80s and 90's, leading up to the financial crisis of 2008, investing without sustainability in mind, still somehow makes sense for the majority of assets in the face of a rapidly changing world. It does not.

Ultimately, the question for me is this: Will our global society willfully self-destruct in the face of the evidence, or will we try to find a positive way ahead?

At times we seem willing to tiptoe along the edge of a cliff, pushing resource and capacity boundaries to their limit in the pursuit of temporary gain or, as many suggest, we are already beyond the limits on crucial issues such as biodiversity and now need to consider adaptation measures first and foremost. Ultimately, I don't believe that we are a self-destructive species. In the face of looming disaster, we rally to the cause, no matter how many lessons it takes in the meantime and no matter the barriers to coming to a common understanding of what's best for future generations, without sacrificing our current needs and dreams.

Innovation is what is required to save the day. Likely we are not much more than a generation away from Kurzweilian sea changes of technology, fission energy breakthroughs, solar at cost, and similar advances that will leave the world of the future unrecognizable to us. If we are not self-destructive, the innovators will see it through, and they will win in the markets as well.

Sustainable investment offers a way to find these winners of tomorrow and not be left behind as investors, stuck as universal owners of all companies, guaranteed to have winners and losers alike. By definition universal owners feel the need to own the entire market—a common phenomenon among the largest US pension funds for example. Certainly, at minimum, using sustainability as a lens to avoid the minefields of the past decade—from Enron through BP, from WorldCom through TEPCO—would seem at minimum essential to factor in to investment strategies. Loss avoidance may be sustainability's greatest contribution to the investing world. Identifying winners is always a challenge for any investor, but as the early shareholders in Microsoft and Google would certainly agree, if you can find the gold nuggets, it is well worth the pursuit, and what else is any investing if it is not attempting to find outperformance through anticipation of trends that you feel the other guy hasn't seen coming? There is, of course, a winner and loser in every transaction.

There is also the short-term versus long-term argument. This is a cliché and can be a barrier to action. We have seen sustainability as a lens lead to outperformance already, and so we discard this argument as irrelevant, especially for those seeking to get ahead of inevitable global trends.

This inevitable trend towards sustainability will also have its own winners and losers, but opportunities remain for all as we speak. Bubbles seem to always form around any coming new realm, from tulips to railroads, radio to the internet. The same has been true for alternative energy in recent times as well. Caution is clearly essential for anyone looking to participate in sustainable investing, as is hard work and an intelligent application of this investment philosophy.

Perhaps some of those who recognize that they will fail will get in the way of what's best for the world—even what's ultimately best for their own families—without realizing it. We have already seen that happen in some ways, with the disinformation campaigns against the significance of carbon emissions contributing to climate change is concerned, but the truth can remain hidden for only so long. Certainly few people actually want to leave a much worse world for their children and grandchildren. This dynamic ensures from an investment standpoint, that everyone has not yet invested accordingly, and so by definition, upside remains for sustainable investing.

Assuming that the average mainstream investor does start to catch on to this opportunity set, finding practical, positive value through a sustainability lens, this represents an opportunity unto itself. If and when sustainability gets more embedded into mainstream investment thinking, as many expect is already starting to occur, we have stumbled on a market inefficiency that eventually will get priced in. Getting ahead of the curve is very much Investing 101, or so the traditional investment world tells us. And as mentioned in the introduction, markets need winners and losers to be efficient after all.

NOTES

1. www.yale.edu/investments/
2. www.youtube.com/watch?v=PZkTlVPgqG4
3. Cary Krosinsky and Nick Robins, eds., *Sustainable Investing: The Art of Long Term Performance* (Earthscan, London, United Kingdom, 2008).
4. Nick Robins, *The Corporation That Changed the World* (Ann Arbor, MI: Pluto Press, 2006).

Sample Curriculum

A s stated throughout this book, there is a great need for more clarification and education as well as a great hunger from students for more material on the subject matter of this book. This appendix contains a potential syllabus regarding a course being taught at the MBA level at the University of Maryland's Robert H. Smith School of Business. The premise is to construct, interactively with students, a sustainable portfolio—one with the attributes of companies we seek and one that can outperform (see Chapter 24) Guest speakers are featured throughout, as well as intensive review and discussion of relevant case studies. A version of this course is taught at Columbia University's Earth Institute, where it was given for the first time in late 2009. The constructed portfolio went on to outperform in 2010, experiencing 18.85% growth on an equally weighted basis versus the Standard & Poor's 500's 12.8% growth and the MSCI World's 5.6% during the same time frame.

Resources on available curriculum and syllabi on related subjects and courses include:

- The Aspen Institute's Beyond Grey Pinstripes is also a useful resource in this regard: www.beyondgreypinstripes.org/index.cfm
- The Initiative for Responsible Investment at Harvard University maintains a growing list: http://hausercenter.org/iri
- This book's Web site, www.sustainabilityandinvesting.com, will be an updated resource.

SYLLABUS

BUFN 758G: Sustainability & Investing
University of Maryland, the Robert H. Smith School of Business

Spring 2011

Saturday 9 AM–6PM

February 5/February 19/March 5

Lecturer: Cary Krosinsky

Background

This course will provide a walk through the framework, analysis, and metrics involved with the growing practice of factoring sustainability into investment strategy, especially as it pertains to financial measurement of environmental, social, and governance risks and opportunities.

Students will actively participate in the construction of a model sustainable equity portfolio as well as studying how sustainability affects other asset classes, while reviewing macro sustainability trends that will likely affect regions, corporations, and public policy.

Bennett Freeman of Calvert Investments and Brunno Maradei of the International Finance Corporation are among the expected in-person guest speakers. Others who will participate in person or virtually include Matthew Kiernan, Stephen Viederman, Graham Sinclair, and Nick Robins.

Additional materials and case studies will be distributed and discussed, including *Newsweek*'s Green Rankings, the recent United Nations–commissioned report of ecosystem valuations and their effects on universal owners, as well as the HBS case study of generation investment management and Wal-Mart.

Textbooks and Readings

Required (should be read prior to class 1):

1. *Sustainable Investing: The Art of Long Term Performance*, Krosinsky/Robins (Earthscan, 2008)

Required (to be read by class 2, if not prior to class 1):

2. *Investing in a Sustainable World*, Kiernan (AMACOM, 2008) (see UM Testudo or Amazon.com for purchasing instructions)

Required—Case Studies:

HBS/Generation: "Generation Investment Management," (HBS, September 2009) To be read prior to class 1, discussed during class 1

HBS and Ivey/Wal-Mart: "Wal-Mart's Sustainability Strategy," (HBS, April 2007), and "Wal-Mart China—Sustainable Operations

Strategy" (Ivey, January 2009) two cases to be read prior to class 2, to be discussed during class 2

Optional Readings

Beyond Growth: The Economics of Sustainable Development, Daly (Beacon, 1997)

Green to Gold, Winston/Esty (Yale Press/John Wiley & Sons, 2008)

Natural Capitalism, Hawken/Lovins/Lovins (Back Bay, 2008)

Prosperity without Growth, Jackson (Earthscan, 2009)

Lectures

February 5: Methodology and Metrics/Setting the Framework

Guest Speaker: Stephen Viederman   Why, from an environmental governance standpoint, sustainability is now essential for investors and public companies alike. Examples of existing metrics are provided as well as:

- Brief history of the 11 different strands of socially responsible investing (SRI)
- How sustainable investing has evolved from the first waves of SRI, which primarily encompassed divestment from South Africa and screening out alcohol, tobacco, and firearms
- Extensive discussions of environmental metrics, with a key focus on Trucost and the *Newsweek* Green Rankings as well as all leading indexes and data sources, such as KLD, DJSI, Bloomberg as well as other key sustainability issues, including social, governance, and quality
- Review of book 1 and discussion of the paper that was presented on the subject to the UN PRI Academic Network event at Carleton University on October 1–3, 2009 www.unpri.org/academic09/agenda.php and related
- Selected review of upcoming chapters of a book with John Wiley & Sons (release in September/October 2011), which highlights best practice investors involved with sustainability
- Review of the HBS Case on generation investment mManagment
- Setting the framework for the underlying project to run through the class: building a maximally sustainable portfolio interactively with students
- First paper and student presentations to be assigned, due prior to class 2

February 19: The Corporate Perspective/How to Start Constructing a Sustainable Portfolio

- Guest Speakers: Bennett Freeman, SVP, Calvert Investments, Bethesda, MD; and Matthew Kiernan, Inflection Point Capital Management/InnovestStudents to present, ten minutes each, examples of individual companies they believe are sustainable and why
- Bennett Freeman to present his and Calvert's thoughts on sustainability and investing
- Matthew Kiernan to discuss his book, his new investment firm's methodology, and industry trends
- How leading corporations increasingly see sustainability as a positive force
- The response from investors, and what is expected in future
- Internal corporate expectations and what corporations can hope to achieve as thought leaders
- Sustainability as a risk factor: how do companies measure themselves —Sustainability 2.0 framework
- Reviewing case studies of corporate efforts in sustainability—focus on Wal-Mart
- What opportunities will present themselves to students—reviewing the implications for sustainability and investingi on the job market today and going forward
- Review of other investors' approaches to sustainability and investing compared to our class's first attempt at a model sustainable portfolio
- How these approaches compare with those of other investors and efforts of other investment classes
- Assignment of the second paper, due before the final class, and the second round of student presentations

March 5: Macro Trends that Affect Sustainability, Implications for Asset Allocation, Developing World Implications, and Final Portfolio Construction

Guest Speakers: Nick Robins, HSBC Climate Change Center of Excellence; Graham Sinclair, AfricaSIF; Brunno Maradei, IFC/Developing Markets; Howard Brown, dMASS   How environmental sustainability is and can be factored into decision making: what is relevant and material, how companies have been and will be measured now and in the future

- The global perspective: emerging markets and sustainability

- Other asset classes: fixed income, microfinance, carbon trading, social and community investing
- Student presentations—final visions of a model sustainable portfolio across the asset classes
- Evolution of civil society, fiduciary duty, and global public policy and new business models and strategies that likely will affect investment
- What opportunities will present themselves to students
- Final discussions and incorporation into a class portfolio

Grading Criteria

20%: Attendance and active participation

25%: First paper

25%: Second paper

30%: Student presentations to class

Additional Resources

Investor Network on Climate Risk	www.incr.com
Newsweek Green Rankings	http://greenrankings.newsweek.com
Pew Center for Global Climate Change	www.pewclimate.org
Trucost Plc	www.trucost.com
UN PRI	www.unpri.org

Investors

Here is an alphabetical list of investors profiled in this book.

Aviva	www.aviva.com
Blue Wolf	www.blue-wolf.com/
Calvert	www.calvert.com/
Domini	www.domini.com/
Generation	www.generationim.com/
Green Century	www.greencentury.com/
Highwater Global	www.baldwinbrothersinc.com/investment/vehicles/ highwater-global
Inflection Point	www.inflectionpointcm.com/
Jupiter Ecology	www.jupiteronline.co.uk/PI/Our_Products/ Green_Funds/SRI_Funds/J3.htm
NEI Investments	www.neiinvestments.com/Pages/Home.aspx
Pictet Water	www.pictetfunds.com/
Portfolio 21	www.portfolio21.com/
SAM	www.sam-group.com/htmle/main.cfm
Trillium	trilliuminvest.com/
Winslow	www.winslowgreen.com/home/

For more information on sustainable fund managers, please see our book's companion Web site, www.sustainabilityandinvesting.com

Index